FAMILY LAW AND LITIGATION
IN BASOTHO SOCIETY

FAMILY LAW AND LITIGATION IN BASOTHO SOCIETY

Sebastian Poulter
M.A., D.PHIL.(OXON)

Lecturer in Law at the
University of Southampton

CLARENDON PRESS · OXFORD
1976

*Oxford University Press, Ely House, London W.*1

GLASGOW NEW YORK TORONTO MELBOURNE WELLINGTON
CAPE TOWN IBADAN NAIROBI DAR ES SALAAM LUSAKA ADDIS ABABA
DELHI BOMBAY CALCUTTA MADRAS KARACHI LAHORE DACCA
KUALA LUMPUR SINGAPORE HONG KONG TOKYO

ISBN 0 19 825335 4

*Printed in Great Britain
by Billing & Sons Limited, Guildford and London*

To
JANE

PREFACE

SOUTHERN Africa is a focal point of world attention. However, while news about South Africa, Rhodesia, Namibia, and Mozambique is almost daily in the world's press the tiny mountain Kingdom of Lesotho tends to find itself overlooked and neglected. Yet an understanding of family life in Lesotho, of the legal rules which regulate it, of the country's continuing economic dependence on South Africa some eight years after independence, of the contribution its labour force makes to the increasing prosperity of white South Africans to the detriment of Lesotho's own social structure—all this is important for a full appreciation of the situation in southern Africa today.

Most Basotho regard their customary law not merely as one of the major assets in their cultural heritage but as virtually indispensable for the continued ordering of their society. People often state quite bluntly that without their law they would no longer exist as a nation. My own research into Sesotho law was first prompted by the lack of detailed information about how the concepts it employed were being applied in the courts. Duncan's admirable introductory work *Sotho Laws and Customs*[1] appeared some fifteen years ago, but the author was at pains to explain in his preface that 'As the writing of this book drew to a close it became clear that its scope is limited. It is the first thing of its kind in Basutoland, and I regard it as merely the first brick on which others will build.'

It cannot be accepted as true today—if it ever was in the past—that at least the Basotho themselves know their law and therefore it is only necessary to record it for the benefit of foreigners. Certainly the general ideas and guiding precepts are known to many Basotho, but the manner in which specific rules are applied, the intricacies and nuances, as well as the way in which the law has evolved over the past hundred years are grasped by only a very few.

This particular study provides the first detailed and systematic account of family law and litigation in Basotho society. Although

[1] O.U.P., Cape Town, 1960.

essentially concerned with presenting the law as it applies in the courts today care has been taken to give the reader a historical perspective and to trace the law's development over the past century and a quarter.

The work is divided into three parts. First there is a general survey of the cultural, economic, social, and institutional framework within which the law operates. Part II contains a description of the substantive rules and principles of Sesotho family law and forms the core of the book. The final part looks to the future and suggests some possible reforms. It had at one stage been hoped to include a detailed analysis of the relationship between the customary law and the received common law, but in order to keep the book to a reasonable length this plan eventually had to be abandoned. The material on 'internal conflicts of law' problems has therefore been held back for publication at some later date. Although this means that those family relationships that are regulated by the common law are not dealt with in this book there is consolation in the thought that they are statistically of very little significance.

I offer my survey of Sesotho family law as a contribution to the state of knowledge about the working of different legal systems and thus of general relevance in the study of comparative law. I also hope that I may have assisted in developing and refining the research techniques employed in the investigation and recording of African customary law. Many, if not most, of the major contributions in this field have hitherto come from social anthropologists and I shall be pleased if one consequence of my work is a reawakening of interest in the subject among lawyers.

However, my chief desire in writing this book has been that I might facilitate the task of those who are confronted with problems of Sesotho law in a professional capacity, for instance the judges in the Court of Appeal and High Court, and the lawyers who appear before them. I have also had particularly in mind the Judicial Commissioner's Court which stands at an intermediate level between the Local and Central Courts and the superior courts and which siphons off a large volume of appeals on matters of Sesotho law.

While my work will at present be of use to very few of the presidents of the Local and Central Courts because of their lack of formal legal training and generally limited knowledge of

English, the policy of the Lesotho government is to integrate the
personnel of these courts with that of the magistrates' courts as
soon as possible. The result should be that during the next few
years there will be a growing number of legally qualified officials
with a good command of English administering Sesotho law in the
customary courts.

Tomorrow's judges and lawyers are today's students and I
hope that this book will also be useful to those who are pursuing
legal studies at the University of Botswana, Lesotho and Swaziland.

By writing down the rules of Sesotho law I do not seek to
fossilize them so that they become difficult to change at a time
when adaptation and modification may come to be matters of
urgent need. I am neither codifying customary law in statutory
form nor providing an official version in the form of an authorized
restatement. Rather I am attempting to provide more detailed
information than has hitherto been available about the application
of the law by the courts at the present time. I hope that as a result
the law will be applied with greater certainty and conviction with a
consequent strengthening of the administration of justice in the
country at large.

Southampton   S. M. P.
September 1974

ACKNOWLEDGEMENTS

Much of the research for this work was undertaken during 1969–71 while I was on the teaching staff of the University of Botswana, Lesotho and Swaziland (U.B.L.S.). The University generously furnished me with a research grant which enabled me to obtain photostat copies of many unpublished cases, to hold a panel discussion on Sesotho family law (and produce a transcript of the proceedings) and also to undertake a small social survey. For all this I am most grateful.

I should like to thank the Judicial Commissioner, Mr. R. F. Thompson, O.B.E., for allowing me unrestricted access to the records of his Court. In addition both he and his chief clerk of court Mr. E. M. Sehalahala gave me much of their valuable time and assistance. So also did Mr. S. L. Makara and Mr. Sesioana.

I owe an enormous debt of gratitude to the nine members of the Panel Discussion who spent five days thinking and talking about Sesotho family law with me in July 1970. They were Chief P. S. Matete, Chief J. M. Mohale, Chief 'Mako Moliboea Molapo, Chief S. M. N. Bereng, Mr. L. S. Noosi, Mr. E. M. Sehalahala, Mr. M. P. Motlamelle, Mr. R. B. Fobo, and Miss J. Bele. Their patience and lively interest seemed virtually inexhaustible and their contribution to my understanding of the law is apparent from many of the pages which follow. The memory of our fascinating exchanges will remain with me for a long time to come. In arranging the Panel Discussion I was fortunate in receiving the closest co-operation from the Minister of Justice and his permanent secretary Mr. L. Qhobela, so that the civil-servant members of the Panel could be allowed a temporary 'respite'—if that is an appropriate word—from their normal duties. Miss Jane Bonvin kindly acted as secretary to the Panel Discussion and since then has done much to sustain me in completing this work. Happily she is now my wife.

I should also like to thank three of my former students at U.B.L.S., Mr. S. Tsoako, Mr. R. T. Makeka, and Miss M. Mamashela, who conducted the interviews for my social survey in 1970–1.

I am very greatly indebted to Dr. Alan Milner, Fellow of Trinity College, Oxford, who supervised the doctoral thesis upon which this present work is based. His penetrating comments and criticisms have done much to improve the quality of my analysis and the style of presentation.

The credit for successfully transforming my untidy manuscript with its scarcely legible depiction of many Sesotho names and words into a respectable typescript belongs to Mrs. Wiltshire in Lesotho, Mrs. Charlesworth in Oxford, and Miss Glegg, Mrs. Dacre, and Mrs. Johnstone in Southampton.

CONTENTS

LIST OF TABLES

TABLE OF LESOTHO STATUTES

TABLE OF LESOTHO CASES

(All cases are unreported unless followed by the reference H.C.T.L.R.)

TABLE OF FOREIGN CASES

ABBREVIATIONS

A.C.	Appeal Cases (U.K.)
A.D.	Appellate Division (South Africa)
All E.R.	All England Law Reports
C.A.	Court of Appeal
C.C.	Central Court (formerly 'A' Court)
Ch.D.	Chancery Division Law Reports (U.K.)
Civ./A.	Civil Appeal
Civ./App'n.	Civil Application
Civ./T.	Civil Trial
C.J.	Chief Justice
D.C.	District Commissioner
E.A.	East Africa Law Reports
G.N.	Government Notice
H.C.	High Court
H.C.N.	High Commissioner's Notice
H.C.T.L.R.	High Commission Territories Law Reports
H.M.S.O.	His (or Her) Majesty's Stationery Office
I.A.I.	International African Institute
J.A.	Justice of Appeal
J.A.L.	*Journal of African Law*
J.C.	Judicial Commissioner
J.C.L.I.L.	Journal of Comparative Legislation and International Law
K.B.	King's Bench Law Reports (U.K.)
L.C.	Local Court (formerly 'B' Court)
N.A.C.(T. and N.)	Native Appeal Cases (Transvaal and Natal)
Nig. L.J.	*Nigerian Law Journal*
N.L.R.	Nigerian Law Reports
P.C.	Paramount Chief
P.C.'s Ct.	Paramount Chief's Appeal Court
P.D.	Panel Discussion transcript
P.E.M.S.	Paris Evangelical Missionary Society
Proc.	Proclamation
R.C.	Resident Commissioner
R. and N.	Rhodesia and Nyasaland Law Reports
S.A.J.E.	*South African Journal of Economics*
S.A.L.J.	*South African Law Journal*
S.C.	Subordinate Court

ABREVIATIONS

S.O.A.S.	School of Oriental and African Studies, University of London
Sol. Jo.	*Solicitor's Journal*
S.R.	Southern Rhodesia Law Reports
T.L.R. (R.)	Tanganyika Law Reports (Revised)
U.B.L.S.	University of Botswana, Lesotho and Swaziland
W.L.R.	Weekly Law Reports (U.K.)
Yale L.J.	*Yale Law Journal*

A NOTE ON TERMINOLOGY

THE African population of Lesotho is comprised almost entirely of people who call themselves *Basotho* (sing. *Mosotho*). The stem '*Sotho*' is generally employed by ethnographers to indicate the peoples of the central high grasslands of southern Africa who constitute a group with a broadly similar culture and language. The Basotho of Lesotho are one of the three major sub-groups and are sometimes referred to as the Southern Sotho because of their geographical location within the wider Sotho grouping. Their language is *Sesotho* and this word is also used by the Basotho to describe anything characteristic of their culture, for instance Sesotho law.

From 1868 to 1966 the country was known as the British colony of Basutoland. During this period the use made of the prefixes added to the stem Sotho was often inconsistent and erroneous. Moreover Sotho was usually spelt Suto, a relic of an earlier orthography. These factors account for the employment of expressions like 'Basuto law' (for Sesotho law) and 'Basutos' (for Basotho). The correct modern forms will naturally be adopted throughout this work save where direct quotations use the older forms.

PART I
GENERAL PART

INTRODUCTION

MODERN Sesotho law draws its inspiration from an ancient African culture. However, while its origins are indigenous many of the modifications that have taken place during the past century are the product of British administration.

At the start of the nineteenth century there were the traditional concepts, customs, practices, and beliefs which were prevalent in a purely agricultural community before the arrival of the missionaries, the advent of colonialism, and the introduction of wage labour. Some of these were enforced by the chiefs' courts while others must have depended for their adherence largely on public opinion. Many disputes must have been resolved within the extended family.

During the colonial period from 1868 to 1966 great changes took place. The pattern of institutions for the settlement of disputes was radically altered and a hierarchy of courts established by statute now exists to enforce the law.[1] Its personnel, procedures, and jurisdiction are all different from anything that existed previously. The substance of individual rules clearly changed too, but it was the restructuring of the judicial process which wrought the most far-reaching innovation for its effect was subtly to transform the very nature and character of Sesotho law.

Throughout this work I shall use the broad expressions 'Sesotho law' and 'customary law' interchangeably to signify the system of rules recognized as obligatory within Basotho society over a long time-span including three different periods—first during the pre-colonial era up to 1868, secondly from the advent of colonialism down to 1938 when drastic changes were made to the court structure, and thirdly from 1938 to the present day. In relation to the modern law I shall be concerned to draw a distinction between legal rules which are enforceable in the courts on the one hand, and other moral and customary norms which, while they are

---

[1] See Ch. 2 below.

usually followed, do not carry the same sanctions if they are disregarded. Naturally there is a large area of overlap because once certain customs and practices had been accepted by the people as having considerable social utility this was a strong justification for enforcing many of them through the courts in the interests of the general public. But as we shall see, by no means all of the modern customary law is derived from customary practices, nor are all customs enforceable as legal rules.

Some indication of the complexity of the interaction between the concepts of law and custom is apparent from Sesotho terminology. *Molao* (law) might superficially be contrasted with *mokhoa* (custom), but a closer examination reveals that there is only a partial convergence of function between the Sesotho words and these English translations.[1] Thus *mokhoa*'s primary meanings are manner, way, fashion, habit, and routine; custom is only a secondary meaning. And *molao* can also mean a commandment or an order. Furthermore, it appears that sometimes the two words can be used virtually interchangeably.

A brief reference is appropriate here to the Laws of Lerotholi.[2] The earliest version of these Laws was drawn up in 1903 by the Basutoland National Council, an advisory body without legislative power, which consisted mainly of chiefs and had been set up by the colonial administration earlier that year. The Laws were named after the Paramount Chief of the time in order to distinguish them from the three published laws of his grandfather Moshoeshoe I.[3] They contained not only sections regulating the chieftainship, the administration of justice and the system of land tenure, but also a number of rules in the sphere of family law. Most, but not all, were of ancient origin. The High Commissioner at once authorized their publication and circulation for the guidance of the chiefs' courts. The original provisions, as well as the many amendments which have been made over the years,

---

[1] Hamnett, 'Some Notes on the Concept of Custom in Lesotho', [1971] *J.A.L.* 271–2; Allott, *Law and Language* (S.O.A.S., 1965), p. 27.

[2] For a full treatment of the origins and development of the Laws of Lerotholi as well as a discussion of the difficulties over their recognition in the higher courts see Poulter, 'The Place of the Laws of Lerotholi in the Legal System of Lesotho' (1972), *African Affairs* 144.

[3] The texts of Moshoeshoe's three published laws on liquor (1854), witchcraft (1855), and trade (1859) are to be found in Theal (Ed.), *Basutoland Records* (Cape Town, 1883–1964), vol. ii, pp. 133, 152–3, and 536–7.

will be examined in detail in subsequent chapters on the substantive law.[1]

As a result of reforms in the administration of the chieftainship
in 1938 the Paramount Chief (then Griffith, the son of Lerotholi)
was empowered by statute to issue, subject to the High Commissioner's approval, 'rules' and 'orders' providing for the peace,
good order, and welfare of his subjects.[2] It was felt desirable to
publish these rules and orders and it seemed convenient to
combine them with the laws carrying Lerotholi's name. As a
result there emerged a new edition of the 'Laws of Lerotholi'
divided into three parts. Part I, which was entitled 'Declaration
of Basuto Law and Custom', basically comprised the laws of
1903 together with amendments and additions agreed to in the
Council since that date. Part II consisted of the Paramount
Chief's rules and included a few provisions which had been
transferred from the 1903 version, for instance those dealing with
compensation for seduction and abduction. Part III contained
the Paramount Chief's orders.

The exact legal status of Parts II and III has always been clear.
They are pieces of delegated legislation. However, owing to a
popular misconception of the true functions of the Basutoland
National Council it came as a considerable surprise when in 1943
Lansdown J., sitting in the High Court, referred to Part I of the
Laws (which he called 'the Lerotholi code') in the following terms:

No legislative authority or official recognition has been extended to
this code; nevertheless it is helpful, though not conclusive, on any
question as to the existence or extent of any customary practice
amongst the Basuto people . . . [It] is in no sense written law. Its
provisions though reduced to print, do not emanate from any law-
giver.[3]

Strictly speaking, this was correct and the position remains the
same today. However, there can be little doubt that so far as the
general public are concerned Part I carries the same authority
as the other parts and the Local and Central Courts do not

[1] See below, Part II. The relevant portions of the most recent version of the
Laws are printed at the end of the book as an appendix.
[2] In terms of the Native Administration Proclamation, No. 61 of 1938,
ss. 8 and 15. On the reforms see below, pp. 37–8.
[3] *Bereng Griffith* v. *'Mantsebo Seeiso Griffith* (the *Regency case*) (1926–53)
H.C.T.L.R. 50 at 58.

appear to draw any distinction between them. It is only in the higher courts that the validity of any of the rules found in Part I is likely to be challenged. The question will then turn on whether the particular written rule embodies an established and recognized custom.[1] Part I constitutes in any event a most important source of information about Sesotho law and if legal technicalities are ignored it represents much more than this and comprises the major primary written source of that law itself.

2. RESEARCH METHOD

Progress towards a consensus of opinion among lawyers and anthropologists as to the most appropriate method of recording African customary law has been slow. In an endeavour to make my study as valuable as possible to lawyers and the courts in Lesotho I have made use of a variety of individual techniques pioneered by other writers but not hitherto employed in full combination with one another.[2] These are

(a) the derivation of information from

   (i) a substantial quantity of cases decided by the lower level customary courts (this being the prime source);

  (ii) the relevant judgments given by the superior courts;

 (iii) any written formulation of the customary law (here, the Laws of Lerotholi);

 (iv) existing ethnographic and legal works; and

  (v) views expressed by knowledgeable persons at a panel discussion; and

(b) presentation in the form of a comprehensive and systematic analysis of legal principles and rules in which

   (i) full and detailed citation of authority is made for every proposition that is found in the text so that the reference can easily be checked (this relates not only to the cases but also to the panel discussion);

  (ii) rules that are enforceable through the courts are distinguished from those that are not;

---

[1] This matter is considered further below at pp. 46–8.

[2] For a full discussion see Poulter, 'An Essay on African Customary Law Research Techniques: Some Experiences from Lesotho' (1975), *Journal of Southern African Studies* 181.

(iii) the historical development of the law is revealed, hence providing an indispensable explanation of its present state; and

(iv) sufficient information about the institutional framework and social background to the legal rules is given for their full significance to be made plain.

3. SOURCES

In my field-work which commenced in 1969 I first read the few existing ethnographic and legal accounts [1] and then proceeded to a collection of case materials. After I had read a large number of cases I held a panel discussion to verify and supplement the information I had already obtained. Finally, I conducted a small social survey. I was already familiar with the general law of the country from my earlier research into the Lesotho legal system.[2]

(a) The Case Records

A diagram of the structure of the official courts appears on p. 8. The bulk of customary law cases is heard in the Local and Central Courts. Here the evidence of the parties and their witnesses is recorded verbatim in Sesotho during the course of the hearings. When an appeal is lodged to the Judicial Commissioner's Court a full transcript of the evidence, together with the judgments of the lower courts and the appellant's grounds of appeal, is forwarded to the Judicial Commissioner's Court where it is translated into English. To facilitate my research I decided to limit my survey of cases in the lower courts to those which proceeded this far on appeal.

Since I was particularly concerned to record the modern law I endeavoured to collect complete sets of proceedings from the start of the case in the Local Court, through the Central Court to the decision of the Judicial Commissioner at the second level of appeal, in every case on family law heard by the Judicial Commissioner's Court between 1963 and 1969. I also obtained a smaller number of cases for the years before 1963, most of them dating back no further than 1950 and about half of them consisting solely of judgments of the Judicial Commissioner's Court.

---

[1] A full list is given in the Bibliography. See also below, pp. 12–14.

[2] The results of that research, which was conducted jointly with Vernon Palmer, were published as *The Legal System of Lesotho* (Michie, 1972). That work contained virtually no treatment of substantive private law.

THE COURTS

Diagram showing the structure of the official courts in matters of Sesotho law

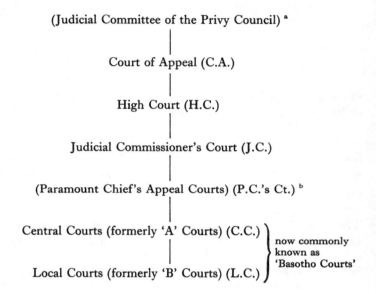

(Judicial Committee of the Privy Council) [a]

|

Court of Appeal (C.A.)

|

High Court (H.C.)

|

Judicial Commissioner's Court (J.C.)

|

(Paramount Chief's Appeal Courts) (P.C.'s Ct.) [b]

|

Central Courts (formerly 'A' Courts) (C.C.) ⎫
| ⎬ now commonly known as 'Basotho Courts'
Local Courts (formerly 'B' Courts) (L.C.)   ⎭

Notes:
(a) Appeals to the Privy Council were abolished in 1970—see below, p. 43.
(b) The Paramount Chief's Appeal Courts disappeared in a reorganization in 1962—see below, p. 43.

In addition to the cases decided in the customary courts and the Judicial Commissioner's Court I have also made use of about thirty cases decided by the superior courts, mostly on appeal. The chart in Table 1 (p. 9) shows the full extent of my case materials.

It might, I suppose, be argued that courts set up by the colonial administration—as all these courts were—can hardly be regarded as the true exponents of the customary law because, even where, as in Lesotho, they were a continuation of the tradition of centralized law enforcement formerly practised by the chiefs, the change in the nature of the judicial process was a relatively profound one. Certainly in Lesotho the new court presidents who took over the role previously held by the chiefs

TABLE I

Analysis of Cases used, by Reference to Courts of Hearing and Date

Years	*Through the Basotho Courts to J.C. and H.C.*[a]	*Through the Basotho Courts to J.C.*[b]	*Hearings in Basotho Courts only*	*Judgment of J.C. only*	*Hearings in H.C. only*[c]	*Total*	
1920–9	1	1				2	
1930–9		3	1			4	
1940–9	13	9		6	1	29	
1950–9	7	21	1	33	1	63	
1960		6		10		16	
1961		8		3		11	
1962		3		2		5	
1963	1	28		1		30	
1964	2	30		3		35	
1965	2	27	1	1		31	
1966		40	2	2		44	} 248
1967		19	2	3		24	
1968	3	17	1	5		26	
1969[d]		13		4	2	19	
1970		3		1	1	5	
1971	2					2	
Total	31	228	8	74	5	346	

Notes:

(a) Cases which proceeded beyond the High Court to the Court of Appeal and Privy Council are included in this group.

(b) References to J.C. before 1944 signify the subordinate courts, presided over by magistrates.

(c) These are cases heard by the High Court at first instance.

(d) The explanation for the fall off in the number of cases from 1969 onwards is that they are classified here according to their set-down number in the J.C.'s Court (unless they went on appeal to the High Court) rather than by their number of hearing. Cases set down in 1969 would usually only have been heard during 1970–1. I ceased systematically collecting judgments shortly before I left Lesotho in March 1971.

were not as well acquainted as the chiefs had been with the histories and personal circumstances of the litigants because they were peripatetic officials, and inevitably this meant some loss of flexibility and informality in the proceedings. However, to argue along these lines is to presuppose the existence of a pristine customary law unsullied by external influences. The truth is that the modern customary law is an amalgam of traditional law and many outside factors, particularly the changes introduced by colonial governments both in the judicial structure and process and in the substantive law. These have had an enormous impact, not only on the courts themselves, but also on other methods of dispute settlement (including the informal chiefly and family tribunals)[1] and any accurate portrait of the current law must take them fully into account.

(b) *Panel Discussion*

In July 1970 I held a panel discussion to supplement the information I had derived from the cases and the existing ethnographic and legal accounts. The seven participants in the discussion had all been recommended to me by the Judicial Commissioner as persons qualified to speak with authority on the customary law and all possessed judicial experience, either as a customary-court president or as a chief or headman or, in one case, as the Judicial Commissioner's interpreter and senior court clerk. They happened by chance to come from five different clans[2] and their family homes were scattered throughout six of the country's eight districts. Their ages ranged from forty-two to seventy-five. They were all men, but one of the girl law students from the university sat in for much of the discussion and did not hesitate to put forward the viewpoint of her sex and generation where she felt it was warranted. The discussion lasted for some twenty-five hours spread over five days. A tape-recording was made and from this I subsequently prepared a transcript to which frequent reference is made in Part II of this work.

The purpose of holding the discussion was fourfold. First, to test and verify the legal rules which I had tentatively deduced from a preliminary reading of a considerable proportion of the cases and most of the ethnographic and legal materials. Secondly, to discover rules that were not covered by these cases and materials

---

[1] Discussed in Ch. 2 below.
[2] For a discussion of the clans see below, pp. 18–19.

and thus to plug some of the gaps. Thirdly, to learn in respect of both the past and the present how far actual practice differed from the stated legal norms. Fourthly, to gain a deeper insight into the way in which Basotho viewed their laws and customs and indeed their whole society, in the hope of reducing the ethnocentricity likely to appear in my expatriate's account.

Much of this was achieved. It soon became clear that the participants conceived of their law as a rational and explicable system of norms and in the main they were well able to distinguish between the law and mere practice. They could cite in support of their propositions both maxims covering general points of principle (ideal norms) and numerous cases which they either knew or had themselves decided, as well as disputes and events in which they had each been personally involved. They were undoubtedly aware of the changes that had occurred in the law and did not regard customary law as immutable. While some soon revealed themselves as conservative in the sense that they did not favour further changes, others recognized the deficiences of the existing rules and were prepared to contemplate new solutions.

(c) *Social Survey*

I concluded my field-work during the period from November 1970 to February 1971 by investigating the incidence of various social activities and events. I wished to know, for instance, how common it is for couples to elope before marriage, the extent to which polygamy survives, the degree to which certain traditional types of marriage still persist, how often widows retain the lands allocated to their late husbands, and whether they tend to re-marry and bear more children. With a view to eliciting information on such matters I prepared a questionnaire which demanded simple answers about the personal lives of informants. Three of my law students at the University of Botswana, Lesotho and Swaziland interviewed some 162 women and filled in the questionnaires with the answers they gave.

The information derived from this survey is presented merely as a rough indication of the situation prevailing in various parts of Lesotho today. It has no claim to statistical accuracy. The women interviewed came from the three villages of Lenono's, Morija, and Manteko's. In the case of Lenono's and Manteko's they represented virtually the entire female population of the villages over the age of eighteen, while for Morija they constituted only about 75 per cent. The villages were selected because they were the homes of the students who conducted the interviews, but they have some small claim to be representative of the general population in that one was predominantly Roman Catholic, one comprised many members of the Lesotho Evangelical Church, and the other seemed to be predominantly non-Christian.[1]

In addition to this survey I spent some time in the office of the Registrar-General of Deeds and Companies collecting statistics on the incidence of civil marriages among the Basotho.

Finally, I flew to the remote district headquarters of Qacha's Nek in the south-east of Lesotho and spent several days listening to cases in the Judicial Commissioner's Court which was on circuit there. I had earlier briefly attended the same court in the capital and also the Local Court at Ralejoe.

(d) *Existing Descriptions and Accounts*

In my view it is extremely important to make a careful attempt to trace the development and evolution of customary law. Only if this is done can the modern law be presented meaningfully so that the trend of legal change is clearly seen. The law as it applies today has been drawn together from a variety of different strands and one of the functions of research should be the analysis of these and the influence they have had in shaping the direction of change. This is not as easy to accomplish as it might at first appear because if, for instance, one's major modern source is in the form of decided cases and these are unavailable for an earlier period a diachronic approach will not necessarily be comparing like with like. This is, in fact, the position for Lesotho. Records of the proceedings of the customary courts are virtually non-existent for the years before 1938 and have only become impressive since the late 1940s. Therefore resort must be had to other sources, including both the written accounts left by ethnographers and other observers as well as to the early memories of the older generation which can be elicited in a panel discussion. These can be supplemented by more formal sources such as written laws

---

[1] The religious affiliations of the Basotho are discussed in Ch. 1 below.

and the reports of government commissions and debates in advisory councils.

More specifically, the brief account given by Ellenberger and Macgregor[1] for the middle of the last century and the evidence supplied by some of the leading chiefs to the Commission appointed to investigate Sesotho law by the Cape Parliament in 1872[2] can both generally be relied upon for accuracy.[3] However, in the case of the latter it has to be remembered that the witnesses may well have been reluctant to speak plainly in every instance for fear that the Cape authorities would abolish by legislation certain laws and customs of which they disapproved—as in fact happened.[4] It therefore becomes necessary to read between the lines at some points. Even so, despite the lack of trust on the part of some of the witnesses[5] the replies to most of the questions are remarkably direct and straightforward.

Turning to the present century, the reports of the proceedings in the Basutoland National Council for the years 1903 to 1958, in which proposed alterations to the Laws of Lerotholi were discussed and debated, afford a particularly valuable insight into the merits and demerits of particular rules.

For the twenty-five years up to 1955 considerable reliance can be placed on the ethnographic accounts of Laydevant,[6] Ashton,[7] and Sheddick[8] and the analysis of colonial administration by Hailey.[9] In the case of Ashton it has to be borne in mind that most of his field-work during the 1930s was conducted among the

[1] *History of the Basuto, Ancient and Modern* (Caxton, 1912), pp. 271–80.
[2] *Report and Evidence of Commission on Native Laws of the Basutos* (Sau. Solomon & Co., 1873; repr. Morija, 1966), hereafter referred to as *1873 Report and Evidence*.
[3] Sekese's work *Mekhoa le Maele a Basotho* (Morija, 1907; repr. in 1953 and 1968) also contains some interesting information on this period. The relevant parts were kindly translated for me by Mr. S. Peete.
[4] See the regulations contained in Cape Proclamations Nos. 74 of 1871 and 41 of 1877.
[5] See the supplementary paper of Mr. Austen, Senior Magistrate, in *1873 Report and Evidence*, p. 60.
[6] 'Étude sur la famille en Basutoland' (1931), 1 *Journal de la Société des Africanistes* 207.
[7] *The Basuto* (O.U.P., 1952; 2nd ed., 1967).
[8] *The Southern Sotho* (I.A.I., 1953); *Land Tenure in Basutoland* (H.M.S.O., 1954).
[9] *Native Administration in the British African Territories*, Part V (H.M.S.O., 1953).

Batlokoa who, as he points out, are closer than other Basotho to the traditional culture of pre-colonial times. Moreover, some of the descriptions he gives must certainly relate to an even earlier period than 1930. Duncan's *Sotho Laws and Customs*,[1] based largely upon the decisions of the Judicial Commissioner's Court from 1944 to 1957, is also generally very accurate.

The most recent major contribution has been Hamnett's work[2] which concentrates mainly on the public side of Sesotho law and the regulation of the chieftainship. However, some aspects of private law are also discussed, notably in the field of inheritance, and I have made reference to his views wherever these are relevant to my study. Finally, there is the short 'Restatement of the Sesotho Law of Marriage' prepared by a panel of court presidents under the chairmanship of Ramolefe.[3] It is of only limited value.

4. MANNER OF PRESENTATION

My approach has been to refer, in the part of this work devoted to the substantive law, to practically all the versions of rules of Sesotho family law for every period from 1850 to the present day that have been recorded or noted down whether by chiefs, councils, missionaries, magistrates, ethnographers, or lawyers. I have analysed and compared them one with another and integrated them with the case records and the views expressed at the panel discussion so as to present the historical development of Sesotho law. I have shown where the sources can be reconciled, and where they differ I have endeavoured to explain the discrepancy. No statement has been made which cannot be supported and the authority for every proposition is given full citation. Only in this way can the reader, whoever he be, evaluate the respective weight of one propounded legal rule against another.[4] This, in my opinion, has been one of the fundamental weaknesses of some previous

---

[1] (O.U.P., 1960).

[2] *Chieftainship and Legitimacy: An Anthropological Study of Executive Law in Lesotho* (Routledge & Kegan Paul, 1975). This book is largely based upon Hamnett, 'Sotho Customary Law' (unpubl. Ph.D. thesis, University of Edinburgh, 1970).

[3] (Cyclostyled, n.d. but *c.* 1968); hereafter referred to simply as the 'Restatement'.

[4] The need to do this has been stressed by White, 'African Customary Law: The Problem of Concept and Definition' [1965], *J.A.L.* 88.

studies of African law. They have paid insufficient attention to the reader's desire to know the source or sources from which any given proposition is derived so that its authenticity can be assessed and its date known.

Four aspects of the way in which I present my material warrant special mention.

First, the mode of citing information derived from the panel discussion is by reference to the relevant page of the transcript.[1] However, this must not be understood necessarily to connote that every member of the panel expressly endorsed the proposition for which the panel discussion is given as authority. Only rarely was this the case. I did not proceed on the basis of putting every question to every member of the panel. This would have extended the length of the discussion beyond the time available. Therefore very often the assent of the majority of the panel has been inferred from their tacit acceptance of the propositions made by one, two, or three of their number on a particular point and from my impression of the tenor of the feeling of the meeting. Where there was a very full discussion of a particular point and the various views were still in conflict at the end of the debate care has been taken to incorporate this dissension in the text. More often, however, the apparent conflicts were resolved and explained in the course of the debate and it is the agreed position that is being relied upon.

The second matter relates to the way in which rules of law have been extracted from the case records. This has been done in the conventional manner in respect of decisions of the superior courts and the Judicial Commissioner's Court since the judges are careful to provide a full explanation of the grounds upon which they reach their decisions and the *ratio decidendi* of each case is readily apparent. The same approach has not, however, been so easy to apply in relation to the lower courts. The fact is that whereas Westernized courts are usually very explicit in their judgments as to the grounds for their decisions, the Local and Central Courts in Lesotho tend to state their decisions very succinctly. This often means that their reasoning is merely

[1] Poulter (Ed.), 'Sesotho Family Law Conference Transcript' (unpubl., 1970). Copies of the transcript are available for consultation at the Judicial Commissioner's Court, Maseru, the library of the University of Botswana, Lesotho and Swaziland, the Bodleian Library, Oxford, and the library of the School of Oriental and African Studies, University of London.

implicit[1] and has to be sought in the questions asked by the court and the parties in the course of the proceedings and in the answers given to them. Despite this, these courts operate with reasonably well-defined concepts, norms, standards, and principles and after hearing the evidence proceed to apply these to the facts as found. The *ratio* of a case is thus located by taking the decision of the court together with the material facts in much the same way as in the common law system.[2]

Thirdly, there is the question of the authority of the decisions referred to in this work. It is important to appreciate that the cases are being used as analytical data and as illustrative devices but, with the possible exception of the few judgments of the superior courts, they are not being cited as binding precedents. There was no system of precedent in the traditional judicial process and the present Basotho Courts are in no position to apply such a doctrine since they have virtually no knowedge of the decisions given by courts above them. However, one can obviously expect courts in the future to attach a certain amount of weight to any previous decisions that are brought to their notice as a result of this work. Hopefully they will also be prepared to take note of statements based on views expressed at the Panel Discussion.

Finally, the manner in which decisions are referred to in the footnotes needs to be explained. Where a case is cited as authority for a given proposition the level of the court from whose decision this proposition is derived is always given in brackets. For instance, in the bulk of cases which I have used, the proceedings have commenced in a Local Court and then gone to two appeals, first in a Central Court and then in the Judicial Commissioner's Court. Because the Judicial Commissioners have nearly all been non-Basotho I have not treated their judgments as exclusively authoritative and therefore the best citation will be to the decisions of all three courts (i.e. 'L.C., C.C., and J.C.' or 'all courts'). However, a citation to one court alone is not an indication that the other courts took a different view; if they did so this will be stated unequivocally. Rather it means either that the decision in those courts was made on different grounds or that no clear *ratio decidendi* can be extracted from the proceedings or very occasionally

---

[1] Fallers found the same situation in Busoga—see *Law without Precedent* (Chicago, 1969), especially pp. 20–1, 31–2.

[2] See Goodhart, 'The *Ratio Decidendi* of a Case', 40 *Yale L.J.* 161 (1930).

that the judgment was so clearly erroneous as not to even warrant mention. With respect to cases before 1961 it often means that only the judgment of the Judicial Commissioner was available.

Of the cases decided in the superior courts only eleven have been reported in the High Commission Territories Law Reports (H.C.T.L.R.). Decisions of the Basotho Courts and the Judicial Commissioner's Court have never been reported.

I

CULTURAL AND ECONOMIC FRAMEWORK

I. CULTURAL HOMOGENEITY

In the process of founding the present Basotho Nation the first Paramount Chief, Moshoeshoe I (c. 1786–1870) brought together under his aegis a number of clans and other tribal groups. Some were of Sotho origin and others of Nguni stock. Most of the former, including his own, were known as Bakoena, and these people have dominated the other groups and have done their utmost to develop a national culture along the lines of their own laws and customs. Just how successful they have been is hard to assess, but one writer has suggested that a considerable degree of cultural homogeneity has now been attained:

Originally, the various groups constituting the Basotho Nation of today each showed specific ethnic characteristics, e.g. the Batlokoa and Baphuthi. In the past certain areas experienced a history slightly different from that of the rest of the country, e.g. the Quthing District. Nevertheless it can be said that, on the whole, regional differences among the population of Lesotho can no longer be explained primarily through differences in historical, political or social characteristics. As a result of the forging of Lesotho's heterogeneous population groups into one Basotho Nation under the great Moshoeshoe I, Lesotho is now already for more than a century one relatively homogeneous area, with its people sharing basically the same historical and political events, undergoing fundamentally the same social and cultural influences and transformations.[1]

Despite this, there are some groups that require special mention.[2] The Batlokoa, who were the subject of particular study

---

[1] Smits, 'The Distribution of the Population in Lesotho and Some Implications for Economic Development' (1968) *Lesotho Notes and Records* 19 at 23.

[2] See generally Sheddick (1954), pp. 14–16.

by Ashton,[1] appear to have held vigorously to some of their
original customs and seem to be regarded on the one hand as
exponents of 'pure' Sesotho law and custom and, on the other,
as extremely conservative. Of the Nguni groups the Vundle,
Thembu, and others have retained their own laws and customs,[2]
some of which are totally at variance with those of the Bakoena,
for instance, the rule prescribing exogamy. Whether the courts
are empowered to give effect to the personal customary laws of
these people does not ever seem to have been decided,[3] but in
any event no discussion of these laws will be found in the present
work. The Nguni groups constitute a relatively small proportion
of the total population[4] and information about them is very scarce
indeed.

Furthermore, since this study is concerned with the Basotho of
Lesotho, no account is taken of those Basotho who have made
their permanent homes in the Republic of South Africa. There
are many, for instance, who live in the border areas surrounding
Lesotho. Clearly their laws were at one time the same as the
Basotho who were living in Lesotho, but the standard South
African textbooks on 'native law' show clearly that the courts
there have so warped and perverted these laws that they have
become, in Ramolefe's apt words 'caricatures of concepts known
to and used by the Basotho of Lesotho'.[5]

2. GEOGRAPHICAL SITUATION

Lesotho is a small mountainous kingdom roughly the size of
Belgium with a population of over 1,000,000 Basotho and only
about 3,000 Europeans. The major centres are the capital Maseru
(population *c.* 20,000) and the eight other administrative headquarters, but none of these has a population of more than 6,000.
The country is thus predominantly rural with the people living in
villages rather than towns.

Lesotho is in the uniquely unfortunate position of being com-

[1] In *The Basuto* (O.U.P., 1952; 2nd ed., 1967).
[2] See Sheddick (1954), p. 16; P.D., pp. 69, 71.
[3] See below, pp. 55–6.
[4] The most recent official census containing any breakdown of the population
in terms of tribal origin was as far back as 1936. This revealed a figure of
475,613 Basotho (presumably of Sotho origin) and 88,586 people of Nguni
origin (Zulu, Thembu, Fingo, Ndebele, and Pondo).
[5] 'Sesotho Marriage, Guardianship and the Customary-law Heir' in Gluckman
(Ed.), *Ideas and Procedures in African Customary Law* (O.U.P., 1969), p. 197.

pletely surrounded by a country whose political philosophy is totally at variance with her own. The fact of this encirclement by South Africa needs to be firmly grasped if the background to everyday life is to be clearly understood. The influence of South Africa is felt in many ways. Political decisions have to be taken with an eye to possible reactions from the South African government. Many of the attitudes fostered by the doctrine of apartheid invade Lesotho through the medium of newspapers and broadcasting as well as in the behaviour of many of the white South Africans who come to Lesotho as officials, businessmen, and tourists. Most of the consumer goods available in the shops come from South Africa which in turn takes most of Lesotho's exports, consisting of livestock, wool, mohair, and diamonds. South African currency (rand) is the only legal tender in Lesotho and all the main financial institutions in the country except the Lesotho Bank are controlled from South Africa. This has the bizarre result that a large part of the personal savings of the Basotho in commercial banks, building societies, and the like are utilized abroad, while the country itself is desperately in need of more capital for development.[1] For the first three years after independence the annual budget had to be balanced by a very substantial contribution from the British government, but greater reliance is now being placed upon the increased revenue provided by the Customs Agreement which was renegotiated with South Africa in 1969. While the receipts under this Agreement appear to provide Lesotho with a large and predictable form of revenue the rates of duty and thus the over-all total are dependent on whatever fiscal policies are adopted for the time being by the South African government.

All these facts tell of the enormous impact that South Africa has on Lesotho but none can compare in economic and social significance with the system of migrant labour under which most Basotho men spend a large proportion of their lives working in South Africa with very little reward.

3. THE SYSTEM OF MIGRANT LABOUR

(a) *Causes*

The real reason why hordes of Basotho travel to South Africa

---

[1] See *Lesotho First Five-year Development Plan 1970/71–1974/75* (Maseru, 1970) (hereafter referred to as *Development Plan*), p. 15.

every year to take employment there is dire economic necessity. The other grounds sometimes put forward are only peripheral, for instance that it constitutes a modern form of initiation process or that it derives from a thirst for adventure and the desire for the glamour of urban life or from the need to escape from burdensome legal or kinship obligations.[1]

The simple truth is first that the land resources of Lesotho are insufficient to support, even at the level of subsistence, the present population. Secondly, there are very few opportunities for paid employment within Lesotho. These stark facts emerge clearly from the figures for the male labour force in 1969:[2]

	Numbers	Percentage
Employment in agriculture in Lesotho	135,000	48
Paid employment in Lesotho	15,000	7
Paid employment in South Africa	120,000	45
	270,000	100

Basotho men go to South Africa, therefore, in order to earn enough to keep themselves and their families alive. They hope to be able to save enough to make purchases of specific articles which are badly needed, such as clothing, furniture, and other household articles and simple items of agricultural equipment. In addition they must set aside enough money to pay their taxes. Last but by no means least, many men will be trying to save enough from their earnings to pay *bohali* (bridewealth) for a wife.

(b) *Historical Development*

Migrant labour is by no means a modern phenomenon for the Basotho and dates back almost as far as their first contact with Europeans.[3] For most of the thirty years up to 1868 they fought skirmishes with, and made raids upon, the Boers who had trekked north from the Cape of Good Hope in search of new lands and freedom from British control. For much of this period the country was in very straitened circumstances and some

---

[1] See generally Ashton, pp. 162–5, and, for comparison with the position in Botswana, the detailed study made by Schapera, *Migrant Labour and Tribal Life* (O.U.P., 1947).

[2] *Development Plan*, p. 11.

[3] Ashton, p. 162.

Basotho went to take employment in Natal and the Cape Colony while fighting was in progress in the Orange Free State and Lesotho.[1]

When the Basotho forces commanded by Moshoeshoe I were on the brink of total collapse in 1868 Lesotho was saved from the ignominy of final defeat by being incorporated as a British colony. However, in return Moshoeshoe was forced to accede to the Aliwal North Convention of 1869 under which the Basotho surrendered their title to a huge area comprising the most fertile lands they had ever possessed, situated to the west of the Caledon River. This fact, coupled with the immediate imposition by the colonial government of a hut tax, led large numbers of Basotho to set out from the barren and mountainous residue of their country to the Kimberley diamond mines which were opened in 1870.

During the years 1930–56 not only did the movement of Basotho workers to and from South Africa increase but large numbers of Basotho made their permanent homes in South Africa, concealing their origins to escape being deported. The 1946 census revealed that the *de facto* population of Lesotho (i.e. excluding those absent in South Africa) showed virtually no increase over what it had been ten years earlier. By 1955 the Tomlinson Report estimated that there were some 220,000 Basotho who had been completely absorbed within South African society and who were permanent residents there.[2]

Since 1963 South Africa has set up border control posts and by requiring everyone from Lesotho to be in possession of valid travel documents and identification papers has at last halted the flow of permanent immigrants.

(c) *The Pattern of Periodic Visits*

Table 2 indicates the numbers of male absentees over a thirty-year period and shows that 21 per cent of all male Basotho were abroad in South Africa on 14 April 1966, the enumeration day for the most recent census. Virtually all of them were in jobs. Table 3 gives an indication of the ages at which workers tend to migrate. It will be noticed that the percentage of migrants starts to rise around the age of eighteen. This is the age at which a man

---

[1] See Hailey (1953), p. 13.

[2] *Summary of the Report of the Commission for the Socio-economic Development of the Bantu Areas within the Union of South Africa* (Pretoria, 1955), p. 40. See also Leistner, *Lesotho: Economic Structure and Growth* (Pretoria, 1966), p. 4.

TABLE 2

*Basotho male absentees abroad in South Africa on the day of the
Lesotho Census (excluding those presumed to be permanently
domiciled in South Africa)*[a]

Year	Male absentees	Total de iure male population	Absentees as a percentage of total male population
1936	78,604	317,309	24
1946	83,419	329,763	25
1956	112,790	383,241	29
1966 [b]	97,529 [c]	465,784	21

Notes:

(a) This table is based upon the figures in the 1936, 1956, and 1966 Lesotho Census Reports and for 1946 on information provided by the South African Union Department of Census and Statistics.

(b) The reason given in the 1966 Census Report (at p. 86) for the fall in the number of absentees was the more restrictive influx control practised by South Africa during the 1960s.

(c) Of these, 92,020 were workers, 1,404 at school, and 4,105 unspecified.

TABLE 3

*Comparative analysis of Basotho males present in Lesotho and
absent in South Africa on the day of the 1966 census, by age*

Age	Present	Absent	Total	Absentees as percentage of total
0–16	205,922	5,260	211,182	2·5
17–19	19,584	5,871	25,455	23
20–39	59,555	61,845	121,400	51
40–9	30,704	14,966	45,660	33
50–64	31,936	6,233	38,169	16
65 and over	19,015	908	19,923	4·5
not stated	1,371	1,267	2,638	—

first becomes liable to pay tax and it is also the minimum age for employment in the South African mines. Of the men aged between twenty and thirty-nine those absent actually exceeded those present in Lesotho. If a working life of forty-seven years is taken, from seventeen to sixty-four, it can be calculated that about 38·5 per cent of the male labour force is absent from Lesotho at any one moment of time. However, this by no means presents a fair reflection of the percentage of people for whom migrant labour is an essential feature of their way of life. This is due to the fact that the visits to South Africa for work are made at periodic intervals according to a relatively stable pattern.

For instance, mine workers go on contract for a specific number of shifts. Basotho miners usually sign up for 180 shifts which take about eight months to complete, though they sometimes extend the period when they find they still have not managed to save from their earnings as much as they need. However, in no circumstances can they continue for more than two years at a time. After eight or nine months it is usual for them to return home to Lesotho for a period of three or four months. People living in different localities tend to migrate at different times of the year because of seasonal variations affecting their farming activities.[1] However, this should not be interpreted to mean that Basotho miners are simultaneously conscientious farmers for, as we shall see, the contribution made by migrant workers to the agricultural production of Lesotho is no more than an empty gesture. In the main they merely return home for rest and recuperation and do not play an active part in farming.

Bearing in mind the periodic nature of most employment in South Africa and the seasonal variations it seems probable that the number of workers abroad at any one time represents between two-thirds and three-quarters of those who migrate at some time every year. This would suggest that about 55 per cent of the male labour force are 'professional' migrant workers and even this figure may be conservative.[2]

These dry statistics are given flesh and blood by the recent investigations carried out by Devitt in the lowland village of Mokhokhong which lies some thirty miles east of the capital.

Most men begin their careers as migrant workers when they are eighteen to twenty years of age, and are seldom seen again in Mokhokhong, apart from periods of a few weeks to a few months every two or

---

[1] Much of the information in this paragraph was kindly supplied by Mr. M. S. Hobson of the Maseru Office of the Mine Labour Organisations (N.R.C.) Ltd.
[2] Leistner, 'Foreign Bantu Workers in South Africa' (1967), *S.A.J.E.* 54, gave an estimate for 1964 of 62 per cent based on statistics provided by the South African Department of Bantu Administration and Development.

three years, until they are about thirty-seven. Migration then becomes less frequent, longer periods are spent at home, until the age of about forty-five when most men have ceased to migrate altogether. At present those over forty-five who are still migrating are either landless or have very good jobs in South Africa. The age of thirty-seven coincides approximately with the time when a man can expect to receive adequate land, two acres or more, to warrant his staying at home to cultivate it. Before this time he cannot support his family without wage earnings, and even with two acres he must find other sources of income.

The most active period of men's lives is therefore spent away from home. The brief 'resting times' spent in Mokhokhong are too short to allow any serious project to be started and established. Men contributed relatively little to agriculture at this time, both because they are often not present during the peak labour-input periods and because they regard the interludes between contracts as times for recuperation.[1]

Around the age of thirty-seven men usually hope their days of migrant labour are over, but as Devitt goes on to point out, they are often compelled to continue the practice.

This frequently happens at the end of a man's career as a migrant. He puts a great effort into his farming to try to make enough to remain at home, but he probably will have a bad season within the first few years, and since he is not quite old enough not to work he returns once more to his work place. This may happen several times until he is too old to continue migrating. But many men return sick, some with phthisis contracted on the mines, and find it impossible to give much energy to the task of domestic reconstruction.[2]

The burden of supporting the family will then be thrust upon able-bodied sons who in their turn must migrate to find employment. It is no exaggeration to conclude from this that the average man's working life is a pathetic cycle of sweated labour abroad followed by inefficient farming at home. The fact that the option of employment in South Africa is available at all prevents most Basotho from making more determined efforts to become efficient cultivators and stock farmers. In consequence bad farming practices reduce the productivity of the land and the value of the

[1] 'The Politics of Headmanship in the Mokhokhong Valley' (unpubl. M.A. thesis, Univ. of the Witwatersrand, 1969), pp. 72–3.
[2] At p. 74.

livestock so that the need to migrate for work becomes ever more pressing and a vicious circle is created.[1]

The statistics from the 1966 Census show that around two-thirds of the migrants were married;[2] yet the vast majority are prohibited by South African legislation from taking their wives and families to live with them and, as will be seen, the whole structure of family life is undermined in the process. However, there are also estimated to be some 20,000 Basotho women working in South Africa as domestic servants, seasonal farm-workers, and the like, at least half of them married.[3]

(d) Conditions and Wages

Most Basotho employed in South Africa work in gold mines and coal mines either in the Orange Free State or on the Witwatersrand. In addition there are many men employed as farm-workers and in private industries such as manufacturing and construction, as well as those in public corporations and in the wholesale and retail trade. Inevitably, the majority can only aspire to unskilled jobs. In 1966 it was estimated that around 94 per cent of migrants had not even completed a primary-school education. Nearly half had never even been to school at all.[4] In any event even for the better qualified the rigid system of job reservation based on racial discrimination would present an insuperable barrier to most skilled and semi-skilled work.

It is common knowledge that the conditions of work are poor and no one will deny that the life of a miner is unpleasant, dangerous, and hard. Despite some dramatic increases in wage-levels during 1973-4 the earnings of unskilled black workers are still appallingly low and the main concern of those espousing their cause is to ensure that they do not fall below the so-called 'poverty datum line'.

(e) Effects

In economic terms migrant labour not only provides wages for a large proportion of Basotho men but also supports their families since relatively large sums are brought back into Lesotho. Indeed, it has been suggested that the total earnings abroad of migrants

[1] See Smit, *Lesotho: A Geographical Study* (Pretoria, 1967), p. 33.
[2] *1966 Population Census Report* (Morija), vol. i, p. 109.
[3] *Development Plan*, p. 11.
[4] See *1966 Population Census Report*, vol. i, p. 107.

are of comparable magnitude to the entire gross domestic product of Lesotho.[1] Even so, the average *per capita* income of the nation as a whole has been estimated at only about R63 which means that Lesotho falls within the United Nations list of the world's twenty-five poorest countries.[2]

On the other hand, the system of periodic migrations leads to inefficient and disinterested farming by those who have land with the result that agricultural production within Lesotho remains at a low level. Ploughing, for example, is sometimes left in the hands of women and children who are too weak to do more than scratch at the surface. Livestock is herded by boys who ought to be at school. Paradoxically, therefore, while the population is too large for the country in terms of subsistence on agricultural production, the country's work force is in fact inadequate for the purposes of increasing this production.

The social consequences are exclusively on the debit side. Men are separated from their wives and children for long periods and the cohesion of the family is disrupted. Wives are placed in an awkward position since they must take additional responsibility for the management of their households when their husbands are absent and then retire into the background when their men return. This calls for considerable tact and self-restraint when husbands are at home and excellent judgment when they are abroad. Sons (and daughters) grow up in villages practically devoid of men for much of the year and this can lead to a loss of parental control and influence. Young boys are prevented from attending school regularly by the need to herd the family's livestock. Both wives and husbands are tempted to be unfaithful to one another and large numbers of children are conceived in adultery.[3] Separated spouses and looser family ties become the natural state of affairs. Kinship obligations are felt to be less binding and family council meetings which were and still are extremely important in the settlement of disputes are made more difficult to arrange. Even the enforcement of the law is hampered since criminal offenders, tortfeasors, and other miscreants can easily escape the net of justice by scurrying across the border.

---

[1] *Development Plan*, p. 6.
[2] Ibid., p. 7.
[3] See Wallman, *Take Out Hunger* (London, 1969), p. 45.

4. AGRICULTURE

Agricultural production constitutes the major *local*, as opposed to external source of income for roughly 85 per cent of the Basotho population.[1] Crops are grown and livestock are kept, but for a variety of reasons farming tends to be unremunerative and does not even provide sufficient for the nation's needs.[2]

(a) *Crop Production*

The most important crops are maize, sorghum, and wheat, but beans, peas, oats, barley, and pumpkins are also grown to a small extent. The maize crop yields as little as two to three bags per acre compared with thirty to thirty-five bags which can be achieved under experimental conditions with irrigated land. Adverse climatic conditions are responsible as well as the very poor terrain and the migrant labour system, but two further factors also contribute to this extremely low level of productivity.

(i) *Population pressure*

As will be explained in Chapter 2, land for cultivation is not owned absolutely by individuals.[3] It belongs to the Basotho Nation as a whole and is allocated by chiefs and headmen to married men for the support of themselves and their families. Allocations are in certain circumstances made to women and to bachelors, but these are somewhat rare occurrences.[4] A married man can expect to receive a residential site on which to build his huts, a garden near by where he can grow fruit and vegetables and also some arable fields for cultivating his crops. Traditionally the amount of arable land depended, as to some extent it does today, on the number of wives. A man with one wife would be allocated three fields, one for himself and two for his wife and children, each field measuring very approximately two or three acres. If he had more than one wife he would receive two extra fields in respect of each additional wife. Such allocations are, however, invariably made to the husband and not directly to his wives and he naturally bears the over-all responsibility for the maintenance of the entire household.

---

[1] *Development Plan*, p. 9.
[2] Lesotho actually has to import maize, wheat, and sorghum.
[3] See below, p. 37.
[4] See below, pp. 186–7, 195–6, 222.

When the country had a small population every Mosotho could expect to obtain a holding of this nature immediately he married and the idea that this was a matter of right became firmly entrenched. However, for many years the growth of population has been outstripping the amount of land available.[1] Men have had to wait a considerable length of time after they have married and their belated allocation has often been well below the standard quota, so that by 1953 Hailey was writing that the occupation of arable land had reached saturation point.[2]

A comparison of the two most recent Agricultural Surveys in 1949–50 and 1960 shows how acute the problem has become. Not only were there more households in 1960 with two fields than those occupying the conventional norm of three,[3] but the number of landless households had risen sharply.

The general pattern appears clearly from the following statistics:[4]

	1949–50	1960
Number of landless households	11,700	14,780
Percentage of landless households	7·2%	8·5%
Average acreage per household of those with lands	5·75	5·4
Percentage of landholders who had less than four acres	35·7%	44·3%

The 1960 Report concluded:

The average size of the majority of holdings is too small to supply the basic requirements of families. Crop yield figures obtained from the census . . . show that most holdings still obtain minimum produce from their lands. This factor combined with the low prices paid to the farmers for their produce indicate that many farming households cannot make a living out of farming.[5]

[1] See e.g. Pim, *Report of the Commission appointed to Inquire into the Financial and Economic Position of Basutoland* (H.M.S.O., 1935) (hereafter referred to as the *Pim Report*), p. 46.
[2] (1953), p. 119.
[3] Morojele, *1960 Agricultural Census, Part 3* (Maseru, 1963), pp. 39–40.
[4] Based on Douglas and Tennant, *Basutoland Agricultural Survey 1949–50* (Maseru, 1952), pp. 27, 95, and *1960 Agricultural Census Part 2*, p. 21; *Part 3*, pp. 10, 14–15, 23.
[5] At p. 11.

While no figures are available to indicate what developments have taken place since 1960 some idea can be obtained from the fact that the current net growth rate for the *de iure* population is estimated to be around 2·5 per cent a year.[1]

In the upshot the law today no longer provides that chiefs and headmen are *bound* to provide their subjects with land to cultivate. These allocating authorities are now merely made responsible for the distribution of the land. This power is not coupled with a duty and a citizen cannot claim any absolute right to be allocated land.[2]

(ii) *The system of land tenure*

There are various aspects of the land-tenure system[3] which might be regarded as placing obstacles in the way of any modernization of agricultural practices and increased production.

We have already seen that titles of individual absolute ownership are not recognized. Arable land cannot be sold or mortgaged[4] and this inability to provide security prevents farmers from obtaining the credit which they badly need for agricultural development and improvement.

Another factor often put forward as inhibiting farmers from investing money and effort in improvements is the risk of being deprived of their lands by the allocating authority. For instance, the law imposes an obligation upon all chiefs and headmen to make frequent (usually annual) inspections of the land-holdings in their areas to discover whether anyone is occupying more land than is necessary for the subsistence of himself and his household. If any person is found to be in this relatively prosperous state the chief or headman is empowered to reallocate the surplus land to those of his subjects who have no lands or insufficient

---

[1] *Development Plan*, p. 1.

[2] Compare s. 8 of the 1903 version of the Laws of Lerotholi with s. 7(1) of Part I of the 1946, 1952, and 1959 versions.

[3] See generally on the subject of land tenure Hailey (1953), pp. 116–21; Sheddick (1954); Duncan, pp. 86–94; Crawford, 'Land Shortage and Land Plenty' (1967), *S.A.L.J.* 437; Cowen, 'Land Tenure and Economic Development in Lesotho' (1967), *S.A.J.E.* 58; Palmer and Poulter, pp. 172–89; Williams, *Lesotho: Land Tenure and Economic Development* (Pretoria, 1972).

[4] Sales and mortgages are now prohibited by statute—see Deeds Registry Act, No. 12 of 1967, ss. 15(1) and 27(1). However, something closely akin to a sale of land can occur by the sale of structures built on the land. The chief's agreement will be needed since he will have to make a reallocation of the residential site to the purchaser of the building—see Hailey (1953), p. 118; Duncan, p. 99; P.D., pp. 172–3, 219.

for their needs.[1] This power is designed to achieve an equitable distribution of the meagre land resources throughout the whole population, but the way in which the law is framed at present does certainly seem to suggest that farmers are in danger of deprivation if they achieve a standard of living higher than bare subsistence. To the extent that the law is designed to give land to as many people as possible even if this means subdividing holdings that are already very small, this may constitute a disincentive to improvement by existing holders. It seems clear that in practice deprivations are very rare, but even the possibility may be decisive if the farmers themselves are disinclined to change their way of life.

Apart from the loss of land following an inspection landholders who fail to cultivate their lands properly for two successive years without sufficient reason may also be deprived,[2] as may anyone who ceases to owe allegiance to the authority who allocated the lands and turns his loyalty to another chief or headman.

Moreover, there is another possible disincentive in the legal principle that arable lands are not inheritable; instead they revert on death to the allocating authority.[3] Again, the objective is to prevent the tying up of lands in families for long periods in case this prejudices an over-all distribution that is fair to everyone.

(b) *Livestock Production*

Bearing in mind the fact that the terrain of the country is more suitable (though hardly ideal) for pastoralism than agriculture, it is not surprising that the Basotho have always kept a large number of livestock. These they use for ploughing and for milk as well as for meat. Three-quarters of Lesotho's exports, running to some R3 million annually, are made up of livestock, wool, mohair, skins, and hides.[4] Despite this the livestock industry is backward and stagnant, plagued by a preference among the people for quantity rather than quality. One of the reasons for this is that the marriage payment of *bohali* is calculated, and commonly paid, in terms of cattle, goats, sheep, and horses, and the quality of the particular animals is of no significance provided they are

---

[1] Laws of Lerotholi, Part I, s. 7(2).
[2] Laws of Lerotholi, Part I, s. 7(3).
[3] Discussed in Ch. 17 below.
[4] *Development Plan*, p. 17.

not diseased or lame. In consequence the country is badly over-stocked, having more than double the number of animals for which there is grazing land available.[1] This leads to rapid destruction of pastures and increased soil erosion.

5. RELIGION

There have been missionaries in the country for 140 years and the impact of Christianity has been so great that ethnographers have found it extremely difficult to reconstruct the traditional religious beliefs of the Basotho. However, these appear to have revolved around a recognition of the influence of the spirits of the departed.[2] The ancestors were regarded as continuing to hold roughly the same positions as they had held when living and they were thought to exercise the same sort of control and protection over their families. Their descendants were under an obligation to care for them and pay homage to them in order to retain this protection. Equally they were under a duty to ensure that the family line was continued so that the ancestors would never be neglected or forgotten. This explains the great importance attached to the birth of children and the numerous legal mechanisms which exist to encourage this. In a very real sense a man's main purpose on earth was seen as forging a link between his ancestors and his own descendants.

Such beliefs persist among many people today although they are often overlaid with aspects of Christian doctrine. The first missionaries arrived in 1833 in response to an invitation from Moshoeshoe I who hoped they would help him in his dealings with the Boers. They were members of the Paris Evangelical Missionary Society (P.E.M.S.) and one of their number was the Revd. Eugène Casalis who subsequently became Moshoeshoe's political adviser.[3] Roman Catholic missionaries did not appear on the scene until some thirty years later, but during this century they have been more successful than any of their rivals and nearly 50 per cent of all Christians are now Roman Catholics. Less than 30 per cent are members of the Lesotho Evangelical Church, the autonomous church which resulted from the activities of the P.E.M.S.

[1] *Development Plan*, pp. 84–6.
[2] See generally Ashton, pp. 112–19; Sheddick (1953), pp. 65–7.
[3] Moshoeshoe was only converted to Christianity a few weeks before his death and was on the point of being baptized when he died on 11 Mar. 1870.

The growth in the number of adherents to Christianity appears from the following figures taken from the official census reports:

Year	Number of Africans professing Christianity	Expressed as a percentage of the de facto African population
1875	6,379	5
1904	50,526	14·5
1921	135,749	27
1936	254,511	45·5
1946	323,913	63
1956	452,925	71
1966	695,002	82

These are high figures indeed, and as might be anticipated by no means all professing Christians put their faith into practice in relation to all the important events in their lives. The average number of civil marriages contracted each year during the decade 1961–70 was only just over 2,500. Of these the vast majority were church weddings, only about 5 per cent being before a District Commissioner.[1] However, if it is assumed that the total marriage rate among Basotho is eight per thousand of population per annum[2] it is clear that only about one-third of all marriages between Basotho are contracted according to civil rites.

One particularly interesting feature has been the approach of the Christian missions towards those Basotho who have wished both to adopt the ceremony of their faith and to retain their traditional practices. Would the missions permit a couple to marry under Sesotho law first and then go through a ceremony of marriage in church afterwards? The major denominations represented in Lesotho took different stances. The P.E.M.S., believing that the payment of *bohali* under Sesotho law signified the purchase of a wife, refused to countenance customary marriages.[3] Anyone paying or receiving *bohali* was liable to be

[1] Private researches in the office of the Registrar-General, Maseru.

[2] This figure seems to be the rough average for those countries (mainly European) for which accurate statistics are available—see *U.N. Demographic Yearbook 1970*, pp. 730–5. No such statistics are kept in Lesotho; only civil marriages are required to be registered.

[3] See Casalis, *The Basutos* (London, 1861), pp. 182–6; V. Ellenberger, *A Century of Mission Work in Basutoland* (Morija, 1938); E. W. Smith, *The Mabilles of Basutoland* (London, 1939), pp. 124, 188, 341–2; Germond, *Chronicles of Basutoland* (Morija, 1967), p. 472.

expelled from church membership forthwith. The Roman Catholic and Anglican churches, on the other hand, were less rigid and took no objection to such 'dual marriages'.[1]

In practice members of the Lesotho Evangelical Church frequently broke the rules and paid *bohali* surreptitiously.[2] In the process they were often compelled to resort to devious disguises for their payments. Some drove the cattle after nightfall and acquired the nickname of 'Christians of the Twilight'.[3] Others paid in cash and the money was then meant to be used to offset the wedding expenses, including the bride's dress and the feast.[4] This payment they called *mpho* (a gift),[5] a transparent cover for what was commonly *bohali*, at any rate in some degree, since not all the money was really spent on the wedding by the bride's family.[6] Other simple techniques of evasion were for parents not to become converts until they had married off all their daughters[7] or else, if already members, to lapse as soon as their daughters became eligible for marriage.

Eventually the Church realized that its attitude had led to even greater evils than those which it had sought to eradicate. Christians were learning to behave hypocritically and were practising constant deceptions on their own clergy. The *bohali* custom had turned out to mean far more to the Basotho than the P.E.M.S. missionaries had imagined and they were steadily losing converts to the other churches.[8] Therefore in 1954 the rule banning *bohali* payments was lifted and the Church of Lesotho officially countenanced what everyone knew had been going on behind the scenes for upward of a hundred years.

[1] See V. Ellenberger, p. 240; *1944 National Council Proceedings*, p. 194; Reuter, *Native Marriages in South Africa* (Münster Westfalen, 1963), p. 238. The Catholic viewpoint was first expressed publicly at a famous *pitso* at Matsieng on 21 June 1888.

[2] Sheddick (1953), p. 37; Reuter, p. 247; information provided by the Revd. Ncholu of Morija, a Mosotho priest of the Lesotho Evangelical Church.

[3] Ashton, p. 71.

[4] Ashton, ibid.; Sheddick (1953), p. 37.

[5] See e.g. *Ntsinyi* v. *Rammoko* J.C. 268/1954.

[6] Sheddick (1953) states (at p. 37) that the *mpho* was not recoverable on divorce.

[7] Paroz, 'Le Mariage au Lessouto' (1946), *Journal des Missions Évangeliques* 17–21.

[8] Ellenberger and Macgregor, pp. 274–5 (note by Macgregor).

2

SOCIAL AND JUDICIAL
INSTITUTIONS

I. SOCIAL ORGANIZATION

(a) *The Family*

THE composition and major functions of the traditional extended family emerge clearly from the following description by Ashton:[1]

> The basic family group is the biological family of parents and children. This widens out to include parents' parents and children's children, together with the brothers and sisters of all these individuals and their wives and children in ever-widening circles. One's close kinsmen are known as '*ba heso*' (the people of our place). They form what is primarily a patrilineal group, composed loosely of one's parents, paternal grandparents, paternal uncles and their wives and children. One is usually brought up among these people, lives and works with them, assists them in ceremonies and domestic and agricultural activities, is helped by them to marry and bring up one's own children. For a woman this connexion with her own people is weakened by marriage, for she then has to go to her husband's village and identify herself with his people; but it should not be entirely severed and in case of trouble with her husband and his people, a woman seeks refuge and help among her own.

Polygamous families are divided up into 'houses'. Each house consists of a wife and her children. Houses possess a considerable degree of independence and property is usually allocated to each one by the husband. There are rules designed to prevent the husband from taking property away from one house and allocating it instead to another and the maxim '*malapa ha a jane*' ('houses do not "eat" one another') is of fundamental importance.[2]

No one doubts that kinship obligations are of less significance

---

[1] At p. 18.
[2] Discussed at pp. 173–5 below.

today than they were in the past. There is a greater emphasis on the individual, and family members are more dispersed and less dependent upon one another than in former times. However, kinship rights and duties are still significant and where they are of legal consequence they will be examined fully in the ensuing chapters.

(b) *The Village*

Most people in Lesotho live in villages or hamlets. There are no large towns and the eight administrative centres (or 'camps', as they are commonly known) have small populations ranging from less than 1,000 up to about 6,000. Only the capital, Maseru, is larger with around 20,000 inhabitants.

The basic residential unit is the household. In its simplest form it comprises a man, his wife, and their children. It becomes more complex where the family head is a polygamist or has other relatives living with him or has servants and other workers residing there.[1] In some villages the households will be related to one another agnatically through their respective family heads, but this is by no means the invariable pattern.[2] The average village contains about fifty households, but many are smaller and some have as many as 300.[3]

(c) *The Chieftainship*

The Basotho have always recognized the authority of hereditary chiefs and headmen.[4] However, both during the colonial period and particularly with the advent of a democratically elected legislature at independence, chiefly powers and prerogatives were considerably curtailed so that today these traditional authorities occupy positions of greatly diminished significance.[5] Nevertheless, in the context of their local communities and the everyday affairs of village life chiefs and headmen still have important functions to perform. In the first place, they are bound to promote the welfare and lawful interests of their subjects. Secondly, they are

[1] See Morojele, Part I, p. 118.
[2] See Sheddick (1953), p. 26.
[3] *Basutoland Village Population Lists* (Maseru, 1960).
[4] For the various classes of headmen see Duncan, pp. 54–5; the post of the lowest level of headman (known as *ramotsana* or village head) is not a hereditary one.
[5] e.g. they have lost their rights to 'place' relatives in positions of authority, to obtain free service in the cultivation of their official lands and to enjoy the revenue of their courts—see Hailey (1953), p. 104.

the local-government agencies for matters such as the collection of taxes, the maintenance of law and order, and the prevention of crime (with the assistance, of course, of the police).[1] They are also entrusted with the task of making a fair and impartial allocation of the land in their areas.[2]

This last prerogative is derived from the King who holds the supreme right of allocation over all land in Lesotho 'in trust' for the whole Basotho Nation.[3] His powers in this respect have, over the years, been delegated down through the hierarchy of principal chiefs, ward chiefs, chiefs, and headmen,[4] so that today in the large majority of cases the particular fields are actually allocated by the subordinate authorities. The main functions of the higher echelons are therefore limited to exercising a general supervision over the allocation process and hearing complaints and appeals relating to land administration.

Chiefs and headmen also have the onerous duty of keeping themselves well briefed on all the important events which occur in their villages. This will improve their chances of settling disputes and enable them to channel information to the appropriate quarter if this is necessary, for instance by giving evidence in a court of law. These matters are considered further below.[5]

2. INSTITUTIONS FOR THE SETTLEMENT OF FAMILY DISPUTES

Each of the networks of social organization described above provides a forum for the settlement of family disputes. If the matter cannot be satisfactorily resolved between the contestants themselves the proper procedure is for the problem to be brought before the *lekhotla la lelapa* or family council. If no acceptable solution emerges from this body a dissatisfied party can take the issue to the local headman's 'court' and from there to the chief's 'court', each of these institutions being referred to as a *lekhotla la tlhopo*.

Before 1938 the traditional courts of chiefs and headmen used

[1] Chieftainship Act, No. 22 of 1968, ss. 6 and 7.
[2] *Laws of Lerotholi*, s. 7(1) of Part I.
[3] These principles were incorporated in ss. 92 and 93 of the Independence Constitution of 1966 and are now to be found expressed in ss. 3 and 4 of the Land Act, No. 20 of 1973.
[4] See Sheddick (1954), Ch. 9; *Lesitsi* v. *Mafa* J.C. 84/1953 (J.C.).
[5] See below, pp. 41–2.

to be given official recognition under Proclamation 2B of 1884[1] and there was no separation of the administrative and judicial powers of the chieftainship.[2] However, serious complaints from the public about the conduct of these courts were widespread during the 1920s and 1930s and were endorsed by Sir Alan Pim in his governmental report of 1935.[3] This report led to the introduction of sweeping reforms. The Native Courts Proclamation of 1938[4] provided that only courts which had been issued with warrants by the Resident Commissioner could exercise judicial powers and thus enforce their decisions. Warrants were then issued provisionally to 1,340 chiefs and headmen out of a total of about twice that number. The next stage was for the finances of these courts to be brought under the supervision of a newly established National Treasury in 1945–6 and this drastically reduced the number of courts so that by 1949 there were only 106. Following the report of a select committee of the National Council in 1951 further pruning took place and there has recently been yet another cut-back. Today there are only forty-eight. They constitute the lowest tier of official courts and are known as the Local and Central Courts[5] or more colloquially as 'Basotho Courts'.[6] They are no longer run by chiefs and headmen and have their own court presidents who fall under a separate department of the central government.

This means that the traditional courts of chiefs and headmen exist today merely as institutionalized forms of mediation and conciliation. They cannot enforce their decisions and it is a criminal offence for a chief to try to usurp the powers of the Local and Central Courts.[7] This demotion has, not surprisingly, proved difficult for the chiefs and headmen to accept. It was a strong indictment of their judicial incompetence and corruption for as Lord Hailey wrote in 1953,

[1] The relevant provision is now styled s. 2 of the General Law Proclamation.
[2] For the history of these courts up to 1938 as well as for details of the criticisms levelled against them, see generally Ashton, Ch. XIV; Hailey (1953), pp. 64–112.
[3] *Financial and Economic Position of Basutoland* (H.M.S.O., 1935).
[4] Proc. 62 of 1938.
[5] The Native Courts Proclamation has been renamed the Central and Local Courts Proclamation.
[6] The expression 'Basotho Courts' was given currency by the Basuto Courts Proclamation (No. 23 of 1958) which never came into force.
[7] Central and Local Courts Proclamation, s. 21.

THE
UNIVERSITY OF WINNIPEG
PORTAGE & BALMORAL
WINNIPEG, MAN.
CANADA   R3B 2E9
SETTLEMENT OF FAMILY DISPUTES   39

Nothing is more typical of the attitude of the more responsible section
of people in Basutoland than the popular support recently given to the
proposal that Chiefs holding administrative charges should not be
permitted to preside over a Native Court within their jurisdiction . . .
As an institution . . . the reputation of the Native Court depended on
the personal character of the Chief, and it has clearly been unable to
survive the test.[1]

In response some chiefs and headmen have sought to under-
mine the reforms by fostering the erroneous belief among their
subjects that no suit or action can be brought in a Local Court
unless it has first been before their own 'courts'. This is entirely
false and any litigant is entitled to take his claim directly to the
official courts. However, these courts are partly themselves to
blame for the popular misconception through failing to stand
their ground against the local chief. Sometimes, for instance,
they may refuse to hear a case unless the plaintiff produces a
letter of authorization from the chief, despite the fact that the
Paramount Chief ordered court presidents to discontinue this
practice as long ago as 1950.[2] In certain circumstances a litigant
may, of course, prefer to go in the first instance to the unofficial
'courts' if he has confidence in them, and in appropriate cases
this is to be encouraged as a way of reducing the load of the
official courts, but it is certainly not obligatory. Whichever method
is used, the existence of more than one judicial or quasi-judicial
authority at the local level clearly can, on occasion, have a dis-
ruptive influence on the village community. There may sometimes
be a tendency for the chief or headman and the Basotho Court
president to strive to dominate one another and whereas in former
times the chief was without peer in his own area, today the court
president stands in the pre-eminent position with the power and
machinery to enforce his own decisions, backed by the independent authority of the Ministry of Justice.[3]

A different situation obtains in relation to bringing disputes
before the family council. This is a *sine qua non* in questions
relating to inheritance and even in other matters the Basotho
Courts, as well as the unofficial 'courts', will tend to refer the
problem back to the family if there is a reasonable chance of

[1] (1953), pp. 137, 143.
[2] See Hailey (1953), p. 109.
[3] See Sheddick (1954), p. 32.

reaching an acceptable solution there and the family has not yet given adequate consideration to the matter.

(a) *The Family Council* [1]

(i) *Composition*

Basotho society is divided into different lineage groups consisting of living persons of both sexes who can show a real or accepted relationship, either by birth or by legal affiliation at birth, in a continuous male line to one common ancestor.[2] A full lineage group would therefore commonly cover a large number of persons who, more especially in modern conditions, would be widely dispersed both geographically and in terms of commitment to one another's nuclear families. The family council might on very important occasions consist of the full lineage groups, but normally it would only comprise a small segment of the group and by no means all of these would be available to attend a particular meeting.

Where the dispute is between members of two different lineages, for instance between a man and his wife, representatives of both lineages are needed to form a joint family council.

Married women, as well as widows, seem to play an important role in these councils, no doubt partly because they are nearly always at home whereas their husbands tend to be abroad. However, despite the inconvenience, migrant labourers commonly do hurry home to Lesotho in times of family crisis thus reflecting the continuing acceptance on their part of their kinship obligations.

Sometimes the chief's representative may attend the meeting but this does not appear as usual now as it was in the past. The advantages of his presence are that he may have some specialist knowledge of law and custom as well as being a skilled conciliator and that he will become well versed in the problem and better able to deal with the matter if it later comes before the chief's 'court'.

---

[1] See generally P.D., pp. 110–13; Hamnett (1970), pp. 284–9; Ashton, p. 225. I should like here to acknowledge the assistance of Mr. John Perry of the Department of Social Anthropology at Rhodes University who kindly allowed me to read the drafts of those sections of his thesis covering the Family Council, the Headman's 'court' and the Chief's 'court'.

[2] See Sheddick (1954), p. 18.

(ii) *Procedure*

The meeting should be summoned by the head of the lineage or lineage segment as soon as possible after the dispute has arisen in order to prevent the parties from taking up hard and fast positions from which they can only be dislodged with difficulty.

The concern of the gathering is to achieve a reconciliation through consensus. Moral and legal norms and family values are usually stressed. The parties, and indeed all the family members, are bound by important ties and it is worth while making a concerted effort to preserve existing relationships intact. Admittedly the power of the family over its individual members has been greatly reduced in recent years because of the growing independence of individuals, the lessening of kinship bonds and the loss among some young people of the belief in the likelihood of punishment by the ancestors. However, this last fear still appears to induce many people to abide by the family court's decision—a surprising fact in view of the large number of Basotho professing Christianity. Apart from this the family court has mainly to rely on the natural respect due to it if it is to achieve a lasting solution since it lacks the power to enforce any decision it reaches. On the other hand, the threat of taking the matter to the official courts may be a factor in inducing a settlement.

It is not only as a mechanism for settling disputes that have actually arisen that the family council plays a vital role in maintaining harmony. It also meets to witness important family events. This serves two related purposes. First, it should provide almost incontrovertible evidence as to the occurrence of a specific event and its significance. Secondly, the validity of certain transactions is actually made dependent upon the matter having been given full family publicity at the time. Typical examples of occasions falling within one or other of these categories are marriages, the making and revocation of gifts and allocations of property, the adoption and legitimation of children, and the disinheritance of a prospective heir.[1]

(b) *The Headman's 'Court' and Chief's 'Court'*[2]

These 'courts' will be dealt with together since they serve the

---

[1] All these matters are discussed when the substantive law is analysed in Part II.

[2] See generally Hamnett (1970), Ch. 3.

same purpose and operate in similar ways. The chief's 'court' hears appeals from the headman's 'court' as well as dealing with matters at first instance.

(i) *Composition*

Following the traditional practice the chief or headman is assisted by a panel of two or more officials, either elected or appointed by himself, who act as his assessors or advisers and who may often deputize for him during his absence or if he prefers not to handle this type of work himself.

(ii) *Procedure*

In general terms both 'courts' act as clearing houses, taking in a wide variety of disputes and problems and then guiding these into the appropriate channels. Sometimes the matter will be sent on to the official courts, and at others it will need to be referred back to a family council. Certain types of problem require the attention of government departments, for instance the police, the Ministry of Agriculture or the Collector of Taxes. These unofficial 'courts' also act as useful filters in creaming off certain disputes which they are in a position to solve themselves, without the matter having to go before the Basotho Courts.

As pointed out earlier they have lost their powers of enforcement and can merely advise, mediate, and hope to reach a settlement which the parties can accept. They have to rely on the public's respect for their traditional authority in order to obtain compliance with their decisions, but it is clear that this has sharply diminished, especially among the younger generation.

(c) *The Official Courts*

(i) *The structure of the judicial hierarchy*[1]

The structure of the official system of courts in matters of Sesotho law has already been set out on page 8 of the Introduction. Although the Basotho Courts date back as far as 1938 they only acquired this name in 1958 and they were not given their present formal titles of Central and Local Courts until 1965. They form the bottom two tiers in the hierarchy, with the Local Courts hearing cases at first instance and the Central Courts having predominantly appellate business. Their respective jurisdictions are circumscribed first by statute, and secondly by the

[1] A more detailed analysis is to be found in Palmer and Poulter, pp. 443–506.

limits, mainly financial, set out in their individual warrants. From 1938 to 1962 three tiers were operating, known as 'B' Courts, 'A' Courts, and the Paramount Chief's Appeal Courts. These last-mentioned courts were discontinued in 1962. Throughout this work, for reasons of convenience, 'B' Courts and 'A' Courts are described in footnote references as Local Courts and Central Courts respectively, even where the case in question was decided before the change of name.

Since 1944 appeals from the Paramount Chief's Courts, and following their demise the Central Courts, have gone to the Judicial Commissioner's Court.[1] Only a handful of cases have proceeded further than this, but appeals lie upwards to the High Court and thence to the Court of Appeal.[2] Appeals to the Judicial Committee of the Privy Council were abolished in 1970[3] and in any event only one such appeal on a matter of Sesotho law was ever heard there.[4]

The personnel and *modus operandi* of each of these courts will be discussed in turn.

(ii) *The Central and Local Courts*

The Central and Local Courts are staffed by presidents all of whom are Basotho. They sit alone and reach their decisions without the guidance of assessors. They are expected to have a good knowledge of the customary law, but they have not had any formal legal education or training and their general education standards are not high. They take judicial notice of Sesotho law and there is no need for rules to be proved by the opinion evidence of 'expert' witnesses.

The practice and procedure of the courts is regulated in accordance with Sesotho law and custom supplemented by the provisions of the Basotho Courts (Practice and Procedure) Rules, 1961.[5] These Rules are designed *inter alia* to ensure that the principles of natural justice are observed and that every party obtains a fair hearing.

[1] Established by Proc. 16 of 1944.
[2] Following the suspension of the Independence Constitution of 1966 which had regulated these courts, they were re-established by the Court of Appeal and High Court Order, No. 17 of 1970 in almost identical form.
[3] By the Court of Appeal and High Court Order (above).
[4] *Mojela* v. *Mojela*, Privy Council appeal No. 93 of 1927, discussed below, p. 161.
[5] G.N. No. 21 of 1961.

The proceedings are conducted by the parties themselves or by their authorized[1] representatives, but lawyers are barred from appearing in civil cases.[2] The parties or their representatives are entitled to address the court and their witnesses are examined and cross-examined and often questioned by the president. Their evidence is taken down in longhand by the president, read back to them and then signed.

The judgment usually contains a review of the evidence and a decision as to who is entitled to succeed. The court does not generally make explicit the process of reasoning by which this conclusion is reached in any but the tersest language. Commonly a single sentence or a bare reference to a provision of the Laws of Lerotholi suffices. Sometimes one may not even get that. As a result it is often only by a careful reading of the evidence— particularly the questions asked by the president and the answers given by the parties and their witnesses—against a background knowledge of the basic issues in the branch of the law under discussion that an assessment can be made of the legal rule that the court is applying. Previous cases are practically never referred to and no system of precedent applies. In any event this would not be feasible because decisions of the Basotho Courts and the Judicial Commissioner's Court are neither published in the law reports nor collected together in such a way as to facilitate easy reference. Save for a very small number of important decisions of the Judicial Commissioner's Court which are given general circulation, each court is completely. oblivious of the decisions of the others except where it is reversed on appeal.

Figures for 1967 show that while only a small proportion of civil cases are taken on appeal from the Local Courts to the Central Courts the proportion of appeals actually upheld by the Central Courts (including judgments varied) is as high as 40 per cent.[3]

(iii) *The Judicial Commissioner's Court*

Of the nine or ten people who have held the post of Judicial Commissioner since it was created in 1944 less than half have

---

[1] Satisfactory proof of authority must be given, but a written authorization is not required—*Mountain Trading Store* v. *Mathaba* J.C. 19/1967 (J.C.).

[2] Central and Local Courts Proclamation, s. 20.

[3] 'Statistics compiled by the Judicial Commissioner from figures supplied by court presidents' (roneoed, 1968).

occupied this position for more than a few months, and some have merely held acting appointments in respect of particular cases. The three notable Judicial Commissioners, all of them Europeans, have been W. G. S. Driver (1944–9 and 1952–9), Patrick Duncan (1950–2), and Rivers Thompson (briefly in the 1940s, briefly in the 1950s, and then from 1959 to 1974).[1] All have shown a keen interest in the customary law and Duncan J.C. wrote the admirable introductory book on the subject which has already been referred to.[2] They have each had to learn about Sesotho law as they went along and have relied considerably on their Basotho assessors for guidance, especially at the beginning of their appointments, but the decision has always been theirs alone. Only Driver J.C. possessed a law degree, but while the lack of formal legal qualifications may have led the others to make occasional ill-informed remarks about the common law, this does not seem to have hampered their administration of the customary law. A lack of rigorous instruction in the principles of the common law may even have constituted a positive advantage.

The Court takes judicial notice of rules of customary law. The Judicial Commissioner relies on his own knowledge and that of his assessor and there is no need for the rules to be proved before the Court,[3] although parties may bring expert witnesses to give evidence if they so wish.[4]

Whereas an appeal to the Central Court takes the form of a retrial, the hearing at the Judicial Commissioner's Court is based almost entirely on the record and fresh evidence is rarely admitted. At this level legal practitioners do have a right of audience in civil actions, but they only appear in a small percentage of cases.

The judgments of the Judicial Commissioner's Court take the form of a review of the evidence followed by a very articulate, if brief, pronouncement of the legal principles upon which the case is being decided. The reasoning which in the Basotho Courts was implicit is at last made explicit. References are commonly made

---

[1] Others have been Collins, Murray, Hennessy, and Ramsden. Elliott, Mohaleroe, and Matete have been acting J.C.s. Ramsden's absurd judgments have been wittily exposed by Hamnett (1971), pp. 267–8.

[2] *Sotho Laws and Customs.*

[3] The statement to the contrary by Evans J. in *Moonyane* v. *Maqoacha* H.C. Civ./A/5/1971, is quite erroneous.

[4] For an example of this see *Bereng Griffith* v. *'Mantsebo Seeiso Griffith* (No. 2) J.C. 245/1945.

to the provisions of the Laws of Lerotholi and, since it was published in 1960, to Duncan's book and the cases cited there. However, apart from these cases and the few on the customary law reported in the High Commission Territories Law Reports hardly any reference is made to earlier decisions because they are neither remembered by name nor easy to trace. Rather the Judicial Commissioner will recall in general terms similar cases he has decided without attempting to have them brought up from the Court archives, and his recollection will fortify him in deciding the instant case on the same principles as the previous ones.

The Court has recently been hearing appeals at the rate of about 250–300 per annum. Of these only a handful proceed to the High Court. If they are to do so it must be upon the certificate of the Judicial Commissioner that they are fit cases for appeal or upon a question of law reserved by the Judicial Commissioner at the instance of either of the parties or of his own motion.[1]

The Court has its headquarters in the capital but travels around the country on circuit, visiting each of the administrative centres at regular intervals.

(iv) *The Superior Courts*

Up until 1974 the High Court and Court of Appeal have always had expatriate judges (as did their predecessors, the Resident Commissioner's Court and the Assistant Commissioner's Court). None of them has been particularly well versed in Sesotho law and sometimes in the High Court they have been advised by assessors, although the decision has always been theirs alone.[2] Their approach to the proof of matters of customary law thus requires investigation.[3]

Sometimes they have taken the view that the same techniques should be employed as with the proof of local customs at common law.[4] Thus a customary rule would only be upheld and applied if by reference to specific instances it could be shown to be certain and reasonable and to have been uniformly observed from an origin dating back to the distant past and perhaps even to time

[1] Proc. 62 of 1938, as amended, s. 28(3).
[2] This is authorized by the High Court Act, No. 4 of 1967, ss. 8 and 9.
[3] For a fuller discussion of this question see Palmer and Poulter, pp. 108–26.
[4] See e.g. Lansdown J. in *Bereng Griffith* v. *'Mantsebo Seeiso Griffith* (1926–53) H.C.T.L.R. 50; de Beer J. in *Bereng Griffith* v. *'Mantsebo Seeiso Griffith* (No. 2) H.C. 9/1946; Evans J. in *Moonyane* v. *Maqoacha* H.C. Civ./A/5/1971.

immemorial.[1] It is submitted that this approach is erroneous for the following reasons.

First, the equation of African customary law with local customs in England or South Africa is a false one. The common law rules are designed to permit local customs to derogate from the general law of the land and therefore strict safeguards have to be introduced, whereas customary law actually constitutes a primary source of the general law applicable in Lesotho.[2]

Secondly, to require that customary law must be unchanging and have been uniform over a very long period of time is to deny to it one of its chief virtues and indeed make nonsense of it. Customary law depends for its validity to a large extent on the practices of the people who are subject to it; as these develop so does the law.[3] Thus to declare that only those rules are valid that have existed from time immemorial is absurd; a more sensible policy is that the court should be satisfied that any given rule is well established, as opposed to undergoing the pangs of birth or being in the final state of decay.[4]

Thirdly, as Sir Carleton Allen has shown, even in English law the courts have been hard pressed to provide the requirement of reasonableness with any meaningful content.[5] In Salmond's view for a local custom to be deprived of legal efficacy it would have to be

. . . so obviously and seriously repugnant to right and reason, that to enforce it as law would do more mischief than that which would result from the overturning of the expectations and arrangements based on its presumed continuance and legal validity.[6]

This approach gives greater specificity to the concept of reasonableness and since the test of 'repugnancy' is applicable to the administration of Sesotho law in the Basotho Courts a discussion about the way in which it should be applied will be

---

[1] For a statement of these requirements in South African law see *Van Breda* v. *Jacobs* 1921 A.D. 330 and in English law see 11 *Halsbury's Laws of England* (3rd edn.), pp. 160–8.
[2] Cf. Allott, *New Essays in African Law* (Butterworths, 1970), p. 258.
[3] See *Monare* v. *Koela* J.C. 89/1959 (J.C.); *Qele* v. *Ndabeni* J.C. 68/1966 (J.C.).
[4] See *Bereng Griffith* v. *'Mantsebo Seeiso Griffith* (1962–53) H.C.T.L.R. 50 at p. 69.
[5] *Law in the Making* (O.U.P., 7th ed.), pp. 129–30, 132–3.
[6] *Jurisprudence* (11th ed.), p. 242.

reserved for the next chapter where the jurisdiction of the various courts is examined.

If the proof of customary law is not to be based on the criteria adopted in respect of local customs, what approach should the superior courts adopt?

In *Angu* v. *Attah*,[1] a Privy Council decision on appeal from West Africa, the following rule was propounded:

As in the case with all customary law it has to be proved in the first instance by calling witnesses acquainted with the native customs until the particular customs have, by frequent proof in the courts, become so notorious that the courts will take judicial notice of them.

This procedure of calling witnesses to give 'expert' opinions was designed for expatriate judges and has been applied in many parts of Africa,[2] particularly during colonial times, as well as in the Lesotho courts.[3] However, the stage does not yet seem to have been reached where the superior courts in Lesotho are taking judicial notice of any well-known customs, no doubt because of the infrequency of decisions on Sesotho law at this level.

Opinion testimony of 'experts' does not have to be given orally, but can also be presented in the form of works of authority on the law. Duncan's *Sotho Laws and Customs* has occasionally been referred to and two South African books, Whitfield's *South African Native Law*[4] and Seymour's *Native Law in South Africa*[5] have also been cited. However, there is a great danger in relying on what has been written about the version of customary law applied by the South African courts. Ramolefe's scathing criticism of the writings of South African authors has already been adverted to[6] and no finer statement of their very limited utility is to be found than this passage from the judgment of Lansdown J. in *Bereng Griffith* v. *'Mantsebo Seeiso Griffith*:[7]

---

[1] [1874–1928] Privy Council 43 at 44 (1916).

[2] See e.g. the authorities cited in Allott (1970), p. 260, from Sierra Leone, Nigeria, Kenya, Uganda, Tanzania, Malawi, and Zambia.

[3] See e.g. *Bereng Griffith* v. *'Mantsebo Seeiso Griffith* (1926–53) H.C.T.L.R. 50; *Motsoene* v. *Harding* (1954) H.C.T.L.R. 1.

[4] (Juta, 2nd ed., 1948.)

[5] (Juta, 2nd ed. 1960; 3rd ed. under the title *Bantu Law in South Africa*, 1970.)

[6] Above, p. 19.

[7] (1926–53) H.C.T.L.R. 50 at 58–9.

It has been contended for the plaintiff that in the determining of any question relating to Basuto law and custom and, in particular, in rules of marriage and inheritance, the Court may in general be guided by the practices of other nations or tribes in South Africa of the Bantu race; and plaintiff's counsel has submitted, as authorities which may be adopted, several decisions of the Native Appeal Courts of the Cape Province of the Union and Mr. Seymour's useful book on *Native Law and Custom* written in 1910, which is, for the most part, based upon the native law and custom as practised in the Transkeian Territories of the Cape Province. Great caution, however, is necessary in seeking any guidance from these authorities. There is, it is true, a general analogy between the practices, particularly in the matter of marriage and inheritance, of the native races of the south and those of the Basuto; but it is clear that there are marked divergences which only careful investigation and comparison of the practices of both can determine. There are in the Matatiele and Mount Fletcher districts of the Cape Province, which are adjacent to Basutoland, some 24,000 Basutos who are under the immediate governance of a Basuto Chief Jeremiah Moshesh, a grandson of the first Paramount Chief, who controls this people in accordance with Basuto law and custom, which also is applied to them by the native Appeal Court operating in that portion of the Cape Province. In so far as that Court purports to administer Basuto laws and customs, its decisions, while not authoritative in this Territory, will, of course, be regarded with great respect. Mr. Seymour, whose book as I have stated deals mainly with the practices of the Transkeian Bantu tribes, has worked in the districts of Matatiele and Mount Fletcher, but he gave evidence in this case from which it may clearly be gathered that, while he was disposed to regard the Basuto law of marriage and succession as practically identical with that operating in the south, there were radical differences to which he had not been enabled to devote attention. Thus he admitted that he had not known of any woman chief in the Transkeian Territories, and it is clear that he had not been enabled to devote attention to the divergences of custom in Basutoland which had resulted from such a practice in that Territory, nor had he studied Basuto customs as set forth in the Lerotholi Code. . . . Great caution must therefore be exercised in accepting as applicable to Basutoland any law or custom operative in other native Territories. For approximately a century the Basutos have been separated off from the remainder of the Bantu peoples, and it is to be expected that their customs, at one time no doubt closely akin to if not identical with those of the great body of Bantu people, have shown divergences and developments.

At present little use is made of judicial precedent and this is probably due to the paucity of reported decisions. But in any event decisions in much earlier cases may not be a reliable guide because the customary law may have altered in the meantime. The courts seem to appreciate that they must reckon with this possibility.[1]

A particularly thorny problem arises over the approach that the superior courts should adopt when hearing an appeal from the Basotho Courts via the Judicial Commissioner's Court, since these latter courts will have taken judicial notice of the customary law rules applicable. Is the High Court to follow suit or should it require rules that have been applied by the lower courts to be proved by the opinion evidence of experts? There are two schools of thought. First, there are those who argue that the appellate court should take judicial notice because this is the common-sense thing to do.[2] They are implicitly giving pride of place to the lower courts as the final arbiters of what the law is.[3] Those who take the opposite view are concerned that the appellate court, which exists mainly to reverse erroneous findings of law by the lower courts, should exercise its function properly and should not merely act as a rubber stamp.[4] It should be prepared to undertake a full investigation into any legal controversy and provide the 'final' solution. It is submitted that the second procedure is preferable to the first. However, what the appellate courts should definitely *not* do is what was recently done by Evans J. in the High Court appeal of *Moonyane* v. *Maqoacha*.[5] He upset the findings of law of the lower courts on the basis that *they* had not heard evidence as to the rule of customary law which was applied and that there was thus no proof of its existence. Either a High Court judge must himself hear expert witnesses because of his own ignorance of the law or he can take judicial notice of it like the lower courts, but he is certainly not entitled to reverse findings of law on this sort of pretext.

If developments in some other parts of Africa are to be regarded as pointers for the future it may well eventually come about that

---

[1] See e.g. *Bereng Griffith* v. *'Mantsebo Seeiso Griffith* (1926–53) H.C.T.L.R. 50 at 54–5, 57, 67 (where the changing status of women was recognized).
[2] See e.g. *Chitema* v. *Lupanda* (1962) R. and N. 290 (Malawi).
[3] For illustrations of this approach see the cases cited by Allott (1970), pp. 281–2.
[4] See e.g. Allott, 'Judicial Precedent in Africa Revisited', [1968] *J.A.L.* 3 at 21.
[5] Civ./A/5/1971.

the superior courts in Lesotho will invariably take judicial notice of the rules of Sesotho law in the way in which the lower courts do and thus the rule in *Angu* v. *Attah* will cease to be applicable.[1] However, before this can happen it will need to be much easier for rules of customary law to be ascertained and either more textbooks, manuals, or restatements will have to be written or else codes will have to be promulgated. The problem will no doubt be eased when more Basotho are on the bench, but it will probably not be solved, because those who fill such positions will certainly have been trained in the common law and may possess only limited knowledge of the customary law.

[1] See Ghana, Courts Decree (1966), para. 65; *Kimani* v. *Gikanga* [1965] E.A. 735 (per Crabbe J.A. dissenting) (Kenya).

3

THE APPLICATION OF
SESOTHO LAW IN THE COURTS

I. THE RECOGNITION OF SESOTHO LAW

DURING the period when the country was annexed to the Cape Colony from 1871 to 1883 only limited and uncertain recognition was extended to Sesotho law and to the authority of the traditional chiefs' courts to administer it.[1] However, on the resumption of direct responsibility by the British government in 1884 this policy was reversed. Proclamation 2B of that year, after providing for the continuation in force of Cape Colonial common law so far as the circumstances of the country permitted, contained a proviso that

... in any suit, action or proceedings in any court to which all the parties are natives, and in all suits, actions or proceedings whatsoever before any Native Chief exercising jurisdiction as aforesaid, native law may be administered . . .[2]

This constituted a clear recognition of the power of both the traditional courts and those established by the Imperial government to apply principles of Sesotho law. This policy has, in the main, been preserved down to the present time and amendments to the proviso have been largely linguistic. The word 'native' has naturally been replaced because of the offensive overtones it carries in southern Africa and, as already explained,[3] the old courts which were run by the chiefs have been deprived of their judicial powers and replaced by 'Basotho Courts' established by statute. The modern version of the proviso therefore runs as follows:[4]

[1] See Poulter, 'The Place of the Laws of Lerotholi in the Legal System of Lesotho' (1972), *African Affairs* 144 at 147-8.
[2] Proc. 2B of 1884, s. 2.
[3] See p. 38 above.
[4] The amendments were contained in the Law Revision Proclamation, No. 12 of 1960, s. 7(2).

Provided, however, that in any suits, actions or proceedings in any Court to which all of the parties are Africans, and in all suits, actions or proceedings before any Basuto Court, African law may be administered . . .

The broad effect of this wording has been to allow the customary law to be applied at all levels of the judicial hierarchy whenever the circumstances of the particular case were appropriate for its use.[1] So far as family law is concerned there are four statutory provisions which buttress the recognition of customary law given in the 1884 Proclamation. The first is section 42 of the Marriage Act 1974,[2] which provides

This Act shall apply to all marriages solemnised in Lesotho save and except marriages contracted in accordance with Sesotho law and custom, and nothing herein contained shall be taken as in any manner affecting or casting doubts upon the validity of any such last-mentioned marriages contracted before or after the coming into operation of this Act.

The second is section 3(b) of the Administration of Estates Proclamation of 1935[3] which provides that the proclamation is not to apply to the estates of Africans which shall continue to be administered 'in accordance with the prevailing African law and custom in the Territory', with the proviso that such law and custom is not to apply to the estates of Africans who have been shown to the satisfaction of the Master of the High Court to have abandoned tribal custom and adopted a European mode of life, and who, if married, have married under European law.[4] Thirdly, the Intestate Succession Proclamation[5] provides that it shall not apply to the estates of Africans unless they fall within the proviso to section 3(b) of the Administration of Estates Proclamation. Fourthly, the Adoption of Children Proclamation of 1958[6] expressly declares that nothing therein contained is to be construed as preventing or affecting the adoption of an African child by Africans in accordance with Sesotho law and custom.

---

[1] It was expressly continued in force on Independence by s. 4(5) of the Independence Order, 1966.
[2] Act No. 10 of 1974.
[3] Proc. 19 of 1935.
[4] This proviso is discussed at pp. 323–4 below.
[5] Proc. 2 of 1953, s. 3.
[6] Proc. 62 of 1952.

2. THE JURISDICTION OF THE COURTS

It will be noted that the proviso in the General Law Proclamation confers considerable discretion on the courts by declaring that African law 'may' be administered; no guidelines are laid down as to how the choice between the two systems should be exercised in particular cases. This presents acute problems for the superior courts, some of which have been analysed by the present writer elsewhere.[1] However, despite the flexible wording of the proviso the Basotho Courts have virtually no discretion. In terms of the Central and Local Courts Proclamation[2] they can only administer the customary law together with a limited range of statutory provisions.[3] They cannot decide cases under the common law. If they consider that any matter ought properly to be determined in terms of the common law they are bound to decline jurisdiction and transfer the case to a subordinate court.[4] More specifically, the Proclamation denies them the power to try cases 'in connection with' civil marriages.[5] This would clearly cover actions for divorce, judicial separation, nullity, the restitution of conjugal rights, and actions for maintenance and the custody of children. Logically it should also cover property disputes including orders in respect of the matrimonial assets upon a decree of dissolution, and indeed the Judicial Commissioner has so held.[6] However, this may lead to anomalous results because, in terms of the choice of law, the proprietary consequences of a civil marriage are not necessarily governed by the common law. Thus while the High Court would be free to apply Sesotho law to determine issues of this nature, the Local and Central Courts would not be entitled to do so. On the other hand, the statute expressly permits the latter courts to hear cases in connection with the payment, return or disposal of *bohali*[7] because this is not an integral feature of civil marriages. The main difficulty here lies in the fact that, as we have seen, it is not uncommon for customary and civil marriages to subsist side by

[1] See Palmer and Poulter, pp. 127–53.

[2] Proc. 62 of 1938, as amended, s. 9.

[3] e.g. Parts II and III of the Laws of Lerotholi, the Partnership Proclamation (No. 78 of 1957) and the Basic and Graded Tax (Consolidation) Act, No. 24 of 1968.

[4] See Basuto Courts (Practice and Procedure) Rules, r. 31.

[5] s. 8(1).

[6] *Mokhutsoane* v. *Mokhutsoane* J.C. 81/1969; *Makhaphela* v. *Makhaphela* J.C. 138/1969.

[7] s. 8(1).

side and the problem posed is which system should regulate which aspects of the marital relationship.

3. THE REPUGNANCY CLAUSE

It was a general feature of British colonial policy only to permit the customary laws of African peoples to continue to the extent to which they did not offend against the British sense of justice, morality, and good conscience.[1] Basutoland was no exception and the Basotho Courts are still only empowered to administer what is described as 'the native law and custom prevailing in the territory', so far as it is not repugnant to justice or morality or inconsistent with the provisions of any other laws in force in the country.[2]

It seems rather anomalous to have retained this anachronism after the attainment of independence, thus running the risk of expatriate judges imposing their own ethnocentric attitudes on the customary law. For despite the fact that the limitation is placed on the power of the Basotho Courts they will rarely, if ever, strike down a rule of customary law for repugnancy since the general and established usage of the people will carry a strong conviction that it is a just and moral rule. The restriction will therefore practically always come into play when a case is taken on appeal to the Judicial Commissioner's Court or the superior courts. Moreover, as already pointed out, the High Court in hearing cases at first instance may in fact be applying the same criteria when determining whether a rule is reasonable or not.[3]

The repugnancy clause is really made up of three component elements and these will be examined in turn.

(a) 'The Native Law and Custom Prevailing in the Territory'

This archaic language can only be referring to Sesotho law as the dominant customary law in the country.[4] However, this may present problems with regard to the small communities of people of Nguni origin who live in Lesotho and who apparently retain their own laws and customs.[5] In the only available case on this question, *Ndlungwane* v. *Setokwe*,[6] the parties were Thembus and

[1] See generally Daniels, *The Common Law in West Africa* (Butterworths, 1964), pp. 266–86.
[2] Proc. 62 of 1938, s. 9(1). There is a discussion of the Lesotho repugnancy clause in Palmer and Poulter, pp. 155–69.
[3] See p. 47 above.
[4] Cf. *R.* v. *Ilorin Native Court* ex parte *Aremu* [1953] 20 N.L.R. 144 (Nigeria).
[5] See above, p. 19.   [6] J.C. 135/1961.

one of them relied on a rule of Thembu customary law which conflicted with Sesotho law. The Local Court upheld the Thembu rule, but on appeal the Judicial Commissioner declared that any suggestion that the Laws of Lerotholi did not apply to all the African inhabitants of Lesotho could not be sustained. It is unclear whether the court intended to draw a distinction in this respect between the Laws of Lerotholi and the rest of Sesotho law or whether the whole of Sesotho law was being held to be universally applicable to all Africans resident in the country.

(b) 'Repugnant to Justice or Morality'

There have been a number of cases on family law in which the Judicial Commissioner's Court and the superior courts have declared a rule to be repugnant. These will be individually examined, as appropriate, in the discussion of the substantive law in later chapters. It will be seen that the clause has been applied to such matters as special forms of marriage,[1] the rule that there is no limitation period for the institution of judicial proceedings[2] and the liability of a father for the wrongs of his adult sons and his corresponding entitlement to their earnings.[3] The courts have also refused to countenance the forcible circumcision of a girl as a punishment for peeping at an initiation school.[4] In so far as the cardinal principles of natural justice are enjoined by the repugnancy clause these have been incorporated in the rules regulating the practice and procedure of the Central and Local Courts.[5] In the remainder of this section it is proposed to consider in somewhat broad terms how the courts ought to approach the issue of repugnancy.

Bearing in mind the colonial background of repugnancy clauses it is hardly surprising that some expatriate judges and lawyers working in Africa have in the past taken the view that the relevant standard of justice and morality was the British one.[6] Today, however, African customs are generally better understood and their social significance is more keenly appreciated as a result of research findings published during the last quarter of a century.

---

[1] See Ch. 12 below.   [2] See p. 128 below.   [3] See pp. 189, 192 below.
[4] *Mothobi Maele* v. *R.* (1963–66) H.C.T.L.R. 218.
[5] See Basuto Courts (Practice and Procedure) Rules, G.N. No. 21 of 1961.
[6] See e.g. *Gwao bin Kilimo* v. *Kisunda bin Ifuti* (1938) 1 T.L.R. (R) 403 (Tanganyika); Abrahams, 'The Colonial Legal Service and the Administration of Justice in the Colonial Dependencies', (1948) 30 *J.C.L.I.L.* 1 at pp. 8, 11.

In view of this, it is submitted that the approach of expatriate judges should reflect increased respect. There is an interesting parallel with the legal recognition of foreign personal laws in England. Until relatively recently a generally hostile stand was maintained against, for instance, polygamous marriages[1] and *talak* divorces[2] because they seemed so alien to the British way of life. However, with the influx of immigrants from various parts of the Commonwealth a much more tolerant attitude has developed as a result of a growing familiarity with these customs and contact with the people who practise them[3] and the English courts have said that their discretion to refuse recognition to a status created by foreign law must be 'most sparingly exercised'.[4] Thus in 1962 in *Cheni* v. *Cheni*[5] Sir Jocelyn Simon declared the true test to be whether the foreign marriage in question, which had been contracted by Jewish rites in Egypt between an uncle and his niece, was

. . . so offensive to the conscience of the English court that it should refuse to recognise and give effect to the proper foreign law. In deciding that question the court will seek to exercise common sense, good manners and a reasonable tolerance. In my view, it would be altogether too queasy a judicial conscience which would recoil from a marriage acceptable to people of deep religious convictions, lofty ethical standards and high civilisation.[6]

More recently in *Mohamed* v. *Knott*[7] the English Court of Appeal had to decide whether a Nigerian Moslem girl of thirteen was being exposed to moral danger in sleeping with a man whom she had married according to Islamic rites in Nigeria. The court upheld an appeal by the husband on the ground that the magistrates

---

[1] See e.g. *Hyde* v. *Hyde* (1866) L.R. 1 P. and D. 130; Re *Bethell* (1888) 38 Ch. D. 220; *Sowa* v. *Sowa* [1961] 1 All E.R. 687.

[2] See e.g. *R.* v. *Hammersmith Superintendent Registrar of Marriages* [1917] 1 K.B. 634.

[3] See e.g. the Matrimonial Proceedings (Polygamous Marriages) Act 1972; *Qureshi* v. *Qureshi* [1971] 1 All E.R. 325.

[4] See *Varanand* v. *Varanand* (1964) 108 *Sol. Jo.* 693 approved in *Qureshi* v. *Qureshi* (above) at 346. A reasonably tolerant approach on the part of a colonial court as far back as 1922 is to be found in the judgment of Tredgold C.J. in the Southern Rhodesian case of *Chiduku* v. *Chidano* [1922] S.R. 55; he declared that the court should only reject 'such customs as inherently impress us with some abhorrence or are obviously immoral in their incidence'.

[5] [1962] 3 All E.R. 873.   [6] At 883.   [7] [1968] 2 All E.R. 563.

had misdirected themselves. The proper approach was laid down by Lord Parker C.J. as follows:

> When [the justices] say that 'a continuance of such an association notwithstanding the marriage, would be repugnant to any decent minded English man or woman', they are, I think, and can only be, considering the view of an Englishman or woman in relation to an English girl and our western way of life. I cannot myself think that decent minded English men and women, realising the way of life in which [the wife] was brought up, and the [husband] for that matter, would inevitably say that this is repugnant. It is certainly natural for a girl to marry at that age. They develop sooner, and there is nothing abhorrent in their way of life for a girl of thirteen to marry a man of twenty-five. Incidentally it was not until 1929 that, in this country, an age limit was put on marriage . . . For my part . . . it could only be said that she was in moral danger if one was considering somebody brought up in and living in our way of life, and to hold she is in moral danger in the circumstances of this case can only be arrived at, as it seems to me, by ignoring the way of life in which she was brought up, and the [husband] was brought up.[1]

We may conclude, then, that the expatriate judges in the appellate courts in Lesotho should place themselves in the position of right-minded members of Basotho society and only strike down for repugnancy those rules whose evil social consequences far outweigh any possible utility contended for them. Admittedly, in practical terms this is by no means an easy task. Where the values of any community are in a state of flux the traditional rules will often appear to many members of the younger generation not only to be outmoded but positively unjust. Equally the more conservative members may see modern innovations in a similar light. Since rules of customary law are derived from practices which the people consider themselves bound to follow, they must to a large degree depend for their validity on widespread popular recognition of both their obligatory nature and their social utility. Provided a customary rule is shown to be well established in the sense of being widely practised in the belief that it is the law, the burden of proving that it is repugnant should be an extremely onerous one. After all, if it is felt that a more abrupt change in the law is required

---

[1] At 568. See also *Dawodu v. Danmole* [1962] 1 W.L.R. 1053 at 1060 (Privy Council).

than occurs through the gradual evolution of popular practice this is better done by carefully framed legislation than through the fortuitous and virtually unpublicized application of the repugnancy clause in particular cases.

The fact that customs and values tend to crumble and shift with time raises a further difficult question, namely whether the repugnancy of a particular rule should be judged by the standards of the period when it was relied upon and complied with or whether the proper criteria are the values prevailing when the matter ultimately comes to court. In *Malofotsane* v. *Mpho*,[1] Elyan C.J. came down emphatically in favour of the latter view, but more recently in *Ntsoele* v. *Ramokhele*[2] Mapetla C.J. gave equally sound reasons for adopting the former approach.

When the courts do find that a specific rule is repugnant it appears, from high authority, that the custom cannot be judicially modified or transformed and then given effect in a watered down form; it has to be rejected outright.[3] However, there does not seem to be any reason why distinct and separate parts of a rule should not be severed one from the other so that the repugnant aspect can be eliminated while the acceptable portion is retained.[4]

(c) 'Inconsistent with the Provisions of any Law in Force'[5]

Rules of customary law have to give way in face of conflicting statutory provisions. Indeed, as indicated in the previous paragraph, where objection is taken to any such rule the best solution lies in the process of legislation. Both forced marriages[6] and ghost marriages[7] have, for instance, been banned by statutory enactment. Where the statute in question does not clearly evince an intention to alter or abolish a rule of customary law it is a moot point whether it has this effect. I have taken the view elsewhere that it does and based my contention on the general principle of statutory

---

[1] (1959) H.C.T.L.R. 107 discussed further at pp. 164–5 below.
[2] H.C.Civ./A/13/1974 discussed further below p. 165.
[3] *Eleko* v. *Government of Nigeria* [1931] A.C. 662 at 673 (Privy Council).
[4] See Palmer and Poulter, p. 163, where the analogy of illegal contracts is suggested.
[5] This is taken to refer only to inconsistency with statute law, not the common law; for the overwhelming arguments in favour of this view, based on the wording of the General Interpretation Proclamation No. 12 of 1942, see Palmer and Poulter, pp. 164–6.
[6] See Marriage Proclamation, No. 7 of 1911, s. 2, now repealed and replaced by Marriage Act, No. 10 of 1974, s. 3 discussed below, pp. 81–2.
[7] See Laws of Lerotholi, s. 34(3) of Part II.

interpretation that the legislature is presumed to know the existing law and legislate with this in mind.[1] However, in dealing with a similar problem in Nigeria Gower has argued cogently that

. . . a statute should be construed as not affecting a transaction governed by customary law unless it expressly or by necessary implication provides to the contrary. The main argument in favour of this conclusion is the manifest absurdity which would otherwise result. This absurdity is especially great . . . when customary courts are not empowered to administer the statute concerned.[2]

Fortunately in the sphere of family law there are no Lesotho statutes of this century where the matter was left open to doubt. However, there are still in force a limited number of acts and ordinances of the Cape Parliament which were introduced into Basutoland *en bloc* in 1884 by Proclamation 2B of that year.[3] There is an additional reason why *these* should not be regarded as affecting Sesotho law, namely that the Cape Parliament obviously did not have the people of Lesotho in mind at the time. In any event the prudent step was taken by the British government of only introducing these enactments so far as the circumstances of the country permitted. Only three of those still in force are of any direct relevance to family law and these are dealt with, as appropriate, in the treatment of the substantive law in Part II.

---

[1] See Palmer and Poulter, pp. 166–8.

[2] 'Nigerian Statutes and Customary Law', (1964) 1 *Nig. L.J.* 73 at 90–1.

[3] Now known as the General Law Proclamation. The Cape enactments were listed in a schedule to the Proclamation.

PART II
THE SUBSTANTIVE LAW

4

POLYGAMY

SESOTHO marriage is potentially polygamous, or to be more accurate, polygynous, thus entitling the husband to have more than one wife if he so wishes. The following discussion focuses on various aspects of the practice in turn—its origin and early popularity, the opposition of the missionaries, the attitude of the government, and the apparent decline of polygamy during the last hundred years.

I. ORIGIN AND EARLY POPULARITY

Mohlomi, the uncle of Moshoeshoe, is generally thought to have been the first Mosotho chief to have had more than four or five wives[1] and he is said to have justified large-scale polygamy to Moshoeshoe on the basis that there were political advantages to be derived from being in a position to lend out wives to prospective followers.[2] Whether such advice was really given or accepted, we cannot be sure, but at all events Moshoeshoe did marry perhaps as many as 100 wives and some of his marriages no doubt cemented useful political alliances during the period when he was moulding together various clans and groups to form the basis of the present Basotho nation.

He justified the practice to Casalis, the first and most famous of the P.E.M.S. missionaries in Lesotho, in the following terms:[3]

[1] Arbousset, *Narrative of an Exploratory Tour to the North-east of the Colony of the Cape of Good Hope* (London, 1852), pp. 379–80; letter dated 1 Oct. 1872 from Casalis to the Governor's Agent, reprinted in *1873 Report and Evidence,* p. 25; Ellenberger and Macgregor, p. 279.

[2] Ellenberger and Macgregor, p. 108; P. J. Laydevant, 'Étude sur la famille en Basutoland', (1931) 1 *Journal de la Société des Africanistes* 207 at p. 244.

[3] Quoted in Germond, p. 516. See also Orpen, *History of the Basutus of South Africa* (Cape Town, 1857), p. 4; 'Being rich in cattle, he purchased wives for the poorer among his people, and bestowed partners upon them on the condition that the cattle received as purchase money for the female children when they married, should revert to him, thus securing the goodwill of the people and at the same time, a source of ever increasing personal wealth to himself. . . .'

Our women age rapidly and we cannot resist the temptation of taking younger ones. Among the older women there are some who become lazy, and they are the first to advise us to take one more wife, hoping to make a servant of her.[1] For us chiefs, it is a means of contracting alliances with the heads of other nations, which helps to preserve peace. Moreover, we receive many travellers and strangers; how could we lodge them and what could we feed them on, if we did not have several wives?[2]

Successive paramount chiefs followed Moshoeshoe's example and the practice spread through the lesser chiefs to those commoners who could afford it (cf. the Sesotho maxim '*Moetlo o qala ho marena oe ho sechaba*' meaning that a law emanates from the senior to the junior, i.e. the commoners copy the chiefs). Estimates as to the exact number of wives married by Moshoeshoe, Letsie I, and Lerotholi unfortunately vary a great deal and figures cannot therefore be given with any sure claim to accuracy.[3]

Among commoners polygamy has always been more limited, its prime purpose being to add to a man's labour force for the expansion of his agricultural holding and thus increase his wealth. A married man has conventionally been entitled to three fields with an extra two in respect of each additional wife. In turn the possession of a number of wives enhanced a man's prestige and gave him a greater chance of accomplishing the vital object of having a male heir to continue his line, perpetuate his spirit, and glorify his memory.

Polygamy also performed the valuable function of providing every woman with a husband and a role to play at a time when the number of men may have been depleted by war, and the scope of a woman's possible alternative activities or careers was very narrow. It was preferable that she should bear legitimate children within marriage rather than illegitimate children outside it.

2. THE OPPOSITION OF THE MISSIONARIES

The first missionaries, those of the Paris Evangelical Missionary

[1] The particular concept of a servant wife or *ngoetsi* is discussed in Ch. 12 below.

[2] This is not, of course, a reference to cannibalism! However, cannibalism *was* practised at a much earlier period of Basotho history when the people were in the direst straits in time of war.

[3] Figures given for Moshoeshoe are 30–40 (Casalis), 60–80 (Ellenberger and Macgregor), over 200 (Laydevant); for Letsie I 80–100 (Ellenberger and Macgregor), 100 (Laydevant); and for Lerotholi 80 (Ashton; Laydevant).

Society who arrived in 1833, were implacably hostile to polygamy as well as to marriages with *bohali*. An idea of the passion with which they opposed these customs can be obtained from an article in one of their publications *The Little Light of Basutoland* which they put forward as part of their evidence to the 1872 Commission on the Laws and Customs of the Basotho which had been set up by the Cape Government. The article, bombastic throughout, reaches a climax at the end:

Cattle-marriages mean polygamy, they mean systematic sensualism and immorality. Take them away, and the whole fabric is broken in pieces,—the native heathen customs become meaningless,—polygamy becomes impossible,—woman is emancipated,—virtue, truth, and honour cease to be empty names, destitute of meaning, and incapable of realization in the mind of a Mosuto,—they cease to be a utopian dream which even the Christian can hardly conceive or believe in. In our attempts, therefore, to introduce and propagate Christianity, our chief blows should be struck at this system. If we wish to reconstitute the family on the Christian mode, to train up 'a righteous seed', to found an indigenous Church, there must be no compromise with this embodiment of evil, this traffic in souls, this chain of bondage under which many a soul, convinced of the truth of Christianity, still groans unable and often, alas! unwilling to cast it off.

We must apologize to our readers for our superficial and summary treatment of the subject. We have only indicated the main line of argument. We have advanced many arguments without giving our proofs, but we can assure the readers that we are well able to prove them. And if we have not adduced more proofs and examples, it is chiefly because they would unveil details too loathsome for a Christian pen to record. Let the churches everywhere unite their efforts to suppress the crying evil, well assured that when once they succeed, the end of South African heathenism will not be very far off. May God shortly bring this to pass![1]

The P.E.M.S. made rules barring polygamists from becoming church members and a polygamist who was converted to Christianity had to separate from all his wives except one and also make proper provision for the others and their children.[2]

---

[1] *1873 Report and Evidence*, p. 37.
[2] See e.g. the Revd. Dyke's evidence in *South African Native Affairs Commission, 1903–5*, vol. iv (1904), p. 423.

Although Moshoeshoe himself was never converted to Christianity, he was prepared to lend the weight of his authority to encouraging the propagation of the gospel and to co-operate in a practical way in relation to those members of his own household who wished to become members of the church. Since his own junior wives would not be admitted to church membership unless they separated from him, he granted them letters of divorce on their conversion.[1] Casalis describes how this occurred:

His decision to separate from these women was not a private arrangement, simply between himself and the women, but it was proclaimed in a great assembly of the people in 1840. Some of the heathen present raised their voice in the meeting to oppose the introduction of the new custom, and even threatened one of the counsellors of Moshesh with instant death for advising the chief to divorce his wives. But Moshesh was firm.[2]

The form the letter of divorce took has also been provided by Casalis:[3]

[Translation]

Separation of Sethepu[4]

This day appeared before me, Eugene Casalis, minister of the Church of Thaba Bosigo, Moshesh Chief of the Basutos, and Nsseriso daughter of Ntimu and of Monoa, an inferior wife of Moshesh, and declared before confirmers (*batusi*) thus:

1st.   Their marriage by which they were formerly united in the manner of *sethepu*[5] shall this day end.

2nd.   Nsseriso is released from the bond (*molao*) of Moshesh, that of a husband, and Moshesh is released from bond of Nsseriso, that of a wife.

3rd.   This day Nsseriso shall return to her relations, and there be at her own disposal or be free (*a ipotoke*); and if she shall again marry it shall not be said she commits adultery; if she remains single, she shall be considered a free woman.

---

[1] Letsie I later followed his father's practice.
[2] *1873 Report and Evidence*, pp. 25–6.
[3] Ibid., p. 26.
[4] *Sethepu* here means a junior wife.
[5] *Sethepu* here means polygyny.

4th. As to the children, they shall be brought up as their parents (*batsuali*, progenitors) shall agree together.
Thaba Bosigo, 21st February, 1843.

E. CASALIS,

MOSHESH, X

NSSERISO, X

Confirmers:
Tsolio x, Ntisnu x, Yorefa Isiu x, Mvanya x, Malitsani x, Ntlama x, Yathua Nan x.

Where a woman after conversion found that her polygamous husband was unwilling to allow her a divorce, or even a separation from him, she could not, during the last century, be admitted to church membership although she could be admitted as a catechumen. The church would not allow her simply to leave her husband and live apart from him since this meant neglecting her children. Many of the missionaries regarded this rule as too harsh and sought to have it changed in 1889. However, the Revds. Mabille and Ellenberger felt that to allow any relaxation of the rule would amount to a compromise with polygamy and successfully resisted the proposed reform.[1] It was not until later that the regulations of the church were amended to allow such a wife to join the church provided she had constantly tried to obtain her husband's agreement to a separation and had spent at least four years as a catechumen and had led a blameless life.[2]

Casalis records that he always approached the subject of polygamy indirectly with Moshoeshoe, appreciating that change could not be achieved instantaneously; rather, reform had to come from a spontaneous acceptance of Christianity by the people.[3] Despite this, some of his less experienced colleagues in the P.E.M.S. were pressing for more drastic action. In 1872 the Revds. A. Mabille and Jousse called for the statutory abolition of polygamy (and marriages with *bohali*) in their evidence to the 1872 Commission.[4]

However, while the Commission was prepared to believe that polygamy was one of the customs most injurious to the Basotho morally, socially and politically, it had no doubt that it was too

[1] E. W. Smith, pp. 342–4.
[2] *The Church of Basutoland: Its Constitution, Rules and Regulations* (Morija, 1927) gives the rules in published form.
[3] Quoted in Germond, p. 515.
[4] *1873 Report and Evidence*, p. 47.

deeply entrenched to be so easily abolished and made its recommendations accordingly.

That will be a question of time; and as by the influence of the Government and the missionaries the people are raised in the scale of civilization, so will these customs disappear.

With regard to the missionaries, your Commissioners would wish respectfully to bring to the notice of Government that they disagree entirely with these zealous men, who have the interests of the natives entirely at heart, but who wish to make Christians of them by legislation, being firmly convinced that this much-to-be-desired object can only be brought about by conviction. At the same time, your Commissioners would strongly recommend that the Government should take every opportunity of showing the Basutos that it does not approve of these heathenish and barbarous customs, and that it would gladly see them abolished.[1]

In 1904 the Revd. Dyke, also of the P.E.M.S., in his evidence before the South African Native Affairs Commission advocated in place of legislation abolishing polygamy, certain government measures to discourage it. First, polygamists should be barred from gaining higher offices in government service. Secondly, a graduated tax should be introduced in place of the existing hut tax so that a man's liability increased in proportion to the number of wives he had.[2]

The Catholic Church which arrived in Basutoland some thirty years after the P.E.M.S. was also vigorously opposed to polygamy and saw it as an even greater stumbling-block to the gaining of adherents than the presence of the rival churches. An article in the *South African Catholic Magazine* of 1914 declared[3] 'The chief difficulty lies in the people themselves (not the P.E.M.S.) and has not been conquered to the present day. The chief cause which prevents Basutos from becoming converted is not want of intelligence. . . Polygamy is *the* great obstacle.'

3. THE APPROACH OF THE GOVERNMENT

Despite the onslaughts from the churches, neither the Cape government during the period 1871 to 1883, nor the British

---

[1] *1873 Report and Evidence*, p. 5.
[2] *South African Native Affairs Commission, 1903–5*, vol. iv, p. 416.
[3] At p. 367.

government in the years 1884 to 1966 made any attempt to legislate the demise of polygamy. Nor has such a step even been considered in the years since independence. Similarly no court has ever declared the practice to be 'repugnant to justice or morality'.

The expectation has always been that polygamy would gradually wither away in the face of economic, religious, political, and social forces. The extent to which this has in fact happened is not easy to gauge with any accuracy since the two most recent censuses in 1956 and 1966 did not investigate the number of polygamists. However, some indication may be gleaned from the table on page 70 based on the official censuses undertaken in the years 1911, 1921, 1936, and 1946.

While the figures do tend to show a decline they are rendered rather inconclusive by the large number of persons for whom the number of wives is not known, especially in 1946. Polygamists may well have been particularly anxious that year not to reveal the number of wives they had because a liability to pay a higher rate of hut tax had just been imposed upon them in respect of each additional wife.[1]

Further evidence is provided by my sample survey in 1970.[2] A total of 125 women who had been married were interviewed. They were asked if their husbands had ever had more than one wife at the same time, and if so, how many. The responses were as follows:

Monogamist husband	2 wives	More than 2 wives	Total
119	6	0	125

4. REASONS FOR THE DECLINE OF POLYGAMY

Various explanations for the probable decline have been adumbrated at one time or another. Special emphasis is invariably placed on the impact made by the 'civilizing agencies' of church and state and the process of education.

The figures presented in Chapter 1 revealed the steady increase in the spread of Christianity so that by 1966 82 per cent of the people officially professed the Christian faith. When account is taken of the fact that girls generally spend more time at school

[1] Hailey, *An African Survey* (O.U.P., revd. 1956), p. 653.
[2] For details see above, pp. 11–12.

The Extent of Polygamy, 1911-46

Married men together with number of wives each

Year	1 wife (monogamists)	2	3	4	5	6	7	8	9	10	11 or more	Not stated	Total
1911	43,843	8,207	1,361	325	106	38	9	7	4	3	11	—	53,914
1921	52,210	8,218	1,194	242	84	29	16	8	8	2	12	2,107	64,130
1936	57,009	6,287	753	190	51	10	4	7	2	1	—	3,850	68,164
1946	63,524	5,337	600	131	33	14	5	1	5	42	—	13,719	83,411

than boys[1] and that virtually all the educational establishments are run by Christian missions it seems extremely likely that the growing antipathy of women towards polygamy must have made a significant contribution to its decline. However, economic factors also played their part. We have seen how the rapid increase in population has put great pressure on the country's land resources so that the number of fields which a family can expect to be allocated has shrunk. In these circumstances there is no advantage in having additional wives since there is insufficient land for them to cultivate profitably, nor can the necessary degree of independence be provided for harmonious relations between them.[2] Nor can additional wives be regarded as wage earners capable of making a cash contribution to the family's assets. Although a large number of married women do migrate to South Africa for work[3] they are generally rootless and rarely bring their savings back to Lesotho. Those who find paid employment in Lesotho have frequently had the benefit of a reasonably long education and would hardly consider marrying a polygamist in any event.

Finally, it is no longer so necessary for all Basotho women to marry in order to fulfil themselves. The range of opportunities has widened dramatically and many spinsters take jobs as teachers, nurses, secretaries, etc.

In view of the limited number of polygamous marriages being entered into today it is appropriate to mention at this juncture the extent to which polygamy has a significance beyond the small proportion of the population who practise it.

First, it should be borne in mind that for purposes of inheritance and succession the repercussions of a polygamous marriage may only finally be worked out a very considerable time after it is contracted.

Secondly, in determining status within a family or a lineage the grading of 'houses'[4] in a polygamous marriage can have great importance for subsequent generations.

Thirdly, the polygamous nature of marriage is deeply embedded

[1] See *Annual Reports of the Director of Education, passim*; Sheddick (1954), p. 82; above, p. 27.
[2] Sheddick (1954), p. 163.
[3] See p. 26 above.
[4] This expression is used to refer to an entity consisting of a wife and her children. See further p. 173 below.

in Sesotho culture. An illustration of this is to be found in the fact that the most recent provisions of the Laws of Lerotholi on inheritance (dating back to around 1950) are drafted mainly with polygamous families in mind and often their application to a monogamous household is left as a matter of inference. In part this is, of course, explained by the family backgrounds of the members of the National Council at that time, but there is no doubt that even today the marriages of the chiefs, who are the main practitioners of polygamy, are matters of great interest to their subjects.

Another example of the strength of the tradition of polygamy is the fact that when a widower or a divorcee remarries he often regards himself as playing the part of a polygamist in taking a second wife. This has important implications in determining how many 'houses' he has created. The impact of these various aspects of polygamy in terms of the modern law will be fully explored in the ensuing chapters.

5

CAPACITY TO MARRY

Various persons are incapable in law of contracting a valid marriage. Sometimes the bar is an absolute one; in other cases it merely restricts the category of possible spouses.

1. AGE

No minimum age limit has ever been fixed for marriage, but it seems clear that very young children cannot marry. The 'Restatement' declares that in the past a child's return from initiation school was a sign of readiness for marriage,[1] but since attendance there was never compulsory this cannot be regarded as a satisfactory test.[2] In traditional society where marriage was far more a matter for the parents, they would have had a good idea of when their children were capable of shouldering marital duties with sufficient responsibility. Even today this must be the test in the majority of cases, for the girl's parents will usually be concerned to assess whether the man has the ability to support his wife, either through tilling the fields or by managing his stock or as an industrial worker or miner in South Africa. In physical terms it would seem obvious that puberty must have been reached.

The 1966 Census tables suggest that the peak marriage age is thirty to thirty-four for men and twenty to twenty-four for women.[3] Whereas in the fifteen-to-nineteen age group there were only 470 married men (or 0·25 per cent of the male population aged fifteen or over), the number of married women in that group was 10,531 (3·5 per cent). The reasons for the comparatively late marriages of men are clearly economic.[4]

2. MENTAL AND PHYSICAL CONDITIONS

A valid marriage may not be contracted by a person who lacks the capacity to understand the nature of marriage and its commitments.[5]

---

[1] At p. 8.   [2] P.D., pp. 15–16.
[3] *1966 Population Census Report*, vol. i, p. 104.
[4] See p. 21 above.   [5] 'Restatement', p. 9; P.D., pp. 16–17.

However, neither physical disabilities such as deafness, dumbness, and blindness, nor physical deformities constitute a bar to marriage.[1]

3. CURRENTLY SUBSISTING MARRIAGES

Since Sesotho law only recognizes polygyny and not polyandry, a woman who is a party to a valid and subsisting marriage may not contract a second or subsequent marriage. She must therefore obtain a divorce in order to be free to remarry. The complicated position with regard to a widow's remarriage is discussed in Chapter 18 below.

4. PROHIBITED DEGREES OF RELATIONSHIP

There is no rule of exogamy among the Basotho such as is found among many other peoples of Southern Africa and all may marry as they choose, within their own clan grouping or outside it and either with other Sotho or with people of Nguni origin or even with persons of a different race.[2]

Certain close relatives may not, however, marry one another. Prohibited marriages include those between brother and sister, mother and son, and father and daughter. Generally speaking cousins may marry one another and such matches are considered by some to be very desirable.[3] They still occur today, but to nowhere near the same extent as in the past.

The following lists of prohibited degrees are based on information provided by the seven members of the Panel Discussion and only indicate a prohibited degree where this was the view of a substantial majority.[4]

(a) A woman may not marry
(i) *Blood relations*
Father
Son
Father's father
Mother's father
Son's son
Daughter's son

(b) A man may not marry
(i) *Blood relations*
Mother
Daughter
Father's mother
Mother's mother
Son's daughter
Daughter's daughter

---

[1] 'Restatement', p. 9; P.D., p. 17.
[2] P.D., p. 18.　　　　　　[3] See pp. 80–1 below.
[4] The members gave written answers to this question and it did not form part of the formal proceedings of the Panel Discussion itself.

Brother	Sister
Brother's son	Brother's daughter
Sister's son	Sister's daughter
Father's brother	Father's sister
Mother's brother	Mother's sister
(ii) *Relations by marriage*	(ii) *Relations by marriage*
Husband's father's father (after death or divorce)[1]	Wife's father's mother
Husband's mother's father (after death or divorce)	Wife's mother's mother
Husband's father (after death or divorce)	Wife's mother
Husband's son by another wife (after death or divorce)	Wife's daughter by another husband
Husband's son's son (after death or divorce)	Wife's son's daughter
Husband's daughter's son (after death or divorce)	Wife's daughter's daughter
Father's mother's husband	Father's father's wife (after death or divorce)
Mother's mother's husband	Mother's father's wife (after death or divorce)
Mother's husband	Father's wife (after death or divorce)
Daughter's husband	Son's wife (after death or divorce)
Son's daughter's husband	Son's son's wife (after death or divorce)
Daughter's daughter's husband	Daughter's son's wife (after death or divorce)

[1] The relationships followed by the phrase 'after death or divorce' would, in the absence of the first husband's death or a divorce, create polyandrous 'marriages' which are prohibited in any event.

6

THE CONTRACTING OF A
MARRIAGE

IN considering the legal requirements for the formation of a valid marriage it is imperative to start with the framework provided by section 34(1) of Part II of the Laws of Lerotholi. This section was transferred from Part I around 1950 and now carries statutory force because it was issued as a rule of the Paramount Chief under the Native Administration Proclamation of 1938.[1]

The relevant part of this provision runs as follows:

A marriage . . . shall be deemed to be completed when:
(a) there is agreement between the parties to the marriage;
(b) there is agreement between the parents of the parties or between those who stand *in loco parentis* to the parties as to the marriage and as to the amount of the *bohali*;
(c) there is payment of part or all of the *bohali*: . . .

To set this provision in its proper perspective a cautionary note should be sounded:

In African native law there is not usually any prescribed formality or set of formalities which can be readily identified as corresponding to the 'solemnization' or 'celebration' of a marriage under European law. The marriage transaction is normally a long-drawn out process, and there is often some doubt, both as to the exact point in that process at which the parties become husband and wife, and also as to which (if any) of the accompanying ceremonies and observances are strictly essential to the conclusion of a valid marriage. Any statutory regulation of the procedure for solemnization of a customary marriage is, therefore, likely to involve a certain degree of interference with native law and custom.[2]

---

[1] No. 61 of 1938. This proclamation, after being restyled the Chieftainship (Powers) Proclamation, was eventually repealed by the Chieftainship Act, No. 22 of 1968.

[2] Phillips and Morris, *Marriage Laws in Africa* (O.U.P., 1971), p. 107; see also Radcliffe-Brown and Forde (Eds.), *African Systems of Kinship and Marriage* (O.U.P., 1950), p. 49, and Gluckman (Ed.), *Ideas and Procedures in African Customary Law*, p. 63.

The ensuing analysis will provide a validation of this statement in the context of Sesotho law and will show the extent to which section 34(1) falls short of a comprehensive and accurate description of the essential requirements of a Sesotho marriage.

I. ENGAGEMENT

Since, under the traditional system, marriages were planned and arranged more by the parents than by the prospective spouses themselves, it is not surprising that parents should sometimes have promised their sons and daughters in marriage while they were still young children.[1] This process of 'infant betrothal' has now virtually died out, since it was linked with the outmoded idea that the will of the head of the family should predominate over the wishes of his children in the choice of a partner in marriage.

Apart from these cases of formal betrothal, the normal situation in the old days must have involved a period of informal engagement between the moment when some agreement on marriage had been reached and the time when the marriage itself was completed. The same is true of marriage in the modern setting.[2]

The main area of legal concern in engagements lies in relation to the repercussions of a decision by one of the parties not to proceed with the marriage. What circumstances give rise to liability? Two preliminary points should be borne in mind. First, in a case where a man is marrying for the first time, both he and his fiancée are, in legal theory at any rate, minors, and the general freedom from personal liability and lack of capacity to make a binding contract apply.[3] Secondly, and flowing from this, it may be said that where the only accord that has been reached is one between the prospective spouses themselves, without any additional agreement on the part of their parents, no liability to pay compensation arises from a change of mind by either party,

[1] See Laydevant, p. 245; Ashton, p. 64; Duncan, p. 21; 'Restatement', p. 2; P.D., pp. 2–6.

[2] The 'Restatement' must be taken to be in error when it declares baldly (p. 2), 'Engagements today are not common'. Information given to me by my students as well as by anthropologists who have done field-work in villages in Lesotho controverts such a statement.

[3] The general rule, in legal theory at any rate, is that a man attains majority only through marriage and not simply upon reaching a specified age; a spinster can achieve majority only through emancipation. These matters are discussed at pp. 185–9, 194–6 below.

regardless of the cause.[1] The reason is simply that neither of them possesses the capacity to enter into a binding agreement giving rise to legal consequences.

The next stage after the private engagement of the couple themselves is for agreement to be reached between their respective parents. The parents must first agree that the marriage should take place and then on the amount of *bohali* to be transferred. As soon as the parents have agreed to the marriage the engagement takes on a new status in terms of liability for its breach. If the man wrongfully breaks the engagement, a beast known as *sesila* may be claimed from his father by the head of the girl's family.[2] Liability is limited to a single beast, the symbolic purpose of which is to cleanse or purify the girl after her misfortune. The basis of the claim seems to be in the nature of compensation for the smear on the girl's reputation and the fact that she may consequently find it more difficult to get married to another man. However, the liability arises irrespective of whether she has been seduced or abducted, although if compensation is claimed and paid under either of these heads the *sesila* beast would, it seems, be included within the award of six head of cattle and not added to it.[3] Liability for seduction and abduction is considered further below.[4]

It seems clear that there is no liability for the *sesila* beast where the man has a just cause for breaking the engagement, for instance if the girl formed an attachment to another man or behaved in an insulting or disrespectful way to the man or his family.[5] In such cases she is to blame and not the man. Where it is the girl who wrongfully breaks off the engagement nothing equivalent to the *sesila* beast is payable to the man's parents; he will have other opportunities for marriage and his chances are not felt to have been jeopardized.[6]

During the engagement period the man has no obligation to maintain or support his fiancée, nor does he acquire the right to sue someone who seduces her; such rights and duties remain with her parents until she is married.[7]

During this period property may have been transferred to the girl's family or herself. It is possible that cattle (or perhaps more commonly a single beast) known as *tebeletso* ('pledge') may have

---

[1] 'Restatement', pp. 2–3; P.D., p. 6.   [2] 'Restatement', p. 3; P.D., pp. 8–9.
[3] P.D., pp. 8–9.   [4] See p. 109 below.
[5] P.D., pp. 8–9.   [6] P.D., pp. 8–9.   [7] P.D., p. 10.

been paid over in contemplation of the marriage by the man's father to the girl's family.[1] *Tebeletso* was commonly given in the old days in cases of infant betrothal and served as a deposit to be included later in the *bohali*, as it does today.[2]

Where the man wrongfully refuses to proceed with the marriage the *tebeletso* cattle are forfeited.[3] On the other hand, where he is justified in his refusal or where the girl or her parents wrongfully break off the engagement the *tebeletso* cattle must be refunded.[4] If the father of the girl has in the meantime sold or slaughtered the particular beasts (as he is entitled to do) he is bound instead to return their equivalent.[5] Where the offspring of the *tebeletso* cattle can be identified, it seems that these too are recoverable.[6]

Aside from the question of *tebeletso* cattle, small personal gifts may have been exchanged between the man and the girl during the engagement period, but these are seemingly not recoverable if the marriage does not proceed.[7]

2. REQUIREMENTS FOR CONTRACTING A MARRIAGE

(a) *Consent of the Parties*

There is strong evidence from early reports that during the last century some couples were forced to marry against their will.[8] A father's control over his sons and daughters was far greater in those days and children were brought up to believe that they had to obey their father's wishes, even in such personal matters as marriage.[9] Such forced marriages were designed to achieve or strengthen desired political and social relationships.[10]

---

[1] Sekese (1968), p. 3; P.D., pp. 2–5.

[2] See Duncan, p. 21.   [3] 'Restatement', p. 2; P.D., p. 3.

[4] *Semandla* v. *Pitso* J.C. 189/1963 (all courts); *Kholu* v. *Nyenye* J.C. 191/1966. (In the latter case the Local and Central Courts and the J.C.'s Court all agreed that the cattle should be refunded; the lower courts awarded them to the man but were overruled by the J.C. on the ground that they should have been awarded to his father.) See also P.D., pp. 3–4 (one member of the panel described how he was betrothed as a child and later decided he did not wish to marry the girl chosen for him by his father; the cattle were not refunded, nor were their offspring); 'Restatement', p. 2.

[5] P.D., pp. 5–6.   [6] 'Restatement', p. 2; P.D., p. 3.

[7] P.D., pp. 7–8; *contra* 'Restatement', p. 3.

[8] See e.g. George Moshoeshoe's barely veiled statement to the 1872 Commission: 'It does sometimes happen that parents compel their daughters to marry men against their wishes by beating them, etc., but this happens only very seldom', *1873 Report and Evidence*, p. 40; ibid., p. 33 (article reprinted from *The Little Light of Basutoland*); Germond, p. 536; Ashton, p. 64.

[9] P.D., pp. 11–14.   [10] Ellenberger and Macgregor, p. 273; P.D., pp. 17–18.

For instance, marriages between cousins were, broadly speaking, regarded as particularly desirable or 'preferred'. This applied to marriages not only between cross-cousins where a man married his mother's brother's daughter or his father's sister's daughter, but also between parallel cousins, where a man married his mother's sister's daughter or his father's brother's daughter.[1]

Such marriages could be expected to be particularly well exploited among the chieftainship which would not only be more interested in maintaining the good standing of the family, but would also possess sufficient wealth to contract preferred marriages as well as 'love-match' marriages.[2] Jones has illustated, with a *fin de siècle* example from the royal family, how the intermarriage of parallel cousins was used to link together rival, or potentially rival chiefly dynasties:

> . . . the most serious potential rival of the Paramount Chief Letsie I was his brother Molapo, the chief of the largest ward in Basutoland. But Molapo's heir, Joseph, and Joseph's full brother Jonathan who later acted as regent for him, were both married to a daughter of the paramount. Thus when Letsie I and Molapo died, Lerotholi, the new chief, was able to intervene very effectively in the internal politics of the Molapo ward as his sisters were married to its ward chief and to its regent and were the mothers of their respective heirs.[3]

However, this practice was by no means confined to the chiefs and it served to cement family relationships among commoners too. As the saying goes, '*Ngoana malome 'nyale ke selibelo ke mafura a lefehloa ha ke fele*' ('Child of my maternal uncle marry me; I am an ointment of melted butter which exists for ever').[4]

Moreover a man's marriage to the daughter of his paternal uncle meant that the *bohali* cattle remained within the extended family. This explains another saying, '*Ngoana rangoane 'nyale*

---

[1] Junod, *The Life of a South African Tribe* (Macmillan, 2nd ed. 1927), pp. 299–300; Ashton, pp. 62–3; P.D., p. 17. Sheddick (at pp. 34–5) points out that there are exceptions in the case of the Bakhatla clan (where marriages to a man's mother's sister's daughter are *prohibited*) and among the Vundle people who are Xhosas (where all cousin marriages are forbidden because of the principle of exogamy). Laydevant (at p. 242) seems to be mistaken in his assertion that parallel-cousin marriages were prohibited for all save the chieftainship.

[2] See Ashton, pp. 62–3, and his Appendix III.

[3] 'Chiefly Succession in Basutoland', in Goody (Ed.), *Succession to High Office* (C.U.P., 1966), 57 at p. 59.

[4] P.D., p. 18.

likhomo li boele sakeng' ('Child of my paternal uncle marry me so that the cattle go back to the kraal').[1]

The statutory abolition of forced marriages was the first blow struck by colonial legislation against the power of a family head. This step was taken in the first marriage regulation made after Basutoland was annexed to the Cape Colony in the following terms:

It shall not be lawful for any person to compel any woman to enter into a contract of marriage against the wish of such woman.[2]

The regulation refers only to the consent of wives but it must not be allowed to mislead. Husbands were dictated to by their fathers almost as much;[3] however in their case, having first married wives selected by their fathers they were then free to marry others according to their choice. This factor apparently outweighed any hardship that might otherwise be thought to exist. However, difficulties arose in determining the line of succession when the husband managed to marry his own choice first, a matter that is dealt with below.[4]

A similar provision to the first marriage regulation was contained in Proclamation 2B of 1884 when the British government took over the direct administration of the country from the Cape and this was later incorporated in the Marriage Proclamation of 1911.[5]

This Proclamation was repealed in 1974 and replaced by the Marriage Act,[6] section 3 of which reads:

No person may be compelled to enter into a contract of marriage with any other person or to marry against his or her wish.

Whereas the 1911 provision was in the general part of the Proclamation and thus applicable to both civil and customary marriages, the 1974 Act is not divided into separate parts and contains a section excluding customary marriages from its ambit altogether.[7] This has the surprising consequence that the statutory

---

[1] P.D., p. 18.

[2] Marriage regulation No. 1 of Proc. 74 of 1871.

[3] For two unsuccessful attempts by fathers to 'switch' their children's spouses immediately after their marriages see *Sempe* v. *Tsepo* H.C.8/1946 and *Molapo* v. *Molapo* C.A.Civ./A/1/1974.

[4] See pp. 102–3 below.   [5] Proc. 7 of 1911, s. 2.

[6] Act No. 10 of 1974.   [7] S. 42.

bar against forced *customary* marriages has been abolished. Probably this is merely the result of an oversight, but in any event it seems clear that any previous rule of Sesotho custom permitting forced marriages must have been abrogated by a century of almost total disuse pursuant to the various statutory prohibitions.

Although forced marriages would not be countenanced by the courts today, they may nevertheless persist to a small extent in the sense of considerable moral pressure being placed on a girl by her family, especially where a wealthy suitor is offering to pay full *bohali* at the time of the wedding, rather than by irregular instalments over the years.[1]

A similar situation might arise where a man abducts a girl against her will and then follows it up with a payment to her father of cattle in excess of the six required by law as compensation.[2] If her father is tempted to accept them (or even to treat the compensatory six cattle as part payment of *bohali*) the girl could come under strong pressure from her family.

In *Tomotomo* v. *Mothae*[3] the plaintiff claimed to have married 'Ma-Sefako in 1945 after abducting her and paying £50 by way of *bohali* to her father. Between 1946 and 1960 she had been living with the defendant and had borne him seven children. The defendant claimed that she had never been validly married to the plaintiff and was in fact married to him. The Judicial Commissioner found that 'Ma-Sefako had been abducted by force in 1945 and had only managed to escape from the plaintiff after persistent requests; since she had never given her consent to the alleged marriage with the plaintiff it was declared invalid.

(b) *Consent of the Parents to the Marriage*

The Laws of Lerotholi require agreement to the proposed marriage from the parents of the parties or else from whoever stands *in loco parentis* towards them.

It would seem that in the reference to the parents the person whose consent is particularly required by the law is the head of the family. Thus, where both father and mother are alive it is the consent of the father which appears to be decisive and opposition from the mother can be discounted.[4] Where the father is dead, his

---

[1] P.D., pp. 11–14. For the payment of *bohali* see pp. 127–8 below.
[2] This situation is discussed further below, Ch. 8.
[3] J.C. 9/1963.
[4] P.D., pp. 25–6.

son and heir, if married and thus a major, takes over responsibility for the marriages of younger brothers. If no son has attained majority, responsibility today generally passes to the father's widow.[1] She ought to consult her deceased husband's relatives in this matter, as in everything else concerning the family. However, if she fails to do so it seems that her child's marriage will be valid in law, whatever dissension her non-compliance with proper procedures may cause within the family.[2]

Sometimes, as will be seen later,[3] a child is brought up by a relative rather than by his or her parents. Such a relative then stands *in loco parentis* to the child (even if not its lawful guardian) and may give the requisite consent to marry. However, where the parents or guardians are alive it seems clear that this relative ought properly to contact them and bring them into the negotiations. Nevertheless, if he fails to do so and acts throughout as if he were the father, it appears that this will not invalidate the marriage, though difficulties will surely arise if he accepts *bohali* in respect of a girl without her father or guardian being notified of it. This matter is considered further below.[4]

The restriction imposed on the freedom to marry by the law's requirement of parental consent has inevitably given rise to impatience among young people, especially as they have grown more independent. Various devices currently in use for evading this prerequisite must be taken into account in placing the parental power in its proper perspective.

First, it has long been common for couples to elope together to force their parents' hands if they feel they are being opposed or that they need to speed up the process of marriage and their parents are being unduly dilatory.[5] In this connection it is interesting to note the reaction, as long ago as 1884, of one of the P.E.M.S. missionaries to this situation which the missionaries themselves had indirectly helped to bring about:

What is certain, is that the Basuto are still too childish to bear certain customs of European importation which have been applied to them like a piece of new cloth to an old one. In former days a Mosuto's marriage was an affair arranged between his parents and his prospective

---

[1] See e.g. *Mothakathi* v. *Ratikane* J.C. 84/1963.
[2] P.D., pp. 27–8.   [3] See p. 238 below.
[4] See pp. 142–4 below.   [5] P.D., p. 36.

bride's, without any one regarding himself bound to consult the young people concerned. This concept was condemned by the missionaries who, with reason, considered that in matrimonial matters, the young people should have a word to say, and that love should be the basis of marriage. There is nothing amiss in that. But our young Basuto have seized upon this excellent doctrine to throw their parents overboard and to have their own way. They have taken from our European customs only that which would be harmful to them, placing the accent on liberty.[1]

As will be seen, elopements are still a frequent occurrence today. In the technical language of the law an elopement constitutes an abduction of the girl by the man for which compensation is due, regardless of the girl's consent. This is discussed fully in Chapter 8, but suffice it to point out here that if, following two successive elopements, parental consent is still not forthcoming, the law has endeavoured to provide a remedy. Section 4(2) of Part II of the Laws of Lerotholi runs as follows:

If the man abducts the same unmarried girl a second time against the wishes of either his or her parents, the amount of compensation to be awarded to the parents of such girl shall be at the discretion of the court and the court may order the dissenting parents to arrange the marriage.

The subsection has not been well drafted and this has given rise to a certain amount of difficulty. The 'Restatement' remarks caustically: 'How the court achieves compliance with its order and what its real implications are is not clear. Most courts have made the order and immediately looked away—performance or no performance!'[2]

Nevertheless, this was not the approach adopted by the Judicial Commissioner's Court in the recent case of *Ralie* v. *Mosoka*.[3] Here a man abducted the same girl on two separate occasions. His father had paid five head of cattle for the first abduction and was sued for a further seven head, i.e. the outstanding beast in respect of the first occasion together with the full compensation of six head for the second occasion. The Local Court awarded the full amount of the claim and proceeded to order the parents to arrange a marriage despite the unwillingness of the man's father. On appeal

[1] H. Dieterlin, quoted in Germond, p. 531.   [2] At p. 6.   [3] J.C. 29/1967.

the Judicial Commissioner upheld the award of seven head, but overruled the lower court's order to arrange a marriage on the ground that orders made in terms of section 4(2) were impossible to enforce unless the parents could reach agreement over the amount of *bohali*. He went on:

... if that law was required to be enforceable it would be better worded that the court may fix [*bohali*] and declare the marriage effective on that basis irrespective of the dissenting parent or parents.

This rather obtuse attitude seems hard to justify save on the basis of an ultra-conservative view of the judicial function. Implicit in the section is surely the intention that the courts should have the power to fix a reasonable *bohali* scale in the absence of parental agreement. The manifest object of the provision is to place a restriction on parental power in the contracting of marriages and for the courts to uphold a father's veto because of the inelegant language of the section is an abdication of judicial responsibility. It is respectfully submitted that this part of the decision in *Ralie* v. *Mosoka* should not be followed. It is in any event inconsistent with an earlier decision of the Judicial Commissioner's Court in *Mashoai* v. *Nkoko*,[1] where Duncan J.C. declared that to force the girl to return to her father and forgo the marriage would be 'repugnant to good morals, modern life and good behaviour'.

A second technique for dispensing with the need for parental consent is for the parties to take themselves out of the *customary* law of marriage entirely. Provided the couple are both over twenty-one they can enter into a valid *civil* marriage without obtaining their parents' consent.[2]

Thirdly, the 'Restatement' describes what it regards as a modern phenomenon, where the husband proceeds to marry according to customary law without the consent, or even knowledge, of his parents:

Following the spate of marriages in recent years in which the husband-to-be has used his friends and people other than his parents to ask a girl's parents for her hand in marriage, there now appears to have emerged and resulted a new agreement: one involving the bridegroom and the girl's parents. The friends and non-parents are the groom's mere representatives and in those cases it is clear that the payment of

---

[1] J.C. 235/1951. See also Duncan, pp. 21–2.
[2] For a recent classic example see *Maqutu* v. *Hlapane* H.C. Civ./A/1/1971.

bohali may be demanded only from the man and that, even were his parents to come to light and their whereabouts be known, the girl's parents cannot proceed against them, instead of going against their son-in-law. The defence open to his parents is to say simply that they were never a party to the negotiations.[1]

In the Panel Discussion[2] it was explained that this type of arrangement is generally confined to the towns since in the rural areas the man and his parents would be living in the same vicinity and the father would inevitably get word of what was going on. Where, in an urban community, a man does succeed in by-passing his parents his reason might be to avoid entrusting his earnings to a spendthrift father who could not be relied upon to use the money for *bohali*. Alternatively he might not be on good terms with his father or he might be marrying a girl his father disapproved of. The Panel did not welcome the advent of such marriages, subversive as they are of the traditional family aspect of marriage and its concomitant pressures to assist in the solution of marital problems through reconciliation.

Some members of the 'Restatement' Panel considered that a marriage without parental consent is 'at best, a limping union inferior in status to that in which such a consent is present', but the 'Restatement' itself reached the conclusion that such marriages are fully valid and that a child of a marriage which lacks the consent of the husband's parents would not be barred from succeeding his father as his heir.[3]

If this is the case section 34(1)(b) is no longer an adequate statement of the law. In any event it lacks completeness since where a man marries a second or subsequent wife there is no need for his parents to consent. He is a major at law, may make the necessary marriage arrangements without assistance and is obliged to pay the *bohali* himself.[4]

(c) *Agreement of the Parents as to the amount of* Bohali

As in the case of consent to the marriage, when the Laws of Lerotholi refer to the agreement of the parents over *bohali* it is that of the respective fathers which is of paramount significance

---

[1] At pp. 4–5.   [2] See P.D., pp. 28–31.   [3] At p. 4.
[4] *Nkoko* v. *Cheli* J.C. 272/1966 (J.C.); P.D., pp. 54–5; cf. 'Restatement' (at p. 8) which while agreeing on the *bohali* question states that the man's parents negotiate subsequent marriages 'because it is considered impolite or improper for the groom personally to do this'.

since they are the heads of their families. After their deaths responsibility passes to their heirs or widows, depending upon the circumstances already noted.

It is quite common for the man's family to send a relative to the girl's people as their representative to undertake the negotiations on their behalf. If such a representative is properly authorized his agreement on the amount of *bohali* will bind the person who sent him and needs no ratification.[1]

It not infrequently happens that children are brought up by persons other than their natural parents. Such people, who are invariably relatives, stand *in loco parentis* and may, in the case of a girl, enter into an agreement on the amount of the *bohali* in addition to giving the necessary consent to the marriage in terms of section 34. Although it might be thought that someone in this position should not be permitted to take any action which might bind the girl's true father without having consulted him, especially in property matters, it has repeatedly been held by the Judicial Commissioner that he may do so. The rationale for permitting such a procedure lies in the need to protect the prospective husband and his family who are the other party to the transaction. Thus in *Jonathan* v. *Mothoana*[2] Thompson J.C. declared:

... it is the custom that when a man wishes to marry a girl he is expected to approach the head of the family with whom the girl lives. He is not expected to know whether the head of the family where the girl lives is the girl's lawful guardian ...

He then went on to explain how the girl's lawful guardian is safeguarded by the law:

The guardian whose ward does not live at his home has the right to sue the family who gives her away in marriage for the [*bohali*] paid to the family head and he can claim the balance from the husband or husband's father once they are aware of the legal guardianship.[3]

---

[1] *Pokonyane* v. *Qekisi* J.C. 137/1964 (L.C., C.C., and J.C.); *Mokhojana* v. *Mokoma* J.C. 112/1966 (L.C., C.C. and J.C.); *Mohale* v. *Selebalo* J.C. 342/1966 (L.C. and J.C.).

[2] J.C. 273/1964.

[3] In this case the L.C. and C.C. judgments do not support that of the J.C. Thompson J.C. reiterated his views in *Ralekabu* v. *Lelimo* J.C. 216/1969 (J.C.). See also pp. 142–4 below.

Payment of *bohali* to the person handing the girl over operates to give the person paying a complete discharge and he cannot later be held liable to pay the same amount again by the girl's true father or guardian.[1] Support for these propositions comes also from the judgment of M. N. Lerotholi, a distinguished court president, in the Tsifalimali Central Court in *Semandla* v. *Pitso*.[2] However, he did stress that when a suitor arrives the proper approach for the person with whom the girl is staying is to direct him to the girl's parents or himself convey the suitor's request to them.

Finally, it should be noted that the agreement on *bohali* does not depend for its validity on formality. The agreement does not have to be in writing to be enforceable in the courts,[3] but the desirability of evidencing it in documentary form is more readily recognized today and written agreements are becoming increasingly common.[4] The following example[5] shows an agreement upon the 'conventional scale',[6] with a payment of the equivalent of ten head of cattle on the wedding day:

AN AGREEMENT OVER *BOHALI* IN RESPECT OF TEFO MASHAPHA POKONYANE, WHO MARRIES THE DAUGHTER OF EDWARD THAPHOKANE, NAMED 'MAMATSEMA: AT MABEFOLANE'S MAPOTENG-POPOPO. ON 20th December, 1952;
Those present on the side of Mashapha Polonyane [the husband's father], by an order of a letter addressed to 'Ma-Jason Mohlebi dated 1.11.1952 were:—Josiel Lefela and Malefetsane Kolotsane, being brought by Khohloane Chabeli and Sematla Kolotsane [i.e. his representatives]. Those on the side of Edward Thaphokane were: 1. Sepalo Hlalele 2. Moholo Qekisi 3. Mokopotsa Thaphokane. A bull which was being

---

[1] *Jakalasi* v. *Letsota* J.C. 283/1963 (J.C.).
[2] The judgment was upheld by Thompson J.C. on appeal (J.C. 189/1963). The facts were that the person with whom the girl had been staying had received a deposit in respect of *bohali* from a suitor, but the girl then decided to marry someone else. All the courts held the payer of the deposit was entitled to recover it.
[3] *Mokhethinyane* v. *Sekonyela* J.C. 60/1963, H.C. Civ./A/7/1964 (all courts); *Mohale* v. *Selebalo* J.C. 342/1966 (L.C. and J.C.); *Limape* v. *Lebona* J.C. 95/1966 (L.C.); P.D., p. 41. There is similarly no need for the agreement on marriage to be in writing—see *Hlehlethe* v. *Lebajoa* J.C. 47/1944 (J.C.).
[4] P.D., p. 41.
[5] Copied from the record of *Pokonyane* v. *Qekisi* J.C. 137/1964.
[6] The 'conventional scale' is explained Ch. 7 below.

prayed for that it be counted at two beasts. Edward Thaphokane said he valued it at one beast. Two horses which he agreed to value at two beasts each. Each donkey was agreed it be valued at a beast each and a foal valued at a beast. For that reason all that made ten head of cattle received at this *bohali*.

Through the mouth of Sepalo Hlalele, Edward Thaphokane declared the scale in respect of the *bohali* as being twenty head of cattle, a horse and ten goats. This statement was made in the presence of Edward Thaphokane. These animals were confirmed by a *bewys*[1] . . . [details of *bewyses* given].

The writers were . . . [names given].

Confirmed by Chief Michael Boshoane Peete's Date Stamp—on 22nd December, 1952.

It has sometimes been contended in court that a *bohali* agreement is invalid and unenforceable unless witnessed by the local chief or his representative. This is obviously extremely desirable for evidentiary purposes, but the courts have ruled that it is not essential.[2]

---

[1] A *bewys* is a document evidencing the transfer of livestock.

[2] *Mokhethinyane* v. *Sekonyela* J.C. 60/1963, H.C. Civ./A/7/1964 (L.C., C.C., J.C., and H.C.); *Lekhanya* v. *Mongalo* J.C. 179/1963 (J.C.).

7

THE AMOUNT OF THE *BOHALI*
AND THE INITIAL PAYMENT

THE amount of the *bohali* payable in respect of a marriage is determined by negotiation and agreement between the families of the bride and groom.

The traditional practice was for the negotiations to be initiated and completed on the wedding day itself and the groom's family would arrive at the home of the bride before the wedding driving the cattle which would form the whole or part of the *bohali*.[1] This would be the first time that any member of the bride's family had set eyes upon the cattle. From this it might seem as if the outcome of the discussions would inevitably be agreement, since if deadlock were reached the marriage could not take place—at any rate for the time being—and the preparations for the wedding would be wasted. However, this was not the case; that there was always a possibility of the negotiations breaking down is clear from two Sesotho expressions, meaning literally that the *bohali* has failed ('*bohali bo hobile*' or '*bohali bo nyopile*').[2]

The same procedure is often still followed today, but an alternative practice of settling the *bohali* scale some time before the wedding has become increasingly common. Where this is done the girl's family may even send a representative to inspect the *bohali* cattle at the man's home to establish their number as well as their quality.

Subject to the application of section 4(2) of Part II of the Laws of Lerotholi which empowers the courts to curb any tendency on the part of the girl's father to make an extortionate demand, it is

---

[1] P.D., pp. 40–1, 195.

[2] See the judgment of President Matete in the Setleketseng Local Court in *Mothakathi* v. *Ratikane* J.C. 84/1963. In *Mohale* v. *Mohale* J.C. 248/1966 thirty head of cattle were driven to the girl's home by the man, but the *bohali* negotiators failed to reach agreement over the future of the girl's pre-marital child and the cattle had to be driven back again. See also P.D., p. 36.

beyond question that it is the family of the girl who have the decisive voice in *bohali* negotiations and bargaining. They have the right to state the amount of *bohali* they require and if the man's family are not prepared to meet this request then the marriage cannot proceed.[1] The only check placed upon the extent of their demand is that if they ask more than the 'conventional amount' (see below) and this is refused, they may find that the court reduces the scale under section 4(2). However, as we have seen, before this section can be invoked the couple must have eloped on at least two occasions.[2]

The remainder of this chapter is devoted first to an examination of the 'conventional scale' of *bohali* which is commonly agreed upon and its exact status in law and secondly, to the final requirement for a valid marriage laid down in section 34 of the Laws of Lerotholi, namely that at least part of the *bohali* must actually have been paid over.

1. THE CONVENTIONAL SCALE OF MODERN TIMES

In Sesotho custom and practice there has existed for many years a *bohali* scale for the daughters of commoners which is agreed upon in so many cases and which is so frequently referred to in conversation and literature, as well as in courts of law, that it may fairly be regarded as conventional.[3]

It consists of the following animals or their equivalent:

(i) Twenty head of cattle;
(ii) Ten sheep or goats known as *setsiba* (loin-cloth or trousers), expressing the old idea that their skins could be used as clothing by the bride's father;
(iii) One horse called *molisana* (the herd boy) for herding the cattle;[4]

---

[1] *Makoa* v. *'Matli* J.C. 45/1964 (J.C.); *Mohale* v. *Selebalo* J.C. 342/1966 (L.C. and J.C.); *Matsemela* v. *Rabukana* J.C. 346/1966 (L.C.); *Mokhojana* v. *Mokoma* J.C. 112/1966 (all courts); *Phatela* v. *Khamali* J.C. 284/1968 (L.C.); *Mtakabone* v. *Ramphobole* J.C. 71/1969 (J.C.); see also P.D., pp. 31–3.

[2] See p. 84 above.

[3] See e.g. Sekese (1953), p. 4; Sheddick (1953), p. 33 (who refers to it as 'a popularly accepted ideal scale' for normal marriages with first wives, and says less may be paid for marriages to subsequent wives); Duncan, p. 23; 'Restatement', p. 6; P.D., pp. 31–2.

[4] Sekese writing in 1907 refers to this portion of the *bohali* as a recent innovation.

(iv) One ox called *moqhoba* (the driver) which is given not to
the bride's parents, but to the women who accompany the
bride to her husband's home.

The total amount of this *bohali* may alternatively be expressed
as twenty-three head of cattle.[1] The scale for the daughters of
chiefs is commonly higher than this and may be thirty, forty, or
even fifty head of cattle.[2]

The conventional scale is high, representing R460 (or about
£260) at the cash equivalent usually employed by the courts and
roughly twice that amount at current market prices for livestock.
The reason why it can still be the agreed amount in so many
marriages today despite the overall poverty of the nation is that
it is not all required to be paid at one and the same time on the
wedding day. The bride's family will invariably accept an arrangement for payment by instalments since *bohali* debts do not
prescribe and are transmitted from one generation to another.[3]
Thus the groom's family can safely be allowed to pay off its debt
as circumstances permit over a great many years. As a result of
this never-never system even a pauper without prospects can enter
into an obligation to pay the conventional scale and his poverty
will not be regarded as grounds for reducing the actual amount
payable.[4]

An indication of the length of time for which such debts tend
to be outstanding is provided by the figures in Tables 4 and 5.
Table 4 analyses the position in Ha Tsiu, a traditionalist village
community situated high in the mountains in a remote part of the
Qacha's Nek district. In every instance the amount of *bohali* was
agreed at the conventional scale of twenty-three head of cattle and
the table shows how the debt is slowly but steadily reduced as the
years go by so that ultimately a very high proportion, if not the
whole amount, is paid.

[1] Cf. Ashton, p. 71, and Wallman, pp. 69–70, who give instead a total of
twenty-five cattle.
[2] See P.D., pp. 35–6, where illustrations were given of marriages of chiefs'
daughters to both chiefs and commoners with *bohali* as high as forty and fifty
head; the daughter of Chief Makhaola Letsie II was married with fifty as was
her mother (see *Letsie II* v. *Bolae* J.C. 182/1964); around 1890 Chief Joe
Qhobela married the granddaughter of Paramount Chief Letsie I with forty
(see *Qhobela* v. *Qhobela* H.C. 24/1943).
[3] See pp. 127, 139–40 below.
[4] P.D., p. 32.

Table 5 presents the position in the lowland village of Mokho-khong which is only about thirty miles from Maseru, the capital. This community is less traditionalist than that of Ha Tsiu. Here it is quite common for the parties to fix a lower scale of *bohali* and out of the sample of twenty-six only eight had reached agreement on the conventional scale. Thirteen had agreed on twenty head of cattle and the remaining five had agreed on amounts between ten and sixteen head. The payments in Mokhokhong do not generally seem to be as well maintained as those in Ha Tsiu so that a *bohali* debt appears to be only rarely completely extinguished, at any rate during the wife's lifetime.

2. HISTORICAL PERSPECTIVE

It is extremely difficult to assess the extent to which the standard amount of *bohali* has risen over the years. Various commentators have given estimates of what was required, but since they made no detailed study their views cannot be relied upon very strongly. On the one hand, we cannot be sure from their writings exactly

TABLE 4

Analysis of payments in respect of 49 bohali agreements in Ha Tsiu village

Date of marriage	Number of marriages studied	Average number of cattle paid up to date of interview (1969)	Percentage
1891–1900	1	20	87
1901–10	2	23	100
1911–20	2	19	82·5
1921–30	3	21	91
1931–40	10	21·5	93·5
1941–50	5	16	70
1951–60	13	14·5	63
1961–8	13	10·5	45·5
	49		

Source: Interviews with families of migrant labourers conducted in 1969 by Gottfried Wellmer, who kindly gave permission for me to analyse the unpublished material he had collected.

TABLE 5

Analysis of payments in respect of 26 bohali
agreements in Mokhokhong village

Date of marriage	Number of marriages studied	Total number of cattle agreed upon	Total number of cattle paid up to date of interview (*1968*)	Percentage
1921–30	3	69	54	78
1931–40	6	116	90	77·5
1941–50	3	59	34	57·5
1951–60	1	10	1	10
1961–7	13	251	108	43
	26			

Source: Interviews with wives and widows conducted in 1968 by Margaret Spencer-Smith who kindly gave permission for me to analyse the unpublished material she had collected.

what period of history they were describing. On the other, it is not clear whether they referred to the amount of *bohali* usually agreed upon or the amount usually paid, which, as we have seen, may not be the same thing at all. Thirdly, they often made no distinction between the marriage of a chief's daughter and that of a commoner's daughter.

The missionary Arbousset writing in 1852 stated that *in earlier times* the figure was two or three head of cattle,[1] and Austen, who was one of the senior magistrates in Basutoland during the period of Cape rule and whose contact with the Basotho stretched back to 1843, has written that the large *bohali* payments current around 1870, which were said by some to be part of ancient Sesotho tradition, were nothing of the sort; rather they had been introduced by Moshoeshoe after the people had grown rich in cattle. A similar development occurred among the Zulus of Natal.[2]

---

[1] At p. 380. Sekese (1968, pp. 70–1) also mentions hoes, beans and tobacco.
[2] See *1873 Report and Evidence*, p. 58.

At all events most writers during the century 1840 to 1940 gave estimates of between ten and thirty head.[1]

3. THE APPROACH OF THE COURTS

There is no rule of law that the 'conventional scale' described above must be agreed upon. The courts have constantly declared that there is no fixed scale of *bohali*.[2] The amount depends entirely on what is settled as a result of the negotiations and examples are available of significant variations both for chiefs and for commoners.[3] Nevertheless the conventional scale has become so familiar that it is likely that many people do regard it has having achieved a greater level of legal recognition. Furthermore, in certain types of case the courts seem almost to have elevated it into a legal norm because of the difficulty of proving an agreement on any other amount. These cases are concerned with situations in which a reduction in the amount of *bohali* would be regarded as justifiable as a result of the following circumstances.

First, it is usually hoped that the bride will be a virgin and although a discussion of this will not feature in the negotiations for obvious reasons, yet where there are clear public indications that she is not a virgin these may definitely be taken into account. She may, for instance, have been seduced and compensation of six head of cattle may have been paid to her father; she may have been married and divorced; she may have been widowed; she may have borne children within or outside marriage. In such cases a reduction would often in practice be asked for and given.[4]

---

[1] See e.g. Maeder (1843, quoted in Germond, p. 524) who said 10–20; Arbousset (1852, p. 380) who said 10–30–100; Casalis (1861, p. 229), who said 25–30; George Moshoeshoe (*1873 Report and Evidence*, p. 40) who said 15–20; Duvoisin (1885, quoted in Germond, p. 536) who said 10–30; Sekese (1907), who said 25–30; Ellenberger and Macgregor (1912, p. 272) who said 15–20; Laydevant (1931), who gave the conventional scale; *1938 National Council Proceedings*, pp. 306–7, where one counsellor said 20; *1944 National Council Proceedings*, p. 198, where another counsellor said that in the old days it was 20; Ashton (1952, p. 71), who said that by the 1930s the scale among the Batlokoa had become fixed at the conventional scale and that for other Basotho the amount had risen to 25.

[2] See *Lekhanya* v. *Mongalo* J.C. 179/1963 (J.C.); *Nyooko* v. *Bolepo* J.C. 271/1963 (J.C.) and the cases cited below.

[3] See e.g. P.D., pp. 43 (Motlamelle demanded sixteen head of cattle for his daughters) and 31 (where Molapo stated that ten head was the proper *bohali*), and Table 5 above.

[4] See P.D., p. 34 where it was thought that it would be reasonable for there to be a reduction of six head if the girl had previously been seduced or

Secondly, where the bride has previously been abducted by another man this is also commonly regarded as justifying a reduction, even though the fact of the abduction itself does not necessarily mean that she lost her virginity in the process. However, it does give rise to a claim by her father for six head of cattle and this may be seen as grounds for a corresponding reduction in the amount of *bohali*.

When the courts are called upon to pronounce on the significance of these factors the question usually arises in the following form. Many years after the marriage the wife's family make a claim for the balance of *bohali* which they allege is due. Those who were actually present at the negotiations may all have died in the meantime and there may be no documentary evidence of what was agreed. The defendant, apart commonly from denying that the amount paid to date is as little as alleged, may argue that the original agreement was for a scale less than that contended by the wife's family. Since there will often be a conflict of evidence as to what the exact agreement was, testimony will be given of one of the factors mentioned above which, if true, might have led the negotiating parties to reduce the scale. Despite the difficulties in the way of reaching satisfactory conclusions as to the facts of such cases the approach of the courts should become clear from the following examples.

In two cases the bride had, before her marriage to her husband, been abducted by another man and compensation of six head of cattle had been paid to her father. In both cases the husband's family contended in their defence that the *bohali* had been agreed at six cattle less than the conventional figure and that the balance due was correspondingly six head less than the claim made by the girl's family. In *Lenonyane* v. *Bohloko*[1] all the courts rejected the defence contention and assessed the balance due on the basis of an agreement on the conventional scale. The Judicial Commissioner pointed out:

While payment of such damages often leads parents to reduce the *bohali*, it is a disconnected matter since the *bohali* depends entirely upon the agreement between the parents.

---

impregnated and an even larger reduction if she had already been married before.

[1] J.C. 94/1963.

Similarly, in *Motiki* v. *Ralilochane*[1] all the courts again found for the plaintiff in terms of the conventional scale without any reduction. Whereas President J. M. Mohale in the Central Court concentrated on the point that cattle paid as compensation for abduction cannot be requested as a loan from the girl's father in the way in which they can in a case where the person who abducted her later marries her,[2] the Judicial Commissioner was content to reiterate that the amount of *bohali* depends upon agreement and that here no agreement on a figure lower than the conventional scale had been proved.

The core of the reasoning of the Judical Commissioner in these cases seems to be that it is not sufficient to establish the fact that there has been a prior abduction with its concomitant payment of compensation; it is essential to go further and prove that as a result of this the respective families actually agreed upon a reduction in the conventional scale of *bohali*. In this sense it may be said that the conventional scale has gained legal recognition as a norm in all circumstances and the burden of proof is thrust upon the party seeking to prove a deviation from it. Putting it another way we may say that there is a strong presumption in favour of the conventional scale.[3] In practical terms, bearing in mind the time that has usually elapsed between the agreement and the instituting of legal proceedings, the chances of successfully rebutting this presumption in the absence of a document evidencing the agreement are not very high.

In the case last referred to President Mohale went on to say, later in his judgment, that the girl whose *bohali* scale is reduced is one who has, before her marriage, already given birth to an illegitimate child. However, two further cases show that the principle here is, in fact, the same as in the abduction cases.

In *Molise* v. *Theletsane*[4] the plaintiff's wife had, before her marriage, had an illegitimate child by another man. The conventional scale of *bohali* had been paid on her marriage, despite this fact. The plaintiff claimed that this meant that he had 'married' this child together with its mother and that he was now entitled to the child. This contention found favour with the Local Court on

---

[1] J.C. 154/1967.
[2] This is discussed at pp. 109–10 below.
[3] See also *Lekhanya* v. *Mongalo* J.C. 179/1963 (J.C.).
[4] J.C. 103/1965.

the basis that this must be the explanation of why the conventional scale was paid despite the fact that the bride was not a virgin. But on appeal both the Central Court and the Judicial Commissioner rejected this argument. Thompson J.C. stated that the payment of the conventional scale for a virgin was not a law but a common practice and stressed that the amount depended purely and simply on the agreement reached. Moreover, the question whether a pre-marital child went with its mother on her marriage was also a matter for agreement at the time of the marriage and no such agreement had been established on the facts of the case.[1]

In *Mohale* v. *Selebalo*[2] the husband when sued for the balance of *bohali* contended that since his wife had, before the marriage, had an illegitimate child by another man, the scale should be reduced. Both the Local Court and the Judicial Commissioner's Court held that the amount depends upon agreement.

The final case is *Mokhanya* v. *Leluma*[3] in which the bride had previously been married and divorced. Eight *bohali* cattle paid in respect of her first marriage had remained with her father because the Court had held that her first husband was responsible for the breakdown of the marriage through failing to accept her as his wife with the result that the marriage was never consummated. The father of her second husband, when sued for the balance of *bohali*, argued that the conventional scale, though already agreed upon, should now be reduced by eight. All the courts rejected this defence, holding that he must carry out the terms of his own agreement. This case is, of course, distinguishable from the others because express agreement upon the conventional scale was clearly established. There could therefore be no grounds for reducing what was agreed simply because a chance of obtaining a reduction during the negotiations had existed but been missed.

However, the general point which emerges from the first four cases may be summarized as follows. Granted that there is no fixed *bohali* scale and that the parties are at liberty to agree as they

---

[1] Cf. *Mahamo* v. *Ramochele* J.C. 197/1964 where the facts were practically identical. Here the Central Court held that payment of the conventional scale indicated that the child had been 'married' together with its mother; however the Local Court and the J.C. held that since nothing was said at the time of marriage about the child, it remained with its mother's family and the husband was not entitled to its custody.

[2] J.C. 342/1966.

[3] J.C. 207/1964.

wish, the courts will tend to imply an agreement on the conventional scale very readily, even where there is evidence to suggest a contrary agreement might have been reached. The decisions are by no means all consistent on the point in the lower courts but the Judicial Commissioner's Court at any rate has never wavered in its view of the situation.

4. MONETARY EQUIVALENTS IN 'BOHALI' AGREEMENTS

Basotho families do not possess as many cattle and other livestock today as they did in the past[1] and in any event money has become just as important as a medium of exchange, if not more so, even in relation to such a traditional occasion as the transfer of *bohali* on marriage. For this reason it is not uncommon to find the agreement providing for *bohali* to be paid either in cattle or in money, as the husband's family may prefer. A trend towards an increased use of money is strongly suggested by the figures in Table 6.

TABLE 6

Analysis of amounts of bohali *paid in cash in respect of 26 marriages in Mokhokhong village*

Date of marriage	Number of marriages studied	Amount of bohali *paid* up to date of interview (*1968*), expressed in numbers of cattle	Numbers of cattle in respect of which the actual payment was made in cash	Percentage
1921–30	3	54	0	0
1931–40	6	90	11	12
1941–50	3	34	9	26·5
1951–60	1	1	0	0
1961–7	13	108	35	32

Source: As for Table 5.

The option to insert a monetary equivalent has been held to be the prerogative of the girl's family.[2] Often they will show their

[1] This can be established by reference to the census reports and the annual reports of the Department of Agriculture. See also P.D., p. 42.
[2] See *Mokhojana* v. *Mokoma* J.C. 112/1966 (J.C.); *Matsosa* v. *Semoli* J.C. 321/1966 (J.C.) and *Makoa* v. *'Matli* J.C. 45/1964 (C.C.); P.D., pp. 41–2.

lack of concern with the materialistic aspect of *bohali* by placing the monetary equivalent well below the market value.

It seems clear that the reason why the marriage payment for so long consisted of cattle was because the people were rich in cattle and Sesotho custom has shown itself predictably adaptable in the face of changing fortunes whenever cattle have run short. The best illustration of this comes from the years following 1896 when the country suffered a rinderpest epidemic which caused the death or destruction of around 100,000 cattle, representing about 90 per cent of the country's herds.[1]

Instead of cattle, people used ploughs, hoes, or grain to pay *bohali*; sometimes they even used stones to represent the cattle which would become payable in the future when the herds grew large again. The way in which this last operation worked was graphically described in 1897 by Adèle Casalis, the daughter of the renowned P.E.M.S. missionary of the same name:

Do you know what they are doing to-day? So-and-so approaches so-and-so to obtain his daughter, whether for himself or his son; they proceed to the kraal. The kraal is empty and contains nothing but dry manure. That makes no difference. Into his kraal the would-be husband brings a number of stones, let us say ten. These ten stones represent oxen, it is a debt of honour, it will be paid when the kraal fills with cattle again. The ten stones are not enough. So-and-so's daughter is comely, there must be fifteen or twenty oxen. The prospective husband solemnly proceeds to consult his friends and relatives who are standing by and, after much debating, gravely brings five more stones which he ranges side by side with the others at the feet of the girl's father or uncle. The latter is not yet satisfied, two more pebbles, young two-year-old bullocks, plus a sheep or two and a blanket, and the affair is settled.[2]

Today, apart from recognizing the monetary equivalent of cattle for purposes of *bohali* transactions, the Basotho also commonly apply a system of equivalence within the category of livestock and with other animals. Thus a cow may take the place of the ten sheep or goats which make up the *setsiba*; one, two, or even three cows may be deemed to represent the *molisana* horse;[3] alternatively

[1] *Pim Report*, p. 30; Hailey (1953), p. 59.
[2] Quoted in Germond, pp. 472–3. See also P.D., pp. 43, 143–4; *1938 National Council Proceedings*, pp. 306–7.
[3] See e.g. the *bohali* agreement set out at pp. 88–9 above.

cattle may be paid in the form of sheep.[1] In one extreme case evidence was given of ten head of cattle being represented by two mules, a cart, and a harness.[2]

There are two schools of thought as to when a cow and its calf can be considered to count as two head of cattle. One school holds that the calf can be regarded as a separate beast for *bohali* as soon as it is on its feet;[3] the other says it only achieves that status when it no longer has to be grazed for by its mother and can graze on its own.[4] I am inclined to favour the first view.

As we have already seen, the girl's family must give their consent to the scale of equivalence and they also have the right to reject a beast that is of very poor quality or too old to be of any use.[5] However, once a beast has been accepted the risk of its death seems to pass to them and another cannot be claimed to replace it.[6]

5. PAYMENT OF 'BOHALI'

The final requirement for the completion of a marriage is that part or all of the *bohali* should actually have been paid. This is specified in section 34(1)(c) of Part II of the Laws of Lerotholi.

It is at this point that the attempt of the Laws to give written definition to such an elusive concept as the completion of a Sesotho marriage begins to present some difficult conundrums. The significance of the provision will be more easily understood if we start by placing it in its historical perspective and appreciate how it came to be incorporated in the Laws.

It seems not unlikely that traditionally there was no need for even part of the *bohali* to have been paid to complete a marriage. It was sufficient if agreement had been reached on the marriage

---

[1] See e.g. *Ramphoso* v. *Thibeli* J.C. 273/1966 (J.C.); *Ntsuba* v. *Shea* J.C. 343/1966 (C.C. and J.C.).

[2] *Maseela* v. *Maseela* J.C. 136/1953.

[3] Chief Kelebone Nkuebe, *1952 National Council Proceedings*, p. 114; P.D., pp. 44–5 (majority view of the panel).

[4] P.D., p. 45 (minority view of the panel). Sekese (1907, p. 117) appears to lend some support to this view in his discussion of the proverb '*ha e fuleloe*' (it does not need to be grazed for) explaining that a calf at this stage of development is regarded as acceptable for *bohali*, In the Panel Discussion Fobo mistakenly interpreted the proverb to mean the opposite—see P.D., p. 44.

[5] See *Khatli* v. *Ramatsabane* J.C. 229/1948 quoted in Duncan, p. 23; *Ntsuba* v. *Shea* J.C. 343/1966 (J.C.); P.D., pp. 44–5.

[6] P.D., p. 44.

itself and upon the amount of *bohali* to be paid in the future.[1] The agreement was the crucial prerequisite, as indeed it continues to be today. This situation gave rise, however, to certain problems in the field of inheritance particularly with regard to succession to the chieftainship. The legal heir was the eldest son of the principal or great wife (*mabatho mofumahali*), but the vital question was how a wife became entitled to this station of pre-eminence. Originally it seems that the order in which the wives were married was the determining factor,[2] but as Ashton has explained, this has not invariably been the position throughout Basotho history.

> Sometimes a young chief was allowed to marry women of his own choice, either with his father's help or at his own expense, and these women were not regarded as potential mothers of the heir. The 'true' wife, the 'mother of the tribe', was chosen by the chief in consultation with his relatives and counsellors . . . and the tribe contributed towards her *bohali* cattle . . . She took precedence over her husband's previous wives and her son was the heir.[3]

Jones has also shown how during the years 1868 to 1920 the definition of a great wife was affected by the status of the fathers of the various wives.[4] Thus the daughters of chiefs took precedence over those of commoners and the daughters of a paramount chief took precedence over all.[5]

The commoners objected to this sytem under which they felt they were being exploited by the chieftainship. They complained that when chiefs married commoners' daughters first, the sons of these wives ought to be the heirs. Instead, the daughters of chiefs who were married later usurped their positions. The justification commonly offered by the chiefs was that an agreement had previously been reached with the second wife's father and thus she had in a sense been married first.[6] This sort of chicanery led a party to exclaim bitterly in one of the chieftainship succession

---

[1] See P.D., pp. 39, 143–5, which discusses the position where stones were lined up to represent cattle.

[2] Jones, p. 69.

[3] At pp. 193–4. The importance of the views of a chief's family on the identity of the great wife is apparent from the case of *Hlajoane* v. *Hlajoane* H.C. 8/1944.

[4] At p. 69.

[5] See also Laydevant, p. 244.

[6] See P.D., pp. 144–5.

cases, 'Everyone does what he likes in his own household and calls it the custom'.[1]

This grievance was eventually remedied by the framing of a section of the Laws of Lerotholi providing for seniority in the succession to the chieftainship to be based upon the order in which the wives were married rather than their rank[2] and later a further section[3] providing in the same terms as the present section 34 that marriages should be regarded as complete only when part of the *bohali* had been paid. Thus the original custom on succession was restored and it was buttressed by the introduction of a new rule defining exactly when a marriage could properly be held to be complete. The mere agreement of the parents was insufficient and a part payment of *bohali* (which was harder to invent) had to be established.

Turning now to the application of the section, a problem arises from the use of the expression 'part' (*karolo*) of the *bohali*, especially in view of the following Sesotho maxims:

(i) '*Khomo tse peli leha li le tharo li ka nyala mosali*' ('two or three head of cattle may marry a woman')[4] and

(ii) '*Monyala ka peli o nyala oa hae*' ('whoever pays two head does marry').[5]

Sekese's comment[6] on the second maxim shows that its original reference point was the early nineteenth century before the Basotho became rich in cattle and the same is probably true of the first maxim. Yet in *Qhobela* v. *Qhobela*[7] Huggard C. J. declared:

I am advised[8] that it is sufficient if only one head of cattle is paid, so long, of course, as there is an obligation to pay the balance, but [*sic*] after the [*bohali*] or part of the [*bohali*] is paid then the marriage is completed.

The case concerned a dispute over the seniority of marriages for purposes of succession and the court held that the principal wife was the one who had been married first, in other words, assuming

---

[1] In *Qhobela* v. *Qhobela* H.C. 24/1943.
[2] Law 1 (1903).   [3] S. 4 of Part I.   [4] See P.D., p. 33.
[5] Quoted in the judgment of President M. N. Lerotholi in the Matsieng Central Court in *Mokotja* v. *Tsepo* J.C. 40/1968, and in P.D., p. 37.
[6] (1968), pp. 70–1.   [7] H.C. 24/1943.
[8] One of his assessors was the future Judicial Commissioner, Mr. Driver.

the necessary consents had been given, the one for whom part of the *bohali* had first been paid.

The 'Restatement' is rather ambiguous on this question since it declares marriage to be complete when 'a part, usually a half, of the *bohali* has been paid'.[1] The reference to half, which probably means ten head of cattle, links up with the importance of the *tlhabiso* ceremony, discussed below.[4] Even so, the 'Restatement' cannot, by such language, be interpreted to mean that a minimum of ten head must be paid for the completion of a marriage in view of its endorsement later in the same paragraph of the saying, 'he who gives two beasts has already married his wife'. However, it does appear that where less than ten head of cattle have been paid questions may still sometimes be raised as to whether any children born to the couple are properly filiated to their father's lineage.

In view of the essentially historical nature of the maxims, it seems only right to recognise the flexibility inherent in the use of the word 'part' in section 34(1) (c) despite the very specific pronouncement of Huggard C. J. in *Qhobela* v. *Qhobela* quoted above.

A further problem is created by the fact that section 34(1) prescribes the payment of *bohali* as a prerequisite for marriage in unambiguous language. The knotty question whether Sesotho marriages without *bohali* can ever be regarded as lawful is investigated below.[3]

It is appropriate to conclude this chapter with some general observations. An inevitable consequence of the succinct wording of section 34(1) is that it describes the processes needed to complete a marriage without specifying what legal consequences flow from proof of the completion. In view of the foregoing explanation we can be sure that one result is that the order of seniority of wives may be determined in this way, but many other questions remain unresolved. It is worth mentioning some of them here as they will be investigated in the ensuing pages.

First, does a marriage automatically legitimate premarital children?

Secondly, does a completed marriage automatically transfer a previously unmarried man from the status of a minor to that of a major for all purposes?

[1] At p. 7.
[2] See Ch. 9 below.
[3] See pp. 149–52 below.

Thirdly, if soon after the marriage has been completed one of the parties dies, is the survivor necessarily a widow or a widower?

Fourthly, is a completed marriage the moment at which rights and duties in respect of the bride which were previously held by her father are transferred to her husband?

Fifthly, if one of the parties changes his or her mind immediately after the marriage, is a divorce required or may the marriage be broken off as if it were merely an engagement? Is there any distinction in Sesotho law between annulment and divorce?

8

MARRIAGES FOLLOWING AN ELOPEMENT

QUITE a high proportion of marriages today are preceded by an elopement. The estimate given by Ashton for the 1930s was more than a quarter of all marriages[1] but the statistics presented in Tables 7–9 suggest that this may be conservative, both for that period and for the present day. Tables 7 and 8 provide information about 122 couples who were interviewed during my sample survey in 1970. They come from three villages, each of a predominantly different faith, selected for reasons of personal convenience rather than as being representative of the country as a whole.[2] These figures suggest that the elopement rate may range from around one-third in communities largely adhering to the strictest of the religious denominations up to two-thirds in predominantly non-Christian villages.

Table 9 analyses eloping couples in relation to the type of marriage they subsequently contract since this, rather than the nature of the particular community, may enable a more soundly based assessment to be made. If these figures—derived from an admittedly small and by no means necessarily representative sample—did happen to provide an accurate gauge of nationwide patterns of behaviour, it would seem that the percentage of couples who elope before they marry may be as high as 55 per cent.[3] These tables do not, of course, take into account the numerous elopements which do not lead to marriage.

What prompts a couple to elope?[4] As already explained, elopement may be used as a device to hasten a wedding which the parents are felt to be delaying, either because they oppose the

[1] At p. 65.

[2] The response rate was virtually 100 per cent of the women over eighteen in Manteko's and Lenono's villages, but only about 75 per cent in Morija.

[3] This figure is based on the information provided about the civil marriages and the assumption made about the total marriage rate above at p. 33.

[4] See generally Ashton, p. 65.

TABLE 7

*Numbers of eloping couples in the three villages of
Lenono's, Manteko's, and Morija*

	Number of married women respondents	Number who eloped	Percentage
1. Morija (Maseru district; predominantly Lesotho Evangelical)	43	13	30
2. Manteko's (Qacha's Nek district; predominantly Roman Catholic)	34	15	44
3. Lenono's (Maseru district; predominantly non-Christian)	45	29	64
	122	57	

TABLE 8

Analysis of eloping couples in Table 7 by date of marriage

Date of marriage	Number of marriages within particular decade	Number who eloped
Unknown (and so probably early)	19	9
1911–20	3	1
1921–30	6	3
1931–40	18	7
1941–50	29	14
1951–60	20	10
1961–70	27	13
	122	57

TABLE 9

Analysis of eloping couples in Table 7 by type of subsequent marriage

	Number who eloped	Number who did not elope	Total	Percentage of elopers
Subsequent civil marriage	19	43	62*	31
Subsequent Sesotho marriage	43	22	65	66
Total	62†	65	127†	

* This figure includes only one marriage before a district commissioner and 61 church marriages.

† These figures includes five dual marriages.

marriage or because they are still haggling over the amount of *bohali*.[1] The couple may be particularly keen to marry quickly if the girl is already pregnant. Another justification for eloping is that in popular culture it is regarded as a sporting thing to do, even where there is not likely to be any difficulty over obtaining parental consent to the marriage. In the old days it was commonly done to try to avoid a forced marriage to someone else who had been selected by the parents, but this must be a rare cause today.

As Ashton has explained,[2] the attitude of parents and relatives to an elopement is somewhat ambivalent in cases where it is clear that the couple are in love and wish to get married. On the one hand, it is deplored as a provocative act directed against the authority of the older generation; on the other, it is seen as a harmless gesture which will probably lead to a perfectly satisfactory marriage when everything has been sorted out. Moreover, many parents did the same when they were young. Of course, where it seems that the man has run off with the girl purely for his own sexual gratification and without any serious long-term intentions the girl's family will be extremely angry, even if the girl herself consented.[3]

The process whereby an elopement leads to a completed marriage gives rise to some complex legal problems and is analysed

[1] See p. 83 above.   [2] At p. 65.

[3] If the girl did not consent the man will have committed a crime—see s. 3 of Part II of the Laws of Lerotholi.

below in some detail with reference to a number of decided cases, but before turning to these, the normal chain of events will briefly be traced. The man commonly takes the girl to his parents' home without the prior knowledge of either set of parents. On arrival he informs his parents of what has happened and the following morning he or his parents notify the girl's parents of the elopement, usually by sending a messenger. They in turn will ask for their daughter to be returned and at the same time will demand compensation of six head of cattle from the man's parents.[1]

This liability arises because the man has committed the wrong of abduction by removing the girl from the control of her parents without their consent.[2] Whether or not the girl has been seduced or impregnated during the course of the abduction is irrelevant to the question whether an abduction *per se* has taken place,[3] and seduction is itself a separate and recognized wrong under Sesotho law.[4] The amount of compensation for abduction is laid down in section 4(1) of Part II of the Laws of Lerotholi as an amount 'not exceeding six head of cattle' but in practice the full amount is always awarded by the courts in the absence of special circumstances.[5]

Ideally the progress towards marriage then follows a pattern in which the girl returns, the compensation is paid in full, the respective parents agree to the marriage and arrange the *bohali* scale, the girl's father allows the man's father notionally to borrow back the six head of cattle so that they become included in the *bohali*, and the wedding then takes place.

In practice, however, it is not uncommon for the girl to remain

[1] See the judgment of Driver J.C. in *Puseletso* v. *Raphoko* J.C. 11/1957; P.D., p. 45.

[2] See generally Palmer, *The Roman–Dutch and Sesotho Law of Delict* (Leiden, 1970), pp. 157–9. If the girl's parents consented to the abduction they clearly have no right of action under the *volenti* principle which is found in s. 3 (3) of Part II of the Laws of Lerotholi—see Palmer, p. 61; however according to the judgment of Thompson J.C. in *Khakhane* v. *Kokana* J.C. 165/1964 the father may sue provided he did not consent even if the mother herself consented.

[3] *Mofolo* v. *Pule* J.C. 43/1965 (J.C.) quoted in Palmer, p. 158.

[4] See Palmer, pp. 153–6. The wrong is committed by anyone having intercourse with a girl regardless of whether she becomes pregnant as a result; there is no requirement that she must have been led astray by the blandishments of the man, nor need she have been a virgin before the intercourse.

[5] Where the girl died or received an injury during the abduction, or was physically or mentally defective or became pregnant and died in childbirth larger sums are provided for by the Laws of Lerotholi, Part II, ss. 4(4), (5) and (6).

living with the man, for less than full compensation to be paid or for an amount of between six and ten head of cattle to be handed over, for no *express* marriage or *bohali* agreement to be reached between the parents and for the situation to remain like this until a dispute over the *bohali*, or occasionally the children, comes to court many years later.

The invidious task for the court is usually to determine whether a valid marriage has ever really taken place and whether any cattle which have been paid ought properly to be regarded as *bohali* or merely as compensation for abduction.

Three initial points may be made.

First, it is the duty of the man's father to approach the girl's family in elopement cases with a view to reaching agreement upon the marriage and the *bohali* in the same way as it is in ordinary cases.[1] If he is dilatory the girl's parents should obviously remind him.[2] However, in view of the provisions of section 34(1)(b) of the Laws of Lerotholi it seems that it is just as essential to obtain agreement in these circumstances for the completion of a valid marriage as it is in the 'normal' type of situation.

Secondly, the process whereby the father of the man is permitted by the father of the girl to borrow back the compensatory payment of six head of cattle and count them as *bohali* is well established.[3] However, this is a matter reserved for the discretion of the girl's family,[4] though it is the almost universal practice to do so.[5] To refuse would, of course, be sheer greediness and would suggest that the girl's father was more interested in the material gain from the marriage than in his daughter's future welfare.

Thirdly, there are conflicting decisions on the question whether or not the six head of cattle paid for abduction are ever recoverable on divorce, even if they have been incorporated in the total *bohali* paid. This matter will be discussed in Chapter 16 but at this point it is sufficient to note that the cases examined below reflect this uncertainty as to the true legal position.[6]

---

[1] *Puseletso* v. *Raphoko* J.C. 11/1957 (J.C.); *Mtakabone* v. *Ramphobole* J.C. 71/1969 (J.C.); *Lekhobola* v. *Mahae* J.C. 175/1963 (J.C.).

[2] *Lekhobola* v. *Mahae* J.C. 175/1963 J.C.).

[3] *Puseletso* v. *Raphoko* J.C. 11/1957 (J.C.); 'Restatement', p. 5.

[4] See the judgment of President J. M. Mohale in *Motiki* v. *Ralilochane* J.C. 154/1967 (C.C.); *Matlere* v. *Raphoto* J.C. 74/1966 (C.C.); 'Restatement', p. 5.

[5] P.D., p. 46.

[6] See also Duncan, p. 24.

The following ten cases on the significance of events arising from elopements are analysed in two sections, the first where more than six head of cattle had been paid, the second where six head or less had been paid.

(i) *Payment of more than six head*

For ease of presentation rather than for any legal distinction these cases have been split into two sub-groups.

The first type of dispute to be examined is where a claim was made for the cattle to be restored, usually because the couple had separated.

In *Lekhanya* v. *Mongalo*[1] ten head of cattle were paid and accepted following an elopement. The girl lived at the man's home for a while but later deserted him and went to South Africa. A claim for the recovery of the cattle was thereupon brought by the man's widowed mother. All the courts took the view that a marriage had been completed, despite the absence of any evidence of an agreement on the amount of *bohali* to be paid. Whereas the Local Court awarded the plaintiff a refund of all the cattle, the Central Court and the Judicial Commissioner's Court both held that the proper person to bring such an action was the husband himself and not his mother, since once married he became a major. He would in effect be petitioning for a divorce. The Judicial Commissioner went on to state *obiter* that if the husband had been the plaintiff he would have been entitled to only four of the ten cattle paid since cattle paid as compensation for abduction were not recoverable.

In *Limape* v. *Lebona*[2] seven head had been paid and accepted and thereafter the couple lived together for nine years. After the man's death the girl returned to her parents' home and was married to someone else. The man's heir thereupon claimed a refund of the cattle from her father. Again all the courts treated the couple as having been married despite the lack of any evidence of an express agreement on the *bohali* scale. While the lower courts awarded the full amount of the claim, the Judicial Commissioner reduced it to a single beast, reiterating that the six head paid for abduction were irrecoverable.

The second type of situation is where the girl's father claims the balance of *bohali* on the basis that a marriage exists.

In *Mtakabone* v. *Ramphobole*[3] nine head of cattle had been paid

[1] J.C. 179/1963.   [2] J.C. 95/1966.   [3] J.C. 71/1969.

and accepted following the abduction, but there was no evidence that the parties had ever reached agreement on the *bohali* scale. The Judicial Commissioner explained what the proper procedure was:

... it is the duty of the father of the boy to go to the father of the girl to conclude that agreement particularly in this case having paid nine head of cattle as a beginning. Having paid nine head of cattle it does appear ... he sat tight and did nothing. ...

Despite this, all the courts held that the marriage was complete, and the Judicial Commissioner awarded a balance of fourteen head of cattle, as claimed, on the basis of the conventional scale. The lower courts disagreed merely on the ground that the plaintiff was not the right person to receive the *bohali*.

In *Lekhobola* v. *Mahae*[1] nine head of cattle were similarly paid and accepted and after the couple had lived together for some time the balance was claimed by the girl's family in terms of the conventional scale even though there was nothing to show that any express agreement had been reached. In the Tsifalimali Central Court President M. N. Lerotholi upheld the claim, declaring

It is a stable Basotho custom, which is still in force that when a young man has eloped with a girl, in addition to the six head of cattle being compensation for elopement the father of the young man should pay a beast or beasts as [an] initial instalment towards *bohali* and if the father of the girl has accepted them, the terms of agreement on the marriage are regarded as complete and the girl is regarded as a member of the young man's family. The father of the girl has every right to claim the balance of the *bohali* cattle.

However, on appeal the Judicial Commissioner held that no valid marriage had been completed because there had been no agreement on the *bohali* scale. In doing so he was following the judgment of the Local Court. In view of the seeming conflict between this decision and the cases discussed above, and more especially that of *Lekhanya* v. *Mongalo* which he had decided only two weeks previously, it is felt desirable to set out the relevant portion of his reasoning. He held that there was a presumption of fact from the circumstances of the payment and acceptance of

[1] J.C. 175/1963.

nine cattle that the parties were prepared at one time to negotiate a marriage. However, the girl's father did not usually lay down the scale upon the receipt of the extra three cattle because he had to consult his relatives before holding negotiations and food would have to be prepared for the gathering. The man's father should arrange for further negotiations and if he was dilatory the girl's father should remind him. The father of the girl could not sue for the balance of *bohali* until he had notified the man's father of the *bohali* scale he desired. Therefore the present action was premature and the plaintiff should call upon the defendant to initiate further negotiations. Lastly, 'if there is a refusal to marry, to effect marriage negotiations at this stage, then a court could fix a [*bohali*]'.

The basis of this reasoning is thus that the payment of extra cattle following an abduction amounts to no more than a deposit and merely indicates an intention to negotiate further towards an agreement upon the *bohali* scale.

This approach gains some slight support from the Panel Discussion where at times the view seemed to be that the additional cattle constituted *tebeletso* and that when they had been accepted the parties had the status of being engaged rather than actually married.[1] However, the impression was one of general uncertainty and it was also stated that the acceptance of a seventh beast by the girl's father meant that the marriage was complete.

As will be indicated later in this discussion it is a mistake to see either position as an invariable one; the significance of the payment will ultimately depend upon the surrounding circumstances.

While it is felt that the Judicial Commissioner's judgment in *Lekhobola* v. *Mahae* was incorrect, a satisfactory rationale remains to be found whereby the other cases referred to may be reconciled with section 34(1) of Part II of the Laws of Lerotholi.

The answer seems to lie in the recognition by the courts that the agreement of the parents required by the section may be implied from their conduct. Acceptance by the girl's father of cattle over and above the six required as compensation will generally be interpreted to mean that he is willing for the marriage to take place and that it will be a marriage with *bohali*. Further, since there is a presumption of fact that the conventional scale is the one agreed

---

[1] P.D., pp. 45–7. The contention that the seventh beast amounted to *tebeletso* was rejected by the J.C.'s Court in *Phera* v. *Pholo* J.C. 134/1953.

upon, with the result that any contrary agreement must be proved,[1] the courts will operate on the basis of this scale where no express agreement has been reached.

However, there seems no reason to rule out the possibility of cases in which the conduct of the parties cannot be interpreted along these lines and therefore where the courts may properly conclude that no valid marriage has been completed. For instance, where there is evidence that the girl's father has asked for a *bohali* greater than the conventional scale which the man's father has not agreed to, there is no justification for applying the conventional scale and, as Thompson J.C. pointed out in *Lekhobola* v. *Mahae*, the parties must negotiate further and any claim brought before then will be regarded as premature. Here there is no room for any agreement to be implied, for the conduct of the parents effectively negatives it. Similarly where the man and the girl themselves do not appear to be consenting parties to the marriage this will nullify all other arrangements on the part of their parents. This seems to be the explanation of two further decisions.

In *Ramarumo* v. *Kala*[2] seven head of cattle were paid after an abduction but the girl later changed her mind and married another man. The abductor's father sued to recover the seven cattle and the Local Court and the Judicial Commissioner's Court awarded him only one beast in terms of the rule previously stated. However, there was no question of disallowing the claim on the grounds that the proper plaintiff should have been the husband, as there should have been if the marriage had been completed. The marriage negotiations would not have reached lawful completion because the girl's consent was lacking.

A case where it was the man who was not a consenting party is *Nkoko* v. *Cheli*.[3] He had abducted the plaintiff's daughter and paid R140, the equivalent of seven head of cattle. The plaintiff then asked him to pay a further three head and come and negotiate the scale of *bohali*. However he never went to negotiate, but continued to live with the girl, who bore him a child. The plaintiff claimed a balance of *bohali* on the basis of the conventional scale, but he contended in his defence that he no longer wished to marry the girl. The Local Court and the Judicial Commissioner both held there was no completed marriage.[4]

---

[1] See above, pp. 95–9.   [2] J.C. 257/1954.   [3] J.C. 272/1966.

[4] The Central Court held that a marriage had been completed and ordered

(ii) *Payment of six head or less*

In *Matlere* v. *Raphoto*[1] and *Puseletso* v. *Raphoko*[2] the courts held that where only six head are paid they will be presumed merely to constitute a compensatory payment for abduction and therefore the onus is thrust upon the man's family to prove that they requested the inclusion of these cattle in the *bohali* and that the girl's father acceded to this request. Since the man's family failed to establish this in either case and since there was no other evidence of an agreement upon marriage the courts held no valid marriage had taken place.

The task of proving a valid marriage where less than six cattle have been paid following an elopement will be just as hard, if not harder, for the parties will still usually be at an early stage in the marriage negotiations.

In *Mokoma* v. *Ralipoli*[3] the equivalent of four head was paid, but the man and the girl had a row on what would have been the wedding day and neither seemed prepared to proceed. The man thereupon sued for the recovery of his cattle. The Local Court held that they constituted *bohali* cattle, not compensatory cattle, and were therefore recoverable, on two grounds.

First, because the *bewys*[4] described them as *bohali* and secondly because the girl's father inspected them at the man's home which is never done with compensatory cattle.

This decision was overruled by the Central Court and the Judicial Commissioner's Court, both of which found that the cattle were merely compensation for abduction and irrecoverable. They held that no agreement had been reached by the parties or their parents on the marriage or on the scale of *bohali*. The Judicial Commissioner disposed of the first reason given by the Local Court by pointing out that the description given in a *bewys* can never be decisive since a *bewys* is commonly obtained by the man's family who unilaterally instruct the *bewys* writer to put the word

---

payment of a balance on the basis of a scale of six cattle less than the conventional scale simply because the girl had borne an illegitimate child by another man. The judgment seems erroneous in both respects.

[1] J.C. 74/1966 (C.C. and J.C.).

[2] J.C. 11/1957 (J.C. overruling L.C.).

[3] J.C. 29/1965.

[4] No stock may be transferred without a *bewys* (stock-permit) issued by a chief or headman—see Stock Theft Proclamation, No. 80 of 1921, and section 17 of Part II of the Laws of Lerotholi.

bohali because they hope the cattle paid as compensation will ultimately be converted into *bohali*.[1] The second reason was outweighed by the fact that the man stated that the agreement on marriage took place at his home, whereas the custom is for the marriage negotiations to be concluded at the girl's home.

In *Ncholu* v. *Ndabeni*[2] four head were paid and the girl's father then gave the man's family a period of six months in which to bring the total up to more than six head of cattle in order to start the *bohali*. However, during this period the girl deserted the man and returned home. Her father would not release her until some *bohali* cattle had been paid. The man's father brought an action in which he claimed that the girl's father should either release her or return the four head of cattle. Both the lower courts held that a marriage had been concluded, the Local Court relying on the maxim '*monyala ka peli o nyala oa hae*' ('whoever pays two head of cattle does marry') and the Central Court basing its judgment on its interpretation of the behaviour of the man's father as tending to reflect his agreement to the marriage. The Judicial Commissioner, however, reached the opposite conclusion and held the marriage was incomplete since the *bohali* scale had never been agreed. He further stated:

If the father of the boy or man does not pay more than the compensation asked he cannot claim that a marriage is complete and that the girl is his wife.

While it is thought the Judicial Commissioner's decision may well have been the correct one on the facts of the case it is submitted that this statement is too wide.

The broad position is this. For any marriage following an elopement to be regarded as complete it must satisfy the requirements of section 34(1). This involves establishing a set of agreements and the payment of at least part of the *bohali*. While it is true that compensatory cattle may be borrowed for inclusion within *bohali* if the girl's father is agreeable, the fact that he has really consented both to this and to the marriage is far more readily established where he has accepted a total of more than six cattle. Even here, this fact of acceptance is far from conclusive proof of a completed marriage. But where six cattle or less have been paid it is clearly

---

[1] See also *Limape* v. *Lebona* J.C. 95/1966 (J.C.) on this point.
[2] J.C. 17/1965.

correspondingly harder to prove his agreement to the marriage. That is not to say, however, that no agreement may ever be reached in such circumstances. A father may well agree to the marriage after only a few head have been paid as compensation because he is keen for his daughter to marry the abductor and he is prepared to incorporate the compensatory cattle within the *bohali* immediately.

9

THE LEGAL SIGNIFICANCE
OF CEREMONIAL EVENTS

I T is often a matter of difficulty to separate what is legally required for the completion of a valid marriage from what is merely the customary procedure, especially where a ceremonial event which falls within the latter category is, in many people's experience, the focal point of the occasion. Moreover, where the ceremonial event is deeply rooted in tradition there may be a tendency today on the part of some informants to overemphasize its legal significance to try to ensure the continuance of Sesotho culture at a time when it is being whittled away on all sides by contact with outside forces.

Various ceremonial events will be dealt with in turn.

I. 'TLHABISO'

The *tlhabiso* ceremony properly involves the slaughtering of an ox during the wedding festivities and the distribution of its meat to relatives and friends of the families of the respective spouses. The ox is provided by the parents of the bride as soon as they have received ten *bohali* cattle from the bridegroom's family. Details of the way in which the different portions of the ox ought to be shared out are available in the writings of ethnographers and will not be repeated here,[1] save to note that the part that is retained by the bride's family is known as *maumo*,[2] which will be discussed further below.[3] The legal aspects of *tlhabiso* will now be examined in their historical perspective.

(a) *Its Traditional Significance in Law*

The fact that *tlhabiso* became due when *ten* head of *bohali* cattle had been paid calls for some explanation. It may well be that there is a link here with the traditional rule that compensation

---

[1] See e.g. Ellenberger and Macgregor, pp. 275–6; Laydevant, p. 247; see also P.D., pp. 66–7.

[2] P.D., pp. 66–7.   [3] See below, pp. 121–2.

for wilful homicide was ten head of cattle[1] and that the bride was seen as completely lost to her own family from the time of her marriage; at any rate as soon as ten *bohali* cattle have been paid Basotho use the expression 'they have completed a head' (i.e. the equivalent of a human being).[2]

In his evidence to the 1872 Commission Sofonia Moshoeshoe declared that the completion of marriage was dependent upon *tlhabiso*. Major Bell put the question to him, 'At what stage of the proceedings is a marriage said to be completed?', and this was his reply:

A marriage is said to be completed when the father of the bride has slaughtered an animal or animals as *'mafura'*, with the fat of which the bride and bridegroom are anointed, and the bridegroom has the gall bladders put around his wrist. If the bridegroom refuses to have the gall bladders put on his wrist it is a sign that he does not like the bride, and the marriage is dissolved, the cattle are returned, and the animals slaughtered by the bride's father are paid for by the bridegroom or his friends.[3]

This evidence was not controverted by any of the other witnesses and in view of the general reliability of the rest of Sofonia's testimony, it seems right to accept it without reservation.

Ashton too, writing about the 1930s, stated that from the legal point of view the tying of the gall-bladders was the culmination of the ceremony and that up to this point the marriage could have been broken off. However, he also seemed to acknowledge that the whole ceremony was dying out and was only continuing to be practised by the upper-class Batlokoa and a few other conservative Basotho; modern couples would tend to use a ring instead, emulating the European fashion.[4]

From the Panel Discussion it seems the practice must last have been widespread around the turn of the century, one member tactfully explaining that it would hardly be very satisfactory once

[1] See *1873 Report and Evidence*, p. 39; Duncan, p. 105; Palmer, p. 114.
[2] P.D., p. 31. This explains why some people (e.g. Chief Molapo in the Panel Discussion) hold that the proper traditional *bohali* used to be ten head of cattle and that the reason why modern *bohali* is greater is that it has become tainted by commercialism. See also *1947 National Council Proceedings*, p. 124, where Councillor Malebanye stated that *bohali* was complete when ten head had been paid.
[3] *1873 Report and Evidence*, pp. 44–5.
[4] At p. 68.

the Basotho had started to wear clothes in place of skins, since it would make them dirty![1]

(b) *Its Place in the Modern Law*

Any evaluation of the legal status of the *tlhabiso* ceremony today must take account of its dual role. On the one hand, the tying of the gall-bladder and the smearing of the bride and groom with ox bile had a religious significance in dedicating the newly married couple to the care and protection of the ancestors[2] and this aspect of the ceremony could be expected to fall into disuse as Christianity spread, quite apart from the problems presented by the modernization of dress.

On the other hand, the slaughtering of the ox to acknowledge and confirm that a significant proportion of the *bohali* had been paid, and its sharing for festive purposes between the two families to publicize this new relationship was likely to continue for as long as *bohali* was an integral part of the normal marriage, although inevitably certain modifications might have to be allowed as more wealth came to be held in money instead of cattle.

It seems safe to conclude that today neither the smearing of the couple with bile nor the slaughtering of the ox is a necessary requirement for the completion of a valid marriage, more particularly in view of the fact that neither process is mentioned in section 34(1) of Part II of the Laws of Lerotholi. The former practice has fallen totally out of use; the latter must now rather be regarded as a legally enforceable obligation flowing out of marriage, to be performed by the wife's family upon the satisfaction of a corresponding duty on the part of the husband's family.[3]

The approach of the courts will now be illustrated.

In *Maseela* v. *Maseela*[4] the Judicial Commissioner declared:

---

[1] See P.D., pp. 59–60; one of the witnesses in the case of *Majara* v. *Majara* H.C. 30/1942 stated that the practice had not occurred for two generations.

[2] Ellenberger and Macgregor, pp. 275–6; P.D., pp. 59–60.

[3] See Sekese (1968), p. 4; P.D., pp. 66, 68. But cf. the decision of the Local Court in *Nyapane* v. *Ratibisi* J.C. 167/1968 (discussed below). However, the statement in the text is supported by three decisions of the 1940s cited by Duncan, p. 26, namely *Mokhele* v. *Lekane* J.C. 421/1947 (P.C.'s Ct.); *Khorula* v. *Lethetsa* J.C. 185/1947, and *Lebajoa* v. *Hlehlethe* J.C. 246/1948, as well as by the 'Restatement', p. 7. (The 'Restatement' is, however, totally misleading in saying that the purpose of *tlhabiso* is 'to smear with fat the feet of those who bring the *bohali*'.)

[4] J.C. 136/1953 (J.C.).

It is commonly known that when ten head of cattle have been paid as [*bohali*] the father of the girl must *hlabisetsa* (kill a beast) for ten head of cattle are known as *hloko ea motho* (head of a person). The meat of the beast killed is shared between the man marrying and the girl's parents.

With *bohali* standing conventionally at more than twenty head of cattle the question arises whether the girl's family are obliged to slaughter another beast after payment of the second ten has been completed. In *Lepelesana* v. *Monyane*[1] the Local and Central Courts and the Judicial Commissioner's Court all held that such an obligation did exist and that it was legally enforceable.

The order that the courts make is that the bride's family should slaughter a beast, not that they should transfer the beast to the man's family, since the meat must be shared between the families.[2] However, with the shortage of cattle and the growing importance of money, attempts to reduce the traditional ceremony to a financial transaction were bound to occur. The way in which the courts handled such a situation in the case of *Nyapane* v. *Ratibisi*[3] is extremely illuminating.

The plaintiff, who was the bride's father, had already slaughtered one *tlhabiso* beast for the defendant when the first ten head of cattle had been paid and in an earlier stage of the litigation had been ordered by the Court to perform the *tlhabiso* ceremony a second time since by then a further ten head had been paid. The Court, however, had framed its order in the alternative, permitting the plaintiff either to slaughter a beast or to pay the defendant the sum of R50. The plaintiff had elected to pay in cash and now claimed from the defendant a payment of R20 out of the sum of R50 to represent the bride's family's entitlement of *maumo*. The defendant resisted the claim on the grounds that R20 was excessive for *maumo*.

President 'Matli in the Makhaleng Local Court pointed out the difficulty of enforcing a judgment in which the slaughtering of a *tlhabiso* beast was ordered and his judgment goes so far as to hold that, for this reason alone, no such claim can be entertained by the judicial courts. However, as has been stated earlier, this view is

[1] J.C. 56/1967; see also the cases cited by Duncan, p. 26, and Sekese (1968), p. 4.
[2] P.D., pp. 66, 69.
[3] J.C. 167/1968.

thought to be erroneous. Turning to the question of a monetary payment being substituted for the *tlhabiso* ceremony, he stated that this was a mistake, but went on to apply a principle of reciprocity to the facts of the case:

. . . this court alone cannot force any of the claimants to fulfil what is required from him without forcing the other claimant to do the same. If the slaughter has been made as a payment of money before the court, *maumo* also must be made in the form of money. . . . It must be got from the same payment which is said to be an ox though it is not . . .

He therefore awarded the plaintiff the sum of R20 as claimed and this was upheld by the Central Court. However, on appeal, Monyake Acting J.C. held that since *maumo* represented the intestines of an ox and these only had a market value of around R3 the award should be reduced to this amount.

2. 'FOMO'

Fomo signifies a sheep that is slaughtered for a feast by the bride's father. Because it is really derived from Nguni practice there is doubt among many Basotho as to its true significance as well as about whether it properly forms part of modern Sesotho custom at all. It often coincides with the *tlhabiso* ceremony and seems to denote mutual satisfaction at the extent to which the *bohali* contract has been fulfilled. It is neither necessary for the completion of a marriage, nor can it be enforced through the courts.[1]

3. HANDING OVER OF THE BRIDE

The bride frequently does not go to her husband's home immediately after the wedding but remains a short time at her parents' home to collect together various household and personal effects.

In *Qhobela* v. *Qhobela*[2] it was argued on behalf of the appellant that a marriage was only complete when the spouses had cohabited together or at any rate when the bride had been formally handed over to her husband. The facts were as follows. Chief Qhobela had married two wives, 'Mamolapo and 'Ma-Jameson. The evidence showed that the first to live with Chief Qhobela was 'Ma-Jameson because 'Mamolapo went off to an initiation school

---

[1] See generally on *fomo* Duncan, p. 29 relying on evidence in *Majara* v. *Majara* H.C.30/1942 and the decision in *Khorula* v. *Lethetsa* J.C. 185/1947; P.D., pp. 70-1.
[2] H.C. 24/1943.

immediately after her marriage and only came to live with her husband after 'Ma-Jameson had already borne him a child.

The respondent, the son of 'Mamolapo, contended that her marriage was completed before 'Ma-Jameson's for the reason that a part payment of *bohali* was made in respect of her marriage before 'Ma-Jameson's. All the courts upheld the respondent's plea and the argument that the spouses must cohabit to achieve a valid marriage, after being rejected in the Assistant Commissioner's Court, was not even pressed on appeal. In the High Court the Chief Justice quickly disposed of the contention that there needs to be a formal handing over of the bride and pointed out that Sesotho law differed in this respect from the laws of a number of other southern-African peoples.[1] One consequence of this is that if the bride were to be seduced between the time of her marriage and her arrival at her husband's home any right of action against the seducer would lie with her husband and not with her father.[2]

4. 'KOAE'

Koae, like *fomo*, signifies the slaughter of a small stock as part of the wedding festivities. However, the two occasions on which *koae* is slaughtered, as well as its underlying purpose, are fundamentally different from *fomo*, though they are liable to be confused.[3]

The most important feast of *koae* is when the bride comes formally to her husband's home for the first time after the wedding, accompanied by her girl-friends.[4] As Ashton has explained:

Her father-in-law kills a sheep for them and gives her a piece of the intestines as a symbol of her acceptance into the family. This is called *koae* (tobacco). Until this has been done, she may not eat anything nor start her marital life. She is received with a similar rite in the case of elopement, should the boy's father be prepared to ask for her in marriage, and also if she comes to live with her husband before the wedding.[5]

Koae in this sense was traditionally called, rather cumbersomely, '*tja-bohobe*' (literally 'something to go with bread', i.e. meat).[6]

---

[1] See also *Moshoeshoe v. Maime* J.C. 138/1952 (L.C. and J.C.); *Makara v. Mokobori* J.C. 164/1955 (all courts).

[2] See *1947 National Council Proceedings*, pp. 112–29 (the voting in favour of this view was 64–9).

[3] See P.D., pp. 70–3. I am greatly indebted to Mr. Colin Murray for saving me from perpetuating the error in my thesis on these topics.

[4] Ellenberger and Macgregor, p. 276; Laydevant, pp. 247–8.

[5] At p. 74. See also P.D., pp. 71–2.   [6] P.D., p. 72 (Molapo).

Secondly, *koae* is also slaughtered, reciprocally, to mark the husband's first formal visit to his in-laws. This occurs at the same time as *tlhabiso*, after ten head of cattle have been paid.

The slaughter of *koae* on these two occasions is neither a prerequisite for the completion of a valid marriage, nor is it enforceable through the courts.[1]

5. 'MOQHOBA'

The *moqhoba* beast is the ox given by the husband's family to the women who accompany the bride when she comes to her husband's home for the first time.[2]

It is included in the conventional *bohali* scale,[3] but there seems to be considerable doubt whether it can be claimed in court. The Basotho Courts commonly award it,[4] but they are invariably overruled by the Judicial Commissioner on appeal.[5]

In Duncan there is found the following statement which has sometimes been cited by the Judicial Commissioner to support his decisions:[6]

On delivery of the bride the women usually ask for the . . . *moqhoba* beast, which is a voluntary gift by the bridegroom to the women, and cannot be demanded as of right (*Mojela* v. *Mojela* Privy Council 93/1927).

This statement, which is attributed to the Privy Council in *Mojela*'s case, did not, however, form part of the Board's opinion. It merely constituted part of the appellant's case before the Board. In view of this and of the fact that in the early case of *Mokhosi* v. *Konya*[7] the Paramount Chief's Court, the District Commissioner's

---

[1] *Majara* v. *Majara* H.C. 30/1942 (per Thompson D.C. in S.C. and see generally the evidence in that case on *koae*); 'Restatement', p. 7.

[2] Ellenberger and Macgregor, p. 276; Duncan, p. 29.

[3] See above, p. 92.

[4] See *Lenonyane* v. *Bohloko* J.C. 94/1963 (L.C. and C.C.); *Nyooko* v. *Bolepo* J.C. 271/1963 (L.C. and C.C.); *Mokhanya* v. *Leluma* J.C. 207/1964 (L.C. and C.C.).

[5] See the decisions of Thompson J.C. in *Lethunya* v. *Rabukana* J.C. 57/1962; *Lenonyane* v. *Bohloko* J.C. 94/1963; *Nyooko* v. *Bolepo* J.C. 271/1963; *Mokhanya* v. *Leluma* J.C. 207/1964; *Matsemela* v. *Rabukana* J.C. 346/1966 (C.C. also agreed here); *Mokhesuoe* v. *Moiloa* J.C. 10/1967; *Sekhopha* v. *Pule* J.C. 81/1967.

[6] At p. 29.   [7] H.C. 1/1941.

Court and the High Court all awarded the *moqhoba* beast as part of the balance of *bohali* without any discussion, the matter must still be regarded as an open question.

6. THE PRESENCE OF THE LOCAL CHIEF

The presence of the local chief or his representative is a common feature of most weddings. He is there as a witness who will be available to give evidence if there is later a dispute; he is there because he needs to keep himself well informed of important village affairs; he is, in any event, always present at large gatherings to ensure good order.[1] However, his presence cannot be regarded as strictly necessary for the validity of the marriage.[2]

It is interesting to note that in 1944 the National Council passed a motion to amend the Laws of Lerotholi by requiring a marriage certificate to be issued by the local chief before a marriage could be deemed to be complete.[3] The idea was to try to obviate some of the difficulties encountered by Basotho in South Africa who needed to be able to establish their marital status. However, no step to implement the Council's recommendation was ever taken.

An example of the type of marriage certificate which may be issued by a chief is shown below.[4]

MARRIAGE CERTIFICATE

There came one Mapheelle Mohlomi conveying cattle for [*bohali*] being paid for his younger brother named Mohlahlola John Mapheelle for the marriage of the daughter of Ntjanatsela Moliea named Nukoana, for 11 head of cattle, a blue beast was added to make 12, whereupon he asked for a fortnight within which to bring . . . *molisana* (horse) to make 13.

On hand there had been 12 given by terms of agreement, hence his wife was handed over to him, with the balance of 11 head of cattle.

Bohali ceremony was rounded off with the slaughter ox, a red ox called Tsoeu-Koto, that brought the marriage to a close, whereupon one Kileng Jack turned up. Witnesses of the lass Leqheku Hlothoane and Tsita Phatela, this being for the marriage of Ntjanatsela Moliea. Witnesses for the lad being Jack Leutsoa Mahasele and the scribe being Tsita Phatela.

[1] P.D., pp. 65–6.
[2] Duncan, p. 29; P.D., pp. 65–6.
[3] *1944 National Council Proceedings*, p. 196.
[4] Copied from the record in *Mohlomi* v. *Molia* J.C. 333/1966.

OFFICIAL STAMP ENDORSEMENT:
> Chieftainess 'Mantsebo Seisa
> Chief of Pheelong
> Mpiti's Administration
> Qacha's nek, Basutoland
> 17 August, 1963.

7. THE PRESENCE OF OFFICIAL WITNESSES

Duncan states that witnesses to the marriage on both sides, known as *bathethesi*, are present and that these are the equivalents of the 'official witnesses' mentioned in the Natal Code.[1] This is inaccurate if it is intended to mean that their presence is a prerequisite for a valid marriage in Lesotho in the way that it is in Natal.[2] Their presence is optional with respect to a Sesotho marriage, but they will almost invariably attend and their evidence in years to come will be the best possible testimony that the marriage took place.[3]

---

[1] At p. 29.

[2] Natal Code, Proc. 168 of 1932, s. 59(1) and see *Mahlolose* v. *Kaba* 1938 N.A.C. (T. and N.) 43.

[3] *Tsiloane* v. *Tsiloane* J.C. 6/1962 (L.C. and C.C.); *Thafeng* v. *Thafeng* J.C. 104/1967 (C.C. and J.C.); *Ramaipato* v. *Rantho* J.C. 221/1967 (J.C.); P.D., pp. 65–6.

BOHALI CLAIMS IN THE COURTS

WITHIN the sphere of family law it can be stated without fear of contradiction that *bohali* claims constitute the largest proportion of court cases. *Bohali* is a never-ending source of litigation. One of the main reasons for this is to be found in the extraordinary power of survival conferred upon *bohali* debts by the law. A variety of defences are commonly put forward against a claim for *bohali*, but very few are recognized by the law, as the following substantive rules show.

I. SUBSTANTIVE RULES

(a) Bohali *Debts do not Prescribe*

It has already been explained that while there is a conventional scale of something over twenty head of cattle which is commonly agreed to, by no means all of this will be paid on the wedding day. As we have seen, payment of the full amount at one and the same time is very rare today.[1]

The balance left outstanding on the wedding day is a liability of the husband's family which they are expected to pay off over the years, as circumstances permit. Furthermore, there is no time fixed for payment and no period of limitation during which the girl's family must make a claim. The rule is summed up in the Sesotho maxim, '*molato ha o bole*' ('a debt never rots or dies').

This rule has generally been applied with consistency by the courts at all levels.[2] Naturally, the burden of proving the existence of the debt will become increasingly difficult with the passing of

---

[1] See pp. 92–4 above.
[2] See *Mokhosi* v. *Konya* H.C. 1/1941 (P.C.'s Ct., S.C. and H.C.); *Ntjeke* v. *Ranthiba* J.C. 61/1959 (J.C.); *Mojake* v. *Litjamela* J.C. 4/1963 (all courts); and see P.D., p. 54. Hamnett (1975, pp. 153–4) has, however, provided some examples where the maxim was not applied by the courts.

time, but successful claims have even been made where the debt was more than forty years old.[1]

Duncan[2] is totally misleading in stating that as a result of the decisions of the Judicial Commissioner in *Seakhi* v. *Seakhi*[3] and *Pulenyana* v. *Matela*[4] and the operation of the Cape Prescription Act[5] the traditional rule has ceased to exist and therefore the maxim can no longer be pleaded in the courts.

In the first place the Cape Act contains no provision covering *bohali* debts. Secondly, these two decisions were not given in cases concerning *bohali*; in the *Seakhi* case the action was for money had and received which prescribes after eight years under the Act, and in *Pulenyana* v. *Matela* the suit was for compensation for abduction. Thirdly, there is no justification for the view expressed by the Judicial Commissioner in those cases that the Sesotho maxim '*molato ha o bole*' is repugnant to justice. The rule helps to maintain the bond between the family paying *bohali* and the family receiving it over a long period of time and an adequate safeguard against false claims is provided by the need to supply sufficient evidence to establish the existence of the debt. The practice thus possesses considerable social utility. However, if the view is to be taken that it is undesirable for debts of very long standing to be enforceable by action such a sweeping change should be brought about by legislation and only after careful thought. Indeed in 1962 a Select Committee of the National Council was asked to look into the desirability or otherwise of retaining the customary rule. It finally recommended that *bohali* debts ought to prescribe after a period of twenty years, in the sense that while the obligation to pay the balance should not itself be extinguished, the right to enforce payment through the courts should cease after that period.[6] However, no steps to implement this recommendation were ever taken.

(b) Bohali *Debts Survive Misconduct of the Wife*

It is no defence to a *bohali* claim that the wife has committed

---

[1] In *Mokhosi* v. *Konya* H.C. 1/1941 it was forty-three years old and in *Mojake* v. *Litjamela* J.C. 4/1963 forty-two years old.

[2] At p. 115.   [3] J.C. 209/1953.

[4] J.C. 242/1954.   [5] Act 6 of 1861.

[6] *Report of Select Committee on Wills, Estates and Marriages* (Maseru, 1962), p. ii.

adultery[1] or deserted her husband[2] or shown lack of respect to her in-laws[3] or even that she arrived at her husband's home already pregnant by another man.[4] Far less so if she has merely *ngala*-ed[5] home to her own parents.[6] All these matters should be raised in divorce proceedings if the husband wishes. So long as the marriage still subsists the balance of *bohali* remains due. However, it does seem clear that the wife's father is not entitled to keep her at his home as a hostage for the balance of *bohali*, as perhaps occurred in the past.[7]

(c) Bohali *Debts do not Cancel one another Out*

A Sesotho maxim states '*melato ha e lefane*' ('debts do not cancel one another out') and this applies to *bohali* as to other debts. The rule operates to maintain *bohali* obligations in existence over long periods and might, at first sight, seem unnecessarily burdensome and conducive to increased litigation. However, Hamnett has explained admirably why any other rule would be inappropriate for *bohali* and inadequate to achieve one of its underlying purposes:

. . . affinal relationships would be exposed to uncertainty if any kind of communal accounting cancelled debts against each other and left only net credits and debits outstanding. A man might find himself owing three head of cattle to a family with whom he had no affinal relationship recognizable to him at all. The rule against set-off ensures that [*bohali*] reciprocities are not cancelled out in this way and that affinal relationships are concretely and individually structured along identifiable and specific transfers of cattle.[8]

---

[1] *Mpoke* v. *Selohlanye* J.C. 5/1952 (J.C.); *Thakafoulo* v. *Motikoe* J.C. 104/1965 (J.C.); P.D., p. 54.

[2] *Mpoke* v. *Selohlanye* J.C. 5/1952 (J.C.); *Lenonyane* v. *Bohloko* J.C. 94/1963 (J.C.); *Thakafoulo* v. *Motikoe* J.C. 104/1965 (J.C.); P.D., p. 54.

[3] *Lekhobola* v. *Mahae* J.C. 175/1963 (J.C.).

[4] *Mokhesuoe* v. *Moiloa* J.C. 10/1967 (J.C.).

[5] See Ch. 15 below.

[6] *Mohlomi* v. *Molia* J.C. 333/1966 (J.C.); *Mokotja* v. *Tsepo* J.C. 40/1968 (all courts).

[7] See *Makara* v. *Mokobori* J.C. 164/1955 (all courts); *Mokonyana* v. *Motumi* J.C. 102/1961 (J.C.); *Mohlomi* v. *Molia* J.C. 333/1966 (J.C.).

[8] (1975), p. 112. He cites (at p. 153) the following cases as supporting the application of the maxim: *Rankali* v. *Thelelisane* J.C. 162/1960; *Mosoeunyane* v. *Khomoeamollo* J.C. 27/1961; *Mokonyana* v. *Motumi* J.C. 102/1961; *Monyana* v. *Ralilochane* J.C. 128/1961.

(d) *The Existence of One* Bohali *Debt is no Bar to the Contracting of Another*

A man who still owes *bohali* in respect of his marriage to his first wife is free to enter into a second marriage despite this and he cannot be compelled by the father of his first wife to extinguish this debt prior to entering into the second marriage.[1]

(e) Bohali *Debts generally Survive the Death of the Parties*

The section that follows this one will show that the death of the person whose obligation it is to discharge a *bohali* debt does not extinguish that debt. Instead the obligation passes to his heir and so on through the generations.

Furthermore, the death of either or both of *the spouses themselves* will not, save in exceptional circumstances described below, have the effect of terminating the debt. In the case of the wife's death section 34(2) of Part II of the Laws of Lerotholi provides specifically:

If the woman dies before all the *bohali* is paid any balance of the *bohali* which remains unpaid shall none the less be payable.[2]

However, although not expressly stated the same position obtains with regard to the husband's death.[3]

The exceptional circumstances that have to be taken into account are where one or other of the spouses dies more or less immediately after the wedding, before the bride has even gone to her husband's home.

(i) *Immediate death of the husband*

Section 34(1)(c) of Part II of the Laws of Lerotholi contains a proviso that if the man dies before the woman goes to his parents' home, the *bohali* shall be returned[4] and the marriage shall be null and void.

The introduction of this proviso originated from a motion in the National Council in 1948 which was proposed by the District

---

[1] *Seoto* v. *Mokhojoa* J.C. 29/1954 (J.C.).

[2] This rule was applied in *Hlehlethe* v. *Lebajoa* J.C. 47/1944 (J.C.) before it became embodied in the Laws of Lerotholi.

[3] P.D., p. 54.

[4] Probably, though the subsection does not expressly say so, any progeny of the *bohali* cattle born after they were handed over would also be returnable — see *Phoofolo* v. *Pongo* J.C. 89/1951 discussed below, pp. 219-20.

Council of Mokhotlong.[1] There was concern that among the Batlokoa the old custom was operating of compelling a woman placed in such unfortunate circumstances to go to her deceased husband's family where she would cohabit with one of its members and bear children under the *kenelo* (or levirate) system.[2] Since *kenelo* had been dealt a sharp blow by the judgment of the High Court in the *Regency case*[3] in 1943 the time was obviously ripe for a clear ruling in the Council that in the event of a husband dying so prematurely the marriage should be annulled. This would counteract any pressures placed upon young widows.[4] The significance of the proviso is that it furnishes an exception to the rule that in the case of a wife the marriage bond is lifelong, continuing even after her husband's death, unless terminated by divorce.[5] It was designed to meet a particular need and operates to terminate the marriage forthwith. However, its wording is not particularly apt in modern conditions since there is reference to the woman going to the man's parents' house whereas, today, by no means all newly married couples make their homes in the village of the husband's parents.

Despite the clearly expressed intention of the proviso one member of the Panel thought that the marriage could still subsist if the woman wished to go and live with the man's family and the curious case of *Molelle* v. *Ramafikeng*,[6] decided in 1957, some years after the proviso had been embodied in the Laws of Lerotholi, may tend to support this view. In that case the marriage was complete in terms of section 34(1) and fifteen head of cattle had been paid as *bohali*. The husband died before the bride arrived at his home, and after his funeral, which she attended, the plaintiff, who was the dead man's father, requested the defendant, the girl's father, to send her over all the same. His grounds for asking for her were summed up in the words 'although my son is dead a man is born of a woman', thus expressing his desire for children who would bear his son's name and constitute an addition to his lineage. The girl came and duly cohabited with

---

[1] *1948 National Council Proceedings*, p. 75. The debate also continued during the 1949 Session, see *1949 National Council Proceedings*, pp. 214–22.
[2] *Kenelo* is discussed in Ch. 18 below.
[3] *Bereng Griffith* v. *'Mantsebo Seeiso Griffith* (1926–53) H.C.T.L.R. 50.
[4] See below, p. 263.
[5] See 'Restatement', p. 1 and pp. 299–308 below.
[6] J.C. 157/1957 (J.C. upholding the decision of the Central Court).

a paternal cousin of the deceased. However, her child was still-born and it was over the rites of mourning for the child that the present dispute arose. She was put in mourning by her father who cut her hair, whereas properly this should have been done by the plaintiff since she was now a member of his family. She had gone to her parents' home for the birth of the child in accordance with the custom, but the plaintiff now refused to allow her to return to his home because of the improper conduct of her father which he regarded as an insult. Since neither of the parties was prepared to make any move towards a reconciliation she lived for many years at her father's home before eventually going to South Africa where she entered into a civil marriage. The plaintiff thereupon claimed the return of the *bohali* paid for her marriage to his son. Throughout the proceedings it was taken for granted that there had been a valid marriage and that the defendant's daughter held the status of a widow under guardian-ship. As Driver J.C. put it,

. . . the death of a husband after the marriage is completed (by payment of part or all of the [*bohali*]) and before the marriage is consummated does not automatically dissolve the marriage for the widow may continue to remain a member of her husband's family.

The Judicial Commissioner's Court upheld the plaintiff's claim for a refund of *bohali* acknowledging that what it was really doing was granting a divorce. This was regarded as quite in order since both the widow (by remarrying) and her father (by not apologizing for his wrongful conduct) had been at fault.[1]

It may be safer to regard this decision as a mere historical explanation of how the widow in this case came to be in the position she was, rather than as a statement of modern law, since the Laws of Lerotholi now seem to provide an automatic safe-guard, suggesting that if the girl still wishes to marry into the dead man's family an entirely new marriage with fresh *bohali* should be arranged.[2]

[1] The J.C. also based his decision on the fact that unless a divorce were granted the girl would be married to two men and polyandry was not permitted in Sesotho law.

[2] During the Panel Discussion (see P.D., pp. 64–5) an example was given of the elder brother of Chief Teko Makhaola who died on his wedding day. Chief Teko married the same girl three months later, but not by *kenelo*, as the *bohali* cattle were all returned on the orders of Paramount Chief Griffith and fresh ones brought.

(ii) *Immediate death of the wife*

The Laws of Lerotholi contain no comparable proviso dealing with the immediate death of the wife and it might therefore be concluded that the marriage continues to subsist and the *bohali* to be payable despite her death, more particularly in view of the express provision, already noted, in section 34(2).

However, this provision is framed in general terms and does not seem to be aimed directly at the problem of a wife's death before she has gone to her husband's home.

There seems to be no judicial authority covering the point and during the Panel Discussion a variety of opinions were expressed. Traditionally the husband might have been able to make an arrangement to marry his deceased wife's sister as *seantlo*,[1] but even this opportunity would hardly have been available in every instance and today *seantlo* is only rarely practised. The majority of the Panel seemed eventually to feel that the marriage could not be annulled nor could the *bohali* cattle be recovered,[2] but that if any *bohali* was still outstanding the balance could not be claimed.[3] The minority, on the other hand, who held that the marriage was void and the cattle returnable seem to me to have equity on their side now that the *seantlo* custom has fallen into decay. Where the wife dies so soon, the payment of *bohali* cattle has not achieved one of its major objectives, namely the addition of further members to the husband's lineage.[4] However, the injustice to the husband's family may be more apparent than real. Since such a small proportion of the total *bohali* is usually paid at the time of the wedding the need for a rule permitting the recovery of these cattle is less important than a rule that the balance is no longer due. Indeed, one of the motives for only making a small payment initially may be to guard against just such an unfortunate eventuality.

2. PROCEDURAL RULES

Common defences to claims for *bohali* are that the plaintiff is not

[1] Discussed in Ch. 12 below.
[2] P.D., pp. 61–4 (per Mohale, Fobo, Bereng, and Molapo, the last two of whom changed their views during the course of the discussion; *contra* Sehalahala and Motlamelle; Noosi did not express a view).
[3] P.D., p. 62. This also seemed to be the view of some of the members of the Restatement Panel—see 'Restatement', p. 7.
[4] See pp. 153–4 below.

the correct person to bring the action and that the defendant is not the one who should be held liable. These two procedural aspects are examined in turn. Investigation of disputes involving these questions provides a sharp insight into family relationships and helps to show how the pattern of interlocking rights and duties maintains the family as a coherent unit.

(a) *The Liability to Pay* Bohali

It should be noted at the outset that an unmarried man has traditionally been regarded as a minor at law, regardless of his age, and that it is upon his marriage that he attains his majority.[1] Furthermore, section 6 of Part I of the Laws of Lerotholi, which is often quoted in *bohali* suits, provides as follows:

> No African shall be liable for a wrongful act or debt of his adult relative or friend, but the head of a family may be held liable for a wrongful act or debt of his minor children (i.e. unmarried children living in his house and under his control).

Two initial difficulties arise because on the one hand some bachelors seem to behave as majors to the extent of arranging their own marriages through their friends in urban areas,[2] and on the other, it does not seem absolutely clear at exactly what point in marriage a man becomes a major for purposes of *bohali* debts. Thus the dichotomy between bachelor minors and married adults, which ought to be clear, is in reality rather blurred today.

(i) *Husband marrying for the first time*

Despite this it may be said that generally when a man marries for the first time the obligation to pay his *bohali* rests upon the head of his family.[3] This person would normally be his father,[4] if alive, and after his death, his heir. The heir might either be the husband himself or his senior brother; alternatively one of his paternal uncles or his widowed mother may take over the responsibility as his guardian, as indicated below. Such persons may be

---

[1] See below, pp. 185–9.

[2] See above, pp. 85–6.

[3] Sekese (1953), p. 8; Duncan, p. 27; 'Restatement', p. 7 and the numerous cases cited below.

[4] Where the man is himself an illegitimate child it will be the head of his mother's family—*Masupha* v. *Rapopo* J.C. 22/1964 (L.C. and J.C.); where the man is an orphan it will be his guardian acting under the supervision of the chief—*Mohanoe* v. *Mohanoe* J.C. 90/1963 (L.C. and J.C.).

said to have the primary liability, but there is no doubt that the husband himself always has a secondary liability. Exactly when this secondary liability arises is one of the problems analysed below.

A father's responsibility for his son's *bohali* is counterbalanced by the fact that in law the son's bachelor earnings belong to his father.[1] Thus the father is always entitled to look to his son for assistance in discharging the debt if he so wishes, more especially if he is not well off. The exact arrangements that are made between them will inevitably vary from one family to another. For instance, during a bachelor's early period of migrant labour he may either pay a substantial proportion of his wages to his father who will then be expected to pay out the equivalent and more on the son's marriage, or the father may allow his son to retain all his bachelor earnings so that they may later be paid as *bohali* through the father.

Again, after the marriage, but while there is still a balance outstanding, the son may either pay further *bohali* directly to his wife's family or go through his father. It was agreed during the Panel Discussion that the son is bound to continue paying his earnings over to his father even after his marriage to enable the father to extinguish the debt. In this sense the son may remain a minor for some time after his marriage has been completed in terms of section 34(1), but the father may only claim his son's earnings for this limited purpose.[2] The son may also be regarded as a minor to the extent that his father, when sued by the girl's family, cannot plead that his son is an 'adult relative' within section 6 and as a result that he (the father) is not liable.[3] It is clear that for the purposes of the application of that section to *bohali* debts a man is indeed a minor until his *bohali* has been paid in full.

Another way of arranging matters where the father is poor is for him to pay the initial instalment on the wedding day and then tell the bride's family that in future they should look to the son for the balance.[4] Then the son's secondary liability will come into operation.

[1] *Seenzile* v. *Seenzile* J.C. 143/1961 (J.C.) and see below, pp. 185–9.
[2] P.D., pp. 48–9, 86.   [3] *Pokonyane* v. *Qekisi* J.C. 137/1964 (all courts).
[4] P.D., p. 86; *1958 National Council Proceedings*, pp. 350–1 (Counsellor Goliath Malebanye); President J.M. Mohale in *Masupha* v. *Rapopo* J.C. 22/1964 (L.C.).

As Thompson J.C. rightly put it in *Molatuoa* v. *Molatuoa*,[1]

It is an accepted convention in Lesotho that sons assist their fathers
to pay their [*bohali*] if their fathers are unable to do so out of their own
wealth, but I have never discovered that it is possible for a father to
force a son to pay all his [*bohali*] himself, and thus save his father from
contributing anything whatever, and a dispute of that nature would
have in the first instance to be dealt with by the family . . . a father
is not in a position to sue his son without the matter being threshed
out in the family in the first instance.

We may summarize the position for the period while the
husband's father is alive by stating that the correct person to be
sued is the father, unless he has made it clear from the outset
to the wife's family that they must look to the husband for the
balance. Even when the father is sued, he is entitled to rely on his
son for assistance and this right is ultimately enforceable in law
if it cannot be resolved within the family.

(ii) *After his father's death*

Where the father has died and the husband is his senior son he
will automatically be the heir. There is no doubt that he is
regarded as a major for this purpose if his marriage is completed
in terms of section 34(1). Here the primary and secondary
liabilities merge and the husband becomes solely liable.

However, where he is unmarried the liability will, at any rate
initially, fall upon his guardian, who will usually today be his
widowed mother, although in the past it would probably have been
his senior paternal uncle.[2]

Where there is a married son in the family who is the heir and
thus senior to the husband in question, the responsibility falls
upon him since, as the heir, he steps into the shoes of their late
father.[3] This principle involves one brother being liable for the
bohali of another and has proved to be a very fruitful source of
litigation. One of the defences raised by the heir in cases where his
junior brother has already been married but where there is a
balance of *bohali* outstanding, is that section 6 of the Laws of
Lerotholi absolves him from liability because his brother is an

---

[1] J.C. 181/1967.
[2] P.D., pp. 47, 52–3.
[3] P.D., p. 47 and see p. 255 below.

adult. However the courts have consistently rejected this defence on the same grounds as when it has been raised by a father.[1]

A second defence has been that the deceased's widow should be made liable, rather than the heir. This, however, is based on a misconception on the heir's part of his true position (or else amounts to an attempt to evade his responsibilities) and has also been to no avail.[2]

Moreover, the fact that the estate is insufficient to cover the balance of *bohali* due is no defence since the principle of onerous succession applies, and the heir's liability is not limited to the extent of the assets in the estate.[3]

Where, before his death, the father publicly notified both the husband and the wife's family that the husband would be responsible for the balance, this will naturally absolve the heir from further liability,[4] but apart from this there is no defence available to him when he is sued for his junior brother's *bohali*. However, this is by no means the end of the matter since the husband has internal family responsibilities to his senior brother, the heir, just as he had towards his father during his lifetime. In *Ramochela v. Sekautu*[5] all the courts held the heir liable for the balance of his younger brother's *bohali* despite the heir's plea that the estate was small and that he had not even finished paying his own *bohali*, but Thompson J.C. went on to set out the over-all legal position with its emphasis upon co-operation between family members:

. . . the man who marries . . . is a surety for his [*bohali*] even though his father is liable for it . . . it is for the family to see that its members assist each other in a circumstance where the head of the family may not be any more wealthy than the other members . . . it is a matter for his

[1] *Mothakathi v. Ratikane* J.C. 84/1963 (C.C. and J.C.); *Jakalasi v. Letsota* J.C. 283/1963 (all courts); *Motsiri v. Lintlhokoane* J.C. 79/1965 (all courts); *Ramochela v. Sekautu* J.C. 224/1969 (all courts).

[2] *Motsiri v. Lintlhokoane* J.C. 79/1965 (all courts); *Rametsana v. Malelu* J.C. 27/1968 (all courts); see further on the relationship between the widow and the heir, below, Ch. 18.

[3] *Matsosa v. Matsosa* J.C. 151/1955 (C.C.); *Mokhojana v. Mokoma* J.C. 112/1966 (C.C. and J.C.); *Ramochela v. Sekautu* J.C. 224/1969 (all courts); P.D., p. 47; and see pp. 254–5 below.

[4] This would seem to follow from what has been said above. In *Lesole v. Moseli* J.C. 148/1965 a mere *private* arrangement within the husband's family was pleaded but all the courts upheld the claim of the wife's family who had not been notified of the arrangement. A private arrangement also failed as a defence in *Motsie v. Sekoai* J.C. 238/1960 (J.C.).

[5] J.C. 224/1969.

family to go into and it does appear . . . the younger member of the family cannot refuse to assist, and if there is unreasonable refusal . . . the younger member can be sued by the heir . . . to assist him. But having said all that, a third party . . . looks to the heir. . . .

Thus, while the heir is the person liable to persons outside his family and therefore must meet the claim from his brother's wife's family, he has a right of recourse within his family against his younger brother whose assistance can be enforced through the courts if necessary.[1] However, this does not mean that the husband should be liable for the whole of his own *bohali* any more than he was during his father's lifetime. After all, the heir does usually have particular advantages, in that he inherits assets as well as liabilities and has the prospect of receiving the *bohali* paid upon his sisters' marriages. Moreover, he is not in practice bound to share the estate with his junior brothers in anything more than a token way.[2] Only in a case of extreme poverty and no prospects should the heir, therefore, be totally absolved.

In *Molatuoa* v. *Molatuoa*[3] the heir had been ordered by the court to pay the balance of his younger brother's *bohali* and had thereupon instituted proceedings against his brother for the same amount. The Local Court ordered the brother to hand over some stock to assist the heir, but the amount was left unspecified. The Central Court, while purporting to uphold the judgment of the Local Court, in fact altered it to render the amount specific at seven head of cattle, which was the exact amount of the balance outstanding. Since the husband had paid virtually everything himself so far this would have meant that the heir was totally absolved. On appeal the Judicial Commissioner reinstated the judgment of the Local Court, saying 'It is not a matter in which this court will give any order as to the amount of help'.

However, in the earlier case of *Matsosa* v. *Matsosa*[4] the Court was more specific, Driver J.C. deciding that of a balance of ten head outstanding the husband should contribute three head to his elder brother. The Local Court had ordered the husband to

[1] *Matsosa* v. *Matsosa* J.C. 151/1955 (all courts); *Motsie* v. *Sekoai* J.C. 238/1960 (J.C.); *Rametsana* v. *Malelu* J.C. 27/1968 (J.C.); *Molatuoa* v. *Molatuoa* J.C. 181/1967 (all courts); P.D., p. 48.
[2] See the statement of Counsellor Mapheleba in *1958 National Council Proceedings*, p. 351; and see below, pp. 257–8.
[3] J.C. 181/1967.   [4] J.C. 151/1955.

pay the full amount, while the Central Court took the view that it was the heir's responsibility to pay and any recourse against his younger brother must first come through the family and not by proceedings in the courts.

The difficult task of attempting to achieve an equitable balance of responsibility between brothers in this situation came before the National Council in 1958 in the form of a motion that if, when the father dies, a balance of *bohali* is owing in respect of the marriages of both the heir and his younger brothers, then each should pay his own *bohali*.[1] The motion was carried, but the proposed amendment does not yet appear to have been incorporated in the Laws of Lerotholi.

(iii) *Husband belonging to a polygamous family*

Where the man marrying comes from a junior house within a polygamous family it seems reasonably clear that after his father's death the proper person to be sued is the heir in the junior house as opposed to the general heir in the senior house, because the *bohali* must be paid from the junior house's property under the rule that houses do not 'eat' one another ('*malapa ha a jane*').[4]

Were the general heir to be sued problems of execution would arise since he could not remove property from the junior house without the junior heir's permission, nor could the court execute upon the junior heir's property if he had not been made a party to the case.[3]

However, where there is no heir yet married in the junior house the senior heir should be sued and here he will have the right, just as his father would have had, to remove property from the junior house, after consulting with the widow in that house, for the purpose of paying *bohali* for one of its members. If, however, there were no property available in that house the heir would have to meet the debt from his own assets including any unallocated property in the estate.

(iv) *After the husband's death*

Where the husband dies after being responsible for the payment of the balance of his own *bohali* (for whatever reason) and himself

[1] *1958 National Council Proceedings*, pp. 350–2.
[2] '*Moleli* v. *Maisa* J.C. 286/1960 (all courts); P.D., pp. 49–53. Similarly a junior house's property cannot be taken for paying *bohali* for a son in the senior house—*Kapa* v. *Orpen* J.C. 120/1964 (all courts).
[3] P.D., pp. 59–63.

leaves an unpaid balance, this obligation will pass to his widow[1] or his heir,[2] as the case may be, under the usual principles of inheritance.[3] This has the curious results that ultimately a wife may be paying her own *bohali* to her own natal family and that a son may be paying off his father's *bohali* rather than the other way round.

(v) *Subsequent marriages and modern urban marriages*

In two sets of circumstances the husband himself always has the sole liability for the payment of his own *bohali*. First, where he marries a second or subsequent wife,[4] and secondly where he contracts a marriage of the new type referred to in the 'Restatement', without notifying his parents.[5]

Duncan states that where a husband has divorced his wife his father may be responsible for paying *bohali* for a second wife.

> If the first wife is divorced, and the cattle all returned to the husband's father, and if thereafter the husband marries again, does he have to find his own [*bohali*], or does his father have to find it for him a second time? . . . Presumably, in equity, since a divorce in which all the cattle are returned is almost certain to be a divorce for which the husband is in no way responsible, the father should find the [*bohali*] a second time, especially as he will have recovered all the first [*bohali*].[6]

However, Duncan is under a misapprehension here since the person entitled to the recovery of *bohali* on divorce is the husband, who is now a major, and not his father.[7]

(vi) *Marriages of chiefs*

When a principal or ward chief marries his senior wife a contribution towards her *bohali* is expected from his subjects.[8] This practice was introduced by Moshoeshoe and serves to

---

[1] *Mokhosi* v. *Konya* H.C. 1/1941 (P.C.'s Ct., S.C., and J.C.).

[2] *Mojake* v. *Litjamela* J.C. 4/1963 (all courts).

[3] See below, Chs. 17 and 18.

[4] *Lethunya* v. *Rabukana* J.C. 57/1962 (J.C.); *Kapa* v. *Orpen* J.C. 120/1964 (all courts); *Mohlomi* v. *Molia* J.C. 333/1966 (all courts); Sekese (1953), p. 8; Duncan, p. 27; 'Restatement', p. 8; P.D., pp. 54–5. There is, of course, no rule actually prohibiting a father from paying his son's *bohali* in such circumstances and he may wish to do so in order to strengthen the links between himself and the bride's father—see *Molapo* v. *Molapo* C.A. Civ./A/1/1974 (H.C. and C.A., overruling J.C.).

[5] 'Restatement', pp. 7–8.   [6] At p. 27–8.

[7] See below, p. 213.   [8] Sheddick (1954), p. 148.

involve the people in a direct way with the hereditary principle of chieftainship and thus leads to its preservation.[1] It seems very unlikely that such a matter would ever be brought before the courts.

(vii) *Voluntary contributions*

Apart from the foregoing obligations people commonly make small payments towards *bohali* in respect of the marriages of sons of their relatives and friends, usually in the expectation that such contributions will be reciprocated at some time in the future.[2] Moreover, the husband's senior maternal uncle (*malome*) will often contribute, as he is expected to do, in order to strengthen the alliance between his family and the husband's father's family.[3] In return he can expect to receive a portion of the *bohali* paid on the marriage of his niece.[4]

(b) *The Right to Claim* Bohali

The right to receive *bohali* is vested in the head of the wife's family.[5] This person will usually be her father, if alive, and after his death, his widow or his heir.[6] The widow will have the right to claim in the absence of a married son and heir, provided that she has not deserted her late husband's family.[7]

The rule '*malapa ha a jane*' operates to safeguard the rights of individual houses where the wife comes from a junior house within a polygamous family.[8] The *bohali* paid on her marriage belongs

---

[1] See *1932 National Council Proceedings*, pp. 57–8.

[2] Sheddick (1954), pp. 23–4; P.D., pp. 57–8.

[3] See *Qhobela* v. *Qhobela* H.C. 24/1943 (H.C.); 'Restatement', p. 20; P.D., pp. 55–6. (Bereng was the only participant to hold that the *malome's* contribution was legally enforceable.)

[4] See pp. 144–6 below.

[5] *'Mutlanyana* v. *Mokhachane* J.C. 91/1964 (all courts). Where the bride is an illegitimate child the head of her family is, of course, not her father but her mother's father or his heir, but see also the case of *Paneng* v. *Paneng* J.C. 111/1957, discussed at p. 196 below.

[6] *Lephole* v. *Lephole* J.C. 15/1958 (all courts); *Mojake* v. *Litjamela* J.C. 4/1963 (all courts).

[7] See the trio of cases *Leluma* v. *Mojela* J.C. 184/1964 (L.C. and J.C.); *Leluma* v. *Mohale* J.C. 216/1968 (all courts) and *Leluma* v. *Leluma* J.C. 103/1968 (L.C. and A.J.C.) discussed at pp. 296–8 below.

[8] *'Mutlanyana* v. *Mokhachane* J.C. 91/1964 (all courts); Duncan, p. 24. For the position where a monogamist remarries after the death of his first wife and the problem as to whether he has two houses—see *Lephole* v. *Lephole* J.C. 15/1958; *Ntoula* v. *Morake* J.C. 227/1960 and *Bolepo* v. *Bolepo* J.C. 296/1966 discussed at pp. 243–7 below.

to her house and if there is a married heir in that house he is the person entitled to claim it for the use of that house, and not the senior heir.[1] The senior heir may bring an action on behalf of the junior house in such a case only if he has been properly authorized to do so.[2] In the absence of an heir in the junior house, the senior heir may only make the claim after consulting with the widow in that house[3] and when the *bohali* is received it must be handed over to her.[4]

It has earlier been pointed out that *bohali* arrangements are sometimes made with a relative of the bride who, while not her father or guardian, stands *in loco parentis* towards her.[5] The Judicial Commissioner has declared that such a relative is entitled to claim the *bohali*, although he must then hand it over to the bride's lawful guardian.[6] It is no defence for the husband's family to point out that they have doubts as to whether the relative is really the wife's lawful guardian; they must pay him and in so doing they obtain a complete discharge which ensures that they cannot later be sued again for the same amount when the identity of the true guardian eventually comes to light.[7] On payment they are obviously wise to take a receipt for purposes of evidence.

The following decisions illustrate clearly Thompson J. C.'s approach to the whole question. In *Mtakabone* v. *Ramphobole*[8] the defendant had refused to pay the balance of *bohali* to the plaintiff because he alleged that the plaintiff was not the bride's father. The plaintiff's relationship with the bride was investigated by a number of Basotho Courts and the facts appeared to be these. The plaintiff had married the bride's mother after she had been widowed, but the bride was a child of the first marriage and thus belonged to her late father's lineage. Both the lower courts upheld the defence on this basis, but were overruled on appeal to the Judicial Commissioner who declared that he was surprised at the lower courts' decisions, adding

---

[1] George Moshoeshoe in *1873 Report and Evidence*, p. 41; P.D., p. 58.

[2] P.D., p. 58.

[3] *Matete* v. *Leluma* H.C. Civ./A/2/1965 (L.C., C.C., and H.C.).

[4] *Kheleli* v. *Kheleli* J.C. 225/1964 (all courts).

[5] Pp. 87–8 above.

[6] Successful claims were brought by the bride's family for the recovery of the *bohali* received by persons *in loco parentis* in *Khakahali* v. *Mafale* J.C. 116/1961 (L.C. and J.C.) and *Monoane* v. *Mahase* J.C. 236/1968 (L.C. and C.C.; J.C. pending).

[7] See p. 88 above.   [8] J.C. 71/1969.

... [*bohali*] goes to the person in whose village and under whose custody or control the girl happens to be. If there is a third party who has a better title then it is for that third party to deal with the head of the village or the head of the family with which the girl stayed and which arranged the marriage of the girl.

The Judicial Commissioner gave the same decision on similar facts in the recent cases of *Ralekabu* v. *Lelimo*[1] and *Phahla* v. *Makoaba*[2] and in the latter case he had the support of the lower courts.

There are two aspects of his approach that are disturbing enough to warrant comment. First, he often relied upon the authority of Seymour's book on South African Native Law[3] on this point and employed the South African term 'kraalhead' or the phrase 'head of a village' both of which are inappropriate in the context of Basotho society. This is, of course, not to say that Thompson J. C. was unaware of the differences between the African peoples living in South Africa and the Basotho; he was extremely conscious of them and it is clear from his judgments in other cases that he knew full well the very limited usefulness of Seymour's book in Lesotho. The point is rather that his assessors seem to have advised him that Seymour is right on this question, even for Sesotho law, and they may not be entirely correct.

Secondly, in *Mtakabone* v. *Ramphobole* and *Ralekabu* v. *Lelimo* his actual decisions involved successful plaintiffs who belonged to quite different lineages from the bride and therefore who could, in the last analysis, have no possible right to retain the *bohali* paid for her. To hold that they may successfully claim the *bohali*, even on the basis that they will pass it on, not only has a tendency to increase *bohali* litigation, but may even encourage sharp practice since an honest man would surely notify the husband's family forthwith of the identity of the person who was lawfully entitled to the *bohali*. Furthermore, it seems inconsistent with other aspects of the relationship between children and persons standing *in loco parentis* towards them, for as will be seen the latter are not always held liable for wrongs committed by children belonging to different lineages.[4]

[1] J.C. 216/1969 (J.C.).
[2] J.C. 309/1969 (all courts).
[3] The relevant reference in the latest edition is *Bantu Law in South Africa* (Juta, 1970), pp. 160–3.
[4] See *Motsoene* v. *Peete* J.C. 78A/1951 discussed at p. 183 below.

The approach adopted by Thompson J. C. does, however, have a measure of convenience in that there may be many situations in which it is hard to tell exactly who is entitled, particularly where the bride's parents have separated or are dispersed owing to the need to work in South Africa or when one or both of them are dead.

At all events this problem is a further illustration of the complexity of the law on *bohali* and it is not surprising that the scale of *bohali* litigation is so high.

(c) *Malome's Portion* (Litsoa)

The bride's senior maternal uncle (*malome*) is in certain circumstances entitled to receive from the head of her family a portion of the *bohali* paid on her marriage. This portion is known as *litsoa*.[1] This practice is of ancient origin[2] and serves to cement the relationship between their two families. The importance of a *malome* in the affairs of his sister's nuclear family is a feature of Sesotho kinship and it will be remembered that a wife goes to her own parents' home (where the *malome* will commonly be) for the birth of her first child. Further, on the death of his nephew the *malome* can claim to inherit a beast from his estate.[3]

The *malome's* right has been expressly provided for in the Laws of Lerotholi since 1919,[4] but the phrasing has been changed slightly over the years. The current provision is section 5 of Part I, which runs:

A maternal uncle shall be given a portion of the [*bohali*] paid for the marriage of his nieces if such nieces be married by African custom and if the maternal uncle contributed towards the maintenance of his nieces. If such uncle fails to contribute towards the maintenance of his nieces he shall have no claim to a portion of the [*bohali*]. The

---

[1] The word has clear etymological links with *setsoa* (abscess) and may express the idea that the *malome* is thought of as a doctor who can cure his nephews and nieces. During the course of the debate in 1917 at the National Council when the law was first debated Councillor Elia stated: 'The root of the word *litsoa* is *setsoa*, an eruption like ulcer. The disease was incurable by the witchdoctors and we hear that maternal uncles used to be called to spit on the ulcer as that was held to be the way of curing it', *1917 National Council Proceedings*, Minutes of 6th day. See also P.D., p. 55 (per Molapo) and *1944 National Council Proceedings*, p. 201.

[2] See evidence of George Moshoeshoe, *1873 Report and Evidence*, p. 41.

[3] P.D., p. 55; see p. 241 below.

[4] *1919 National Council Proceedings*, Minutes of 8th day.

portion of the [*bohali*] to be paid to the maternal uncle shall be based upon the amount of the [*bohali*] received. NOTE—'Contributing towards the maintenance' means contributing towards the clothing, initiation and entertainment, etc., of the nieces or contributing towards the [*bohali*] for the marriage of the brothers of such nieces.

Assuming that the *malome* has qualified for his entitlement by performing his duties the amount he gets is determined by the amount of *bohali* received. It is clear from the debate at the National Council in 1944 when the wording of the section was being discussed, that the intention was neither to lay down a fixed amount nor to leave the matter entirely in the discretion of the bride's father, but to place the responsibility at the door of the courts for achieving a just and equitable assessment.[1] The courts are, however, put in a further difficulty by the fact that usually not all the *bohali* is paid at once and there is the problem of deciding at what stage a payment to the *malome* can be justified.

In the old days it seems as if the *malome* was entitled to take as many cattle as he saw fit, though obviously he would be expected to act with moderation and common sense.[2] A tendency of some maternal uncles to take excessive portions may have led to the tightening up of the law in making *litsoa* conditional on the proper performance of their duties[3] while leaving the traditional flexibility in the determination of the proper portion.

A few decision of the courts will be given on the question of amount, but these can only be regarded as illustrations of the way in which judicial discretion is being applied.[4] In *Sempe* v. *Lepolesa*[5] four head were awarded to the *malome* out of a total of eighteen cattle and ten small stock which had been received. In *Shemane* v. *Molingoana*[6] four were again awarded, but the exact number of *bohali* cattle received does not appear from the judgments. In *Sebetha* v. *Thethana*[7] the Local Court awarded six, but was overruled on appeal on the ground that the niece had not been validly married and therefore the *malome* had no entitlement whatever.

---

[1] *1944 National Council Proceedings*, p. 198.

[2] See Ashton's remarks about the Batlokoa, p. 72; P.D., pp. 55–6.

[3] P.D., p. 55.

[4] Duncan (at p. 26) states that the courts will award anything up to a maximum of eight out of twenty, but gives no example other than *Sempe* v. *Lepolesa* J.C. 433/1947.

[5] J.C. 433/1947 (all courts).

[6] J.C. 84/1954 (L.C. and J.C.).

[7] J.C. 267/1964 (L.C.).

Finally, mention should be made of the case of *Matlosa* v. *Setlai*.[1] Thompson J.C. laid down the following principles:

Section 5 . . . cannot be used to enforce the paying over of a definite proportion of the [*bohali*] and . . . if the parties do not agree then it is for the maternal uncle to show exactly what expenses he has been put to in assisting in the upbringing of the child . . . The respondent has not put in evidence a statement showing what expenses he has been put to. He has merely mentioned certain clothing etc. the value of which he does not give.

The *malome*'s claim was for nine cattle out of a total *bohali* of nineteen head received and he provided details of all the clothes and school books he had bought for his niece. The three lower courts all granted him the full amount of his claim and the Judicial Commissioner was perhaps being rather too legalistic in absolving him from the instance. Surely the value of the *malome*'s contribution does not need to be specified with exactitude in monetary terms and, even if it were, there is no reason to believe that he should be refunded the same amount out of the *bohali*. If this was the intention the Laws of Lerotholi would have so provided. Instead the determining factor is stated to be the total amount of *bohali* received.

3. PROBLEMS OF MONETARY EQUIVALENCE IN EXECUTION

Because of the recognition that *bohali* may be paid in the form of money or other animals a plaintiff may frame his claim for cattle or other animals or money in the alternative, even though no consensus had been reached at the time of the original *bohali* agreement as to what the scale of equivalence should be.

The Judicial Commissioner has sometimes laid down that it is not the task of the court to determine the equivalence or to give an award couched in language such as 'ten head of cattle or R200', unless the parties themselves have agreed in these terms.[2] The court order should refer simply to the number of cattle or *setsiba* or *molisana*, as appropriate. If the defendant fails to comply with the judgment then it is the duty of the messenger of the court to

[1] J.C. 81/1959.

[2] *Letsie II* v. *Bolae* J.C. 182/1964 (J.C.); *Mothakathi* v. *Ratikane* J.C. 84/1963 (J.C.). But cf. *Maqutu* v. *Hlapane* J.C. 32/1969 where the J.C. confirmed the judgment of the Local Court expressed with a monetary equivalent in the alternative.

follow rule 58 of the Basuto Courts (Practice and Procedure) Rules[1] when he levies execution. This rule states:

> The messenger of court shall not attach more of the property or stock of a judgment debtor than is, in his opinion, sufficient to cover the debt and costs.

If, following the execution, there is any argument as to the value in terms of cattle of what the messenger has attached this must be resolved by the court.

Ultimately, at any rate, the president may have to reach a monetary estimate of the value of a cow and there seems to be some doubt as to whether the courts should follow the fluctuations in market value or maintain a fixed valuation. In 1948 there was a complaint during the National Council session that in some cases the courts were valuing beasts at £3 which was regarded as quite unrealistic, their market value then being about twice that amount.

The Council decided that court presidents should be instructed to use their discretion in making valuations, but that these should bear some relation to the prevailing market price.[2] A motion before the Council in 1952 to fix a maximum value for a beast was heavily defeated.[3]

In the Panel Discussion[4] President J. M. Mohale stated that he thought the courts always valued a cow at £10. The 'Restatement', however, remarks that courts have frequently decided cases with reference to the current market value which is about twice this figure.[5] In one case in 1963 the Local Court awarded certain beasts valued at £20 and others at £16[6] and this was left undisturbed on appeal to the Judicial Commissioner's Court. More recently in a leading case heard during 1970 all the cattle were valued at R20 by the courts.[7]

The question whether the courts should adhere to the market value touches on the significance of the payment of *bohali* and the question of its growing commercialism and it is to this that attention will now be turned.

---

[1] G.N. 21 of 1961.   [2] *1948 National Council Proceedings*, pp. 452–9.
[3] *1952 National Council Proceedings*, pp. 109–19.   [4] P.D., p. 43.   [5] At p. 6.
[6] *Jakalasi* v. *Letsota* J.C. 283/1963. Lesotho used £ sterling before changing to the South African rand and many Basotho continue to speak in terms of the £.
[7] *Maqutu* v. *Hlapane* J.C. 32/1969 (L.C., C.C., and J.C.). This aspect was not dealt with by the High Court on appeal (H.C. Civ./A/1/1971).

11

THE FUNCTIONS OF *BOHALI*

THE origins and nature of cattle payments made upon marriage in various parts of Africa have been the subject of discussion in many quarters for a long time but no leap into the quicksands of comparative analysis will be dared here. Nor will any further time be wasted in refuting that old red herring of missionaries and racists that marriages involving the transfer of cattle amounted to a sale of the bride.[1]

Since there is no sure way of knowing how and why the *bohali* custom originated, the treatment here has the more profitable purpose of attempting an assessment of its function in modern Basotho society and family life. This will, of necessity, involve an understanding of the way in which the payment is regarded by the people themselves.

Various aspects will be looked at in turn.

1. 'BOHALI' AS THE VALIDATION OF MARRIAGE

A Sesotho maxim declares '*khomo e kopanyo batho*' ('the beast joins people together'). It is a truism to say that *bohali* stands at the heart of the Sesotho marriage. This is not just a statement about the past; it is an accurate reflection of the position today. Often indeed the word *bohali* is used to signify marriage itself. After being presented with the choice of a Sesotho marriage or a civil ceremony for over a hundred years, a large majority of Basotho still choose to marry in the customary way.[2]

In terms of section 34(1) of the Laws of Lerotholi it seems abundantly clear that *bohali* serves to validate a Sesotho marriage

[1] See e.g. the article in *The Little Light of Basutoland* submitted as part of the evidence of the P.E.M.S. to the 1872 Commission in *1873 Report and Evidence*, pp. 31–7; Casalis, p. 182; cf. the opposite view put to the Commission by Austen, a magistrate, at p. 57, and Ellenberger and Macgregor, p. 273. See also Radcliffe-Brown and Forde (Eds.), *African Systems of Kinship and Marriage*, pp. 46–7.

[2] See p. 33 above.

in the sense that it is an essential element for the completion of such a marriage. However, despite the express wording of that section it has on a number of occasions been stated that it is perfectly possible to have a valid Sesotho marriage without any agreement on, or payment of, *bohali*. The evidence on both sides of this controversy needs close examination. If customary marriages without *bohali* are recognized as valid, then section 34(1) is an inadequate statement of the law and we shall not be able to conclude that *bohali* is the validating factor in all Sesotho marriages.

The authorities for the proposition that all Sesotho marriages do require *bohali* will first be set out.

First, Chief Maama, a junior brother of Paramount Chief Lerotholi, stated that this was so in his evidence to the South African Native Affairs Commission.[1]

Secondly, the High Court in *Molapo v. Molapo*[2] declared:

To constitute a marriage there must be actual payment . . . and acceptance of the [*bohali*] . . . where there is no payment of [*bohali*] there can be no marriage.

This categorical assertion must however be placed in its proper context. The circumstances of the case were, unfortunately, somewhat obscure and the most significant event of all was open to a number of possible interpretations. Chief Setsomi had married Nyane, the daughter of Chief Moliboea, but she had borne him no children. Setsomi thereupon requested Moliboea to permit him to marry Nyane's elder sister, Baholo, as well. It was not clear whether Moliboea agreed or not, but at all events when Setsomi later sent him fifteen head of cattle as *bohali* he drove them away and refused to accept them. Soon afterwards he committed suicide. No further developments took place in relation to the *bohali* cattle which remained with Setsomi. Nevertheless, Baholo continued to live with Setsomi and bore him children, including the plaintiff, who claimed to be Setsomi's legitimate son, the issue of a valid marriage. Exactly why Moliboea refused to accept *bohali* cattle was never established, although a number of hypotheses were put forward in the course of the proceedings. He may, for instance, have regarded fifteen head of cattle as insufficient for the daughter of a chief, though if this had

[1] See vol. iv (1904), p. 391.
[2] H.C. 10/1943.

been his reason he could have accepted them as a first instalment of *bohali* and called for more. Alternatively he may have been opposed to the marriage taking place at all, either because Baholo herself seems to have expressed some unwillingness to marry a polygamist or because he had originally offered Baholo (not Nyane) to Setsomi but Setsomi had chosen the younger of the two sisters. This last explanation, at any rate, was the one accepted by the High Court. It is possible, of course, that there was no rational reason for Moliboea's action and that his mind was disturbed, as indicated by his suicide soon afterwards.[1]

The Paramount Chief's Court, the District Commissioner's Court, and the High Court all held that there had been no valid marriage of Setsomi to Baholo. It seems clear that the *ratio decidendi* throughout was that it had not been established that any agreement had been reached with her father either in respect of the marriage itself or in relation to the amount of *bohali*. The case therefore should properly be interpreted as authority for the proposition that such agreement is required, not for the assertion that all marriages without the passing of *bohali* are invalid.

Another statement from the High Court on this point came in an *obiter dictum* from Jacobs C.J. in the very recent case of *Maqutu* v. *Hlapane*.[2] He declared:

The payment of or an expressed or implied agreement to pay [*bohali*] is and always has been an essential to the validity of a marriage according to Basuto custom and this is laid down in so many words in the Laws of Lerotholi . . .

The case concerned, however, a claim for *bohali* following a civil marriage, not a customary one.

In opposition to these assertions stand some of the evidence given to the 1872 Commission, Duncan's book and the views expressed at the Panel Discussion, but I know of no judicial pronouncements.

It seems that two of Moshoeshoe's sons, Sofonia and Selebalo,

---

[1] Duncan (at p. 25) states that it is generally believed that Moliboea's motive was that he did not wish any *bohali* to be paid, but this point was nowhere raised in the proceedings. Furthermore Chief 'Mako Moliboea Molapo, who is a member of the same family, stated in the Panel Discussion that this was not a case where there was an agreement that no *bohali* should be paid—see P.D., p. 37.

[2] H.C. Civ./A/1/1971.

were married without *bohali*[1] and when Sofonia and George Moshoeshoe gave evidence to the 1872 Commission they both mentioned the possibility of such marriages validly taking place, although they emphasized that the general rule was to pay *bohali*.[2] Sofonia said: '. . . those that are married without cattle do so by a private arrangement between the parents of the parties'.

Now, on the one hand these statements may mean no more than that by 1872 some Basotho had been converted to Christianity by the P.E.M.S. missionaries and therefore married *civilly* without *bohali* because this was one of the rules of the church. As we have seen, the other churches did not impose a ban on the passing of *bohali* side by side with a Christian marriage and thus the practice of 'dual marriages' grew up.[3] But in 1872 the really dominant church was the P.E.M.S. and Christian marriages and *bohali* were almost certainly generally regarded as incompatible.[4] Further, Sofonia married the daughter of Moshoeshoe's brother Jobo, who was a pillar of the church.[5] It is inconceivable that these marriages would not have taken place in church and thus must have been purely civil marriages and not Sesotho marriages at all. However, one of Moshoeshoe's daughters was married customarily and without *bohali* to a son of Chief Moorosi Baputhi, with a view to achieving an alliance between them[6] and one of the reasons mentioned during the Panel Discussion for marriages without cattle was to create friendship between families.[7]

Duncan, apart from referring to the evidence before the 1872 Commission and agreements not to pay *bohali* arising out of church membership, gives two further possible situations, namely where the girl's father disowns her or where he disapproves of the man she is proposing to marry.[8] However, this is not at all convincing; no father willingly disowns a daughter for whom he can obtain *bohali* and disapproval of her husband is simply not a satisfactory justification for a father to deprive himself of the *bohali*.

[1] P.D., p. 36.   [2] *1873 Report and Evidence*, pp. 40, 43.   [3] Pp. 33–4 above.
[4] In 1875 out of a total of 6,379 African converts to Christianity 6,272 were members of the P.E.M.S. and only 107 Roman Catholics—*Cape Government Census of British Basutoland, 1875*.
[5] P.D., p. 36.
[6] See letter dated 25 Feb. 1847 from the Revd. Schrumf to the P.E.M.S. Committee in Paris, (1847) *Journal des Missions Évangéliques* 293–4.
[7] P.D., p. 37.   [8] At p. 24.

In the Panel Discussion it was thought that parents might well be willing to forgo *bohali* where their daughter's chances of marriage were not very favourable, for instance where she had already borne one or more illegitimate children and was in danger of getting beyond parental control;[1] indeed, it was stated that such marriages definitely had occurred.

It might be thought that where the man's family were poor the girl's parents might be prevailed upon to waive their right to *bohali*, but this is not the case. The girl's parents will not be amenable to such a suggestion because a better solution is provided by an agreement to pay based upon the mutual recognition that payment will inevitably be spread over a long period of time, even generations.[2] They hope that fortunes will change and enough stock or money will come in from various sources to enable the debt to be reduced bit by bit until it is eventually extinguished. It is not uncommon to hear reference being made to the possibility of the *bohali* received on the marriage of the husband's daughter being used to pay off his own *bohali*.[3]

When Paramount Chief Letsie I was giving his evidence to the 1872 Commission the Governor's Agent asked him the following question:

'If a man married a woman without cattle, who do the children belong to on the death of the husband?'

He replied, 'To the husband's heirs; there are several precedents for this'.[4]

Since, as will be shown, it is a valid marriage which has the effect of ensuring that a woman's children belong to her husband's lineage, this seems to furnish further evidence for the view that marriages without *bohali* are valid.

Assuming that Sesotho law does recognize marriages without *bohali* as valid, for it is difficult to be sure one way or the other, what significance does this have in assessing the function of *bohali* as providing a validation of Sesotho marriage?

---

[1] P.D., p. 38.

[2] P.D., pp. 37–9 and above, pp. 127–8, 139–40. But cf. the personal statement of Molapo, P.D., p. 43.

[3] See e.g. P.D., p. 37.

[4] *1873 Report and Evidence*, p. 48; cf. Sheddick (1953) who states (at p. 37) that as long as cattle are not handed over the wife's family has a prior claim to the children. In the Panel Discussion the general opinion was in accordance with Letsie's view—see P.D., p. 37.

The answer seems to be that in the usual case where the marriage is agreed upon as one involving the transfer of *bohali* the payment of part, at any rate, has the effect of legalizing the union in terms of the Laws of Lerotholi. For a marriage without *bohali* to be valid it needs the agreement of the two families to this special arrangement. Furthermore, it would seem that the courts will presume that all marriages are with *bohali* and therefore require clear proof of any agreement to the contrary.

In South Africa there are two conflicting views on how the obligation to pay *lobolo* (the equivalent of *bohali*) arises. Seymour[1] holds that it arises from a contractual agreement, while others take the view that it flows automatically from the marriage agreement. Such a polarization of extremes is inappropriate for Lesotho where the obligation to pay *bohali* seems basically rooted in the marriage agreement, but allowance is made for its exclusion by express arrangement between the parents.

Where a part payment of *bohali* has not been made, and in the absence of such contrary agreement, the relationship between the parties will amount to no more than concubinage with corresponding disadvantages to the woman and any children she may have.[2]

2. 'BOHALI' DETERMINING RIGHTS IN RESPECT OF CHILDREN

It is often thought that the payment of *bohali* affects the location of rights over children, hence the famous statement of Jeffreys that '*Lobolo* is child-price'.[3] Certainly in patrilineal Basotho society the children of a marriage in which *bohali* has been paid belong to the lineage of the husband, including, at any rate theoretically, children conceived in adultery and children conceived after the husband's death. Such children are regarded as legitimate at law and are entitled to inherit the estate of their mother's husband on his death, whereas children born before marriage or outside it are illegitimate, and belong to their mother's lineage and inherit there, if at all, unless subsequently legitimated.[4]

It hardly seems possible to say that a child must always be illegitimate if *bohali* has not been paid on the marriage of its

---

[1] At p. 153.   [2] See pp. 234–7 below.
[3] '*Lobolo* is child-price' (1961), *African Studies* 145. The 'Restatement' (at p. 16) refers to the Sesotho maxim that 'children are begotten by the cattle'.
[4] See pp. 181–3, 235–7 below.

mother, if marriages without *bohali* are recognized as valid in Sesotho law. Nevertheless, it may still be concluded that *bohali* does usually ensure that the children belong to the husband's lineage in the sense that *bohali* is an integral part of the vast majority of marriages and it is marriage, not paternity, which is the determinant for legitimacy. Suffice it to conclude therefore that the concepts of marriage, *bohali*, and legitimacy are all closely intertwined.

There are various other features of Sesotho law that tend to recognize the importance to the husband's family of the birth of legitimate children from a marriage, and these may all be interpreted, as they have been by Jeffreys, to mean that *bohali* is really child-price.[1] For instance, special types of marriage used to exist, the issue of which belonged to the family that paid the *bohali*, even though the normal features of a marriage were not present. Ghost marriages which fell into this category are discussed below.[2]

Further, in a *seantlo* marriage a man whose wife has died without bearing children may be permitted to marry her younger sister upon payment of a reduced scale of *bohali*;[3] and under the *kenelo* system widows were inherited by their deceased husband's brothers without further payment of *bohali* in order that they should bear more children for his family.[4]

Moreover, as will be seen, the rules about divorce reflect the impact that the movement of *bohali* has upon rights over children.[5]

3. 'BOHALI' AS A MEDIUM OF PUBLICITY AND A MEANS OF STRENGTHENING FAMILY BONDS

Marriage is an important event in all societies and as a *rite d passage* is given due publicity. The actual transfer of cattle adds to the publicity and is a feature that is marked and remembered by those participating. The contributions made within the husband's family serve to strengthen the natural ties between donor and recipient and a similar process occurs when the cattle are distributed within the bride's family. Furthermore, the

---

[1] Sheddick (1953) states (at p. 33) that *bohali* is more accurately expressed as child-price than bride-price; see also the judgment of President Nena in *Peete v Peete* in the Bela Bela Local Court C.C. 21/1960 to the same effect.

[2] See pp. 163–6 below.   [3] See Ch. 12 below.

[4] See Ch. 18 below.   [5] See pp. 213–20 below.

continuing payments that are usually made after the wedding until the full debt is extinguished give concrete structure to the relationship brought about by the marriage.[1] Where money is used in place of cattle the publicity aspect obviously loses some of its importance.

4. 'BOHALI' AS A COMPENSATORY PAYMENT TO THE BRIDE'S PARENTS

Upon marriage the bride's parents lose a member of their family who might otherwise have provided them with useful domestic services. They have been put to the expenses of her upbringing and education and now they will have to fit her out with a trousseau to take to her new home. Traditionally two cattle known as *selelekela* have been specifically regarded as due to the bride's mother and father for bringing the bride into the world and rearing her.[2] For these reasons Basotho parents commonly see the *bohali* they receive for their daughters as a form of compensation.[3] They may also need to maintain their daughter and her children in the future if her marriage breaks up through her husband's ill-treatment or neglect and she is forced to return to their home.[4]

5. 'BOHALI' TENDING TO DISCOURAGE DIVORCE

Bohali is usually returnable upon divorce if the wife is held largely responsible for the breakdown of the marriage, and since her parents will be loath to part with the cattle this may serve to keep the marriage intact.[5] The wife's parents have a direct proprietary interest in the success of the marriage and can therefore be expected to urge her towards a reconciliation of differences with her husband as opposed to a break upon the flimsiest pretext.

Bohali also ties a wife strongly to her husband's family after his death and a widow's remarriage is rendered extremely difficult.[6]

6. 'BOHALI' AS A REMINDER OF TRADITIONAL CULTURE

Basotho value the *bohali* custom as a distinctive mark of their

[1] See Hamnett (1975), p. 112 quoted on p. 129 above.
[2] Sekese (1968), p. 4. The 'Restatement' (at p. 19) refers only to the mother's beast (*seholoholo*).
[3] Ashton, p. 73.
[4] See Chs. 15 and 16 below.
[5] Ashton, p. 73; Reuter, p. 247.
[6] See pp. 299–308 below.

culture and its payment, as well as the negotiations that precede it, are relished as occasions when old traditions are re-enacted and the participants consciously act as they imagine their fore-fathers did. It thus helps to preserve the uniqueness and identity of the Basotho Nation. As the practice grows more commercialized and money replaces cattle this aspect is naturally dying out.

12

SPECIAL TYPES OF MARRIAGE

IN this section a brief analysis is made of various special types of marriage. These are very rarely encountered today and many of them have been expressly prohibited by legislation or curtailed by the courts. Their inclusion here is warranted by the fact that they help to explain the over-all family pattern of traditional Basotho society and their decay is a reflection of the development which has been taking place in the law.

1. 'SEANTLO'

A *seantlo* marriage occurs where a wife dies and her sister (or possibly another close relative)[1] then takes her place as a substitute wife. Both the sister and her father must naturally consent to the marriage,[2] but the *bohali* is usually reduced or none is paid at all. The main rationale is that the new wife should step into the shoes of her late sister to perform her family's obligation of adding children to the husband's lineage and simultaneously take over her late sister's seniority for purposes of succession.

Seantlo now seems to have fallen into almost total disuse.[3] No doubt this is partly due to the modern emphasis on genuine freedom of choice of partners in marriage. Moreover, its objective in terms of conferring seniority for purposes of succession has ceased to be sure of enforcement through the courts.

The circumstances under which *seantlo* may validly occur are

---

[1] Ashton (at p. 83) mentions that the substitute wife could equally well be the deceased wife's father's brother's daughter or her brother's daughter. The 'Restatement' (at p. 1) refers to 'any younger female blood relation' of the deceased wife. In the Panel Discussion Molapo and Mohale said that the sisters need not be of the same house and an illustration was given—see P.D., pp. 73, 76.

[2] *1873 Report and Evidence*, pp. 41, 44 (evidence of George and Sofonia Moshoeshoe); P.D., p. 73; evidence of expert witnesses in *Khabele* v. *Khabele* J.C. 319/1948 (J.C.).

[3] I have gained this impression from the dearth of any modern examples. Neither the Panel Discussion, nor my class of students could give any recent examples. None of the 125 married women interviewed in my survey in 1970 was a *seantlo* wife.

not entirely clear. In *Likoto* v. *Pule*[1] Duncan J.C. overruled the
lower court and held that *seantlo* could only take place where the
first wife had died without issue. There is an element of logic in
this since the major purpose of the custom seems to be to provide
the husband with children and thus ensure that the *bohali* payment is fully productive.[2] Moreover, George and Sofonia Moshoeshoe in their evidence to the 1872 Commission specifically discussed *seantlo* in the context of a wife who died without bearing
children.[3] However, the view of the Panel Discussion was that
the concept is not so restricted and that another of its purposes is to
ensure that children borne by the first wife are well cared for
after her death.[4] This raises a further question in relation to the
amount of *bohali* payable for a *seantlo* wife. George and Sofonia
Moshoeshoe declared that the payment was half the *bohali* paid
for the deceased wife,[5] but other commentators have given different
versions, often distinguishing between cases where issue have been
born and where there has been no issue.[6] No doubt the law permits
a degree of flexibility and the basic position, as with *bohali* paid
for ordinary marriages, is probably that the amount ultimately
depends in each case on the agreement of the parties.

Ashton has written that *seantlo* marriages were only agreed to
in the case of senior wives of important people,[7] but the opinion
was voiced during the Panel Discussion that they were neither
confined to the senior house,[8] nor restricted to chiefly families.[9]

[1] J.C. 67/1951 (J.C.) discussed in Duncan, pp. 33-4.

[2] See P.D., p. 75 and p. 154 above.

[3] *1873 Report and Evidence*, pp. 41, 44.

[4] P.D., pp. 74-6 (though Noosi at p. 73 stated that it was restricted to cases
where there was no male issue in the first house); and see Ashton, p. 82;
'Restatement', p. 2.

[5] *1873 Report and Evidence*, pp. 41, 44.

[6] Ellenberger and Macgregor (at p. 278) stated there was no further payment
if no children had been born; Laydevant (at p. 243) agreed, but stated that if
there were children ten cattle were payable; Ashton (at p. 82) stated that if
there was no issue less *bohali* (usually half) was payable, but that if there were
children full *bohali* was payable; in the Panel Discussion it was thought that
bohali would be reduced to ten cattle regardless of whether children had been
born—P.D., pp. 73, 76. In the leading case of *Khabele* v. *Khabele* J.C. 319/1948,
thirty head of cattle were paid for the first wife and twenty for the *seantlo*;
Duncan (at p. 32) is incorrect in saying that ten were paid for the *seantlo*.

[7] At p. 82.

[8] At p. 75 (Molapo).

[9] At p. 75 (Molapo and Mohale, *contra* Bereng). The case of *Khabele* v.
Khabele above concerned a chiefly family, but there was a conflict between the
expert witnesses on the question whether *seantlo* applied only to the first house.

Various authorities emphasize the desirability of giving due publicity of a *seantlo* marriage to members of the husband's family and any wives married prior in time, as well as the chief, so as to avoid disputes over succession and inheritance on the husband's death.[1] Whether such publicity is a *sine qua non* for the validity of such a marriage is not, however, entirely free from doubt.

Attention must now be turned to the succession rights which flow from a *seantlo* marriage and particularly to the leading case on the subject, *Khabele* v. *Khabele*[2] which was a dispute over succession to a chieftainship.

The lower courts had held that the son of a *seantlo* wife was entitled to precedence over the son of a wife married prior in time to the *seantlo*, but the Paramount Chief's Court and the Judicial Commissioner both reached the opposite conclusion. Whereas the Paramount Chief's Court overruled the lower courts on the basis that the purported *seantlo* marriage was in reality just an ordinary marriage, the Judicial Commissioner after finding that it was indeed a *seantlo* marriage and that such marriages were still extant and valid, refused to permit the son of the marriage to take precedence. His ground for so holding was that the practice was repugnant to justice and morality in terms of the legislation authorizing the application of Sesotho law.[3] It was unjust that a *seantlo* wife should supersede other wives who were already married at the time when she herself arrived at her husband's home.

During the course of the proceedings one of the expert witnesses, Chief Mahala Molapo, stated in his evidence that the *seantlo* custom tended to cause great family disputes in polygamous households and that Law 1 of the original version of the Laws of Lerotholi had been designed to solve the problem by making the order of marriages the determining factor in chiefly succession. It is interesting to note that while the Judicial Commissioner accepted that this explanation was reasonable, he did not base his judgment on the express wording of Law 1.

Duncan has severely criticized the decision on the basis that the *seantlo* custom was very well known and that wives other than

[1] Laydevant, p. 251; Ashton, p. 81; P.D., p. 89.
[2] J.C. 319/1948.
[3] Proc. 62 of 1938, as amended, s. 9, discussed at pp. 55–9 above.

great wives always knew that if the great wife died childless her place could be filled by her sister. 'They are married on those terms, so, if those terms are carried out it is difficult to see where the injustice or immorality lies.'[1]

I have endorsed Duncan's criticism elsewhere[2] and also take the view that *Khabele*'s *case* was not a proper one for the application of the 'repugnancy clause'. Rather, if it was desirable to deny recognition to the custom for purposes of succession, reliance should have been placed on the section of the Laws of Lerotholi which regulated inheritance by reference to the chronological order of marriages.[3] An opportunity was lost of giving a progressive interpretation to the Laws, without imposing the slightest strain on their literal meaning, so as to keep them in line with the sentiment of the times.

Be that as it may there was a general feeling at the Panel Discussion that the effect of the Judicial Commissioner's decision coupled with the relevant provisions of the Laws of Lerotholi has been to bar any further claims to seniority on the basis of a *seantlo* marriage. Furthermore, the members seemed to agree that this was only right and proper in modern conditions.[4]

Apart from this, however, there seems nothing to impair their validity as ordinary marriages to a deceased wife's sister with an agreement on a reduced scale of *bohali*.

2. 'MALA'

A *mala* wife is one married as a 'seed-raiser' for a barren wife who is still alive.[5] A barren wife may even prompt her husband to take this step because she is anxious not to lose her position of seniority to a junior wife who might otherwise bear the heir.[6] Her own status is retained because the *mala* wife and her children form part of the barren wife's house and do not create a new house of their own.[7] For this reason a *mala* wife is also known as a *seriti* (or 'shadow') because she lives in the shadow of the wife to whose house she is attached.[8] *Bohali* is paid for her in the usual way.[9] The purpose is thus to produce a male heir, usually for the senior house.

[1] At p. 33.
[2] See Palmer and Poulter, p. 162.
[3] S. 2 of Part I.
[4] P.D., pp. 73–5, 79.
[5] 'Restatement', p. 1; P.D., p. 79.
[6] P.D., pp. 80–1.
[7] 'Restatement', p. 1; P.D., p. 80.
[8] 'Restatement', p. 1.
[9] P.D., p. 80; *contra* Ashton (at p. 83) who says the *bohali* is only half the usual amount, *sed quaere?*

Mala marriages, like *seantlo* marriages, tend to give rise to disputes over succession. However, the only court case I have come across is the very early one of *Mojela* v. *Mojela*[1] which has the distinction of being the only appeal heard by the Judicial Committee of the Privy Council on a question of Sesotho law. The disputing parties were the sons of the late Chief Mojela and the point at issue was the right to succeed to the chieftainship of the ward of Makhauta. None of the first four wives of the late chief had borne a male child. In terms of the chronological sequence of marriages the respondent Thabo was the son of the fifth wife and the appellant Molapo the son of the sixth. However, Molapo contended that his mother, 'Mamolapo, took precedence because she had been married by a plan (*morero*) to provide an heir in the first house.[2] This argument found favour with the Assistant Commissioner's Court, but was rejected by the Paramount Chief's Court, the Resident Commissioner's Court and ultimately by the Privy Council. The reason given by the last two courts was that some of the necessary formalities to create such a marriage had not been complied with. The difficulty with the judgments, however, is that they do not specify the exact nature of these formalities. One would expect that publicity and the payment of *bohali* might have been regarded as two such formalities, but it appears that consent to the marriage was given by the head of the husband's family and by his first wife and that 'Mamolapo was taken to the first wife's hut. *Bohali* had, moreover, been paid, partly by Chief Mojela and partly by the Paramount Chief himself. The decision is not therefore very illuminating.

The example given here may tend to suggest that *mala* marriages were largely confined to the higher chieftainship.[3] Like *seantlo* marriages they have probably virtually disappeared by now and it does not seem likely that claims to seniority can any longer be upheld in view of the provisions of the Laws of Lerotholi regulat-

[1] Privy Council Appeal No. 93 of 1927. Unfortunately the illustrations of *mala* marriages within the royal family given by Molapo during the Panel Discussion (see P.D., p. 80) are not entirely accurate. For the position with regard to Senate see Jones, pp. 70–1, and Atmore, 'The Passing of Sotho Independence 1865–70' in Thompson (Ed.), *African Societies in Southern Africa* (London, 1969), p. 299.

[2] The claim referred to 'Mamolapo as a *ngoetsi* wife, but it seems more correct to regard her as a *mala* wife on the basis of the facts before the court (this is the approach adopted by Duncan, p. 31). For *ngoetsi* see below.

[3] See also P.D., pp. 81–2.

ing succession in terms of the chronological sequence of marriages.[1]

3. 'NGOETSI'

Ngoetsi were married as junior wives by chiefs who were large-scale polygamists and they were attached to the houses of the more important wives. The word *ngoetsi* literally means 'daughters-in-law' because they were regarded as servants or helpers of the senior wives in the same sense as a daughter-in-law serves and assists her mother-in-law.[2]

The husband cohabited with the *ngoetsi* if he wished to and they were also lent out to others, but all their children were regarded as legitimate and belonged to the house to which each was attached.[3]

Moshoeshoe had many *ngoetsi*, following the example of his uncle Mohlomi,[4] but with the decline of polygamy practised on such a grand scale it is doubtful whether there are many *ngoetsi* being married today. The large majority of the remaining polygamists have only two wives.[5]

4. 'LEFIELO'

A *lefielo* is a servant wife in the sense that *bohali* is paid for her by the family of a *wife* who is already married so that the *lefielo* may go and work for her at her husband's home.[6] Only in the sense that *bohali* is paid for a *lefielo* can she be said to be 'married'. *Lefielo* literally means 'a broom' and her function is to carry out household duties. She is found particularly in cases where the wife is not fit and well and where her family are sufficiently wealthy to be able to afford the *bohali* for such a servant.[7]

Strictly the husband is not supposed to cohabit with a *lefielo*, though other men may do so.[8] Her children have no right to inherit in the husband's family although they belong to him and take his name.[9]

---

[1] Sections 2 (succession to the chieftainship) and 11(1) (inheritance of property) of Part I.

[2] Ellenberger and Macgregor, pp. 279–80; Sheddick (1953), p. 38 (he describes them as *serethe*); P.D., p. 83.

[3] Ramolefe (1969), p. 199.　　[4] See p. 63 above.

[5] See p. 69 above.　　[6] 'Restatement', pp. 1, 6; P.D., pp. 82–3, 87.

[7] See Ramolefe (1969), p. 198.

[8] Jones, p. 70; P.D., p. 82. Ramolefe (1969), p. 198 would seem to be wrong in saying that a *lefielo*'s children must be begotten by the husband.

[9] Jones, pp. 69–70; P.D., pp. 82–3, 87–8.

The practice of *lefielo* seems to have been confined in the main to the chieftainship and examples were given in the Panel Discussion of Chief Nkuebe's daughter, Moselakoto, taking a *lefielo* with her on her marriage to Chief Tau Jonathan and of Chief Moloche's daughter doing likewise.[1]

Lefielo marriages would seem to be rare today, but two court presidents stated at the Panel Discussion that they would give recognition to the custom if an appropriate case came before them.[2] One of them, however, admitted that it was not a good custom and seemed only to wish to safeguard the rights of a *lefielo*'s children by treating them as being adopted within the husband's family, despite the fact that he did not pay *bohali* for her.

In so far as the *lefielo*'s own position is concerned she seems virtually a slave (*lekhabunyane*) and the principle of the practice should therefore be treated by the courts as repugnant to justice and morality and they should not enforce it. However, in so far as the children of a *lefielo* belong to the husband he should clearly have a duty to support them, although they cannot logically be allowed to inherit his estate in the absence of a proper adoption satisfying the necessary legal requirements. It would seem that any rights they may have in this respect must come through the wife's family.[3]

5. 'LEBITLA' AND 'LEBOTA'

Lebitla signifies a person already deceased and the Sesotho expression '*ho nyalloa lebitla*' means 'to be married for the grave'. If a young man died before he had married, his father might nevertheless pay *bohali* for a wife for him and a relative would be appointed by the father to cohabit with the bride.[4] In this way, it was hoped, a son and heir would be born who would maintain the line of succession and perpetuate the spirit of the deceased and glorify his name.

This type of arrangement was taken a stage further in the case of a marriage to a *lebota* or fictitious person. Here the father had never had a son at all and, pretending that he had, he thereupon

---

[1] P.D., pp. 87, 89.
[2] P.D., p. 89 (Mohale and Noosi).
[3] See Ramolefe (1969), p. 198.
[4] Ellenberger and Macgregor, p. 277; P.D., pp. 92–3.

paid *bohali* for a wife for the imagined son.[1] The purpose was exactly the same as with a marriage to a *lebitla*.

Such ghost marriages were strongly criticized in the National Council in 1949 on the grounds that they led to dissension within the family over rights of inheritance, that they brought disgrace upon the children and that it was a heathen custom which lowered a man's prestige.[2]

Soon afterwards a new provision was introduced into section 34 of Part II of the Laws of Lerotholi to prohibit them. Section 34(3) reads:

A form of marriage purporting to be entered into whereby a woman is married to a fictitious person (*lebota*) or to a person already deceased (*lebitla*) is expressly forbidden.

The section has been considered by the courts in at least three cases.

In *Malofotsane* v. *Mpho*[3] Janefeke had married three wives but the only male issue was a still-born child of the first wife. He was determined to have a son and heir and in 1912 after consulting his father and other members of his family he paid *bohali* for a woman, 'Mamphokho, to marry the still-born son. He then appointed his brother's son to cohabit with her and she gave birth to a son. Later on he himself married a fourth wife who bore him a son and the question for the courts to decide was who was entitled to inherit on his death. The four courts reached their decisions through a variety of routes.

The Local Court applied section 34(3) and held the fourth house should inherit; the Paramount Chief's Court reversed this decision on the basis that the arrangement made by Janefeke had not been challenged by the fourth house during the lifetime of his son and was only now being questioned by this son's widow. On appeal the Judicial Commissioner reinstated the Local Court judgment and this was upheld by the High Court.

Curiously both the higher courts doubted whether the custom of *lebitla* had ever existed, perhaps under the influence of 'progressive' assessors. The High Court held that even if it did operate it was repugnant to morality. Elyan C.J. held that the question

[1] Sheddick (1953), p. 38; P.D., p. 93.
[2] *1949 National Council Proceedings*, pp. 223-5.
[3] (1959) H.C.T.L.R. 107.

of repugnancy should be determined in relation to the time of the hearing and not to the time when the *lebitla* arrangement was made, more than forty years earlier.

> The determination of what is repugnant to morality . . . necessarily varies from time to time with the principles which for the time being inform public opinion. To invite this court to take the view that the test of such repugnancy should relate back to the time of the marriage in question is to invite the court to enforce a claim founded upon a transaction which the Court and the Assessors view as being repugnant to morality judged by present day standards, whatever may have been the view in the past. In my opinion, as to this, it suffices if the marriage in question is repugnant to morality as judged by present day standards in Basutoland for such marriages to be in conflict as aforesaid. And that it is so repugnant is the view of the Court and the Assessors.[1]

However, in the recent case of *Ntsoele* v. *Ramokhele*[2] Mapetla C.J. took a different view. Here the *lebitla* arrangement was made not with a still-born child but with a young man who had died during his engagement to his fiancée. Many years later the question arose whether the son born of this 'marriage' could have lawfully succeeded to the chieftainship and hence whether his widow in her turn could properly succeed him on his death. The learned Chief Justice pointed out that the *lebitla* 'marriage' had taken place not only prior to the introduction of section 34(3) but also before the enactment of the 'repugnancy clause' in 1938. He therefore held that there was no legislative basis for applying present day standards of justice and morality and refused to strike down the custom retroactively. The arrangement in *Malofotsane* v. *Mpho* had, of course, similarly occurred long before 1938, but this point was not taken by Elyan C.J.

In the third case of *Polo* v. *Polo*,[3] the parties were disputing the right to receive the arrears of wages due to Moketane who had died in a mine accident. The defendant contended she was entitled because she had been Moketane's wife, but this was denied by the plaintiff who was Moketane's mother. The plaintiff alleged that in 1960 the defendant had been married to Moketane's younger brother *after* the latter's death and that Moketane had

---

[1] At p. 109.
[2] H.C. Civ./A/13/1974.
[3] J.C. 137/1966.

merely been appointed to cohabit with her and bear children. Both the Central Court and the Judicial Commissioner's Court dismissed the plaintiff's claim and relied on the prohibition in section 34(3).[1]

A further type of fictitious marriage used to occur whereby a widow who had no children would pretend that she was a man and pay *bohali* for another woman. The latter would then cohabit with a male relative appointed by the widow and the children would belong to her because she had paid *bohali*.[2] An attempt to accomplish this was made by 'Mathabo, Chieftainess of Patlong, and her action eventually led to the litigation in *Sekake* v. *Tautona*.[3] However, the Sehapa Sekake family council refused to accept a son who had been born in this way as the successor to the chieftainship on 'Mathabo's death.

[1] The Local Court treated the case as one of *kenelo*, but was clearly in error since in *kenelo* widows are inherited by younger brothers, not elder brothers as here—see Ch. 18 below.

[2] Ellenberger and Macgregor, p. 278.

[3] J.C. 15/1959.

13

HUSBAND AND WIFE

THIS chapter deals with the legal aspects of the relationship between the spouses and examines both personal and proprietary matters. To understand their full significance it is first necessary to set the marital relationship in the wider social context of an extended family based upon the lineage of the husband.[1] It is true that the strength of kinship ties is waning under the weight of modern influences,[2] but they are still buttressed by certain economic and residential factors. Thus it is much easier for a married man to obtain land rights at his father's village than elsewhere and for this reason it is quite common for the couple to live near the husband's kin although there is no fixed rule requiring this.[3] Moreover, newly wed couples often cannot afford to set up their own separate establishment immediately and the wife may therefore even live at the husband's parents' home for a year or so while the husband migrates to South Africa to earn sufficient for them to make a start on their own.[4]

All this means that a wife usually has far greater contact with her in-laws than a husband has with his. The point is often made that a wife is married not just to her husband but to 'those people', i.e. the husband together with his family.[5] She takes over their rituals in place of those of her own family and she has the responsibility of cooking, washing, and performing other household duties for them as well as for her husband.[6] She owes them respect and a very formal relationship with her father-in-law and other senior male relatives of her husband is enjoined.[7] She should treat them with great deference and under the *hlonepha* custom she should not use their names nor other words which are very similar, either in speaking directly to them or in general

---

[1] See pp. 35–6 above.   [2] Devitt, pp. 67–8.
[3] Devitt, pp. 69–71; P.D., p. 93.   [4] Devitt, ibid.
[5] See Ellenberger and Macgregor, p. 274; Duncan, p. 37; 'Restatement', p. 13.
[6] Laydevant, p. 249; Restatement', pp., 12–13, 16.
[7] Sekese (1968), p. 9; Devitt, pp. 69–70.

conversation.[1] Instead she should refer to them as 'father of so-and-so' and if their names are ordinary words in everyday use she should always employ a synonym. While this traditional practice is clearly breaking down today,[2] the emphasis upon a wife's duties to her in-laws remains very much in evidence. Further, during her husband's absences abroad, she is meant to consult his relatives before undertaking various actions and she is, up to a point, regarded as under the control of her father-in-law, especially where her husband sends his earnings to his parents rather than directly to her.[3]

I. THE HUSBAND'S RIGHT TO CONSORTIUM

A husband has an exclusive right to his wife's consortium[4] and he has a right of action against any third party who commits adultery with her or abducts or harbours her. A wife, on the other hand, has no such corresponding rights with respect to her husband.[5]

(a) *Adultery*

The Laws of Lerotholi describe the action for adultery as one for the seduction of a married woman, but the wife's consent is no defence.[6] In *Sempe* v. *Salakae*,[7] however, it was held that a wife-swapping agreement between two husbands did constitute a bar to an action for adultery and thus it would appear that a consenting *husband* will be met by the maxim '*volenti non fit injuria*'.

The scale of compensation is specified in the Laws of Lerotholi as not more than three head of cattle and this maximum amount seems to be awarded almost as a matter of course.[8] However, a certain amount of doubt surrounds the possible award of an extra beast where the wife was suckling a child at the time of the adultery. Certainly a claim for one beast for 'weaning the child' has been recognized for a long time.[9] Custom forbids the wife to have sexual intercourse, even with her husband, for a period of about a year after the birth of a child during the period of suckling,[10]

---

[1] Kunene, 'Notes on *Hlonepha* among the Southern Sotho', (1958) *African Studies* 159.

[2] Kunene, ibid; Laydevant, p. 249.   [3] Devitt, p. 70.

[4] 'Restatement', p. 12.   [5] Palmer, p. 161.

[6] Part II, s. 8.   [7] J.C. 116/1967 (L.C. and J.C.).

[8] See Duncan, p. 108; Palmer, p. 161 and the cases cited there.

[9] See Sekese (1968), p. 30.

[10] Ashton, pp. 30, 34 and see the evidence in *Nko* v. *Nko* H.C. Civ./T/3/1968.

and the view expressed by some members of the Panel Discussion was that this practice is still strictly adhered to today by many people.[1] No doubt the original purpose was to prevent another conception and thus protect the health of mother and child in conditions of poverty and malnutrition, and these are circumstances which still prevail today.

Duncan[2] and Palmer[3] express the view that a fourth beast cannot now be awarded despite the express contrary decision in *Tsoeu* v. *Mothobi*.[4] Reliance is placed instead upon the cases of *Ramataletse* v. *Phatela*[5] and *Mona* v. *Tsoene*.[6] In the recent case of *Limema* v. *Lekola*[7] the action itself was recognized by all the courts, including the High Court, as still subsisting, although the beast was not awarded because the alleged adultery was not established on the facts. It was not entirely clear, though, whether any of the courts would have been prepared to award the beast in addition to the standard three head of cattle. The question would therefore still appear to be an open one.

Section 8(2) of Part II of the Laws of Lerotholi provides that if the same man again seduces the same married woman the compensation awarded shall not exceed *five* head of cattle. No case on the interpretation of this subsection is known, but presumably it is designed to provide for situations where a judgment in respect of a first instance of adultery has already been given before the second seduction. It would hardly seem to be open for a husband to claim eight head of cattle (or thirteen or eighteen *ad infinitum*) in respect of two or more acts of adultery on first instituting judicial proceedings.

(b) *Abduction*

Abduction of a married woman by removing her from her husband's control without his consent amounts to both a criminal offence and a civil wrong. Section 7 of Part II of the Laws of Lerotholi provides:

Any person who abducts a married woman or causes any such woman to be abducted shall be liable on conviction to a fine not exceeding R100 or to imprisonment for a period not exceeding twelve months or to both such fine and imprisonment; and in addition the court

---

[1] P.D., p. 237.   [2] At pp. 108–9.
[3] At p. 162.   [4] J.C. 105/1947 (C.C. and J.C.).
[5] J.C. 305/1947.   [6] J.C. 64/1964.
[7] H.C. Civ./A/4/1969.

hearing the case may award to the husband compensation not exceeding ten head of cattle.[1]

Liability for abduction has been extended by the courts to encompass various acts which tend to encourage infidelity on the part of a wife or which are conducive to disharmony in the matrimonial home.[2]

In *Ramakhaleng* v. *Setai*[3] during the plaintiff's absence in South Africa his wife took employment working in the defendant's fields without the permission of the plaintiff or his parents. She lived in the same house as the defendant during her employment and continued to do so for four years. The courts awarded the plaintiff compensation for what the Judicial Commissioner described as 'constructive abduction'.[4]

Another case of a wife being employed without her husband's permission is *Matlala* v. *Ntipe*.[5] Here she was asked by the chief's assistant to act as a *bewys*-writer during the absence of the regular writer and told to forge the latter's signature. The assistant was held liable to pay compensation to the husband.[6] However, the Judicial Commissioner explained that the husband's right to be consulted was not absolute:

. . . a married woman cannot be employed without her husband's permission if her husband is supporting her. It is however difficult to extend this principle to every circumstance in which a married woman assists another person voluntarily. For instance it is common practice for women to assist each other voluntarily in the lands at

[1] The existence of this provision seems to have been completely overlooked by Palmer, p. 159.

[2] See e.g. *Tlokotsi* v. *Koaesa* J.C. 273/1963 (all courts), where the defendant was held liable for writing letters to the wife encouraging her not to return to her husband and using terms of endearment. The Local and Central Courts awarded three beasts and this was reduced to one beast by the Judicial Commissioner. Cf. *Tsemane* v. *Hlalele* J.C. 216/1967 (all courts), where the plaintiff's action failed.

[3] J.C. 44/1965.

[4] The Local and Central Courts awarded ten head of cattle, but this was reduced to five by the Judicial Commissioner because the husband's conduct towards his wife had left something to be desired.

[5] J.C. 71/1959.

[6] The Local Courts awarded him 15s.; the Paramount Chief's Court however gave no award on the ground that the husband had suffered no loss; on appeal the Judicial Commissioner awarded £4 which he unrealistically categorized as nominal damages.

each others' request and no absent husband would cavil at such happening. Further when a woman is left to her own devices by her husband who goes away for a long period and neglects her maintenance again it is commonsense that she is thus entitled to undertake paid employment in order to enable her to obtain the necessaries of life.

2. THE WIFE'S RIGHT TO MAINTENANCE DURING MARRIAGE

Numerous court decisions testify that a husband is legally obliged to support and maintain his wife.[1] He should clothe her, feed her, and provide shelter for her. Since most Basotho subsist, at any rate partially, off the land the courts commonly order husbands to plough the lands for their wives or to make cattle available for this purpose. In *Mountain Trading Store* v. *Mathaba*[2] it was held that a wife is entitled to pledge her husband's credit for necessaries without his knowledge even in a case where he could easily have been consulted before the account was opened.

Where a wife feels she is being neglected there are a number of courses of action open to her for rectifying the situation.[3] She may appeal in the first instance to her husband's family to put pressure on him to support her or ask them to maintain her themselves.[4] Secondly, she may return home to her own parents (*ngala*) and seek a confrontation between the two families to resolve the crisis.[5] If necessary a joint family meeting should be called with a view to reaching a reconciliation. If this fails she can pursue her claim through the courts, being possessed of the necessary *locus standi* for this purpose.[6]

The Deserted Wives and Children Proclamation of 1959[7] has further strengthened her position by providing her with a remedy in the subordinate courts as well as in the Central and Local

[1] See e.g. *Vova* v. *Vova* J.C. 110/1949 (all courts); *Tlale* v. *Tlale* H.C. 3/1951 (H.C.); *Molapo* v. *Rabothata* J.C. 167/1951 (J.C.); *Makhakhe* v. *Makhakhe* J.C. 7/1963 (all courts); *Likotsi* v. *Likotsi*, Maphutseng C.C. 191/1965 (C.C.); *Mothae* v. *Sekutu* J.C. 98/1966 (L.C. and C.C.). See also Duncan (at p. 36) who curiously describes the action for maintenance as one for the restitution of conjugal rights; and P.D., p. 120.

[2] J.C. 19/1967 (L.C. and J.C., *contra* C.C.).

[3] See *Mapheha* v. *Masasa* J.C. 67/1960 (J.C.).

[4] *Molapo* v. *Rabothata* J.C. 167/1951 (J.C.) cited in Duncan, p. 7.

[5] For *ngala* see further Ch. 15 below.

[6] See 'Restatement', pp. 18–19.

[7] Proc. 60 of 1959. Applied in *Malebo* v. *Malebo* H.C. Civ./A/13/1969 (S.C. and H.C.).

Courts without great expense or cumbersome procedures, in cases where she has been deserted. Desertion is established by showing that her husband has failed or refused to supply her with food, clothing, lodging, or medical aid when able to do so and that as a result she is now living apart from her husband and his family.[1] If the court is satisfied that she is without adequate means of support it may make a maintenance order directing the husband to pay a reasonable sum at specified intervals.[2] In order to cater for husbands who are abroad there are provisions for substituted service, judgment *in absentia*, and reciprocal enforcement of orders in South Africa.[3]

Ultimately if the marriage has really broken down and it is clear that her husband will never support her properly she can obtain a divorce.[4]

3. THE MARITAL PROPERTY REGIME

In discussing this question it should be reiterated that while only a small proportion of marriages are actually polygamous today, polygamy will have to be taken into account for some considerable time in the law of property for two particular reasons. First, because the effects of polygamy continue to be felt even after the deaths of the spouses themselves in questions of inheritance, and secondly because the practice is so much a part of traditional culture that when a widower or divorcee remarries he may behave as if he is a true polygamist in his dealings with family property.[5]

It is proposed therefore to start by analysing the position in a polygamous household and then to turn to monogamous marriages.

(a) *Polygamous Households*

In the *Regency case* Lansdown J. described the broad pattern of traditional family life as follows:

Under the early Basotho social system, which was wholly polygamist, the husband was the head of the family, with some limited authority over him by his father if still living; each of his wives had a House of her own with cattle assigned to it; and the property of one House could not be used for the purposes of another; the first wife held a position of seniority in relation to the junior wives which entitled her to the respect of the latter.[6]

[1] S. 5(1).   [2] S. 8.   [3] Sections 7, 8(1), and 17.
[4] See Ch. 16 below.   [5] See pp. 243–7 below.
[6] *Bereng Griffith* v. *'Mantsebo Seeiso Griffith* (1926–53) H.C.T.L.R. 50 at 54. See also Ellenberger and Macgregor, p. 271; Duncan, p. 2; 'Restatement', p. 17.

He went on to explain that although the structure was patriarchal, a wife's position was not an entirely powerless one since she had remedies available if she was neglected and she had a certain amount of independence in respect of the property attached to her 'house'.

The central feature of polygamy is its system of separate 'houses', each comprising a wife and her children together with the husband. The husband allocates land and other property to each of his houses, but often retains certain property himself (commonly referred to as 'unallocated property'). This division continues even after the husband's death and is summed up in the maxim *malapa ha a jane* ('houses do not "eat" one another'). This principle is recorded in section 12(4) of Part I of the Laws of Lerotholi which provides as follows:

Where property has been allocated to any particular house and the wife in that house predeceases her husband, the property allocated shall remain with that particular house to be inherited upon the death of the father by the eldest son of that house and to be shared by him in accordance with Basuto Law and Custom with his junior brothers in his own house.

The maxim is equally applicable where the husband predeceases his wives and is discussed further below.[1]

Once established a house derives property not only from allocations by the husband but also from *bohali* received for its daughters and earnings derived from the labour of all its members.[2]

Property transactions within a polygamous household fall into three categories. First, dealings by the husband with unallocated property. In this sphere it would seem that the husband has a free hand and is not restricted by the need to consult with any of his wives although greater harmony may be achieved if he keeps his first wife informed of what he is doing. Moreover, his son and heir will tend to watch these transactions with a jealous eye because the unallocated estate passes to him on his father's death and he is naturally concerned to discourage any diminution or dissipation of it, especially to the houses of favourite junior wives.[3] However, although this can be a source of ill feeling it

---

[1] See below, pp. 242–3.   [2] 'Restatement', p. 17.
[3] Ellenberger and Macgregor, pp. 271–2.

seems the heir has no power to veto his father's actions.[1] The father is thus entirely free to pay *bohali* for further wives and allocate property to the new houses so created as well as to enter into commercial transactions.

Secondly, there are the actions he takes with regard to property belonging to a particular house and these fall into two separate categories. On the one hand, there are transfers of property between different houses and on the other, transactions with persons outside the family altogether. Dealings of the latter type are subject to the same rules as all dealings with household property in monogamous marriages and are discussed below. The present concern is with inter-house transactions.

It is in this area that a wife's rights have generally been reckoned to be particularly strong, despite her husband's over-all authority. Lansdown J. stated that the property of one house could not be used for another house, but does this amount to an absolute bar? This is extremely unlikely since there can be no reason why one house, i.e. the husband together with his wife and children in that house, should not agree to give some of their property to another house which is in need of it.[2] But the more difficult problem is whether a husband is entitled to take such action alone in the general administration and management of his total household or whether the wife in the house concerned must also give her consent. Since on occasion there may be rivalry and jealousy between the different wives, this is a point of some practical significance.

The 'Restatement' takes the position that if a husband wishes to make over part of one house's property to another he may do so only by way of passing it as a loan because of the maxim '*malapa ha a jane*'. He cannot just make a gift of it.[3] This explanation coincides with the principle that such transfers automatically give rise to an inter-house debt, which is the view taken by Seymour of the South African position[4] and which was endorsed as applicable in Sesotho law by at least one member of the Panel Discussion.[5] The alternative possibility is that the wife has an absolute veto over such transactions by her husband, but this

[1] But see *Peleha* v. *Peleha* J.C. 251/1947 discussed at pp. 320–1 below.
[2] See 'Restatement', p. 17.   [3] Ibid.
[4] See *Bantu Law in South Africa*, pp. 128–33.
[5] P.D., pp. 100–1 (especially Matete).

would seem to exaggerate the strength of her rights.[1] A compromise solution would be to hold that where the husband's act is totally unreasonable in all the circumstances the wife has a right to claim the immediate return of the property, but that otherwise a debt is created between the houses which must be repaid at a later date.[2] There is then the added difficulty of determining exactly when this debt must be extinguished. It must be confessed that there is a dearth of material on the whole question which renders a dogmatic conclusion quite impossible. Attention can only be drawn to the general consideration that the husband is the head of the family and that he is responsible as the over-all administrator of family property and for the management of all his houses.

(b) *Monogamous Households*

In a monogamous household there is no room for the concepts of allocated and unallocated property, strictly so called. There is no need for specific allocation since there is only one house. Difficulties do however arise when a monogamist remarries following the death of his first wife or divorce because there may be issue of both marriages and the husband may tend to regard them as forming two separate houses as if he were a polygamist. Such problems are explored under the law of inheritance since it is only after the husband's death that the question falls to be determined by the courts.

Not all the property of the spouses is household property. Personal effects including clothing are regarded as the individual property of each spouse and this will include, on the wife's side, part of her trousseau.

So far as household property is concerned those Basotho who have heard of the Roman–Dutch law system of community of property often explain that Sesotho law employs the same concept.[3] In reality, however, there are wide divergences between the two marital property regimes, but the picture which such informants seek to portray is one of joint property administered by the two spouses in consultation together. In most households

---

[1] Probably *land* given by a husband to his wife cannot be retaken without her consent—see Duncan, p. 90 and the cases cited there.

[2] See P.D., pp. 100–1 (Matete).

[3] See e.g. P.D., pp. 95–7. This point was also made by numerous educated Basotho who gave evidence to the National Council Select Committee on Wills, Estates and Marriages in 1962.

a significant proportion of the family wealth is derived from the labour of both spouses on their lands and they have equal rights to the produce.[1] To supplement this many husbands migrate to South Africa for work in the mines and industries and wives sometimes also take employment, either in Lesotho or abroad, for instance as domestic servants. The arrangements made about such earnings will naturally vary in detail from one family to another, but it seems clear that it is quite a common practice for each spouse to retain some of his or her own earnings and to spend them on purchases of personal effects without prior consultation with the other spouse.[2]

Apart from this the general rules seem to be these. First, a husband ought to consult his wife before he disposes of household property, though legally he does not need her prior consent; he is the sole administrator of the joint estate and in the last analysis his view predominates in household affairs.[3] However, that there is a strong customary and moral obligation on him to consult his wife[4] is clear from the case of *Mapheha* v. *Masasa*.[5] Without consulting his wife the husband had disposed of ten bags of mealies which were the product of lands which they had worked jointly. The lower courts upheld her claim that she was entitled to be consulted. The Judicial Commissioner, on appeal, also stressed the husband's 'moral duty' to consult his wife before disposing of house property, but went on to point out that once that property had been transferred to a third party the wife had no right to recover it. Instead she must pursue her remedies against her husband if she felt she was being ill-treated or neglected. However, the court did censure the husband's 'high-handed' action by awarding the wife costs.

A similar conclusion in relation to a transaction which the husband had completed with a third party was reached in *Moabeng* v. *Moabeng*.[6] Here the husband had removed some of the household furniture during his wife's temporary absence following a row between them. Part he had sold and the rest he had burnt. On her return she sued him for compensation and succeeded before the Local Court. However, the husband's appeal was allowed by the Central Court on the ground that the Court could not order

<hr/>

[1] 'Restatement', p. 13.   [2] Ashton, pp. 177–8; P.D., pp. 95–9.
[3] Ashton, pp. 79, 180–1.   [4] Ashton, pp. 170–1.
[5] J.C. 67/1960.   [6] J.C. 60/1962.

the husband to return the property; it could merely advise him to do so in the hope that the differences between the couple might be patched up. When the case came before Thompson J.C. he distinguished its facts from the situation where a husband takes property from one house and transfers it to another house. In those circumstances, he said, a wife could successfully claim its restoration to her house. However, where the husband had parted with the property to a stranger the position was entirely different.

> . . . in this case the furniture is not in the husband's hands. The property was their joint property and the husband had the main control over it. While this action is morally wrong the custom . . . is such that since the furniture is no longer in the husband's hands the court cannot assist the wife.

The Judicial Commissioner did conclude, nevertheless, by ordering the husband not to remove any more of the joint property without consulting his wife.

In the earlier case of *Ramakesi* v. *Ramakesi*[1] the husband had loaned out some of his goats to a third party under a *mafisa* contract. His wife complained to the court that she had not been consulted and that her husband was using the stock without her knowledge. The lower courts upheld the *mafisa* contract but stated that if the husband wished to dispose of any of the stock he should decide the matter jointly with his wife; further the wife had a right to inspect the animals if she wished to. On appeal Driver J.C. reversed the lower courts, holding that the stock must remain in the house to which it belonged. The *mafisa* contract was set aside on the ground that it was not easy for the wife to look after the stock when they were out of her immediate control.

This decision was criticized by one member of the Panel Discussion who considered that the court should have determined whether the husband's act was reasonable in all the circumstances.[2] Thus if the wife was being properly maintained with money or other livestock she could have had no cause for complaint. Probably the decision does go too far in granting a wife a virtual veto in connection with the management of house property.

Secondly, a wife has no right to dispose of household property

[1] J.C. 126/1953.
[2] P.D., p. 97 (Matete).

herself without her husband's authorization save in exceptional circumstances. In *Tukisi* v. *Mofolo*[1] the husband and wife were both earning and the wife made a gift of money to her brother without consulting her husband. Both the Local Court and the Judicial Commissioner held that the brother must refund the money. The Judicial Commissioner declared that a wife's earnings were normally subject to her husband's administration and she must consult him before handing them over to someone else. There might be an exception where she had returned home to her parents as a result of her husband's ill-treatment, but this was not the position here.

Similarly in *Matobole* v. *Makhakhe*[2] a wife transferred a cow to her brother during her husband's temporary absence without consulting him. She alleged she had sold it, but it appeared that she might in fact have given it away. All the courts ordered the return of the cow.[3] It was clear that the husband was supporting and maintaining his wife. The Judicial Commissioner pointed out that where a wife is stranded and there is an emergency and she needs to sell property during her husband's absence she should consult his relatives if they are available, and if they are not, then the local chief or headman.

The system under which husbands migrate for extended periods to South Africa and leave their wives and children behind must give rise to some acute practical problems in the administration and management of family property. A wife's position is a particularly ambivalent one.[4] An opportunity is offered which can confer a large degree of responsibility on her which she may well be in a position to bear without undue strain because of her generally better schooling.[5] However, in legal theory she should consult either her husband or, if this is not feasible, his relatives,[6] and if she elects to take the initiative on her own she risks incurring their displeasure, or even, as we have seen, having her actions nullified by the courts. On the other hand, correspondence with her husband in South Africa may take too long and consultation

[1] J.C. 289/1966.   [2] J.C. 64/1965.
[3] The same opinion was expressed by the Panel—see P.D., pp. 103-4.
[4] See Devitt, pp. 55, 76-7.
[5] The 1966 Census revealed that while 72 per cent of the female population had attended school at some stage only 50 per cent of the male population had done so. Boys, it will be recalled, often spend their days as herdsmen.
[6] See P.D., p. 105.

with his relatives may lead to unwelcome interference in the domestic affairs of her nuclear family.

A further decision suggests that where the action she takes without consultation is one that benefits the family then the husband will be bound. In *Mosela* v. *Lebona*[1] the wife had hired a herdboy during her husband's absence. All the courts held that on his return the husband was bound to pay the herdboy his wages. Similarly it would seem that where the wife engages in work that brings in money to the household the husband cannot object[2] unless the employment amounts to constructive abduction or could redound in the husband being held liable for his wife's wrongs or to his discredit.[3] Perhaps again the true test is the reasonableness of the act. The 'Restatement' thus declares that she may stand in for her husband in share-cropping agreements, hiring transport, letting out oxen and ploughs and the services of the children, and the acquisition of necessaries for the support of herself and her children.[4]

4. A HUSBAND'S LIABILITY FOR HIS WIFE'S DELICTS

A husband is liable in respect of delicts committed by his wife because for this purpose she is regarded as a minor.[5] Thus in *Sekoboto* v. *Possa*[6] a husband was held liable for his wife's assault and in *Mohlomi* v. *Mokhutsoane*[7] for her defamatory statements.

5. 'LOCUS STANDI IN JUDICIO'

A wife does not have *locus standi* to appear in court as plaintiff or defendant in actions where her husband (or, during his absence, a male relative) should properly be there in her stead, for instance in household matters where there is no dispute between the spouses. He it is who is the proper person to bring and defend actions relating to e.g. *bohali* in respect of their children's

---

[1] J.C. 252/1966.   [2] P.D., pp. 105–6.

[3] P.D., p. 106, where it was stated that brewing beer needed her husband's consent; but if it was not obtained what sanction would there be?

[4] At pp. 15–16. In *Mountain Trading Store* v. *Mathaba* J.C. 19/1967 it was held that necessaries purchased on credit by a wife without her husband's knowledge must be paid for by the husband even though he was available in Lesotho and could easily have been consulted before the account was opened (L.C. and J.C., *contra* C.C.).

[5] 'Restatement', p. 14.   [6] J.C. 74/1964 (all courts).

[7] J.C. 119/1964 (J.C.).

marriages, their stock and household effects, and delicts committed by or against members of the family.[1]

However, in four types of case she does have *locus standi*. First, in matrimonial disputes against her husband, for maintenance and divorce.[2] It seems she may also sue the head of her own family for maintenance during the period she has returned home (*ngala*-ed) in protest at her husband's ill-treatment.[3] However, one wife may not sue another whom she alleges is gaining too much of their husband's attention.[4]

Secondly, it seems from the Panel Discussion that a woman may perhaps have *locus standi* to sue in her own name in respect of her professional activities, e.g. if she was a herbalist and wished to claim payment for her services.[5] However, it may equally be argued that her husband is the administrator of the joint estate and thus he should bring the claim.

Thirdly, a wife may appear where her husband is unable to conduct the case through sickness or absence, and there is no male relative available to appear instead.[6] This is obviously necessary in cases of urgency where it is impossible to await the husband's return from abroad or recovery from illness.

Fourthly, a wife can be authorized by her husband to appear on his behalf, whether he is available or not.[7] However, in such cases the husband is the plaintiff and the action is brought or defended in his name. His wife merely appears as his representative[8] and he may still be called upon to give evidence in person.

[1] *Regency case* (1926–53) H.C.T.L.R. 50 at 57; *Malatela* v. *Sefale* J.C. 42/1961 (C.C. and J.C.); *Mountain Trading Store* v. *Mathaba* J.C. 19/1967 (J.C.); Duncan, pp. 6–7, quoting J.C. 34/1944 (P.C.'s Ct.); 'Restatement', p. 18.

[2] *Ncheke* v. *Ncheke* J.C. 262/1963 (C.C. and J.C.); *Ralenono* v. *Ralenono* J.C. 135/1966 (J.C.); 'Restatement', pp. 18–19; P.D., p. 103.

[3] *Machela* v. *Lethunya* J.C. 98/1968 (all courts).

[4] *Ncheke* v. *Ncheke* J.C. 262/1963 (C.C. and J.C.).

[5] P.D., p. 232.

[6] 'Restatement', pp. 13–14; P.D., p. 129.

[7] 'Restatement', p. 15; P.D., p. 104.

[8] '*Mutlanyana* v. *Mokhachane* J.C. 91/1964 (J.C. overruling lower courts).

14

THE FAMILY HEAD
AND HIS CHILDREN

1. LEGITIMACY

THE distinguishing feature of legitimacy is that it places a child
in the lineage of its mother's husband and it is his family that has
rights and duties in relation to the child. Illegitimate issue, on the
other hand, belong in the family of their mother's father or his
successor.

Before turning to the legal effects of this distinction the criterion
of legitimacy will be examined. It should, however, constantly
be borne in mind that one of the most significant practical aspects
of the whole question is the right of inheritance, and the decisive
factor here is often the collective view of the family rather than
any formal legal rule. The way in which legitimacy or illegitimacy
affects rights of succession and inheritance will be examined in
Chapter 17.

The valid marriage of its mother is the basic determinant of a
child's legitimacy. Provided that her marriage still subsists and
that she has not been divorced, all the children she bears will be
legitimate.[1] This applies not only to children fathered by her
husband, but also to children born of adultery.[2] As the Sesotho
maxim puts it, '*Mosali ea nyetsoeng ha a tsoale sekhaupane*' ('a
married woman has no bastard').

Since marriage almost invariably takes place with *bohali*, it is the
payment of the *bohali* that is commonly regarded as the determinant of legitimacy.[3] This is reflected in expressions such as
'*ngoana o tsoaloa ke khomo*' ('cattle beget children') and '*ngoana*

---

[1] P.D., pp. 136–7. This was also the view of seven of the nine district councils
at the 1952 National Council—see *1952 National Council Proceedings*, pp. 244,
248.

[2] *Tomotomo* v. *Mothae* J.C. 9/1963 (L.C. and J.C.); *Molapo* v. *Molapo*
H.C. Civ./A/8/1973 (J.C.); P.D., pp. 118, 136.

[3] P.D., pp. 136, 151.

ke oa khomo' ('the child belongs to the beast'). *Bohali* can be seen as operating to confer legitimacy upon the children in the sense that it is a necessary element of virtually all marriages and it is a valid marriage, and not paternity, which confers legitimacy.

Traditionally a woman was regarded as married even after the death of her husband and in some respects this remains true today. In the past she was expected to continue bearing children under the *kenelo* custom with her deceased husband's younger brother. Such children would naturally be considered legitimate and probably also issue fathered by other men, on the same principle as when her husband was still alive.[1]

In the recent High Court case of *Mothebesoane* v. *Mothebesoane*[2] the plaintiff had given birth to a son ten years after her late husband's death and the question arose whether he was entitled to be recognized as the deceased's heir. She had continued to live with her in-laws throughout this period but had not entered into a *kenelo* union. The court after noting that the deceased's father had always accepted the child as a member of his family and allowed it to be given his own name, upheld its claim to be the heir.

Pre-marital children are clearly illegitimate at their birth, even if their parents were already engaged at that time.[3] However, they may be legitimated by the subsequent marriage of their parents or even of their mother to another man.[4] The mother's later marriage to the father must occur quite often in practice and since it is a matter commonly kept private within the family no dispute usually arises. Nevertheless, there do seem to be some specific formal rules concerning legitimation and if eventually there is litigation and such a child's status is challenged, the child

[1] *Sekake* v. *Tautona* J.C. 15/1959 (P.C.'s Ct. and J.C.). See also *1955 National Council Proceedings*, pp. 228–48. The nine district councils were asked whether a posthumous son, not fathered by the chief, could succeed on the chief's death. Six of the districts held that he would succeed, regardless of whether the widow had been formally *kenela*-ed or not. One district was divided and another held that there had to be formal *kenelo*. Ramolefe (1969), p. 198 describes the children of *kenelo* as legitimate. The point seems to have escaped Lansdown J. in the *Regency case* (1926–53) H.C.T.L.R. 50 at 57.

[2] H.C. Civ./T/12/1970.

[3] Duncan, p. 30; P.D., pp. 137–43.

[4] Duncan, p. 30. In the Panel Discussion this seemed at times to be doubted by Bereng and Sehalahala (and by Molapo in the case of another man's child), but the general view was as stated here—see P.D., pp. 89–92, 137–43.

is likely to be declared illegitimate unless these formalities have been properly complied with.

The best known case on this point is *Motsoene* v. *Peete*.[1] The defendant was sued for compensation in respect of repeated abductions of the plaintiff's daughter by a young man called Thabo. Thabo was a pre-marital child of the defendant's wife who was taken with them at the time of their marriage and who spent the whole of his youth at the defendant's home. It appears that the defendant came to have doubts as to whether he had really fathered Thabo and he defended the present case on the basis that Thabo was not his child and therefore he was not responsible for his wrongful acts.

Both the Paramount Chief's Court and Duncan J.C. held that Thabo was illegitimate at birth and that there was no proof that he had ever been properly legitimated on the subsequent marriage of the defendant to Thabo's mother. The Judicial Commissioner held that the mere fact that Thabo had accompanied his mother on her marriage instead of being left at her parents' home was not conclusive. The essential requirements were that the two sets of parents should reach agreement on the future status of the child[2] and that this agreement should be given full family publicity[3] and not merely be a private arrangement. The payment of further cattle to 'marry' the child together with its mother was stated to be optional.[4] Duncan has also written that it is at the discretion of the mother's parents whether they permit the child to go with its mother.[5] Where it remains at home it is known as a *lesala lapeng*.

2 . CUSTODY

A single decision of the Judicial Commissioner's Court suggests

[1] J.C. 78A/1951, discussed in Duncan, p. 30 and in P.D., p. 140.

[2] So held also in *Mahamo* v. *Ramochele* J.C. 197/1964 (L.C. and J.C.); *Molise* v. *Theletsane* J.C. 103/1965 (C.C. and J.C.); *Mosoang* v. *Mosoang* J.C. 234/1966 (all courts). In this last case Thompson J.C. pointed out that the father's own senior relatives could not force him to agree to legitimate the child.

[3] See also *Mosoang* v. *Mosoang* J.C. 234/1966 (C.C. and J.C.); P.D., pp. 139–40.

[4] Restated in Duncan, p. 30. In *Mosoang* v. *Mosoang* J.C. 234/1966 the Salang Central Court seemed to regard it as compulsory, but the general impression gained from the Panel Discussion is that it is optional and depends on the bride's parents who would normally not ask for more *bohali*, at any rate where the husband is the father of the child—see P.D., pp. 89–91, 139–40.

[5] At p. 30, relying on *Matsatsi* v. *Kori* J.C. 173/1954 (J.C.).

that the right to custody of legitimate children does not inhere exclusively in the husband as head of the family but in husband and wife jointly.[1] This may be right and certainly if a wife complains of ill-treatment and returns to her parents' home taking her children with her, the husband will not be entitled to claim the recovery of his children without at the same time co-joining his wife so that her future position can be taken into account by the court.[2] Nor will the head of the wife's family be guilty of child-stealing under section 10 of Part II of the Laws of Lerotholi by simply receiving his daughter and her children at his home.[3] The husband must first call a family meeting and attempt a reconciliation with his wife before applying to the court to divest his wife of the children in divorce proceedings. The factors which the courts take into account in determining the destiny of the children are considered in Chapter 16.

However, where a child has been unlawfully removed from its guardian's custody the courts will order its immediate return.[4]

In the case of an illegitimate child the right to custody and guardianship is vested in the head of the mother's family[5] and he ultimately carries the responsibility for the maintenance and upbringing of the child.[6]

3. GENERAL RIGHTS AND DUTIES OF PARENTS AND GUARDIANS

Parents and guardians are obliged by law to support, protect, and maintain their children by feeding and clothing them and providing them with a home, but there is no legal obligation to send them to school.[7] In return the children can be required to perform various household services for their parents, and sons will often be called upon to herd cattle. Parents may punish their children

---

[1] *Mafale* v. *Khakahali* J.C. 80/1960 (J.C.).

[2] *Sekese* v. *Moshoeshoe* J.C. 23/1969 (C.C. and J.C.).

[3] *Mafale* v. *Khakahali* J.C. 80/1960 (J.C.).

[4] Duncan, p. 2, relying on *Samosamo* v. *Paulusi* J.C. 236/1951 (J.C.).

[5] *Masupha* v. *Rapopo* J.C. 22/1964 (J.C.); *Mahamo* v. *Ramochele* J.C. 197/1964 (L.C. and J.C.); *Ntebele* v. *Letsie* J.C. 110/1964 (L.C. and J.C.).

[6] P.D., p. 142. He is also liable for wrongs committeed—see *Cheoane* v. *Masokela* J.C. 87/1969 (C.C. and J.C.). He also has rights and duties in respect of the *bohali* payable on the child's marriage—see *Sekoto* v. *Kou* J.C. 70/1964 (all courts) and *Masupha* v. *Rapopo* J. C. 22/1964 (L.C. and J.C.) and pp. 134, 141 above.

[7] P.D., pp. 108–10. See also Ramolefe (1969), p. 198, to the same effect.

for their wrongdoings by administering moderate chastisement.[1]

Where a child is being neglected this will usually be noticed by a relative who should thereupon call together a family meeting in order to remind the parents of their responsibilities. If this fails to achieve any improvement in the situation action can be taken under the Deserted Wives and Children Proclamation which provides for a maintenance order to be made against a husband who has deserted his children in the same manner as where he has deserted his wife.[2]

4. BACHELORS, PROPERTY, AND THE ATTAINMENT OF MAJORITY

In traditional law bachelors could not own any property apart from a few personal effects because they were minors and whatever they acquired belonged to the head of the family.[3]

However, bachelors have been migrating to South Africa for employment for over a hundred years and although the correct procedure was, and in legal theory still is, for them to bring their earnings home and hand these over to their parents, this has met with growing resistance as a result of the pressures and habits of urban life.[4]

As Ashton observed in the 1930s,

Popular opinion in this matter is changing and unmarried men and women are now often allowed by their parents to keep private earnings and even their wages from continuous employment as domestic servants, school teachers and mineworkers. They may also own stock and be allocated land. . . . But this change has not yet achieved full legal recognition and if a father uses his unmarried child's property . . . without his or her consent the courts would support him in any action brought by the aggrieved person, provided the property was used for some legitimate family purpose. . . . For this reason some men working away from home do not remit their money to their parents for safe-keeping or investment in stock, but prefer to send it to a friend.[5]

An assessment of the present position reveals little change during the last forty years. The courts continue to emphasize the rights

---

[1] 'Restatement', p. 16.   [2] Proc. 60 of 1959, see pp. 171–2 above.
[3] The 'Restatement' (at p. 12) presents this as the modern position, but is too conservative.
[4] See P.D., p. 176.   [5] At pp. 178–9.

of a family head to the earnings of his minor children.[1] Property may be allocated to junior sons by their fathers directly or in-directly by allowing them to spend their earnings on purchases, but only subject to stringent safeguards. There is considerable authority to the effect that the allocation must receive full family publicity and that the prospective heir must be notified, and unless this can be clearly established such allocations are liable to be upset by the heir after the father's death.[2]

Secondly, the Judicial Commissioner has held that a bachelor who has handed over his earnings to his father has no claim after his marriage to recover any surplus remaining after the payment of his *bohali*.[3]

Thirdly, minors are denied *locus standi* on their own before the courts in civil cases[4] on the ground that since they own no property execution must be levied against the head of the family and this cannot be done unless he is made a party to the pro-ceedings.[5]

However, the pressures placed upon the conservative attitude of the courts are increasing. It is pointed out[6] that bachelors who are over twenty-one possess the vote,[7] they are bound to pay taxes,[8] they can succeed to the chieftainship,[9] and they are entitled to make contracts of employment (especially for migrant labour).[10] Further, they are sometimes allocated lands by the local headman although it is true that they do not have nearly as strong a claim as married men.[11] This is justified on the basis that if a bachelor has stock he must obviously have somewhere to keep his animals; if he has a concubine he needs a separate establishment from that

[1] *Seenzile* v. *Seenzile* J.C. 143/1961 (J.C.); *Chokobane* v. *Chokobane* J.C. 69/1966 (J.C.); and see P.D., p. 176. The frequent economic dependence of a father who is too old for migrant labour upon his sons' earnings must not be overlooked—see p. 25 above.

[2] See pp. 311–13 below.

[3] *Seenzile* v. *Seenzile* J.C. 143/1961 (J.C.).

[4] See Duncan, p. 3.

[5] *Kholu* v. *Nyenye* J.C. 191/1966 (J.C.).

[6] See e.g. P.D., pp. 175–9.

[7] 1966 Constitution, s. 43(2)(b).

[8] Basic and Graded Tax (Consolidation) Act, No. 24 of 1968, s. 2(1)(a).

[9] Chieftainship Act, No. 22 of 1968, s. 13(1). The present King, Moshoeshoe II, acceded to the Paramount Chieftainship at twenty-one while still unmarried.

[10] See pp. 22–3 above.

[11] Sheddick (1954), pp. 69, 164; P.D., pp. 204–5. Duncan (at p. 87) is probably too conservative in saying that this was only done for bachelor soldiers after the Second World War as a temporary expedient and has now died out.

of his parents; if he is young he can be useful to a chief in running errands and doing odd jobs;[1] furthermore, if he were not allotted any land he would be under even greater compunction to migrate in order to earn enough to pay his taxes and keep himself. However, despite this a motion before the National Council in 1947 that bachelors over the age of twenty-one should receive at least one field was defeated, albeit by a narrow margin.[2]

Taking all this into account it hardly seems apt to continue to regard all bachelors as minor children under the control of their parents, especially those over twenty-one.

In the context of judicial proceedings it has been contended that the customary rule that majority is only attained upon marriage cannot continue to be applied by the courts for two reasons. First, because it is inconsistent with the Age of Majority Ordinance[3] which provides that '. . . all persons when they shall attain . . . the full age of twenty-one years shall be deemed to have attained the legal age of majority'. And secondly because it is 'repugnant to justice and morality' in terms of the statutory provision permitting Sesotho law to be administered in the Basotho Courts.[4]

However, the Age of Majority Ordinance has been declared inapplicable by the Judicial Commissioner's Court on at least two occasions[5] and it is quite apparent that the Basotho Courts are completely oblivious of its very existence. The Ordinance was one of the Cape Colonial statutes imported into Basutoland in 1884 and it is clear from the wording of the General Law Proclamation[6] that such statutes can only be administered subject to the condition that the circumstances of the country permit their operation. Palmer has explained the origin of the Ordinance as follows:[7]

The received statute had itself been enacted in the Cape in 1829 in order to reduce the age of majority prescribed at Roman Dutch common law (twenty-five years) to twenty-one years. In my view the reason for

[1] P.D., pp. 204–5.
[2] See *1947 National Council Proceedings*, pp. 69–74 (by 43 votes to 40).
[3] Ordinance 62 of 1829.
[4] See pp. 55–60 above.
[5] *Chaule v. Makae* J.C. 166/1963; *Mopeli v. Rathebe* J.C. 238/1964.
[6] Proc. 2B of 1884, s. 2.
[7] *The Roman–Dutch and Sesotho Law of Delict*, p. 74.

the reception of the identical statute in Basutoland basically coincided with this original statutory intent, namely to alter the received Roman–Dutch common law and thereby to create a uniform age of majority for those subject to Roman-Dutch law, both in Basutoland and in the Cape. . . . Essentially European, the statute was designed to remedy a mischief of the Roman-Dutch law. Despite its apparently universal terms, the statute has never been thought, even in the Cape itself, to have modified customary law.

He concludes that Sesotho law continues to subsist unscathed by the Ordinance.[1] The only difficulty with this interpretation is that in 1877, during the period of annexation to the Cape, a regulation in the same terms as the Age of Majority Ordinance was introduced by the colonial administration directed specifically at the Basotho rather than at the Europeans.[2] When the Ordinance was made applicable to Basutoland in 1884 it was no doubt seen as merely continuing in force an existing provision whose intention had been to override the customary law. However, despite this, it has always been a dead letter so far as the courts are concerned in relation to those Basotho leading a customary mode of life.

Quite apart from this inappropriateness for such people, the fact that the Local and Central Courts have not been empowered to administer it would seem to militate against its extended operation. So many family disputes which come before the customary courts turn on the personal status of one of the parties that it cannot be imagined that the intention was to place these courts constantly in the dilemma of having to say that on the one hand they cannot apply the customary rule of majority because of the Ordinance and on the other that they cannot apply the Ordinance because they have no jurisdiction to do so.

The Judicial Commissioner has also rightly pointed out that if bachelors did attain their majority at twenty-one this would mean that their fathers would be absolved from the responsibility of paying *bohali* on their subsequent marriage.[3] This debt, like any other, would fall upon the husband himself since he would

---

[1] The same view was expressed by the present writer in Palmer and Poulter, p. 203.

[2] See Proc. 41 of 1887.

[3] See *Hlake* v. *Monare* J.C. 70/1969.

already be an adult with full property and contract rights of his own.

On the question of repugnancy to justice the decisions are not entirely consistent. In *Nako* v. *Nako*[1] the plaintiff widow who was the head of the family claimed that the defendant, her bachelor stepson aged thirty, should hand over his earnings to her so that she could pay his debts and the *bohali* for his marriage. Driver J.C. overruled both the lower courts which had given judgment in the plaintiff's favour, and held that the defendant was entitled to retain his earnings and was now responsible for his own debts. The ground for the decision was that to treat such a man as a minor was contrary to justice.

It is submitted that this decision is a further inappropriate application of the repugnancy clause because the rule is an entirely rational one in the context of the reciprocal rights and duties which bind together a family head and his minor sons. To remove only one part of the structure is to render what remains meaningless and anomalous. Furthermore the decision is inconsistent with a whole line of judgments from other Judicial Commissioners on the point.[2]

5. VICARIOUS RESPONSIBILITY FOR THE DELICTS OF MINORS

In the same way that the courts have been generally reluctant to take account of modern developments in relation to the property rights of bachelors, they have been equally loath to interfere with the traditional rule that because the head of the family was the only adult[3] he was automatically liable for the wrongs of his minor children and dependants. In the distant past this may even have extended to the imposition of punishments upon fathers in respect of crimes committed by their sons,[4] but the higher courts have declared this aspect of the practice repugnant to justice, and rightly so because of the stigma attaching to a conviction.[5]

[1] J.C. 141/1949.

[2] See e.g. *Kokota* v. *Kokota* J.C. 374/1947; *Seenzile* v. *Seenzile* J.C. 143/1961; *Chokobane* v. *Chokobane* J.C. 69/1966.

[3] Ellenberger and Macgregor, p. 268; Duncan, p. 3.

[4] But the Judicial Commissioner reached the conclusion in *Malefane* v. *Court of Morija* J.C. 264/1947 that this was not true Sesotho custom.

[5] *Malefane* v. *Court of Morija* J.C. 264/1947 (J.C. quashing fine imposed for attempted rape) (the same case is referred to *sub nom. Libothe* v. *R.* in Duncan, p. 3); *Ntsibi* v. *Goliath* J.C. 415/1956 (J.C. quashing fine imposed for setting grass on fire) cited in Duncan, p. 103.

The principle of vicarious liability was incorporated in the original version of the Laws of Lerotholi in 1903 and the modern version provides in section 6 of Part I:

No African shall be liable for a wrongful act or debt of his adult relative or friend, but the head of a family may be held liable for a wrongful act or debt of his minor children (i.e. unmarried children living in his house and under his control).

On this basis fathers have been held responsible to pay compensation for the delicts of their minor children in a variety of cases, particularly for seductions and abductions of girls committed by their sons.[1]

The principle of vicarious liability for delicts of minor children has come under increasing criticism over the years particularly from parents of sons who are over twenty-one and who have been leading relatively independent lives. Motions in the National Council proposing that bachelors over a certain age should bear responsibility for their own wrongs go back at least as far as 1923[2] and it has even been suggested there that delinquent bachelors should be forced to go and work in South Africa to pay damages for their wrongs and that their wages should be attached at the mines for this purpose.[3]

In the old days the principle of a father's responsibility to pay compensation for his son's wrongs and *bohali* upon his marriage was delicately balanced against his son's obligation to render services to the family and increase the prosperity of the household by handing over whatever property or income he acquired. With the freedom and independence conferred upon sons by the opportunities of earning cash wages in South Africa this harmony became distorted. However, one might have expected that the courts would restore the equilibrium by a careful interpretation

[1] See e.g. *Phakisi* v. *Makoa* J.C. 196/1953 (all courts; seduction); *Molefe* v. *O'Brien* J.C. 113/1964 (J.C.; negligence); *Mopeli* v. *Rathebe* J.C. 238/1964 (all courts; abduction); *Makhooane* v. *Ntatloe* J.C. 181/1965 (all courts); *Rannehela* v. *Pharoli* J.C. 80/1966 (J.C.; damage to property); *Phanyane* v. *Mohlalefi* J.C. 156/1966 (L.C. and J.C.; assault); *Ramaipato* v. *Rantho* J.C. 221/1967 (all courts); *Motsoane* v. *Noosi* J.C. 34/1969 (all courts; abduction); *Hlake* v. *Monare* J.C. 70/1969 (all courts).

[2] *1923 National Council Proceedings*. The motion was defeated as were similar motions in 1944 and 1952—see *1944 National Council Proceedings*, pp. 207–9, and *1952*, pp. 80–102.

[3] See *1938 National Council Proceedings*, p. 308; *1943*, pp. 81–2.

of section 6 of the Laws of Lerotholi. This provision expressly declares that the only minor children for whose wrongful acts a father is liable are those 'living in his house and under his control'. This wording afforded the courts an opportunity of distinguishing between a minor who genuinely fell within the clear meaning of those words and one who led a relatively independent life and kept his own earnings, perhaps even maintaining a separate establishment. Instead, in a long line of cases the Basotho Courts have unfortunately adopted a far too liberal construction of holding the father liable in every instance and this policy has been upheld by the Judicial Commissioner.[1] Thompson J.C. summarized the position recently in *Moseme* v. *Masiu*[2] by saying

In his house has been interpreted widely. A minor working far away still belongs to his home or father's house. As for control, the head of the family in legal theory is supposed to have such control over all the unmarried members of that family.

Moreover, this was a particularly strong case for a differentiation since the minor had been set up in his own separate business by the family head and he did not pass on his earnings.

The Judicial Commissioner further elaborated on his view in *Maqutu* v. *Hlapane*[3] as follows:

The father may have set his son up and given him assistance in starting life; that does not absolve the father from his liability for his son's delicts in the normal course of events. If the father does not get his son to assist him by surrendering some of his wages or by assisting his father it does not mean to say that the son is automatically a major in customary law.

Faced with such a rigid interpretation of section 6 defendants have sought to rely on a number of alternative contentions.

First, reliance has been placed on the express wording of the

---

[1] See e.g. *Chaule* v. *Makae* J.C. 166/1963 (all courts; son kept own wages); *Phanyane* v. *Mohlalefi* J.C. 156/1966 (L.C. and J.C.; daughter living with her maternal grandfather); *Motsoane* v. *Noosi* J.C. 34/1969 (all courts; son lived apart from father); *Cheoane* v. *Masokela* J.C. 87/1969 (C.C. and J.C.; son lived apart from father); *Moseme* v. *Masiu* J.C. 94/1969 (all courts).

[2] J.C. 94/1969.

[3] J.C. 32/1969. This point was not discussed when the case came before the High Court on appeal in Civ./A/1/1971.

Age of Majority Ordinance, but as we have seen this argument has met with no success whatever.

Secondly, in *Hlake* v. *Monare*[1] the defendant father sought to escape responsibility for his son's delict by applying for the case to be transferred to a subordinate court where principles of the common law could be applied, under which he would not be held liable. All the courts refused to allow the transfer, the Judicial Commissioner explaining that if a defendant were free to choose the forum in such a case the whole of Sesotho law would quickly become optional and there would be utter confusion.

Thirdly, it has been contended that the principle of a father's vicarious responsibility for his children's delicts is 'repugnant to justice and morality' and therefore unenforceable. This argument was summarily rejected by Thompson J.C. in the recent cases of *Mofae* v. *None*[2] and *Moseme* v. *Masiu*.[3]

The only crumbs of comfort held out by the Judicial Commissioner to fathers of wayward sons who do not marry and who continue to commit wrongs are that they have the legal right to claim their earnings[4] and, if that seems inappropriate in the circumstances, they are entitled as a last resort to disinherit or compulsorily emancipate their recalcitrant sons.[5] The latter course of action is said to require sufficient grounds and can only be valid if it takes place with family agreement and general publicity, including notification of the local chief or headman.[6] The idea seems to be that such emancipation should be made known to the general public and particularly the prospective injured plaintiff,[7] though this is surely an unrealistic expectation in modern conditions.

---

[1] J.C. 70/1969.   [2] J.C. 93/1967.   [3] J.C. 94/1969.

[4] *Seenzile* v. *Seenzile* J.C. 143/1961 and see p. 135 above.

[5] *Mofae* v. *None* J.C. 93/1967; *Hlake* v. *Monare* J.C. 70/1969; *Moseme* v. *Masiu* J.C. 94/1969. A similar point was made by the Nkuebe Central Court in *Thokoa* v. *Seliane* J.C. 111/1966 (C.C.), where President 'Mabathoana stated that if the minor refused to contribute his earnings the head of the family could go to court and obtain an absolution from further responsibility for the minor's wrongs. Ramolefe (1969), p. 198, also holds that an incorrigible ward can be disowned, so that his guardian will no longer be liable for his delicts, basing this presumably on the evidence of Chief Jobo to the 1872 Commission — see *1873 Report and Evidence*, p. 50.

[6] *Mofae* v. *None* J.C. 93/1967; *Hlake* v. *Monare* J.C. 70/1969; *Moseme* v. *Masiu* J.C. 94/1969. See also *Semoli* v. *Semoli* J.C. 159/1967 discussed at p. 240 below.

[7] *Maqutu* v. *Hlapane* J.C. 32/1969 (J.C.).

Whether such a right of absolving himself from liability is really available to a family head in Sesotho law is very much open to doubt. There are no known decisions on the point, merely a string of *obiter dicta* to this effect by Thompson J.C. Even if there were such a right it is submitted that its application by the courts would lead to far greater difficulties than are warranted by the present state of the law as recorded in section 6 of Part I of the Laws of Lerotholi. Such acts of emancipation would be challenged after the family head's death and the whole question of inheritance would be opened up for debate. Litigation would be fomented, whereas a proper application of section 6 to each case would provide much-needed finality.

It is my contention that the courts have missed an excellent opportunity of striking a golden mean between the competing interests of a family head and his bachelor sons in the difficult conditions of modern times. To hold fast to the traditional rule of vicarious liability regardless of the circumstances can only lead to unnecessary hardship for the family head in some cases and encourage irresponsible behaviour among some bachelors. On the other hand, to jettison the traditional rule completely by adopting the automatic attainment of majority at twenty-one is perhaps to go too fast in the opposite direction, for selfish fathers may be tempted to abandon their responsibilities to their children prematurely. What is probably needed is a compromise. Where the son has taken the initiative and begun to create an independent life for himself outside his father's household he should accept the obligations along with the benefits. Individual material advantages should carry with them the corresponding individual responsibilities.

As if the express provisions of section 6 were not clear enough guidance for the courts in defining the limits of the family head's liability, the National Council in 1952 gave even greater discretion to the courts by deciding that the Sesotho version declaring in mandatory terms that the family head 'shall' be liable was incorrect and that the word should be 'may' as in the English version.[1]

6. LIABILITY UNDER MINORS' CONTRACTS
Section 6 of Part I of the Laws of Lerotholi refers not only to a

---
[1] *1952 National Council Proceedings*, pp. 80–102.

wrongful act of a minor child but also to a debt, for which the family head may equally be held liable.

It seems that in strict legal theory a third party should not normally enter into a contract with a minor without the consent of the latter's family head.[1] However, such contracts are a common occurrence today, especially contracts of employment and ordinary purchases from shops and stores. In many cases a dispute would fall to be decided under the common law or a statutory provision because of the nature of the transaction,[2] but not to the complete exclusion of the customary law.

In *Phasumane* v. *Mohapi*[3] the plaintiff lent the defendant's minor daughter £100 and later sued for its recovery. The Local and Central Courts upheld the claim on the basis that the defendant knew of the loan. On appeal the decision was reversed by the Judicial Commissioner on the ground that the defendant was ignorant of the loan. He held that where the family head does not know of a loan to a minor under his control he can only be held liable on it if it was made for an essential purpose, e.g. to purchase food.

Apart from this case information is scanty on the subject, presumably partly because of the limited opportunities of contracting which were available to minors in traditional society and the fact that the common law rules have tended to be applied in modern situations.

Probably the family head should be held liable only where he has consented to the contract either expressly or impliedly or where he has obtained a benefit from the contract.

The minor, on the other hand, neither is liable nor can he claim rights under the contract. Where the minor has performed his part of the agreement his family head can probably claim some performance from the other side on the basis of unjust enrichment.

7. THE EMANCIPATION OF UNMARRIED WOMEN

Bearing in mind the degree of emphasis placed upon women's rights in Sesotho law it is hardly surprising that the law should recognize the possibility of an unmarried woman becoming emancipated from the control of her father or his heir.

[1] See P.D., pp. 107–8.
[2] For a discussion of criteria for the choice of law see Palmer and Poulter, pp. 135–54.
[3] J.C. 205/1964.

The leading case on the subject is *Monyake* v. *Monyake*[1] which concerned the position of a single woman who was a qualified nurse and had held the post of matron at Quthing Hospital. Her father had been the local headman before his death and he had allocated her a site on which she had built a house out of her earnings. After her father's death her brother disputed her right to the house and the argument turned to the question of whether the concept of female emancipation was known to Sesotho law. The relevant portion of the Judicial Commissioner's judgment is set out in full as it provides an excellent analysis of the problem.

I am assured by my assessor Chief Mabina Lerotholi that what we consider as emancipation under European law . . . is not identical with custom. He states that it is not a new procedure or that the custom is being varied in that women may own property, but from long ago when a woman passed the marriageable age and remained unmarried she could not be expected to live and sleep in the same hut with other children but was given a room or building of her own. She was not only given a house but also a *serapa* (small land) on which to live so that if she had illegitimate children she should maintain herself and them on this *serapa*. He further goes on to state that a father even went to the extent of earmarking a beast for his daughter and that any money she may earn remains her own property. The only difference is that she has to consult her parents in all she does. This advice on custom has been given to this court on prior occasions. I cannot now refer to similar cases . . . but I know of cases where girls returned to their homes from the villages of their husbands and were allotted lands at their homes to live on. There have been cases before this court where girls were actually allotted houses to live in. On the advice I have received from my assessor and the experience I have obtained as President of this Court, unmarried girls are entitled to own property.

This view was endorsed at the Panel Discussion[2] where it was stated that to be emancipated a woman must have left her parents' home, be leading a modern type of life and be doing a career job suitable for an educated person.[3] She could hold land in her own right as well as other property and could sue and be sued in her own name in the Basotho Courts.[4]

However, it seems very much open to doubt whether the status of a *feme sole* possessing such extensive rights is limited

[1] J.C. 293/1953.   [2] P.D., pp. 155–6.
[3] P.D., pp. 237–8.   [4] P.D., pp. 238–9.

to a small educated section of the community living in the modern sector. Thus in two cases decided since *Monyake* v. *Monyake* the courts have allowed unmarried women to claim *bohali* on the marriages of their illegitimate daughters without proof of education or career. In *Paneng* v. *Paneng*[1] the plaintiff had been expelled from her parents' home and neglected by her family for twenty years during which time she had been working to support herself and her daughter. The Local Court held that her father's heir, as head of the family, was entitled to the *bohali* despite this, but was overruled by the Central Court and the Judicial Commissioner's Court. The latter held that she had been emancipated simply by the expulsion and long period of neglect.

More recently in *Nkoko* v. *Cheli*[2] an unmarried mother was also successful in a situation in which she seemed to have no male relatives still alive, and it was held that she did not need any assistance in conducting her case in court.

The Panel was of the opinion that unmarried women who had means could be allocated land, more especially where they had illegitimate children, but there was disagreement on whether the allocation would be made to the woman herself or to her guardian on her behalf.[3] Sheddick states categorically that while she may be granted a residential title directly, an unmarried woman can never claim rights to arable fields and grazing,[4] but Duncan takes the opposite view.[5]

[1] J.C. 111/1957.
[2] J.C. 272/1966 (C.C. and J.C.).
[3] P.D., pp. 206–8.
[4] (1954), p. 164.
[5] At p. 87.

15

NGALA

As will be seen, divorce has always been rare among the Basotho and there are three likely explanations for this state of affairs. The *bohali* is often required to be refunded and this must provide a disincentive to some extent. Further, where a man is attracted by another woman he may marry her as a second wife without divorcing his first wife. In any event extra-marital sexual relations on the part of husbands and wives do not seem to be frowned upon to any great extent and certainly do not always lead to divorce. Thirdly, the low divorce rate must also be due in part to the importance the Basotho attach to the maintenance of the marriage bond and the mechanisms that exist to safeguard it.

One of these mechanisms is the *ngala* custom which operates to resolve marital difficulties and protect a wife against ill-treatment by her husband, particularly where she has failed to get satisfaction from him or his relatives after making a complaint.

Its original form was described by George Moshoeshoe in his evidence to the 1872 Commission.[1]

If a woman is ill-treated by her husband she has the protection of her parents and relatives to whom she can fly, and if the case of ill-treatment by the husband is proved he will have to pay a fine before his wife is returned to him.

After the wife has *ngala*-ed her husband should go to his parents-in-law and seek her return.[2] They have a duty to try to effect a reconciliation[3] and it may even be necessary for a meeting with representatives from both families to be summoned. Where the husband has been in the wrong he must undertake to mend his ways in future if he is to be entitled to the return of his wife. He

[1] *1873 Report and Evidence*, p. 40.
[2] *Makhooane v. Makhooane* J.C. 43/1956 (J.C.); *Ralipoli v. Lephallo* J.C. 138/1960 (J.C.); P.D., p. 121.
[3] *Ralipoli v. Lephallo* J.C. 138/1960 (J.C.); *Mositoane v. Chabalala* J.C. 20/1963 (J.C.); *Lebesa v. Khotlele* J.C. 35/1967 (J.C.).

will probably be rebuked for his misconduct,[1] but the practice of exacting a fine has now disappeared.[2]

Where a wife *ngala*s she does not usually intend to desert her husband permanently or bring the marriage to an end. Rather, in most instances, she is applying pressure on him to treat her with greater love and respect. He must face a confrontation with her parents before he can get her back and inevitably suffers some loss of dignity in the process. There is, then, a sharp distinction between a situation in which a wife leaves her husband and returns home to her parents and one where she deliberately deserts him by going off to South Africa or to live with another man.[3]

The *ngala* custom is thus designed to lead to reconciliation and an improved relationship, but a wife's return home can equally indicate that the marriage is on the point of final collapse. She may be leaving her husband in circumstances that give her a right to divorce him. Alternatively her husband may have driven her out with a view to obtaining a divorce himself. Moreover, since Sesotho law permits divorce on the simple ground that the marriage has completely broken down, the wife's return to her parents may form part of the evidence of this very breakdown. Only by taking full account of such factual differences can seemingly inconsistent court decisions be satisfactorily explained. Some judgments may appear to suggest that it is only after a reconciliation has been attempted that a claim for divorce can be made,[4] but the true position is that it depends entirely on the circumstances of the individual case. Where only the flimsiest justification for a divorce is put forward the tendency of the courts will be to stress the need for a reconciliation if there appears to be any chance of this being successfully achieved.[5] On the other hand, where good reasons exist and the marriage has clearly broken down completely, a formal attempt to reconcile the spouses is not a prerequisite.[6]

---

[1] *Ranamane* v. *Ranamane* J.C. 172/1965 (L.C.).

[2] Duncan, p. 35.

[3] A point made during the *1932 National Council Proceedings*, p. 67; see also *Leboela* v. *Leboela* J.C. 5/1960 (J.C.).

[4] *Ralipoli* v. *Lephallo* J.C. 138/1960 (J.C.); *Mositoane* v. *Chabalala* J.C. 20/1963 (J.C.).

[5] *Leboela* v. *Leboela* J.C. 5/1960 (C.C. and J.C.; L.C. considered there were grounds for divorce and no family meeting was necessary); *Mokatja* v. *Mokatja* J.C. 211/1968 (all courts).

[6] *Ranamane* v. *Ranamane* J.C. 172/1965 (L.C.); *Rantsane* v. *Rantsane* J.C. 140/1967 (all courts).

In any event it does not seem as if the mere fact that the wife is not followed to her parents' home for a long time will give rise to an automatic dissolution; the proper formalities of divorce must be gone through.[1]

It is necessary at this stage to draw attention to an important distinction between the granting of a divorce and the restoration of the *bohali*. We have seen that the payment of *bohali* is an integral part of practically all marriages. There is no corollary, however, that the restoration of *bohali* is a *sine qua non* for divorce, although, as will be shown, there have been some misapprehensions on this question as a result of false comparisons drawn with the situation in South Africa.[2] The position in Lesotho is set out in the next chapter, but it is appropriate at this point to mention that a very relevant consideration in determining whether a husband can obtain the return of *bohali* on divorce is whether or not an attempt at reconciliation has been made.

As the Judicial Commissioner explained in *Pulumo* v. *Mofephe*,[3]

. . . there are many previous judgments of this court to the effect that a [*bohali*] holder cannot be divested of his [*bohali*] unless he is in some way put in the wrong. A husband who is deserted, if he is going to follow custom correctly and obtain a refund of the [*bohali*] . . . must follow his wife to the home of his parents-in-law . . . If he had sought the assistance of his father-in-law to recover his wife [and] if his father-in-law had failed to help him, then the father-in-law would be bound to return the [*bohali*] cattle . . . [*Bohali*] is no guarantee of a wife's faithfulness nor a guarantee against her desertion. If [her] parents fail to exercise their good offices to effect a reunion when the husband asks them for help then they put the [*bohali*] cattle at risk and render the [*bohali*] holder liable to restore the [*bohali*]. A wife's fault in itself is no cause for restoration of [*bohali*] until the parents are put in the wrong too. . . .

The limits of this doctrine must now be examined. Unless the husband's conduct has been so bad as to justify the wife in obtaining a divorce, it would seem that what is expected of her father is more than just a vague attempt to persuade her to return

---

[1] See P.D., pp. 121–2.
[2] See pp. 304–5 below.
[3] J.C. 25/1960; see also *Mothepu* v. *Ferene* J.C. 31/1961 (J.C.); *Tsosane* v. *Makhoabenyane* J.C. 108/1965 (J.C., *contra* L.C.); *Mojapela* v. *Nkibane* J.C. 305/1966 (J.C.); *September* v. *Monyamane* J.C. 250/1966 (J.C.).

to her husband if he is not to be forced to return the *bohali* in appropriate circumstances.[1] Provided the husband has shown a genuine desire to maintain the marriage by following his wife and a readiness to treat her properly in future, the presumption is that the *bohali*-holder should have no difficulty in inducing her to return. Assuming that he has had an opportunity of communicating with her and that she has not by-passed her parents' home completely[2] he must generally succeed in sending her back if he is not to be regarded as at fault.

Sometimes the Basotho Courts have ordered a wife who has *ngala*-ed to return to her husband,[3] but the Judicial Commissioner has held that such an order, being unenforceable in itself, must be coupled with an alternative of divorce,[4] rather along the lines of the Roman–Dutch law concept of an order for the restitution of conjugal rights. In doing so he relies on the following statement of George Moshoeshoe to the 1872 Commission.[5]

If a woman refuses to live with her husband there is no law to compel her to do so, and the only remedy the husband has is to demand that his cattle . . . be restored to him.

If the wife fails to return within a reasonable period of time after such an order then the husband should not be ordered to readmit his wife to the matrimonial home because of the difficulty of enforcement and the likelihood of violence.[6] Again, the remedy ultimately lies in obtaining a divorce if a reconciliation proves impossible.

---

[1] These circumstances are discussed in Ch. 16 below.

[2] See P.D., pp. 134–5.

[3] *Ralipoli* v. *Lephallo* J.C. 138/1960 (L.C. and C.C.).

[4] *Ralipoli* v. *Lephallo* J.C. 138/1960 (J.C.); *Ralekabu* v. *Lelimo* J.C. 216/1969 (J.C.); see also Duncan, pp. 35–6.

[5] *1873 Report and Evidence*, p. 40.

[6] *Mokhutsoane* v. *Mokhutsoane* J.C. 73/1961 (J.C. overruling lower courts).

16

DIVORCE

1. EXTENT OF DIVORCE

DIVORCE seems to have been recognized from earliest times, but was at first so infrequent[1] that the view is sometimes expressed today that it only started with the introduction of the common law, and that Sesotho law had to adapt itself to encompass this new concept.[2] However, a sharp impetus was certainly given to the practice in the middle of the nineteenth century by the rules of the Paris Evangelical Missionary Society requiring a polygamist, upon the occasion of his conversion to Christianity, to put away all his wives except one.[3]

An idea of the rate of divorce over the past sixty years, as it appears from the official census reports, is given in Table 10. Two important reservations should, however, be noted about the accuracy of the figures. First, the 1966 figure includes 'separated persons' while for the other years there is no indication whether such people were included or not. No discrete category of separated persons appears in the earlier reports and these people may have classified themselves either as married or as divorced in their responses. Secondly, none of the census figures indicates whether the marriages in question were by civil or customary rites and thus the number of divorces from Sesotho marriages cannot be quantified.

If these deficiencies are borne in mind, the figures do suggest that the divorce rate is increasing.

---

[1] Ellenberger and Macgregor, p. 269; *1947 National Council Proceedings*, p. 101 (statement by Paramount Chief's representative).

[2] 'Restatement', p. 20; P.D., p. 130.

[3] See pp. 66–7 above.

TABLE 10

Number of Basotho divorcees, 1911–66

Year	Divorced persons			Percentage of total de
	Men	*Women*	*Total*	facto *population*
1911	3	8	11	0·0027
1921	339	1,932	2,271	0·46
1936	720	2,341	3,061	0·55
1946	917	2,216	3,133	0·56
1956		no statistics available		
1966	3,410	7,037	10,447	1·22

2. FORMALITIES OF DIVORCE

Two questions which have generated particular controversy concern the method by which a divorce may be obtained. The first is whether the return of *bohali* is a *sine qua non* for a valid divorce, and the second whether a divorce must of necessity be granted by a court of law. The former issue was actively debated a hundred years ago and the latter is still the subject of dispute.

(a) *Must the* Bohali *be Returned?*

In 1872 a lively exchange of correspondence took place between Griffith, the Governor's Agent, and the Revds. Casalis and Mabille of the Paris Evangelical Missionary Society over the guardianship of the children of one Pauluse Matete. Matete, a polygamist, had been converted to Christianity and abiding by the rules of the church he had given all his wives, save one, letters of divorce. He was thus following the example set by Moshoeshoe I when some of his wives became Christians.[1] On Matete's death his children by these former wives were claimed by his heir and this claim brought a strong reaction from the church. The dispute came before Griffith in his capacity as Chief Magistrate, and Mabille made representations to him by letter. In his reply Griffith summed up the legal position, as he saw it, as follows:[2]

As to Matete's writings of divorce which he gave to his two wives, they may have held perfectly good, simply as between himself and the two women; but neither in Sesuto nor in English law can they be regarded as anything more than a private mutual agreement by consent

[1] See pp. 66–7 above.
[2] Letter dated 29 July 1872, reprinted in *1873 Report and Evidence*, p. 22.

of parties. They could not give Maphoka and Masekwai the right to marry again. For by Sesuto law it would have been necessary that simultaneously with Matete's giving his wives letters of divorce, the cattle which he gave for them in marriage should have been restored to him. Then, and then only, could the divorce have been declared complete (in Sesuto law), and the wives could have married again, and their children by Matete would no longer have been his property or that of his heirs.

Casalis countered on behalf of the P.E.M.S., relying on his own long experience.[1]

We believe, sir, that it will not be difficult for us, even now, nearly thirty years after these letters were given, to obtain satisfactory proof that the cattle paid as [*bohali*] were not returned, and yet these divorces were held legal in the eyes of the Basutos, and that women furnished with them did re-marry. If, therefore, in olden times, it was even true that there was by Basuto custom an impossibility to obtain a divorce without restitution of cattle, what we have here said abundantly proves that for thirty years the custom of divorcing and giving permission to re-marry without restoration of [*bohali*] by the family has been established.

He went on:

. . . we still deny that by heathen Sesuto custom it was a *sine qua non* that cattle should be returned. When the relations of a woman wished to obtain possession of such woman and all her children, the cattle were returned as a custom. But frequently one or two girls were left to the husband and considered sufficient compensation in lieu of the cattle. If the husband sent away the woman or 'threw her away' he lost his right to the cattle, but he could retain some or all of his children.

Casalis's view was vindicated only eight weeks later when George and Sofonia Moshoeshoe and also the new Paramount Chief, Letsie I, all gave evidence to the 1872 Commission (of which Griffith was the chairman) indicating that divorces could validly occur without the restoration of *bohali*.[2]

Since then the courts have occasionally still held the return of *bohali* to be necessary,[3] usually in cases concerning the remarriage of widows[4] and these judgments are subjected to criticism in

[1] Letter dated 1 Oct. 1872, reprinted in *1873 Report and Evidence*, p. 27.
[2] Ibid., pp. 40–1, 44.
[3] See e.g. *Sekhonyana* v. *Letuka* J.C. 46/1953 (J.C.) quoted in Duncan, p. 39.
[4] See e.g. *Molapo* v. *Mahooana* (1926–53) H.C.T.L.R. 309 (H.C.); *Noosi* v. *Mohapi* J.C. 70/1957 (J.C.).

Chapter 18 as being based on a false comparison with South
African law.[1] In any event Griffith's contention has become completely untenable since the enactment of section 34(5) of Part II
of the Laws of Lerotholi which gives the courts a discretion as to
what order they make with respect to the *bohali*.

The true position is and always has been that the right to a
return of the *bohali* hinges upon the allocation of responsibility for
the breakdown of the marriage and the decision about the custody
of the children. These questions are examined further below.

(b) *Must the Divorce take place in Court?*

The traditional position, as he saw it, was described by Casalis
in his letter to Griffith in 1872 as follows:[2]

To break these marriages, there was no civil process before a native
tribunal required; the matter was generally very simple and private.
The man had the right to do as he judged best for himself, or, at any
rate, if his family were called in, they did all that was needed, without
reference to chiefs. Of course the chiefs, especially those of the present
day, would wish every case, relating even to family arrangement, to
pass through their hands, and they may pretend such and such forms
are required to give legality to any step. This would greatly add to
their importance, and give them a far greater power over the people; but
such is not Sesuto custom.

It is not surprising therefore to find that Chief Maama in his
evidence to the South African Native Affairs Commission stated
that all divorces did have to be taken to the chiefs' courts.[3]

It will be recalled that under the 1938 administrative and
judicial reforms the chiefs' courts were replaced by statutorily
constituted Native Courts, the precursors of the present Central
and Local Courts. Although these new courts were granted jurisdiction to hear cases in connection with Sesotho marriages including *bohali* questions, nothing was expressly said about divorce.[4]

The clearest judicial statement that divorces can only be granted
by the courts is to be found in the judgment of the High Court in

---

[1] See below, pp. 304–5.
[2] Letter dated 1 Oct. 1872, reprinted in *1873 Report and Evidence*, p. 27.
[3] Vol. iv (1904), pp. 391–2.
[4] Central and Local Courts Proclamation, s. 8(1).

Motsoene v. *Harding*[1] in 1940 where Huggard C.J. after hearing the evidence of witnesses declared:

Chief Molise states that there can be no legal divorce without an order of court, and I am satisfied that this is correct.

More recently, further uncertainty seems to have resulted from the loose wording of section 34(4) of Part II of the Laws of Lerotholi, which was introduced in 1951. It provides that dissolution of a marriage 'may' be granted by Basotho Courts. Whereas in *Mpoke* v. *Selohlanye*[2] in 1952 Duncan J.C. declared that extra-judicial divorce was possible if it took the form of a family agreement, during 1961–3 Thompson J.C. held on at least three occasions that in view of the wording of the section divorces could only be granted by the courts.[3] However, in *Kobefo* v. *Kobefo*[4] late in 1963 Thompson J.C. did a complete volte-face and held that it was not necessary to go to court after all.[5]

The 'Restatement' makes it very clear that it regards divorces arranged and agreed upon by the spouses' parents as just as valid as judicial decrees,[6] and the members of the Panel Discussion were, after some debate, also of the same opinion.[7] In such divorces it seems that both sets of parents ought strictly to be involved in the arrangement,[8] but perhaps it is sufficient for only the woman's parents to be parties. They inevitably need to be brought in because of the repercussions of the divorce upon the guardianship of their daughter and her children and upon the *bohali*.

Furthermore, wide publicity must be given to the event.[9] For this reason it will be usual to call in the local chief or headman as a witness in case there is a dispute later on.[10] Ashton has drawn attention to the difficulty of getting the necessary family agreement on the contentious issues of the *bohali* and the children and has

---

[1] Owing to an oversight the case was not reported until (1954) H.C.T.L.R. 1. A contrary viewpoint is, however, implicit in the judgment of de Beer J. barely six years later in *Sempe* v. *Tsepo* H.C.8/1946.

[2] J.C. 5/1952.

[3] *Mokonyana* v. *Motumi* J.C. 102/1961; *Khakahali* v. *Mafale* J.C. 116/1961; *Lekhanya* v. *Mongalo* J.C. 179/1963. See also *Makhakhe* v. *Makhakhe* J.C. 7/1963 (L.C.).

[4] J.C. 259/1963.

[5] See also now *Mothea* v. *Mothea* H.C. Civ./A/7/1974 (J.C. and H.C.).

[6] At p. 21.   [7] P.D., pp. 123–7.   [8] P.D., pp. 127–8.   [9] P.D., pp. 127–8.

[10] Information provided by Mr. John Perry (private communication).

suggested that in practice nearly all divorces do go before the courts.[1] This is probably true and in any event the courts certainly provide a wife with a safeguard against any parental veto on divorce.

3. JUSTIFICATIONS FOR DIVORCE

(a) *Reconciliation and the Recognition of the Need for Divorce if the Marriage has Totally Broken Down*

Investigation into the grounds for divorce recognized in Sesotho law reveals little or no consensus of opinion. Probably the reason for this is that traditional law was not concerned to specify particular 'grounds' for divorce. Although the Basotho were opposed to the notion of divorce and concentrated their efforts on reconciling estranged spouses,[2] they did permit husbands to throw away their wives[3] and wives to repudiate their husbands, being realistic enough to appreciate that there was no point in refusing a divorce in a situation where the marriage had broken down completely and where attempts at reconciliation had become utterly futile. This approach has carried through to the present day and is admirably summarized in three judicial pronouncements since 1960.

In *Peete* v. *Peete*[4] the Bela Bela Local Court in granting a divorce declared:

. . . where love has come to an end between man and woman or both of them no one or no group of people can reawaken such love.

The same theme is apparent from the judgment of the President of the Mapoteng Local Court in *Kubu* v. *Kubu*.[5]

. . . I would like to indicate that . . . even if there are no reasons, if only one of the married persons does no longer desire to stay with the other, and as long as no mention is made about the return of the *bohali* cattle, such a marriage is bound to be dissolved.

In *Ralenono* v. *Ralenono*[6] the Judicial Commissioner granted a divorce and declared:

[1] At p. 87. [2] See Ashton, p. 85. [3] See Casalis, p. 184.
[4] C.C. 21/1960. [5] J.C. 26/1965.
[6] J.C. 135/1966; see also *Abram* v. *Abram* J.C. 148/1960 (J.C.); *Moalosi* v. *Moalosi* J.C. 124/1963 (C.C. and J.C.; *contra* L.C.); *Khatseane* v. *Khatseane* J.C. 46/1964 (L.C. and J.C.).

What is absolutely clear, be it the one or the other being in the right or wrong, is that the marriage cannot subsist. There is no hope of success in the future.

However, it should be stressed again that the emphasis has always been, and continues to be, concentrated initially on an attempt to save the marriage by a process of reconciliation. Recent decisions of the courts tend at first sight to convey an impression of inconsistency, sometimes granting and at other times refusing divorces on what appear to be similar facts. This may be explained partly by differences in family situations which are apparent to the judge who actually hears the witnesses and partly also by the individual court president's attitude towards divorce.

In the light of the general desire for the marriage bond not to be too lightly broken it seems appropriate to refer to a notable judgment handed down by the Leribe Local Court in 1951. In *Nkhasi* v. *Nkhasi*[2] the husband had initiated proceedings for a divorce on the grounds that his wife had gone to Johannesburg without consulting him, had been seen kissing a man, had fought with him and bitten his finger, had broken a window in their house, and had incurred debts without his permission. The wife defending, pointed to her husband's neglect which had caused her to leave him. The marriage had subsisted for twenty-five years and none of the courts was prepared to grant a decree of divorce. The court of first instance stated its reasons as follows:

The court [does] not find any reason why it should dissolve elderly persons like you who should lead an exemplary life . . . who I understand . . . are to have a daughter-in-law whom they are to give moral instructions about living with [their] son till death. Remember you, Mansel and Makeretsoane that the reasons produced before the court are not sufficient for this court to dissolve the marriage. . . . The judgment of this court is: go and keep peace in your house and give [a] good example to your children.

Similar cases are to be found of quarrels between husband and wife which have led one or other to institute proceedings for a divorce, but where the divorce has been refused on the ground that there should first be an attempt at reconciliation by the two families. In *Mohale* v. *Mohale*[1] the husband claimed a dissolution

---

[1] J.C. 241/1953.   [2] J.C. 248/1966 (all courts).

of his marriage mainly on the ground that his wife was making life unpleasant for him by claiming that her eldest son was his heir, while he contended that he was not the true father of the child. The petition was refused.

In *Mokatja* v. *Mokatja*[1] the wife had *ngala*-ed to her parents saying that she no longer wished to live with her husband. All the courts held this was insufficient ground for granting her husband a divorce.

(b) *The Introduction of Section 34(4)*

In 1951 section 34(4) was added to Part II of the Laws of Lerotholi and this modern superimposition upon the basic structure must now be examined. The relevant part runs as follows:

Dissolution of marriage . . . may be granted by Native Courts on the application of either party on the grounds of the wilful desertion of the other party, or to the wife for the persistent cruelty or neglect of her husband or other cause recognised under Basuto Law and Custom.

The broad effect of this provision has recently been considered in the case of *Mothea* v. *Mothea*.[2] The plaintiff husband had brought an action for divorce on the grounds of his wife's adultery. His evidence, though slender, was accepted by the two Basotho Courts and the divorce was readily granted. On a further appeal, however, the Judicial Commissioner held that the alleged adultery had not been established and he refused the divorce. His decision was in turn upheld in the High Court. The significant point to emerge from the judgment of Thompson J.C.—endorsed to a large extent by the High Court—was the suggestion that whereas a divorce may be achieved extrajudicially by means of a family agreement on the basis of incompatability or simply because one spouse wishes it, a decree of dissolution should only be ordered by a court if proper 'grounds' can be established in terms of section 34(4). Here the plaintiff had failed to prove the ground he had sought to rely upon and his case could not therefore succeed in a court of law. Such an interpretation of section 34(4) is, of course, rather a narrow one in that it involves excluding from the construction of the word 'cause' those situations where all that can be shown is that the marriage relationship has totally broken

---

[1] J.C. 211/1968 (all courts).
[2] H.C. Civ./A/7/1974.

down. It is also inconsistent with the three judicial pronouncements quoted earlier.[1]

(i) *Wilful desertion*

Deliberate desertion was traditionally recognized as warranting divorce, for instance where husbands had deserted their wives in favour of other women living near by.[2] In recent years the courts have been prepared to grant divorces where wives had left their husbands either in favour of other men with whom they had borne adulterine children,[3] or by remaining at their parents' homes without just cause.[4] However, the main problem has arisen in relation to husbands (or more rarely wives) who have gone off to South Africa for long periods and lost contact with the spouse whom they left behind in Lesotho. It was concern in the National Council over this all-too-common situation which provided the main impetus for the introduction of section 34(4).[5]

Since the majority of Basotho men have long had to migrate to South Africa for extended periods of time in search of work and since their wives have usually been prohibited by South African legislation from accompanying them, the separation of spouses has always been regarded as a natural state of affairs in Lesotho. It was certainly not formerly treated as an adequate justification for divorce, however long the husband stayed away. One reason for this was probably the difficulty of determining easily at any given moment of time whether the husband was still engaged in waging the grim battle against exploitation, poverty, and oppression, with a view to bringing wealth home to his family, or whether he had really abandoned his wife. He was therefore given the benefit of the doubt and never held to be in legal desertion sufficient to justify his wife in obtaining a divorce.[6] The same applied in the reverse situation where the wife left her husband. Life was in each case rendered tolerable for the deserted spouse because he or she simply resorted to lovers, and husbands could, of course, always take

[1] A similar statement to these three was made by the Local Court in *Mothea's case*.
[2] Ashton, p. 86.
[3] See e.g. *Mphaki* v. *Mphaki* J.C. 39/1964 (L.C. and J.C.).
[4] See *Makara* v. *Mokobori* J.C. 164/1955 (J.C., *contra* C.C.) and *Tlelima* v. *Tiro* J.C. 71/1961 (all courts). Both decisions were endorsed by the Panel Discussion—see P.D., pp. 129–30.
[5] See *1947 National Council Proceedings*, pp. 94–102.
[6] Ashton, p. 86; Sheddick (1953), p. 39; P.D., p. 128.

additional wives if they so wished. A wife was not, however, free to remarry.[1] In any event, as already explained, she was regarded as married to her husband's family and not exclusively to him.

It is difficult to know whether the new section has had the effect of altering the law in this regard. A wife may still find it hard to obtain a divorce on the grounds of her husband's long sojourn abroad because she needs to establish that it amounts to wilful desertion. However, if she can establish the fact of his absence over a considerable number of years and that he does not intend to return to her, she must presumably succeed, and vice versa where the husband is the plaintiff.

(ii) *Cruelty and neglect*

The other grounds mentioned in section 34(4) are persistent cruelty and neglect on the part of the husband. Divorces have been granted to wives in a number of cases on these grounds, both where a husband has driven his wife away or failed to follow her when in desperation she has *ngala*-ed to her parents[2] and where she has managed to remain in her husband's home despite gross ill-treatment or neglect.[3] In many cases, of course, the faults are apparent on both sides.[4]

Cruelty naturally encompasses physical assaults on a wife, including beating her excessively as a punishment for wrongdoing.[5] Probably a husband is still permitted in theory to administer moderate physical chastisement to an errant wife,[6] but in practice, as a girl student reminded the male members of the Panel Discussion, 'Today they don't do it because we hit back'.[7]

(iii) *Adultery*

It is interesting to note two further points about section 34(4). First, it reflects a degree of uncertainty on the part of the draftsman

[1] Ashton, p. 86.
[2] See e.g. *Abram* v. *Abram* J.C. 148/1960 (all courts); *Kubu* v. *Kubu* J.C. 26/1965 (all courts); *Ralenono* v. *Ralenono* 135/1966 (L.C. and J.C.; *contra* C.C.); *Rantsane* v. *Rantsane* J.C. 140/1967 (all courts); '*Makolane* v. '*Makolane* J.C. 248/1968 (all courts); *Moahloli* v. *Moahloli* J.C. 52/1970 (L.C. and J.C.).
[3] *Likotsi* v. *Likotsi* J.C. 247/1966 (all courts).
[4] See e.g. *Matsepe* v. *Matsepe* J.C. 90/1956 (all courts); *Moalosi* v. *Moalosi* J.C. 124/1963 (C.C. and J.C.; *contra* L.C.); *Khatseane* v. *Khatseane* J.C. 46/1964 (L.C. and J.C.).
[5] P.D., p. 120.
[6] Ashton, p. 85; 'Restatement', p. 19; P.D., pp. 94–5.
[7] P.D., p. 95 (Bele).

as to exactly what grounds for divorce existed previously since he employed the vague words 'or other cause recognised under Basuto Law and Custom'. Secondly, these other causes appear from the wording of the section only to avail the wife. This seems unlikely to have been the draftsman's real intention and thus the provision must be criticized as rather ineptly phrased.

It is noticeable that adultery in particular was not mentioned in section 34(4). It was specified as a traditional ground for divorce by George and Sofonia Moshoeshoe in their evidence to the 1872 Commission,[1] but Ashton has referred to it as merely affording a husband the right to beat his wife and sue the adulterer for compensation.[2] During the Panel Discussion the view was expressed that only if the wife had repeatedly committed adultery could her husband have obtained a divorce under traditional law.[3] However, it was suggested that the modern customary law might be moving into line with the position under the Roman–Dutch common law,[4] where a single act of adultery amounts *per se* to a ground for divorce. So far as the husband's adultery is concerned the 'Restatement' does not even discuss it under the heading of divorce, but elsewhere rather unhelpfully declares:

She [the wife] cannot prevent her husband from marrying other women but promiscuity and brazen illicit unions with other women [are] not permitted.[5]

Perhaps such conduct merely affords the wife a ground for *ngala*-ing home to her parents.[6]

In the last analysis it would appear that adultery is just a factor to be taken into account by a court in determining whether a marriage has irretrievably broken down. Even here it does not seem to rank as a particularly significant factor. Probably the Judicial Commissioner was not far from the truth when he remarked in *Leboela* v. *Leboela*.[7]

. . . adultery does not constitute a ground for divorce in itself unless the accompanying conduct of the wife constituted a repudiation by her of the union.

---

[1] *1873 Report and Evidence*, pp. 41, 44. Sheddick (1953), p. 39, also mentions it as a ground.

[2] At p. 86.   [3] P.D., p. 113.   [4] P.D., pp. 117–19.   [5] At p. 12.

[6] Duncan (at p. 37) refers to *Ramathe* v. *Ramathe* P.C. 19/1949 where the P.C.'s Court did not grant a divorce for adultery because the wife had not *ngala*-ed.

[7] J.C. 5/1960. See also *Mothea* v. *Mothea* H.C. Civ./A/7/1974.

A fortiori must this be the case where the husband has committed adultery.

(iv) *Other possible justifications*

In the Panel Discussion the following factors were regarded as insufficient in themselves to give grounds for divorce—criminality, insanity, the contracting of a contagious disease, and sterility, though it was felt that inability to consummate the marriage might provide a ground if it was not disclosed at the time of the marriage.[1] If such a ground does exist it seems to be based at least in part on the concept of fraudulent non-disclosure. Similarly a husband may possess the right to claim a divorce where his wife is at the time of the marriage already pregnant by another man if he only discovers this after the marriage.[2] It is possible that he may also have sufficient grounds if, believing at the time of the marriage that his wife had been chaste, he subsequently discovers otherwise.[3] There is, however, the difficulty of proof. Where either of these discoveries is made by the husband both he and his family may often feel that it is preferable to keep the information to themselves rather than bring it to the public notice by claiming a divorce.[4]

Where the matter complained of already existed at the time of the marriage, for instance inability to consummate, non-virginity, or pregnancy *per alium*, it is possible that instead of constituting a ground for divorce this renders the marriage voidable at the instance of the other party.[5] It is far from clear whether Sesotho law draws any distinction between these two concepts and in any event the legitimacy or otherwise of the children would not be affected. However, it might be relevant in determining the extent of the obligation to restore the *bohali* and this question is discussed further below.

[1] P.D., pp. 130–1, 141–2. Casalis (at p. 185) mentions sterility of the wife as a ground for the husband.

[2] See *Mokhesuoe* v. *Moiloa* J.C. 10/1967 (L.C.); P.D., pp. 113–16 (the Panel seemed divided on the question).

[3] Sekese (1968), p. 7; P.D., p. 116; *contra* Ashton, p. 75. Laydevant (at p. 248) stated that he had not heard of a divorce on this ground during the twenty-five years before 1931, though it was a common occurrence earlier.

[4] P.D., p. 114.

[5] See P.D., p. 115, where Bereng states that cases of pregnancy *per alium* are not called by the name of divorce. Duncan (at p. 35) refers to annulment of marriage but the two cases he cites in support are not apposite—see below, pp. 218–19.

The 'Restatement' mentions that a wife may be divorced by her husband's parents if she fails to treat them with respect and look after them properly on the basis that she is married not only to her husband but to his family as well.[1] However, bearing in mind the decline of *kenelo*[2] such a statement seems totally unacceptable as an exposition of the modern law.

4. THE EFFECT OF DIVORCE UPON THE CHILDREN AND THE 'BOHALI'

The governing provision is section 34(5) of Part II of the Laws of Lerotholi which runs as follows:

A court granting dissolution of such a marriage shall make an order regarding the retention or return of [*bohali*] cattle, and to whom the children, if any, shall belong, as may seem just in accordance with the circumstances in which the dissolution is granted.

The subsection reflects the fundamental link between children and *bohali* which has already been noted[3] and brings out the need to treat both matters together in divorce proceedings.[4]

(a) *Procedural Rules*

It will be appreciated that in most divorce cases two different suits are closely intertwined. First, there is the divorce action to which the parties are husband and wife. Secondly, there is usually an action for the return of the *bohali* in which the parties are the husband and the '*bohali*-holder'.

The proper person to make any claim for the return of *bohali* upon a dissolution is undoubtedly the husband. The fact that the *bohali* was paid by his father or that other relatives contributed to it is irrelevant since they are treated as having parted with it permanently and have no right to sue to recover it.[5]

The person against whom the action lies is the holder of the

---

[1] At pp. 12–13.   [2] See Ch. 18 below.

[3] Ch. 11 above. See also P.D., p. 132, where reference was made to the maxim '*Likhomo ha li moo bana ba leng teng*' ('cattle are not where children are').

[4] See also *Rafutho* v. *Rafutho* J.C. 114/1964 (C.C.).

[5] *Nkhatho* v. *Mokhanya* J.C. 214/1951 (J.C.); *Mothepu* v. *Ferene* J.C. 31/1961 (two out of three of the lower courts and J.C.); *Mokonyana* v. *Motumi* J.C. 102/1961 (J.C.); *Lekhanya* v. *Mongalo* J.C. 179/1963 (C.C. and J.C.); *Morapalla* v. *Tsilo* J.C. 217/1963 (all courts); *Mokhesuoe* v. *Moiloa* J.C. 10/1967 (J.C.); *Lebesa* v. *Khotlele* J.C. 35/1967 (J.C.). See also evidence of George Moshoeshoe, *1873 Report and Evidence*, p. 40; Duncan, p. 38 and the cases cited there.

bohali, i.e. the wife's father or his heir, or her former guardian. Thus where the husband is claiming a divorce and the recovery of *bohali*, the *bohali*-holder will be a co-defendant with the wife. On the other hand, if the divorce action is brought by the wife the *bohali*-holder's status in the proceedings will depend on whether or not he supports her.[1]

Where the court takes a decision with respect to the *bohali*, the *bohali*-holder must naturally be made a party because he is directly materially affected by an order for the restoration of the cattle. There is also the additional consideration that on divorce the wife is not emancipated but falls back under the guardianship of the head of her family, and the same applies to her children if she is allowed to take them with her.[2] Despite this the lower courts generally pay insufficient attention to this requirement and their orders have on numerous occasions had to be upset on appeal by the Judicial Commissioner.[3]

Section 34(5) is framed in mandatory terms so that strictly speaking a court granting a divorce *must* make an order about the *bohali* and the children. However, in hearing appeals the Judicial Commissioner has not tended to upset decrees of dissolution or orders as to the custody of children where the lower courts have omitted to deal with the question of the *bohali* in disregard of the provisions of the section.[4] Instead a separate action becomes necessary if the parties cannot reach agreement in respect of the *bohali*. The same applies in the case of the children, if no order has been made about them at the time of the dissolution.[5]

Where there has been a 'dual marriage', both customary and

---

[1] *Lebesa* v. *Khotlele* J.C. 35/1967 (J.C.); *Moahloli* v. *Moahloli* J.C. 52/1970 (J.C.).

[2] *Khatseane* v. *Khatseane* J.C. 46/1964 (J.C.); *Tholoana* v. *Machela* J.C. 6/1965 (J.C.); *Vova* v. *Vova* J.C. 279/1960 (J.C.); *Kholu* v. *Shataka* J.C. 200/1966 (J.C.); *Mohale* v. *Mohale* J.C. 248/1966 (J.C.).

[3] *Abram* v. *Abram* J.C. 148/1960; *Kubu* v. *Kubu* J.C. 26/1965; *Rantsane* v. *Rantsane* J.C. 140/1967; *'Makolane* v. *'Makolane* J.C. 248/1968. See also *Vova* v. *Vova* J.C. 279/1960 (J.C.); *Mothepu* v. *Ferene* J.C. 31/1961 (J.C.); *Moalosi* v. *Moalosi* J.C. 124/1963 (J.C.); *Mphaki* v. *Mphaki* J.C. 39/1964 (J.C.); *Raphutho* v. *Raphutho* J.C. 114/1964 (J.C.); *Ralenono* v. *Ralenono* J.C. 135/1966 (J.C.); *Likotsi* v. *Likotsi* J.C. 247/1966 (J.C.); *Mohale* v. *Mohale* J.C. 248/1966 (J.C.).

[4] *Mothepu* v. *Ferene* J.C. 31/1961; *Mphaki* v. *Mphaki* J.C. 39/1964; *Kubu* v. *Kubu* J.C. 26/1965.

[5] *Kholu* v. *Shataka* J.C. 200/1966; *Rantsane* v. *Rantsane* J.C. 140/1967. The Judicial Commissioner was earlier opposed to the separation of the actions, see *Moalosi* v. *Moalosi* J.C. 124/1963.

civil, such a division of actions is in any event necessitated by the separate jurisdictions of the various courts. While only the High Court can hear divorce proceedings in respect of a civil marriage, Basotho Courts do possess the necessary jurisdiction over the *bohali* paid pursuant to the customary marriage. Section 8 of the Central and Local Courts Proclamation provides:[1]

Subject to any express provision conferring jurisdiction no local or central court shall have jurisdiction to try cases in connection with marriages other than a marriage conducted under or in accordance with Sesotho law and custom, except where and in so far as the case concerns the payment or return or disposal of dowry.

(b) *Substantive Rules*

The traditional position was described by George and Sofonia Moshoeshoe in their evidence to the 1872 Commission[2] and may be reduced to the following principles:

(i) If there were any children of the marriage (and one was sufficient for this purpose), the husband could never claim both them and the return of the *bohali*.[3]

(ii) He could thus choose to claim either the children or the *bohali*, except where he had no justification for divorcing his wife, when he was merely entitled to keep his children and did not possess the option of claiming the restoration of the *bohali*.[4]

(iii) It was open to the parties to agree together on a division of the children and the *bohali*.

(iv) If no children had been born, the husband had a right to recover the *bohali*, except where he had no justification for divorcing his wife.

Ashton, writing of the 1930s before section 34(5) was included in the Laws of Lerotholi, put forward similar propositions, showing how the destinations of the children and the cattle were

---

[1] Proc. 62 of 1938, as amended. The section has been applied by the Judicial Commissioner in *bohali* claims arising out of dual marriages in *Ramatsella* v. *Mosoeu* J.C. 280/1963 and *Tsosane* v. *Makhoabenyane* J.C. 108/1965.

[2] *1873 Report and Evidence*, pp. 40–1, 43–4.

[3] See also Ellenberger and Macgregor, p. 279.

[4] See Casalis, letter dated 1 Oct. 1872 to Governor's Agent, reprinted in *1873 Report and Evidence*, p. 27; P.D., p. 125. In both cases reference is made to husbands simply throwing away their wives.

basically contingent on one another but adding that the allocation of fault was also a determining factor.[1] He gave a modified version of (iv) above stating that if there were no children, the amount of the *bohali* that the husband was entitled to recover depended on who was responsible for the break up of the marriage and how long the parties had been married, i.e. the longer they had been married and the greater his fault, the fewer cattle he could recover. He also made the further general point that very young children would be allowed to remain with their mother until they were able to do without her and only then would they go to their father if they were allocated to him. Those children who remained permanently with their mother would become full members of her family and would adopt her clan name and clan affiliation.[2]

To what extent have the courts in the exercise of the wide discretion conferred upon them by section 34(5) to do what is just, followed the traditional criteria? Have they tended instead to apply new principles, for instance emphasizing the importance of the welfare of the children?[3]

These are extremely difficult questions to answer on the basis of the score of cases available to me. Since questions in relation to the children and the *bohali* are often decided in separate proceedings from the divorce action and even from one another, the cases do not always reveal all the facts which would seem to be crucial for an over-all assessment. Thus a court may make an order in relation to the children and not the *bohali* and here it is impossible to tell what the attitude of the court would be if subsequent proceedings were brought over the *bohali*. Similarly, it is often not clear from the record in an action to recover *bohali* whether there are any children of the marriage and if so what decision or agreement has been reached in respect of them.

If these limitations are borne in mind, the cases do suggest the following tentative conclusions.

First, it is clear that the courts commonly divide up the children, allocating some to the husband and others to the wife's family. The wife tends to get the younger children[4] and those conceived

---

[1] At p. 87. See also the 'Restatement', pp. 20–1.

[2] See also P.D., p. 132.

[3] See P.D., ibid., where the view was expressed that the modern courts were tending to consider what was in the best interests of the children.

[4] See e.g. *Matsepe* v. *Matsepe* J.C. 90/1956 (L.C., P.C.'s Ct., and J.C.); *Moalosi* v. *Moalosi* J.C. 124/1963 (J.C., *contra* C.C. which awarded all children

in adultery,[1] but this is not invariably the case.[2] The question of fault does not seem to be a decisive factor in such cases and the decisions show significant differences in this respect.[3] Nor is the *bohali* necessarily also divided between the parties, though this may be done.[4]

Secondly, there are cases where the wife's family has been awarded all the children either because the husband is held to be unfit to look after them[5] or where they were conceived in adultery[6] or where the husband has been found so much at fault for the breakdown of the marriage that he has also forfeited the *bohali*.[7]

Thirdly, the cases reflect the husband's right to reclaim the *bohali* cattle provided it is his wife who has been at fault and not he himself and provided he is not claiming any children.[8] A recent

---

to wife's family); *Mphaki* v. *Mphaki* J.C. 39/1964 (L.C. and J.C.); *Tsosane* v. *Makhoabenyane* J.C. 108/1965 (C.C.); *Ralenono* v. *Ralenono* J.C. 135/1966 (L.C. and J.C.).

[1] See e.g. *Moalosi* v. *Moalosi* (above); *Mphaki* v. *Mphaki* (above); *Ralenono* v. *Ralenono* (above) (L.C., *contra* J.C.).

[2] See e.g. *Ralenono* v. *Ralenono* (J.C.) where the J.C. awarded the eldest of five adulterine children to the husband because he had been living at the husband's home despite the fact that the spouses had long been separated.

[3] In *Abram* v. *Abram* J.C. 148/1960 and *Tsosane* v. *Makhoabenyane* J.C. 108/1965 the husband was at fault; in *Matsepe* v. *Matsepe*, *Moalosi* v. *Moalosi* and *Ralenono* v. *Ralenono* both parties were at fault.

[4] In *Matsepe* v. *Matsepe* there was no refund, but the balance was not held payable; in *Moalosi* v. *Moalosi* there was no refund; in *Tsosane* v. *Makhoabenyane* the *bohali* was adjusted so that a total of 10 out of 20 were retained by the wife's family. See also 'Restatement', p. 19.

[5] *Kubu* v. *Kubu* J.C. 26/1965 (all courts).

[6] *Khatseane* v. *Khatseane* J.C. 46/1964 (J.C.); *Peete* v. *Peete* J.C. 27/1965 (all courts); *Rantsane* v. *Rantsane* J.C. 140/1967 (L.C. and C.C.) but cf. *Ranamane* v. *Ranamane* J.C. 172/1965 (L.C. and C.C.) where the wife's adulterine children were awarded to the husband.

[7] See e.g. *Makhooane* v. *Makhooane* J.C. 43/1956 (L.C. and C.C.); *Kubu* v. *Kubu* (L.C. and C.C.); *Rantsane* v. *Rantsane* (L.C. and C.C.); see also P.D., p. 132. Cf. *Moahloli* v. *Moahloli* J.C. 52/1970 where the Local Court held that though the children should stay with their mother for the time being they ultimately belonged to the husband since the *bohali* had not been reclaimed.

[8] See e.g. *Makara* v. *Mokobori* J.C. 164/1955 (all courts); *Ralipoli* v. *Lephallo* J.C. 138/1960 (J.C.); *Tlelimo* v. *Tiro* J.C. 71/1961 (all courts); *Morapalla* v. *Tsilo* J.C. 217/1963 (all courts); *September* v. *Monyamane* J.C. 250/1966 (L.C.; part only held recoverable). In *Ranamane* v. *Ranamane* J.C. 172/1965 he did claim the children as well as the *bohali* and the Central Court, overruling the Local Court, held that he could not succeed because the children and the cattle could not be kept in the same home. In similar circumstances in *Ramatsella* v. *Mosoeu* J.C. 280/1963 the J.C. held that since the husband had elected to keep his son he must pay the outstanding balance of the *bohali*.

decision also suggests that despite the husband's fault he may be able to recover a part of the *bohali* where his wife keeps the children.[1]

Fourthly, where the husband has not been at fault and the wife has borne an adulterine child who might otherwise become the husband's heir, the husband is entitled to repudiate the child, which will then be transferred to its mother's family, and to recover part or all of the *bohali*.[2]

There are four further matters for discussion. First, it remains unclear whether cattle originally paid as compensation for abduction and later incorporated within the *bohali* can ever be reclaimed by the husband on divorce. The decisions of the courts, as explained earlier,[3] are not consistent. The lower courts tend to allow such cattle to be recovered and are then overruled by the Judicial Commissioner.[4]

Secondly, there is the problem of whether restoration of the cattle merely involves the return of an equivalent number of animals or extends to cover any natural increase as well. Since during the currency of the marriage the *bohali* cattle are the property of the wife's family and it is they who have to bear any losses,[5] it would seem to follow that any offspring should accrue to them and thus be irrecoverable on divorce.[6] Indeed in only two cases that I have come across has any action for the recovery of *bohali* included a claim in respect of progeny and both of them give rise to considerable difficulties.

In *Malebanye* v. *Mohale*[7] the Paramount Chief's Court ordered the return of the *bohali* together with six calves which had been born while the cattle were in the possession of the wife's family

---

[1] *Ralisa* v. *Masia* J.C. 285/1968 (all courts awarded the return of about half of a *bohali* of R400).

[2] See *Chaka* v. *Chaka* J.C. 210/1966 (J.C.).

[3] See p. 110 above.

[4] See e.g. *Mothepu* v. *Ferene* J.C. 31/1961 (J.C., *contra* L.C. and C.C.); *Lekhanya* v. *Mongalo* J.C. 179/1963 (J.C., *contra* L.C. and C.C.); *Ramarumo* v. *Kala* J.C. 257/1954 (L.C. and J.C.); *Mokoma* v. *Ralipoli* J.C. 29/1965 (C.C. and J.C.); *Limape* v. *Lebona* J.C. 95/1966 (J.C., *contra* L.C. and C.C.); *September* v. *Monyamane* J.C. 250/1966 (J.C., *contra* L.C. and C.C.); *Matsie* v. *Seetsa* J.C. 38/1969 (J.C.). Duncan (at p. 24) relying on *Phoofolo* v. *Pongo* J.C. 89/1951 (J.C.) prefers the view that abduction cattle are irrecoverable and this was shared by all the Panel members—see P.D., p. 135.

[5] See p. 101 above.

[6] This was the view of Ellenberger and Macgregor, p. 269.

[7] J.C. 149/1945 (erroneously cited as J.C. 149/1949 by Duncan).

and this award was upheld on appeal by the Acting Judicial Commissioner. The full facts of the case unfortunately do not appear from the record, but according to Duncan's account[1] the wife never went to live at her husband's home. At all events the *bohali* had been in the possession of the wife's family for four years by the time the husband's father claimed their return and by then the wife had gone her own separate way. Duncan treats this as a case of annulment rather than divorce and explains that it is for this reason that the calves had to be returned as well as the cattle.[2] Although it is true that if the case had been one of divorce the action should properly have been brought by the husband and not his father, it is hard to see why the marriage should be treated as void simply because the bride changed her mind before ever going to her husband's home. As we have seen, a marriage is complete if the requirements of section 34 of Part II of the Laws of Lerotholi are satisfied and there is no additional requirement that the bride must be handed over to her husband.[3] Nor can this be a case where the marriage was voidable on account of some unknown defect existing at the time of the wedding (if indeed this concept is recognized by Sesotho law at all); rather it was a situation of wilful refusal to consummate or desertion justifying a divorce.[4]

The second case of *Phoofolo* v. *Pongo*[5] concerned the position of a young widow. As we shall see in Chapter 18 the status of widows is a controversial subject, but it seems almost certain that a widow can obtain a divorce from her deceased husband's family if the *bohali* paid for her is refunded. In the present case the husband had died within three years of marriage and the widow wished to sever herself from his family and return to her own parents. The Local Court, whose judgment was upheld through two appeals, held that two calves, in addition to the five *bohali* cattle which had been paid, must be returned to the husband's family.[6] The plaintiff had actually claimed five calves but only two

[1] At p. 35.
[2] Ibid. The other case mentioned by Duncan in this connection, *Mabote* v. *Ntseke* J.C. 12/1949 did not in fact concern the progeny of *bohali* cattle at all.
[3] See pp. 122–3 above.
[4] *Makara* v. *Mokobori* J.C. 164/1955, in which a similar situation arose, was treated as a case of divorce. No claim was made in respect of progeny.
[5] J.C. 89/1951.
[6] Six additional cattle which had been paid as compensation for abduction were held to be irrecoverable.

of them could definitely be established to be the offspring of the right cattle.[1]

It is clear that neither of these cases can by any means be regarded as providing an authoritative solution of the question. Logically there is little justification for allowing the recovery of progeny either on divorce or where a voidable marriage is annulled. However, where the cattle have only been in the possession of the wife's family for a relatively short time and their calves are easily identifiable there may perhaps be something to be said for allowing the calves to be recovered as well.

Thirdly, the question arises whether the *malome* has to return his share, known as *litsoa*, when a refund of *bohali* on divorce is ordered by the court. The matter is a controversial one, but the better view seems to be that the wife's parents must refund the full amount, if required to do so, and have no right of recourse against the *malome*.[2]

Fourthly, it would seem from the Panel Discussion that where the children go with their mother on a divorce the father's obligation to support and maintain them comes to an end and this responsibility is transferred to the head of the mother's family.[3]

5. PROPRIETARY CONSEQUENCES

This topic is conveniently divided into three parts, covering the separate property of the spouses, household property, and rights over land.

(a) *Separate Property*

It is clear that on divorce the spouses retain their own individual property consisting of clothing and other personal effects. In the case of the wife she may have brought to the marital home as part of her trousseau (*phahlelo*) various items including blankets, clothing, articles for household and domestic use, as well as presents for her in-laws. Traditionally it seems that all this

---

[1] The need for sufficient proof of identity was explained in P.D., p. 54. However, unfortunately the question was not placed before the Panel Discussion in its widest aspects but only in relation to facts similar to those in *Malebanye* v. *Mohale*; the Panel thought the progeny were recoverable if they were identifiable.

[2] Ellenberger and Macgregor, p. 269; *1919 National Council Proceedings*, Minutes of 8th day; P.D., p. 135; cf. George Moshoeshoe in his evidence, *1873 Report and Evidence*, p. 41. The 'Restatement' (at p. 22) leaves the matter open, as does Duncan, p. 26.

[3] P.D., p. 133.

property belonged, strictly speaking, to the husband's parents, although they would naturally hand over part to the husband and his wife.[1] The 'Restatement' says that today the wife is entitled on divorce to keep 'feminine' items from the *phahlelo*, including any property acquired by her while she was single,[2] while the husband is entitled to retain animals bought with his earnings,[3] though presumably this does not include household stock.

(b) *Household Property*

Traditionally the husband may well have been entitled to retain the entire household property on divorce, virtually regardless of fault, and there are some comparatively recent decisions to suggest that this is still the basic position today.[4] In *Khatseane* v. *Khatseane*,[5] for instance, the Judicial Commissioner overruled the lower court's decision to divide up the joint estate and declared:

. . . for a divorced woman to obtain a division of her husband's property there would have to be exceptional circumstances where all the fault is with the husband and none with the wife.

However, the modern tendency would seem to be in the direction of giving a divorced wife a broader right to a share of the property in appropriate circumstances. Duncan has written:[6]

From enquiries I have made I understand that it is possible for a woman to be awarded part of the joint estate on divorce, and that each case should be decided on its merits.

This statement was endorsed by Thompson J.C. in *Kholu* v. *Shataka*[7] and he added that the important factor to take into account in weighing up the merits was the allocation of responsibility for the collapse of the marriage.[8] Thus in *Matsepe* v. *Matsepe*[9] where both parties were at fault there was a general division of the joint property and in *Likotsi* v. *Likotsi*[10] the courts awarded all the joint estate to the wife since she was found to be in no way responsible for the breakdown of the marriage.

---

[1] P.D., pp. 97–8, 142.

[2] At pp. 11–12; see also *Khatseane* v. *Khatseane* J.C. 46/1964 (J.C.).

[3] 'Restatement', p. 22.

[4] See e.g. *Sekhonyana* v. *Letuka* J.C. 46/1953 (P.C.'s Ct. and J.C.).

[5] J.C. 46/1964.   [6] At p. 42.   [7] J.C. 200/1966.

[8] See also *Mothea* v. *Mothea* H.C. Civ./A/7/1974 (H.C.); P.D., pp. 135–6.

[9] J.C. 90/1956 (C.C., P.C.'s Ct., and J.C.).

[10] J.C. 247/1966 (all courts).

(c) *Land Rights*

Rights to residential sites, gardens, and arable lands are invariably allocated by the local chief or headman to the husband despite the fact that the purpose is to provide for the whole family and that the married status of the man is almost a condition precedent of the allocation.[1] The 'Restatement' therefore propounds the anticipated rule[2] which is reflected in a number of court decisions:[3]

Rights in soil—such as those attaching to fields and the site on which stand the house and the vegetable garden continue to vest in the husband regardless of whose fault brought about the severing of the marriage bond.

However, the matter does not seem to be as simple as this. On the one hand, the husband may be deprived of at least some of his arable lands by the local chief or headman following an inspection on the basis that he has more land than he needs now that he does not have a wife to support.[4] On the other, the courts have sometimes permitted divorced women to continue to live in the matrimonial home if the husband has gone to live elsewhere.[5] Alternatively, it seems possible for a divorced wife to be allocated new lands in her own right at her parents' home if she decides to return there.[6]

[1] Sheddick (1954), p. 160.

[2] At p. 22.

[3] See e.g. *Khatseane* v. *Khatseane* J.C. 46/1964 (J.C.); *Tholoana* v. *Machela* J.C. 6/1965 (C.C. and J.C.; *contra* L.C.). For doubts about whether this is an invariable rule see *Mothea* v. *Mothea*, above (H.C.).

[4] Laws of Lerotholi, s. 7(2) of Part I and see *Tholoana* v. *Machela* J.C. 6/1965 (J.C.); P.D., p. 136.

[5] See e.g. *Matsepe* v. *Matsepe* J.C. 90/1956 (L.C., P.C.'s Ct., and J.C.) (both parties at fault); *Peete* v. *Peete* J.C. 27/1965 (all courts); *Likotsi* v. *Likotsi* J.C. 247/1966 (all courts) (husband solely at fault).

[6] See *Koali* v. *Koali* J.C. 4/1944 cited by Duncan, p. 87.

17

INTESTATE INHERITANCE

1. INTRODUCTION

No legal analysis of the Sesotho law of inheritance starts off on the right footing unless it stresses the time-honoured rule now enshrined in section 14(4) of Part I of the Laws of Lerotholi:

Any dispute amongst the deceased's family over property or property rights shall be referred (for arbitration) to the brothers of the deceased and other persons whose right it is under Sesotho law and custom to be consulted. If no agreement is arrived at by such persons, or if either party wishes to contest their decision, the dispute shall be taken to the appropriate court by the dissatisfied person.[1]

There are really two aspects to this vitally important provision. First, it contains a procedural requirement that before such disputes come before the courts they must have been hammered out within the family; if this has not been done they will usually be remitted to the family council by the court.[2] In *Chobokoane* v. *Chobokoane*[3] the Judicial Commissioner expatiated upon this aspect of section 14(4) in a dispute about whether certain property had been allocated to a particular house and declared:

There is no doubt that it is a recording of ancient custom. In a family matter the first court in Sesotho custom is that of the family itself. [The plaintiff] told this court that that would be difficult to arrange because the family was dispersed. It is true that nowadays most families are dispersed and do not live all in the same village as they used to, but nevertheless it is possible to get a meeting of those members of the family who are available, particularly the senior ones and to have the matter threshed out by the family.

[1] The provision was incorporated in Part I in 1948 following a debate in the National Council: see *1947 National Council Proceedings*, pp. 157–76.

[2] See, out of numerous examples, *Libete* v. *Ntsekhe* J.C. 686/1952 (J.C.); *Masunyane* v. *Masunyane* J.C. 43/1953 (J.C.); *Tseole* v. *Tseole* J.C. 39/1962 (J.C.); *Tjotsi* v. *Tjotsi* J.C. 4/1965 (J.C.); *Motsoene* v. *Motsoene* J.C. 198/1966 (J.C.); *Chobokoane* v. *Chobokoane* J.C. 292/1966 (C.C. and J.C.).

[3] J.C. 292/1966.

Thompson J.C. went on to specify the advantages of this method of settling disputes:

It means that both parties must co-operate with the family to enable the members to reach an equitable decision. It ought to be possible for the family to ascertain questions of allocation by [the parties' grand-father] during his lifetime better than a court. Furthermore as to the arrangements of marriages and remarriages by individuals it is easier for the family to know the precise status of the various wives and their descendants. . . .

The second and more substantive aspect of section 14(4) has recently been examined by Hamnett. He has drawn attention to the great emphasis which the law places on the need for the family to reach agreement upon a solution to the dispute.[1] It is this agreement that actually establishes the legal rights of the parties rather than specific legal precepts. 'The law, in the ideal case, defines certain parameters within which the anticipated agreement operates . . .',[2] but it does not inflexibly determine the outcome.

This means that in looking at the legal rules propounded by the courts it has to be remembered that they are often no more than rough guidelines for family councils, and that the general expectation is that the family will reach a solution without the matter reaching the courts. Where the family fails to reach agreement and the matter is finally referred to the courts this represents, in Hamnett's words 'a situation not where the law is at last made clearly visible but rather one where it is most distorted and obscured'.[3] However, this last statement rather exaggerates the point, for there are certainly some cardinal legal principles which families feel bound to follow and if one member will not accept their application his claim will be rejected. Furthermore, although the courts will naturally be concerned to uphold decisions reached by the family, they will sometimes reverse such decisions if the aggrieved party can point to the violation of some principle which the court regards as important and if his claim is fully made out on the evidence. In such instances the family decision will often be found to have been based not so much on principle as on the strength of individual members or factions.

The ensuing treatment will attempt to set out the guiding principles of the law while taking into account the freedom of

---

[1] (1975), pp. 51–2.   [2] Ibid., p. 52.   [3] Ibid., p. 52.

manoeuvre enjoyed by the family council. A brief outline of the contents of the next three chapters will give an indication of the way the family council, the courts, and the legal rules all interact to resolve disputes over the inheritance of property.

The two major objectives of the Sesotho law of inheritance (appropriately reflected in the emphasis placed on them in the Laws of Lerotholi) are first to identify the person who is designated the 'heir' (*mojalefa*) and secondly to spell out and enforce his rights and responsibilities in relation to other members of the deceased's family. With regard to the family at large the death of one of its members commonly means that property that was formerly administered for the family's benefit by one of its members must now be managed by another. They all therefore have a direct concern in the practical application of the law of inheritance.

So far as the first objective is concerned the law has now developed to the point where the identity of the heir can usually be established by reference to a clear written rule. This means that in the vast majority of cases there is no room at all for the family council to recognize as the heir anyone other than the person defined as such in terms of section 11 of Part I of the Laws of Lerotholi.

On the other hand, in matters relating to the attainment of the second objective, namely the management of the estate for the benefit of the family, the law is extremely flexible. Inevitably the members of each individual family will know best how an equitable solution can be found to the problem of balancing the various needs of its members and ensuring that the estate is not dissipated by one person while the others are neglected. The law has always operated a system of checks and restraints on the abuse of power and has stressed the need for mutual consultation. Thus, as will be shown, the deceased's widow and his heir must work together in harmony. If one attempts to exploit the other or fails to provide for the children of the family it is the duty of the deceased's brothers to intervene and if this does not achieve the desired result, or if the brothers are exploiting their own position, an appeal can always be made to the local chief or the courts.

It will be explained at the end of this chapter and in Chapter 18 how the Laws of Lerotholi have attempted to spell out in some degree of detail just how the estate should be administered in a variety of different circumstances. Chapter 18 is devoted exclusively to an examination of the position of a widow and her relationship with the members of her deceased husband's family. Inevitably, however, the law cannot be expected to envisage every possible family situation and the members may often be uniquely well equipped to take account of personalities and the particular assets comprised in the estate. While an attempt will be made to analyse the relevant provisions and the interpretations of the law to be found in judicial decisions, it should be recognized from the outset that this approach, being orientated towards written law and court judgments focuses on but one aspect of the law of inheritance as it operates in practice.

The present chapter will be devoted to an examination of intestate inheritance rules because nearly all Basotho die without leaving any form of will, and such testamentary instruments are in any event modern developments. These are discussed in Chapter 19 together with 'allocations' of property made by the deceased during his lifetime. Such allocations have always been normal practice and, as we have seen, commonly take the form of transfers of property by a polygamist to his various houses. The effect of this is that very often the amount of property comprised in the deceased's unallocated estate is comparatively small. In a monogamous household, on the other hand, the unallocated property is usually much greater, if indeed it does not make up the whole estate. Testamentary dispositions and allocations have this in common, then, that they both reduce the amount of property that is governed by the rules of intestate inheritance.

2. THE PERSONAL PROPERTY OF MINORS

The bulk of the present chapter is devoted to the position where the person who has died was a married man or family head. The distribution of the personal property of other persons may be disposed of quite shortly at this juncture. Bearing in mind what has already been said to the effect that this is very much a question for the individual family to decide, the following general principles may be propounded.

(a) *Wives*

When a wife dies the only property that is solely hers, as opposed to household property, is made up of her personal effects, for instance her clothing, jewellery, blankets, etc. Whereas the household property will continue to be used by her husband for the benefit of her children, it appears that her personal effects are supposed to be distributed between the relatives of both her own family and her husband's family.[1]

In the case of *Morakabi* v. *Mabote*[2] there were very special facts. The wife had deserted her husband and returned to her parents' home but had not been followed. She had lived there for twenty years before she died but no divorce had ever taken place. During that time she had earned money by brewing beer and at her death she possessed three huts and a large quantity of household effects. Her own family had helped to set her up in business and obtain a residential site on which to build. The Local Court held that her estate passed to her own family on the ground that she was a divorcee, despite the lack of any evidence to support this conclusion, and on appeal both the Central Court and the Judicial Commissioner held that she was still a married woman. Accordingly they decided that her estate belonged to her husband.[3]

(b) *Widows*

A widow's personal effects pass to the heir who distributes them among the relatives as he thinks fit.[4] The household property comprised in her deceased husband's estate is discussed below.

(c) *Spinsters and Divorcees*

Their property, which will mainly consist of personal effects, passes to their parents, who may distribute particular items to other close relatives.[5] If the parents are dead then their fathers' heir inherits. If the deceased had expressed a wish that a specific article should go to a named person that wish will normally be carried out.[6]

---

[1] *Hlehlethe* v. *Lebajoa* J.C. 47/1944 (J.C.); Ashton, p. 182. Sheddick (1953), p. 64, states that the position is not quite clear and this is amply illustrated by the general disagreement among the members of the Panel Discussion—see P.D., pp. 215–18.

[2] J.C. 58/1966.

[3] There would seem to be some problem in the fact that the houses would pass to her husband while the residential site would probably belong to her father. The husband would not be entitled to be allocated the site since he would owe allegiance to the chief in his own village; perhaps he could claim the money spent on the houses instead—see P.D., pp. 218–21.

[4] P.D., p. 221.

[5] Ashton, p. 182; Sheddick (1953), p. 64; P.D., p. 206.

[6] See *Shashapa* v. *Shashapa* J.C. 73/1965 (L.C. and J.C.); P.D., p. 215.

Where an unmarried woman has an illegitimate child the position is more complicated and is discussed further below.

(d) *Bachelors*

A bachelor's personal effects are inherited by his father (or if he is dead, his heir), who may distribute certain items among the other relatives.[1] However, some specific articles are the entitlement of the deceased's *malome* (senior maternal uncle) and go to him. These are listed below since they are also taken by the *malome* if the deceased was a married man.

3. THE PROPERTY OF A FAMILY HEAD

(a) *The Line of Inheritance*

(i) *Identifying the heir*

In comparison with many other less efficient systems in southern Africa which leave the appointment of the heir an open question until after a man's death and entrust the decision to the discretion of a family council, Sesotho law has been at pains to establish the heir's identity at an early stage with a large degree of specificity.[2]

However, this does not mean that difficulties never arise over the identification of the heir in Lesotho simply because the law is designed to achieve a measure of certainty in advance of a person's death as to who will succeed him. Even today the members of the family council possess a limited power of selection and the legal definition of the heir contains sufficient ambiguity to ensure that the question cannot always be resolved by the automatic application of a rule.

Section 11(1) of Part I of the Laws of Lerotholi provides:

The heir . . . shall be the first male child of the first married wife, and if there is no male in the first house then the first born male child of the next wife married in succession shall be the heir.

The essential feature of this definition of the heir was incorporated in the original version of the Laws in 1903[3] and was the

---

[1] Ashton, p. 182; Sheddick (1953), p. 64; P.D., p. 204; *Mosaase* v. *Mosaase* H.C. Civ./T/77/1973 (H.C.). If the bachelor was an illegitimate child, his mother's father would of course inherit.

[2] See Jones, pp. 59–61.

[3] S. 14. Ellenberger and Macgregor (at pp. 271–2) refer to this principle as having operated in much earlier times.

same as that adopted for regulating the succession to the Paramount Chieftainship.[1] Even though it is recognized as a cardinal principle of Sesotho law there have been many deviations from it in the field of chiefly succession[2] and there can be little doubt that the same situation has obtained in cases of private inheritance of property.

It will be noticed that the system differs from one of strict primogeniture in two respects. First, it restricts the inheritance to males and secondly it determines seniority in polygamous families not by priority of birth but by the priority of the mother's marriage to the deceased.

The admirable succinctness of the rule stated in section 11(1) leaves a number of questions wide open and it is here that the flexibility of the law can be fully utilized by the deceased's family council to select a person of their choice who is suitable for the position of heir. Whether this opportunity for the family to play a decisive role usually has a successful outcome or whether it produces unnecessary uncertainty and encourages litigation is hard to assess.

It will be recalled that before the framing of the original version of section 11(1) in 1903 the rule was to the effect that the heir was the first male child of the 'great wife' and this constituted an ambiguity in itself since there was no consensus on what qualified a person to be a 'great wife'. To remedy the grievances of the commoners it was decided that the law should define the great wife as the first married wife and to make part payment of *bohali* a precondition of a completed marriage.[3]

Despite this clarification there are still two possible areas where conflicting claims can present acute problems.

First, it can happen that a man dies without male issue and that a son is later born to his widow out of a relationship with a lover and not within a *kenelo* union. *Kenelo* has in any event virtually died out, as will be shown below.[4] The question will be to decide

---

[1] Laws of Lerotholi (1903), s. 1, discussed by Duncan, pp. 44, 49. See also p. 103 above.

[2] See Ellenberger and Macgregor, pp. 57–9, and Ashton, p. 193. Ashton also refers (at pp. 184–5) to a possible exception to the general rule among the Batlokoa chiefs whereby the deceased's senior grandson became the heir in preference to his son; however he doubted whether this was ever implemented in practice.

[3] See p. 103 above.

[4] See pp. 261–3 below.

whether this son is the rightful heir, particularly where there is no blood relationship between the child's genitor and the deceased. Ashton, after pointing out the theoretically rightful claims of the son, and speaking of the 1930s, wrote:

In practice these rights are likely to be ignored or incompletely admitted, unless the widow was properly *kenela*ed by her brother-in-law.[1]

With regard to succession to the chieftainship an attempt to resolve the question has recently been made by the enactment of the Chieftainship Act.[2] This provides that only a 'legitimate' son may succeed to the office of chief[3] and the intention of the statutory amendment was clearly to exclude such posthumously conceived children.[4] However, the rules as to the inheritance of property were expressly left untouched[5] and so far as *private* rights of inheritance are concerned the offspring of a *kenelo* union at any rate, may still gain recognition as the heir.[6]

A second difficulty is encountered when the person claiming to be the heir is known to have been conceived in adultery during the lifetime of the husband, for instance where one of the spouses has been in desertion for a substantial length of time or where the husband has been absent for a long period of work in South Africa. As we have seen[7] such a child is theoretically legitimate and thus entitled to be the heir. However, it seems that the family council may well decide not to recognize the child as the heir after the husband's death, particularly if the husband did not recognize the child as his during his lifetime.[8] The general opinion of the members of the Panel Discussion was that in practice the husband would never reject such a child,[9] but it certainly appears that he

[1] At p. 84. In the Panel Discussion Molapo mentioned the difficulty encountered by Chief Mathealira, the brother of the present King, in being recognized, since he was born after the death of Paramount Chief Seeiso—P.D., pp. 20–1. Contrast this with the recognition given over a century earlier to the grandfather of Moshoeshoe I, Peete, who was neither the natural son of Sekake, Chief of the Bakoena, nor the issue of *kenelo*, but of an irregular union of Sekake's widow with a member of the Amahlubi tribe (see Laydevant, p. 254; P.D., p. 85).

[2] Act 22 of 1968.   [3] S. 10(1).

[4] See *Molapo* v. *Molapo* H.C. Civ./A/8/1973 (H.C.); P.D., pp. 23–4.

[5] S. 39.

[6] *Sekake* v. *Tautona* J.C. 15/1959 discussed at pp. 263–4 below.

[7] P. 181 above.

[8] Mr. John Perry kindly furnished me with a most interesting example of such an occurrence. It dated back to the 1920s and was related to him by Mr. S. J. Jingoes who is a member of the family in which it happened.

[9] P.D., p. 118.

may divorce his wife in some circumstances and ensure that the child is transferred permanently to its mother's family so as to prevent it from inheriting in his family.[1]

The responsibilities of the family council also come into prominence where the heir's whereabouts are unknown, for instance when he has been absent for many years abroad. Here the family should meet in order to make a temporary appointment of a curator of the estate while investigations proceed with a view to making contact with the heir.[2] If no agreement can be reached within the family the matter will have to be resolved by the court.[3]

Where the heir is a minor at the time of his father's death he does not inherit at once, but falls under the guardianship of his widowed mother or a male relative of his father. He only takes control of the property when he marries and in the process attains his majority.[4] This matter is discussed fully in Chapter 18.

Before tracing the line of inheritance in cases where the deceased had no male issue and thus no heir (in the narrow sense of the word), it should be pointed out that if an heir is born and attains majority through marriage but predeceases his father, the inheritance passes to the heir's own heir[5] and if there is none, to his widow.[6] This can have the result that when a man dies his estate may be inherited by his son's widow rather than by his own widow. The seeming injustice of such a situation was pointed out in a debate in the National Council in 1938,[7] but it is mitigated by the right of the deceased's widow to be maintained during her lifetime out of the estate.[8]

(ii) *Where there is no male issue*

If the deceased died without any male issue there is no heir

[1] See *Chaka* v. *Chaka* J.C. 210/1966 (J.C.) and p. 218 above. See also *Molapo* v. *Molapo* H.C. Civ./A/8/1973 (H.C.) where there are *dicta* suggesting that an adulterine child who had been repudiated by the husband would not have an automatic right to succeed to the chieftainship.

[2] *Manyeli* v. *Manyeli* J.C. 82/1950 (C.C. and J.C.); *Malatela* v. *Sefale* J.C. 42/1961 (J.C.); *Moliko* v. *Moliko* J.C. 228/1963 (C.C. and J.C.).

[3] *Manyeli* v. *Manyeli* J.C. 82/1950 (J.C.); *Malatela* v. *Sefale* J.C. 42/1961 (J.C.); Duncan, p. 13.

[4] See p. 281 below and section 14(3) of Part I of the Laws of Lerotholi applied in *Masobeng* v. *Masobeng* J.C. 36/1965 (L.C. and J.C.) in relation to allocated property.

[5] *Tsita* v. *Rantote* J.C. 98/1959 (all courts); P.D., pp. 148–9.

[6] *Mokorosi* v. *Mokorosi* (1954) H.C.T.L.R. 24 (L.C., C.C., J.C., and H.C.).

[7] *1938 National Council Proceedings*, pp. 267–90.

[8] Discussed fully in Ch. 18 below.

stricto sensu, unless one is born posthumously through the *kenelo* system or otherwise and, even so, such a son may not necessarily gain recognition today as the heir.

Next, in descending order of precedence come the people listed below; if any person within the appropriate category is alive at the deceased's death he or she succeeds to the estate in preference to those in subordinate categories:

(1) The deceased's widow in terms of section 11(2) of Part I of the Laws of Lerotholi;[1]

(2) the deceased's father;[2]

(3) the deceased's grandfather;[3]

(4) the deceased's brothers,[4] in the following order of precedence[5]—

    (a) the eldest brother in the deceased's own house;

    (b) the eldest brother in his father's senior house;

    (c) down through the order of houses from senior to junior; within any house the eldest in age taking precedence over younger members.

Where any brother has died before the deceased, leaving male issue alive, such a son will inherit in his place. Similarly in the absence of a son, that brother's widow will take.[6]

(5) The nearest male related to the deceased by blood.[7]

(6) In the unlikely event that no such relative can be found it appears that the chief holds the estate property as a curator, in case a relative is later discovered.[8]

Although Chief Jobo in his evidence to the 1872 Commission declared that a daughter could inherit her father's property if there were no collateral male heirs (i.e. no one in category (4)

[1] See the discussion below, pp. 288–90.

[2] *Malatela* v. *Sefale* J.C. 42/1961 (J.C.); P.D., pp. 153–4. Duncan (at p. 12) specifies the parents, relying on *Mokhejane* v. *Seisa* J.C. 155/1950 (J.C.), but this case does not appear to establish the point. The deceased's mother would appear to have no right to inherit.

[3] P.D., p. 154.

[4] *Lethaha* v. *Lethaha* H.C. 22/1943 (P.C.'s Ct.; H.C.); *Selalia* v. *Selalia* J.C. 9/1952 (J.C.); Sheddick (1953), p. 33; Duncan, p. 12. See also *Hlongoane* v. *Lebelo* J.C. 64/1963 (all courts).

[5] P.D., p. 154.   [6] P.D., pp. 154–5.

[7] The deceased's *malome* would not, of course, qualify—see P.D., p. 156.

[8] P.D., pp. 157–8.

above),[1] it is doubtful whether he was correct.[2] While there is no case available to me which appears conclusively to deny the right of a daughter to inherit, two decisions do provide strong grounds for believing this to be the position.

In *Lethaha* v. *Lethaha*[3] the plaintiff, a daughter of the deceased, disputed the estate with his younger brother's son. The Paramount Chief's Court divided the property between them. However, the justification for doing this was that the defendant had totally failed in his duty to look after the deceased's widow during an illness which had proved fatal and the court did not doubt that strictly he was the legal heir to the estate. On appeal to the High Court the Chief Justice reversed this decision and awarded the whole of the property to the defendant on the simple ground that he was the heir. One repercussion of this decision was that a motion was brought before the National Council proposing that where a person died leaving daughters but no sons his estate should be divided equally between his daughters and his brothers. The motion was heavily defeated.[4] The *ratio decidendi* of *Lethaha's case* goes no further, of course, than to establish that the deceased's brothers and their issue take precedence over his daughters; it does not lay down a principle that daughters can never under any circumstances inherit, for instance if there were no collateral male heirs.[5]

In *Malatela* v. *Sefale*[6] the dispute was between a married daughter of the deceased and a son of the deceased's sister. The decisions of the various courts through which the case proceeded are rendered inconclusive by the lack of any consensus about the facts. Neither party's claim rested purely upon his or her natural relationship to the deceased. The daughter relied upon an allocation or a will in her favour, while the nephew contended that he had been adopted by the deceased as his own son and heir and had been recognized as such by a family council. In the upshot the Judicial Commissioner gave limited confirmation to the decision of the family council but held that neither party had an outright

---

[1] *1873 Report and Evidence*, p. 50.
[2] P.D., pp. 156–8.   [3] H.C. 22/1943.
[4] *1943 National Council Proceedings*, pp. 85–9.
[5] The same conclusion was reached in *Moletsane* v. *Lebakeng* J.C. 15/1970 (L.C. and J.C.; C.C. awarded the estate to the daughter but this was because she was not being properly maintained by the deceased's brother's son).
[6] J.C. 42/1961.

claim to the estate since there was probably a son of one of the deceased's brothers who, when located, would have a prior right.

One aspect of this question which was referred to by the Central Court in this case merits further comment. While it seems not improbable that daughters, whatever their marital status, are barred from inheriting their fathers' estates, there would appear to be a stronger objection to claims brought by daughters who are married. The reasons are twofold. First, that this would involve the transfer of property from one lineage to another without a sufficient cause such as is provided in the case of the payment of *bohali*. Secondly, that a married woman should look to her husband for her support and not to her natal family.

However this may be, it seems that the only way in which a father can satisfactorily provide for his daughters is by allocating property to them during his lifetime or by making some form of testamentary disposition in their favour.[1]

(iii) *Concubines* (linyatsi)

What is the position of a woman who has lived with a man for a considerable period of time but not married him? The courts seem to have been torn between the strictly legal position which would deny them any rights at all and a desire to do justice in particular cases. Thus in *Thebe* v. *Sofonia*[2] where the parties had lived together for thirteen years the Central Court awarded the *nyatsi* five head of cattle because the man was acting harshly in driving her out after she had cared for him and his household well for such a long period. Similarly in *Makhebesela* v. *Makhebesela*[3] where the cohabitation had lasted for fifteen years the courts came to the rescue of the *nyatsi* when she was turned out.[4] The Central Court ordered that all the products of their joint labours should belong to her including the furniture and livestock they had purchased, the crops they had reaped, and the huts they had built. The man was only to be left with the lands allocated to him and his clothes. On appeal, Driver J.C. felt this was hardly just to the

---

[1] Discussed in Ch. 19 below.

[2] J.C. 248/1947 referred to in Duncan, p. 42. The J.C. on appeal did not deal with this aspect of the dispute.

[3] J.C. 271/1954.

[4] She has no right to remain in her lover's house if he orders her out—see *Mohapi* v. *Noosi*, Motjoka C.C. 223/1959 (C.C.).

man and so altered the judgment to allow the assets to be shared equally between them.

However, where the *nyatsi* has claimed a right to inherit upon her lover's death she does not seem to have been so successful. In *Sebata* v. *Sebata*[1] a *nyatsi* disputed the deceased's estate with his widow (who was acting on behalf of his minor heir). The concubine contended that she was entitled to part of the estate because a large portion of the property had been acquired through her own effort and earnings. Her claim was dismissed by the Central Court, the Paramount Chief's Court, and finally by Thompson J.C., who cast doubts upon the correctness of the reasoning of Driver J.C. in *Makhebesela* v. *Makhebesela*.[2]

Ramolefe, protesting at the injustice of such an outcome, has suggested that the *nyatsi* might perhaps succeed if she framed her claim as one for the sharing of joint assets on the dissolution of a partnership[3] and this idea did gain some support from members of the Panel Discussion.[4] However, it would undoubtedly be a novel step in the evolution of Sesotho law if a claim on this basis were to be upheld by the courts and it would seem both preferable and possible for the principle in *Makhebesela's case* to be followed in appropriate circumstances.

(iv) *Illegitimate children*

Only legitimate children can inherit from their fathers[5] and thus the foregoing discussion has taken it for granted that the heir is a legitimate son, albeit perhaps conceived posthumously or in adultery. It has already been explained that the category of illegitimate children is a restricted one, being limited to those children born to an unmarried woman or a divorcee who have not been legitimated by their mothers' subsequent marriage or remarriage coupled with the appropriate formalities.[6] Such a child belongs in the family of its mother and the question arises as to whether it has any rights of inheritance there.

In *Rasethuntsa* v. *Rasethuntsa*[7] the mother of two illegitimate children had built three houses with the assistance of her son Tom, who claimed to inherit them on her death. His right to do so was challenged by Buller who was the son of Tom's elder

---

[1] J.C. 269/1960.   [2] J.C. 271/1954.
[3] (1969), pp. 204–5.   [4] P.D., pp. 158–9.
[5] *Mosoang* v. *Mosoang* J.C. 234/1966 (all courts); Duncan, p. 11; P.D., p. 147.
[6] See pp. 181–3 above.   [7] J.C. 216/1947.

brother. The Judicial Commissioner, overruling the lower court, held that neither was entitled to inherit since the deceased was a minor and her property therefore passed to her father or his heir.[1] It was further stated *obiter* that if the deceased had had any daughters the *bohali* paid on their marriages would have belonged not to Buller or Tom but to the head of the deceased's father's family.

The situation is more complicated where the illegitimate son marries and becomes a major and a family head himself. In *Tsoele* v. *Nqhae*[2] the question arose whether such a person could be held liable for a seduction perpetrated by his younger unmarried brother. Thompson J.C. held that he could, because on marriage he became the head of the family and was thus entitled to any *bohali* paid for his sisters. However, a mere six months later in *Mahomed* v. *Lempe*[3] Thompson J.C. reached the opposite conclusion on similar facts, holding this time that it was the seducer's mother's father's heir who was liable and absolved the elder brother of the seducer. He reversed the decision of the Central Court and relied on *Rasethuntsa's case*. He went on to state that the only circumstance in which an illegitimate child could inherit was where there was no male survivor of his maternal grandfather's family.

In 1947, the same year in which *Rasethuntsa's case* was decided, it was held in *Thabo* v. *Makopela*[4] that the estate of the deceased passed to his junior brother rather than to his daughter's illegitimate son, despite the deceased's stated desire that his grandson should inherit. These two decisions prompted moves among members of the National Council to improve the plight of illegitimate children. A motion was introduced calling for illegitimate children to be given the right to inherit from their maternal grandfathers in the absence of maternal uncles or their issue, but in precedence over any brothers of their grandfathers.[5] This motion was opposed by many members who raised the spectre of an increase in the illegitimacy rate and the appointment of chiefs who were illegitimate. As a result it was defeated. A second motion along the same lines was proposed in 1952 and its sup-

---

[1] For the inheritance of a minor's property see pp. 226–8 above.
[2] J.C. 73/1964.   [3] J.C. 227/1964.
[4] J.C. 360/1947 (J.C.).
[5] *1947 National Council Proceedings*, pp. 85–9.

porters argued that justice favoured the illegitimate son above the deceased's brother because the former had at least worked for the family and contributed his earnings, while the latter had not. However, the motion was again lost.[1]

Many of those who gave evidence before the National Council's Select Committee on Wills, Estates and Marriages in 1962 expressed the view that illegitimate children ought to be allowed to inherit in their mothers' families and the majority of the members of the Panel Discussion were also unhappy with the present position, suggesting that it was repugnant to justice, morality, and good conscience and ought to be changed.[2] A few even thought that the law had already evolved beyond this point through the practices of the people; particularly where the mother had a separate establishment of her own and where her illegitimate son was married he would take charge of the affairs of her household, merely notifying his grandfather of what he was doing. In effect he would be a joint guardian of his mother with his grandfather and would usually inherit her property on her death.[3]

(v) *Adoption*

Where a married man has no male issue he may adopt a minor son of one of his brothers or another close relative. All parental rights and duties will automatically be transferred to the adopter, and this child may later inherit as the adopter's heir when he dies.[4] Adoption almost invariably occurs within the extended family and is practically unknown between strangers.[5] The legal validity of the act depends upon the satisfaction of two conditions. First, there must be agreement between the child's natural father (or guardian) and the prospective adopter.[6] There is no need for the agreement to be recorded in writing for purposes of evidence[7] owing to the second requirement which is that full family publicity

[1] *1952 National Council Proceedings*, pp. 71–80.
[2] P.D., pp. 147–8.
[3] P.D., pp. 208, 212–15.
[4] See P.D., pp. 197–201.
[5] Laydevant, p. 257; Duncan, p. 8; P.D., pp. 197–9.
[6] *Phamotse* v. *Phamotse* H.C. 22/1952 (all courts); *Mofammere* v. *Mofammere* J.C. 90/1965 (J.C.); *Peete* v. *Phantsi* J.C. 275/1966 (J.C.); *Tseole* v. *Tseole* J.C. 136/1967 (L.C. and J.C.); Duncan, p. 8; P.D., p. 199.
[7] *Phamotse* v. *Phamotse* (J.C.; *contra* C.C. and P.C.'s Ct.). A proposal to make a written agreement obligatory was defeated in the National Council in 1944—see *1944 National Council Proceedings*, pp. 204–7.

must be given to the event.[1] In some cases it has been stated that the local chief must be notified,[2] but while it would be desirable for the adopted child to be pointed out to the chief as the prospective heir for evidentiary reasons, it is not thought to be a *sine qua non*.[3] However, it would seem essential that any person who would have inherited the deceased's estate but for the adoption should have been told.[4]

It is not sufficient to show that the deceased brought up the child and treated him as his own, for instance by paying the expenses of his circumcision or compensation for his delicts or *bohali* on his marriage.[5] These are equivocal acts and may represent no more than kindness and it is a very frequent occurrence for children to be reared by their uncles or grandparents or other relatives without the permanent transfer of parental rights or duties.[6] This latter practice is often found convenient for personal or economic reasons and serves to cement family relationships;[7] it is only temporary and the child may be recalled at any time by its parents. When the child eventually leaves, a single beast known as *khomo ea seotla* is payable to compensate the family which has looked after the child for the cost of its maintenance and upbringing.[8] This is a fixed payment and no greater claim can be made on the basis that greater expenditure has actually been incurred unless this was expressly authorized.[9]

Through the process of adoption even a child which was

[1] *Monne* v. *Monne* J.C. 125/1951 (C.C. and J.C.); *Phamotse* v. *Phamotse* (L.C., J.C., and H.C.); *Mofammere* v. *Mofammere* (C.C. and J.C.); *Noko* v. *Noko* J.C. 187/1966 (L.C. and J.C.); *Peete* v. *Phantsi* (C.C. and J.C.); *Tseole* v. *Tseole* (L.C. and J.C.); Duncan, p. 8; P.D., p. 199.

[2] *Noko* v. *Noko* J.C. 187/1966 (J.C.); *Tseole* v. *Tseole* (L.C. and J.C.).

[3] See Duncan, p. 8. A motion before the National Council in 1944 to make it necessary for the Paramount Chief's approval of the adoption to be obtained was lost—see *1944 National Council Proceedings*, pp. 204–7.

[4] *Phamotse* v. *Phamotse* (H.C.); P.D., p. 199.

[5] See *Phamotse* v. *Phamotse* (L.C., C.C., P.C.'s Ct., and H.C.); *Mofammere* v. *Mofammere* (C.C. and J.C.; *contra* L.C.).

[6] See Laydevant, pp. 256–7.

[7] P.D., pp. 201–2.

[8] *Teleki* v. *Teleki* H.C. 38/1951 (L.C., P.C.'s Ct., J.C. and H.C.); *Letsepe* v. *Lekitla* J.C. 47/1961 (all courts); Duncan, pp. 8–9; P.D., pp. 202–3. Some members of the Panel Discussion were of the opinion that the *seotla* beast was only payable in respect of girls because their upbringing was more expensive than that of boys and they were less serviceable.

[9] *Teleki* v. *Teleki* (L.C., P.C.'s Ct., J.C., and H.C.); Duncan, pp. 8–9; P.D., p. 203.

illegitimate at birth may come to inherit. He might, for instance, be adopted by his maternal grandfather, in which case he would inherit in his mother's family,[1] or by his paternal grandfather or paternal uncle, in which case he would inherit in that family.[2] In the latter case cattle may be paid to the family of the child's mother since the child is being transferred from one lineage to another in a manner similar to cases where the father of a pre-marital child pays extra *bohali* to 'marry' the child with its mother.[3] However, the payment of cattle would not seem to be necessary to make the adoption valid.[4] Sometimes an adopted child will be allotted some stock by his natural father to take with him to his new home to give him a start in life.[5]

(vi) *Disinheritance*

It has earlier been explained that where a husband divorces his wife and she is proved to be at fault, for instance by giving birth to an adulterine child, the husband may recover his *bohali* and the children may sometimes be permanently transferred to their mother's family.[6]

The question arises whether, short of this, a man can ever disinherit his prospective heir and, if so, under what circumstances. The members of the Panel Discussion were adamant that the law did not recognize such a procedure and that even if a father attempted it his family would not implement his decision after his death and thus his heir would still inherit.[7] However, recently Thompson J. C., relying strongly on the opinions of his assessors, and after having initial doubts,[8] has held fast to the view that disinheritance is permissible, and his judgments contain a number of *obiter dicta* to this effect.[9] Ramolefe also subscribes to this opinion.[10]

[1] See the *obiter dictum* of Thompson J.C. in *Moletsane* v. *Lebakeng* J.C. 15/1970.
[2] See *Monne* v. *Monne* J.C. 125/1951 (C.C. and J.C.).
[3] See *Monne* v. *Monne* where ten head of cattle were paid by the adopter in respect of a child fathered by his younger brother before his marriage to its mother.
[4] Duncan, p. 8.   [5] P.D., p. 201.
[6] P. 218 above and see P.D., p. 193.
[7] P.D., pp. 192–3.
[8] See *Seenzile* v. *Seenzile* J.C. 143/1961 where he took the contrary view soon after commencing his appointment.
[9] See pp. 192–3 above.   [10] (1969), p. 205.

The best analysis of the circumstances under which disinheritance can occur, if at all, is to be found in the judgment of President T. J. Molapo in the Maja Central Court in *Semoli* v. *Semoli*.[1] The case was not one of disinheritance *simpliciter*, but rather of the revocation by a father of an *inter vivos* allocation to his heir, and the President's remarks were therefore *obiter*. He declared:

According to the law the heir may be excluded from his rights of heirship. This is a very big step and . . . we find that it is not common; even in cases where it has been attempted it is often found it fails. A person who wishes to exclude the heir from his rights has to summon all members of the family and accuse the heir in his presence and then ask the family to exclude him from his rights. Should the family find a just cause for so doing it will uphold the request which will be notified to the chief. If this procedure is followed the heir may be excluded from his rights. Conditions upon which an heir may be excluded from his rights are not many, but serious misbehaviour which humiliates the parents may be the reason . . . [P]roperty does not belong to one person only but to all his family. The family has placed this property in the hands of someone to accomplish all family obligations with it. An heir is a person who is to enhance the name of his father.

On appeal to the Judicial Commissioner's Court, Thompson J.C. stated that he could not improve upon this formulation of the position.[2]

In the absence of any authoritative decision on disinheritance it cannot be stated categorically what the true legal position is. Disinheritance is recognized as possible among the Sotho peoples living in South Africa and this fact may conceivably have misled those who assert its existence in Lesotho;[3] on the other hand, this fact may equally be regarded as a strong indication that it also forms part of Sesotho law.

Aside from the possibility of being barred from the inheritance by misconduct, an heir does not have to satisfy any requirements in order to qualify for his position. He acquires the status by right of birth. Even insanity would not appear to be a disqualification

---

[1] J.C. 159/1967.

[2] The preconditions referred to by Ramolefe (1969), p. 205 are virtually the same as those laid down in the Central Court judgment, except the notification of the matter to the chief; perhaps this is not an essential requirement.

[3] See Whitfield, *South African Native Law* (2nd ed.), pp. 346–9, and Seymour, *Native Law in South Africa* (2nd ed.), p. 149, both of which were referred to by Thompson J.C. in *Semoli's case*.

though the heir will inevitably need a guardian to supervise the management of estate property and carry out any functions of office, e.g. chieftainship administration. However, such a guardian will not himself take over the heirship.[1] An illustration of this situation is found in relation to the chieftainship of Leribe. When Chief Molapo, the second son of Moshoeshoe I, died in 1880 his senior son and heir Joseph was insane. As a result, his second son Jonathan took over the management of his affairs, but when in turn he died, the chieftainship passed not to his own son Mathealira, but to Joseph's son Motsoene.[2]

(b) *The Division of the Estate*

Not all the property that was held by the deceased at the time of his death passes automatically to his heir and thus the regime is by no means one of universal succession.

It is convenient to examine the various categories of property in turn.

(i) *Personal property*[3]

This consists, broadly speaking, of items that were not primarily held or used for, or on behalf of, the deceased's family or household. It includes clothes, some blankets, accessories such as a watch or a ring, a horse and saddle, any weapons, and other private possessions received or acquired in a personal capacity rather than as the head of the family. These personal effects are distributed by the deceased's senior relatives. The *malome* (senior maternal uncle) has pre-eminence over all the other relatives in taking particular items. He is entitled to select for himself some articles of clothing and to take a horse and saddle as well as things such as a gun or a watch. He should also be given a beast in return for slaughtering one of his own to 'settle his nephew's grave'.[4] The senior maternal uncle's rights are, however, contingent upon his having performed his kinship obligations towards the deceased during his lifetime.

After the *malome* has taken his share the rest of the personal effects are distributed to other male relatives of the deceased. His

---

[1] *Mokhesi* v. *Mokhesi* J.C. 230/1945 (P.C.'s Ct. and J.C.).

[2] See P.D., pp. 193–4. *Chere* v. *Sekara* J.C. 137/1947, cited in Duncan (at p. 49), turned on the validity of an allocation of a chieftainship.

[3] See Ellenberger and Macgregor, p. 270; Laydevant, p. 253; Ashton, p. 182; Sheddick (1953), p. 64; P.D., pp. 209–12.

[4] The beast given to *malome* is called *pelesa ea likobo*—see Duncan, p. 10.

widow will also receive some articles which will be of use in her home, for instance blankets.

The foregoing can only be regarded as a statement of the formal traditional position. Every family will deal with the distribution in a way which is most appropriate to its own circumstances and the introduction of a greater variety of personal articles has meant that the need for a flexible approach is more apparent today than in the past.

From what has been said it will be clear that the personal property of the deceased forms no part of the inheritance which passes to the heir.

(ii) *Household property*

This comprises wealth in the form of cash, livestock of all kinds, agricultural implements, the produce of the land including crops, fruit, and timber, pieces of furniture, the cooking and kitchen utensils, and all other articles used to support the family and its enterprises.

Such property does form part of the heir's inheritance, although as will be seen he does not have the right to do exactly as he likes with it. There is no formal handing over of the estate.[1] The assets of the estate are not turned into money and there is no concept akin to the process of winding up within a fixed time.[2] The heir merely steps into his father's shoes and carries on where the latter left off. He will call upon his father's debtors to pay what is presently due and should also extinguish any immediate liabilities to creditors.[3]

He inherits future rights of action such as claims for damages for, e.g., the seduction of one of his unmarried sisters or an assault upon one of his bachelor brothers. He will also be entitled to receive the earnings of all minors in the family and any *bohali* paid upon the marriages of his sisters.[4] The heir's responsibilities towards other members of the family are analysed below.

The situation is more complicated where the deceased was a polygamist with various houses to whom he would almost certainly

---

[1] *Malefane* v. *Selebalo* J.C. 191/1949 (J.C.) cited in Duncan, p. 14.

[2] *Rametsana* v. *Malelu* J.C. 27/1968 (J.C.).

[3] Ramolefe (1969), p. 206, who points out that *bohali* debts are not immediately paid or called up but continue to be extinguished in the normal way.

[4] Ramolefe, 'Customary Law Inheritance and Succession' (1965–66), *Basutoland Notes and Records* 18 at 19.

have allocated certain household property during his lifetime. Here there will commonly be one principal heir (in the senior house in which there is male issue) and junior heirs in the other houses. The legal position is set out in section 13(1) of Part I of the Laws of Lerotholi which provides that the principal heir inherits all the unallocated property, in addition to the property allocated to his own house. Property allocated to other houses is inherited by the heirs in those houses so as not to offend against the maxim '*malapa ha a jane*' ('houses do not "eat" one another').[1] Such house property naturally includes rights to e.g. *bohali* payable in respect of future marriages of girls in a particular house.[2]

Considerable difficulties arise where the deceased has married a second wife while remaining a monogamist, for instance after his first wife's death or following a divorce. The question which then arises is whether he has left two houses or only one. Strictly speaking, separate houses are created by polygamists and therefore there can only be a single house. This may, however, lead to undesirable consequences if the view is taken, as it was by the Court of Appeal in *Khatala* v. *Khatala*,[3] that the concept of allocation is inappropriate to monogamous marriages. The result will be that the whole of the deceased's estate will be treated as unallocated property which is inherited by the heir and thus the widow and children of the second marriage may be placed at a disadvantage *vis-à-vis* the son of the first marriage.[4] Arguably this should not be allowed to happen because both marriages were monogamous and the second wife was in no sense a more junior wife than the first. It will, however, be strongly contended in a later chapter that the concept of allocation is by no means restricted to houses but can take place in favour of individuals.[5] In this way, therefore, the second widow and her children can be adequately safeguarded by the husband during his lifetime and property allocated to them will, subject to certain conditions, be placed beyond the grasp of the heir of the first marriage. But leaving this question aside for the present, the problem of deciding on the number of houses remains.

---

[1] Ashton, p. 182; Sheddick (1953), p. 63.
[2] See pp. 141–2 above.
[3] (1963–66) H.C.T.L.R. 97, discussed in Ch. 18 below.
[4] See p. 277 below.   [5] See Ch. 19 below.

The courts have by no means been consistent on the question. Sometimes they have held that there is only a single house,[1] but more commonly they have taken the view that there are two houses, seeking in this manner to protect the second widow and her children by the application of the '*malapa ha a jane*' rule.[2] Certainly this upholds the intention of the husband whose behaviour often suggests that he believes himself to be a genuine polygamist.[3]

While the former decisions are technically correct, the latter may be regarded as a slightly erroneous means of recognizing the validity of allocations to the individual second widow or her children. The courts seem particularly ready to do this where there is very clear evidence of an allocation, e.g. by earmarking livestock,[4] but as will be shown this is certainly not a *sine qua non* for the validity of an allocation.[5]

A good example of this situation is provided by the case of *Bolepo* v. *Bolepo*.[6] The deceased has divorced his first wife on the ground of desertion after she had borne him two sons, the eldest being the plaintiff in the present case. He then married the defendant, by whom he has a son and two daughters. Before his death he made a written declaration in which he expressed a wish that the residue of his estate should go to the defendant, stating that he had already allocated a large number of livestock to the plaintiff and his younger brother. The plaintiff brought an action in which he asserted a claim to the entire estate including the stock which had been paid as *bohali* on the marriage of the defendant's daughters. He based this upon the contention that there was only one house to which he was the heir.

All the courts rejected the claim and held that there were two

---

[1] See e.g. *Khatala* v. *Khatala* (J.C., H.C., and C.A.); *Chalete* v. *Mbohla* J.C. 76/1967 (C.C.). The impression of a single house can often be created from the fact that the second wife will normally use the same hut and plough the same fields as the first wife, but this is more a matter of practical common sense than of legal significance.

[2] See e.g. *Sebotsa* v. *Sebotsa* H.C. 23/1940 (all courts); *Lephole* v. *Lephole* J.C. 15/1958 (C.C.); *Ntoula* v. *Morake* J.C. 227/1960 (L.C. and C.C.); *Bolepo* v. *Bolepo* J.C. 296/1966 (all courts); *Chalete* v. *Mbohla* (L.C. and J.C.); *Lephoi* v. *Lephoi* J.C. 264/1968 (C.C. and J.C.).

[3] See P.D., pp. 182, 196–7.

[4] See *Sebotsa* v. *Sebotsa*; *Bolepo* v. *Bolepo*; *Chalete* v. *Mbohla*; *Lephoi* v. *Lephoi*.

[5] See pp. 312–13 below.   [6] J.C. 296/1966.

houses and that the principle '*malapa ha a jane*' applied. Thompson J.C. declared:

[T]he deceased took specific steps to donate livestock to his son and heir by his first wife . . . he did that as an advance part of the inheritance of his eldest son . . . and he furthermore . . . thereafter differentiated his earmark from that used by [defendant's son] and made it clear that what was left was for the maintenance of his second wife . . . I think this case of what may have been a monogamous husband clearly allows his creating two houses by a specific division and allocation and ear-marking of livestock. . . . According to custom he was entitled to create a second house after separating from his first wife.

In a number of judgments in cases of this nature recognition has been given to a custom whereby the husband takes his second wife for the express and stated purpose of having her bring up the children of the first marriage.[1] This practice resembles in some respects the special form of marriage known as *seantlo* discussed in Chapter 12, although in *seantlo* the second wife has to be a relative of the first, which is not the case here. The second wife is seen in both, however, as stepping into the shoes of the deceased wife and taking her place in every way. The inevitable repercussion is that the courts will treat the husband as having but a single house.

The leading case on this custom is *Maseela* v. *Maseela*,[2] which came on appeal before the High Court in 1954. The deceased had first married 'M'a-Enea by whom he had a son Enea. 'M'a-Enea then deserted him and never returned. The deceased later married Mabel by whom he had a son David. After serving with the allied forces in the First World War the deceased returned home and presented Mabel to his family in the presence of Enea and announced that she was his wife and that she would bring up Enea because his mother was in desertion. From this time up to the deceased's death Mabel helped build up the nucleus of a considerable business in Maseru which she developed further on her own after his death. The question which fell to be decided was who should inherit the estate on her death, her son David or

[1] See e.g. *Lephole* v. *Lephole* (L.C. and J.C.); *Ntoula* v. *Morake* (J.C.); *Khatala* v. *Khatala* (C.C. and P.C.'s Ct.); *Lephoi* v. *Lephoi* (L.C.); *Mothebesoane* v. *Mothebesoane* H.C. Civ. /T/12/1970 (H.C.).
[2] (1954) H.C.T.L.R. 48.

the senior son, Enea. Certainly Enea had a strong prima facie claim since he was the eldest son of the first wife and thus the principal heir. However, David contended that when the deceased married Mabel he had created a second house and further that the estate consisted of property belonging to that house in which he was the heir. Enea countered by saying that there was only one house and thus only one heir, namely himself. The Judicial Commissioner accepted this latter argument, pointing out that Mabel was not married as a second wife but was married to *kenela* the rights of (i.e. take the place of) 'M'a-Enea.

. . . if he had married Mabel as a second hut he would have followed the customary procedure when presenting her to his people and mentioned what property was to belong to Mabel's house, namely he would have given her her own earmark.

This finding was upheld on appeal by the High Court.

The decision has been criticized by Ramolefe on the ground that only *seantlo* and *ngoetsi* wives can lawfully take over the rights of a deceased wife.[1] He therefore denies the very existence of the alleged custom. However, the judicial acceptance of the custom in a considerable number of cases during the last twenty years culminating in the High Court decision in *Mothebesoane* v. *Mothebesoane*[2] in 1971 cannot be so lightly dismissed.

Where *Maseela's case* is possibly open to attack is on the basis that the second wife was married at a time when the husband's first marriage was still in existence.[3] The question arises whether the custom can operate where the first wife is still alive and has not been divorced.[4] Bearing in mind that the object of the second marriage is to bring up the young children of the first marriage and that this is publicly acknowledged, there seems no reason in principle why this should not be possible in circumstances such as a long period of desertion.[5] The husband will thus be a polygamist

[1] (1969), p. 199.

[2] H.C. Civ./T/12/1970 and see the other cases cited in note 1, p. 245 above.

[3] See P.D., pp. 145–6. One of the assessors in the High Court recorded his dissent from the decision of the Chief Justice.

[4] Duncan (at p. 1) is in error in stating that the parties in *Maseela's case* had been divorced.

[5] The custom was recognized in these circumstances in *Lesitsi* v. *Mafa* 84/1953 (J.C.).

and yet have but a single house. The situation is therefore analogous to marriage to a *ngoetsi* or a *mala* wife rather than to *seantlo*.[1]

Where the courts do uphold this custom it is clear that no allocation can be made to the second wife and her children as a separate house. However, it is submitted that this does not bar recognition of the possibility of allocations made to them as individuals.[2] In *Maseela's case* Driver J.C. concentrated on whether the second wife had been given her own earmark but this can only be relevant in relation to livestock. Since the dispute concerned the assets of a business the court should have been ready to look for other evidence of allocation.[3] In a sense, therefore, the search for one or two houses in cases like these is a misguided one. The more important task is to discover whether or not a valid allocation has been made. If it has then this reduces the property which is unallocated and therefore available for the heir. This proposition admittedly flies in the face of the High Court decision in *Lekaota* v. *Lekaota*[4] where it was held that allocations could only be made to a house but it is respectfully submitted that this finding was erroneous.[5]

(iii) *Houses and other buildings*

The deceased's huts or houses (in the sense of physical structures) are inherited today by the heir as part of the estate.[6] Sheddick has suggested that in the past they were inherited by the deceased's youngest son despite the fact that the residence rights in respect of the land on which they stood passed to the heir.[7] The reason for this was that the heir would have built or acquired houses of his own. The youngest son, on the other hand, would have continued to live with his parents according to the custom and when his parents died he would have remained in possession as '*toeba ea lithako*' ('the mouse among the ruins'). Whether this really was the traditional position does not seem clear and it may be that the youngest son was merely permitted to continue his occupation with the leave of the heir, as is equally possible today.[8]

---

[1] See Ch. 12 above.
[2] Discussed further in Ch. 19 below.
[3] See *Tsosane* v. *Tsosane* H.C. Civ./A/6/1968, discussed at p. 314 below.
[4] (1963–6) H.C.T.L.R. 38 (H.C.).
[5] See p. 309 below.
[6] Duncan, p. 14; P.D., pp. 147, 234.
[7] (1953), p. 63.   [8] See P.D., p. 234.

(iv) *Residential sites, gardens, and tree plantations*

These assets are all inheritable in terms of section 7(7) of Part I of the Laws of Lerotholi:[1]

On the death of a person who has been allocated the use of land for the growing of vegetables or tobacco, or for the purpose of planting fruit or other trees, or for residential purposes, the heir, or in the absence of the heir the dependants of such deceased person shall be entitled to the use of such land so long as he or they continue to dwell thereon.

In the earlier version of the Laws published in 1946 the following additional words were to be found at the end of the section: '. . . or in the immediate vicinity', thus enabling a person who lived in the same village as the deceased to inherit. Although this phrase has been omitted from the current edition the courts do not seem to have altered their earlier policy of recognizing the claims of heirs or dependants living nearby[2] and this seems eminently sensible because the intention is merely to prevent anyone inheriting who lives elsewhere and thus owes allegiance to another chief or headman.[3] Generally speaking, no one can owe allegiance to two different chiefs or headman, and the acquisition of residential rights depends upon the willingness of the subject to recognize the authority of the chief or headman of that area. The one exception to this rule seems to be where a person has one home in a reserve in an urban area (for instance because he works there) and another one in the countryside which he regards as his family home.[4] Apart from this it appears that, as a concession, some chiefs are prepared to grant residence rights to persons who already possess similar rights under another chief in the countryside.[5]

[1] Applied in *Chitja* v. *Monnanyane* J.C. 304/1963 (J.C.); *Letsae* v. *Letsae* J.C. 8/1965 (C.C. and J.C.); *Peete* v. *Phantsi* J.C. 275/1966 (all courts); *Raseipone* v. *Raseipone* J.C. 14/1967 (J.C.); *Maqoacha* v. *Moonyane* J.C. 2/1969 (J.C.) and see Duncan, pp. 95, 98–9.

[2] See *Chitja* v. *Monnanyane* (J.C.); *Mokhomo* v. *Mokhomo* J.C. 202/1966 (J.C.); *Sekatle* v. *Sekatle* J.C. 221/1964 (J.C.).

[3] This point does not seem to have been appreciated by Evans J. in *Moonyane* v. *Maqoacha* H.C. Civ./A/5/1971.

[4] *Maile* v. *Maile* J.C. 170/1965 (J.C.); *Sekatle* v. *Sekatle* (J.C.); P.D., pp. 173–4; *contra semble Tlebele* v. *Malimatle* J.C. 65/1944 cited in Duncan, p. 68.

[5] *Sekatle* v. *Sekatle* (all courts); *Moabi* v. *Mokhethi* J.C. 120/1965 (J.C.); *Raseipone* v. *Raseipone* (J.C.); Ramolefe (1966), p. 19; and see P.D., pp. 173–4.

Where a person 'removes' from one area to another and thus transfers his allegiance from one chiefly authority to another he will automatically forfeit his rights of occupation and user.[1]

In the recent case of *Moonyane* v. *Maqoacha*[2] the Judicial Commissioner held that before the local chief reallocated a residential site on the death of the occupier he should consult with the deceased's relatives in case there was an heir or dependants who were entitled to inherit it. In the High Court Evans J. held that no such rule had been established to exist, but since his criteria for the proof of customary law were erroneous his decision carries little weight.[3]

Similar rules of inheritance apply to the occupation of cattle posts for as long as the deceased's heir possesses stock and continues to make use of the post.[4]

(v) *Arable lands*

Lands for cultivation are allocated by the local chief or headman to family heads for the maintenance and support of their households. As has already been explained, this process not only has the function of preserving the traditional authority of the chieftainship in the political and social structure of society but is also intended to achieve an equitable distribution among the people of the sparse land that is available. In order to accomplish the latter objective satisfactorily it is necessary to prevent lands being tied up irrevocably for very long periods and thus the chiefs have the power to deprive landholders of their fields in certain specified circumstances mentioned earlier in Chapter 1.[5] Furthermore, in pursuance of this over-all policy there is a principle that, subject to necessary safeguards for any widows and minor children, on the death of the family head the lands that have been allocated to him revert to the chieftanship for reallocation. As the Sesotho maxim graphically puts its, '*ts'imo hase lefa*' ('arable lands are not an inheritance'). The heir is *not* therefore entitled to inherit his

---

[1] *Maile* v. *Sekhonyana* (1963–66) H.C.T.L.R. 67 (J.C. and H.C.); *Letsae* v. *Letsae* (C.C. and J.C.); *Mokhomo* v. *Mokhomo* (J.C.); Duncan, pp. 98–99; Ramolefe (1966), p. 19. For the rights of removers to take the materials of their huts with them or sell them, see s. 9 of Part I of the Laws of Lerotholi; Duncan, pp. 68–9; *1944 National Council Proceedings*, pp. 218–24.

[2] H.C. Civ./A/5/1971 (H.C.).

[3] See p. 50 above.

[4] See *Molahlehi* v. *Daemane* J.C. 214/1947 (J.C.) cited in Duncan, p. 85.

[5] See above, pp. 30–1.

deceased father's lands as part of the estate.[1] However, this is really to state the position too baldly because there is a further equally clear principle that land belongs to a family and not just to an individual person and for this reason the married sons of the deceased head of a family can expect to receive preference over all others when the chief comes to reallocate the lands.

Unfortunately some chiefs have been known to violate this last principle and to allocate lands instead to their favourites. When challenged they have sought to justify their actions by relying on the formalism of the first principle and ignoring the guiding spirit of the second. With a view to combating such abuses the National Council amended the wording of Part I of the Laws of Lerotholi in 1948 to provide that 'On the death of a person who has been allocated the use of property consisting of lands . . . his heir . . . shall be entitled to the use of such property'.[2]

Five years later the validity of this amendment fell to be considered by the Judicial Commissioner's Court in the important case of *Lesitsi* v. *Mafa*.[3] The dispute was between the deceased's widow and his son and heir by an earlier marriage. The son based his claim on the recent amendment while the widow relied on the prior law. The means by which Driver J.C. was able to reject the son's claim were identical to those employed by Lansdown J. in the *Regency case*[4] ten years earlier. First, the National Council did not possess legislative power[5] and secondly, the new 'rule' did not constitute a valid custom because it had obviously not been observed since time immemorial.[6]

There was an initial feeling of outrage in the Council when members learnt of the decision, but after a long debate the Council rejected a proposal to ask for the 1948 amendment to be transferred to Part II of the Laws and decided to bring the land provisions in Part I back into line with the traditional position.[7] As a consequence section 7(5)(a) of Part I now states plainly:

On the death of the father or mother, whoever dies last, all arable land

---

[1] Ramolefe (1966), p. 19 is grossly in error in his statement to the contrary.
[2] Section 7(5); see Sheddick (1954), p. 168.
[3] J.C. 84/1953.
[4] *Bereng Griffith* v. *'Mantsebo Seeiso Griffith* (1926–53) H.C.T.L.R. 50.
[5] See above, pp. 4–5.
[6] For criticism of this test for the validity of a customary rule see p. 47 above.
[7] *1955 National Council Proceedings*, pp. 155, 226.

allotted to them shall be regarded as land that has become vacant and shall revert to the Chief or Headman for re-allocation.

There is no question of the deceased's relatives having to surrender the land. It reverts automatically by operation of law.[1]

Although arable lands are not inheritable as a matter of law they do nevertheless commonly pass through the generations from father to son. How does this occur? First, through the operation of the important principle of land reallocation already mentioned which is presently enshrined in section 7(5)(b) of Part I of the Laws. This states:

In the re-allocation of lands which have reverted to the Chief or Headman on the death of the previous occupier and after the needs of any minor dependants have been satisfied . . .[2] the Chief or Headman shall give priority, as regards the allocation of the remaining lands should there be any, to the requirements of any adult son or sons of the deceased provided such son or sons reside in the village of the deceased.

The justification for such a provision lies in the recognition that lands are a family asset which the sons will probably have worked on and perhaps improved. It is only fair therefore to give them a right of first refusal. They are naturally subject to the general rule that the chief may deprive them of lands if they have more than sufficient and this would commonly occur if they were to retain their own lands as well as inheriting their fathers'. Thus basically if they choose the latter they will have to surrender all or some of the former. They are also subject to the rules of allegiance already mentioned.

The second method whereby land can pass from father to son is by a private and informal transfer. This can be achieved without documentation by the father during his life and is ratified by the chief or headman at the time.[3] Technically this is a process of surrender by the father and reallocation by the chief to the son.[4] It is often done because the family fears that after the death of both parents the chief may rely on the principle of reverter and

[1] *Seghlolo* v. *Phatela* J.C. 41/1968 (J.C.); *Molungoa* v. *Marakabei* J.C. 102/1969 (J.C.); *contra, Lesitsi* v. *Mafa* (J.C.).
[2] The needs of minor dependants are discussed on p. 254 below.
[3] See *Lesitsi* v. *Mafa* (J.C.); P.D., p. 170.
[4] See *Lesitsi* v. *Mafa* (J.C.).

violate the precept contained in section 7(5)(b), choosing to allocate the land to one of his favourites instead. As we have seen, it was in response to just such corrupt practices that the National Council was induced in 1948 to pass the motion designed to make land inheritable.[1]

No examination of this topic would be complete without making reference to Hamnett's critical comments on the judgment of Driver J.C. in *Lesitsi* v. *Mafa*.[2] In Hamnett's view the court made a grave error in seeming to place the rule that arable lands are not inheritable in an entirely 'different juristic universe' from the sons' right of first refusal on reallocation. The latter right, he asserts, became reduced to a pure question of administrative discretion into which the judicial courts were instructed not to inquire. This amounted to a complete perversion of Sesotho law and its effect was

. . . to polarise the law into a judicial aspect that can be enforced in specific terms, and an administrative aspect that is left to the 'discretion' of the chief. This fails to reflect the delicacy and subtlety of the customary situation, in which both norms involved (the non-inheritance of land, and the legitimacy of an heir's claims) are maintained, without the one being sacrificed to the other or the two being institutionally, procedurally and juristically separated into distinct categories of right.[3]

He points out that the impact of the decision was quite widespread because the judgment was circulated to the Basotho Courts many of which thereupon endeavoured to apply it, and because it soon came to be heavily relied upon in the Judicial Commissioner's Court itself. As a result, he alleges, the law has been plunged into confusion which in turn has led to injustice.

It is not easy to determine to what extent Driver J.C.'s judgment has had these dire practical repercussions and consequently to assess the validity of Hamnett's criticism. Certainly Driver J.C. constantly reiterated that arable land was not inheritable despite the attempts of the National Council to make it so. However, his sole reference to any 'discretion' vested in the chieftainship was set in the context of the retention of lands by minor children, and while clearly erroneous, related to a rather different question.

---

[1] See *Lesitsi* v. *Mafa* (J.C.).
[2] (1975), pp. 77–82.   [3] Ibid., p. 78.

Secondly, the bulk of the judgment is devoted to deciding whether a widow is entitled to the lands as against the heir after her husband's death and not whether the heir is entitled as against the chief when both parents are dead. It does not really seem justifiable to say, as Hamnett does, that the principle of non-inheritance was 'overinterpreted' by Driver J.C. On the one hand, he merely rejected the purported introduction of the principle of inheritance by the National Council. On the other, he was concerned to safeguard the rights of widows which were already clearly protected by section 7(4) of Part I of the Laws of Lerotholi.

Thirdly, the only case[1] relied upon by Hamnett to reflect the chaos caused by *Lesitsi* v. *Mafa* can be very well explained on other grounds. So many different issues were involved and so many questions were left undetermined that no satisfactory conclusions can be drawn from it. As Hamnett himself admits, the conflicting decisions given by the various courts in that case are explicable in a great variety of ways.

Fourthly, Hamnett refers to the chiefs' administrative discretion in relation to the process of reallocation being contained in section 7(5)(b) of the Laws[2]. This is incorrect. At the time when *Lesitsi* v. *Mafa* was decided there was no provision at all dealing with the right of first refusal of sons of the deceased. This new subsection was drafted *after* the decision when the land provisions were being reframed in the light of Driver J.C.'s judgment and his rejection of the purported change effected by the National Council. Driver J.C. himself was involved in the drafting process[3] and the rule that finally emerged as section 7(5)(b) is the complete opposite of the administrative discretion so strongly emphasized by Hamnett. It states in mandatory terms:

In the re-allocation of lands . . . the Chief or Headman *shall give priority* . . . to the requirements of any adult son or sons . . . [italics added].

Therefore the only period of time during which the Basotho Courts might have been misled into assuming that the administrative authorities were to have *carte blanche* was between 1953 and 1959 when this subsection was incorporated in the new edition of the Laws.

---

[1] *Thipane* v. *Thipane* J.C. 183/1960.   [2] (1970), p. 213.
[3] See *1957 National Council Proceedings*, pp. 72–3.

Minor children. Where upon the death of the surviving parent there are minor children these will be looked after by a paternal uncle or some other close relative who will act as their guardian under the general supervision of the chieftainship.[1] In terms of section 7(5)(a) of the Laws of Lerotholi the guardian has the responsibility of reporting their presence to the chief or headman who must make provision for them during their minority from the lands of their deceased parents. The subsection then proceeds:

If the minor dependants are sons the Chief or Headman shall, on such sons attaining majority, confirm them on the land or lands used for their benefit during the period of their minority.

It seems that in practice there might sometimes be too many sons and too little land for this instruction to be carried out to the letter. Presumably, therefore, the chief may have on occasion to allocate some sons lands elsewhere.[2]

(c) *The Responsibilities of the Heir*

(i) *The principle of onerous succession*

In the previous section the extent of the assets inherited by the heir was described. In return for this privilege he also takes over the liabilities of the deceased. As the Sesotho maxim expresses it, '*nt'so salla o salle ba melato*' ('the successor succeeds to the liabilities too').[3]

Furthermore, after earlier doubts[4] it now seems clear that the inheritance is onerous rather than beneficial in the sense that the heir's obligation to satisfy the deceased's debts is not limited to the

[1] Laydevant, p. 256; Duncan, p. 2; P.D., pp. 203-4.

[2] See P.D., pp. 171-2. Duncan's statement (at p. 92) to the effect that the rights of orphans on the land terminate when they reach majority seems to be based on the position before section 7(5)(a) was introduced and is therefore out of date. At all events the decisions he relies upon are from the years 1945-7, i.e. *Ramarothole* v. *Tsibane* J.C. 40/1945 (J.C.); *Lehehle* v. *Joel* J.C. 181/1947 (J.C.) and *Mareka* v. *Sebalabala* J.C. 350/1947 (J.C.).

[3] Quoted in *Matsosa* v. *Matsosa* J.C. 151/1955 (C.C. and J.C.). Basotho often speak of the heir as 'the one who eats and pays'—see *1957 National Council Proceedings*, p. 110; P.D., p. 169.

[4] The contrary was held by Driver J.C. in *Tekete* v. *Khotlela* J.C. 190/1957 and other cases. In *Thokoa* v. *Seliane* J.C. 111/1966 Thompson J.C. pointed out that the decisions since 1944 in the Judicial Commissioner's Court had not been consistent on this question, for instance in *Peleha* v. *Peleha* J.C. 251/1947 Driver J.C. held succession to be onerous.

extent of the assets comprised in the estate.[1] He is bound to extinguish all these liabilities even if this involves utilizing his own property.

Ramolefe has suggested that the heir may escape from such a possibility by refusing to accede, but he is forced to admit that there is no recorded instance of this ever having happened.[2] Certainly in *Bereng Griffith* v. *'Mantsebo Seeiso Griffith* (No. 2)[3] de Beer J. described the heir as resembling in many respects the Roman law *heres* who did have the right to refuse the heirship, but this has recently been doubted for Sesotho law by the Judicial Commissioner's Court.[4]

The explanation for the principle of onerous succession is probably to be found in the fact that since there is no winding up of the estate and since future assets and liabilities also fall to the heir, there is no simple method of determining in advance whether there will in fact be a surplus or a deficit. The heir takes over the liability to pay compensation for future delicts committed by members of the family who are minors (including the deceased's widow) and he also has the responsibility of paying the *bohali* due on the marriages of his younger brothers.[5]

A temporary curator or administrator of the estate who is merely standing in for the heir during his absence is, however, only liable up to the extent of the assets in the estate.[6]

(ii) *Responsibilities towards members of the family*

It is a cardinal feature of Sesotho law that the heir does not possess unfettered and absolute rights over the estate.[7] He has far-reaching obligations towards other members of the family. The property he has inherited belongs not so much to him as to the

[1] *Bereng Griffith* v. *'Mantsebo Seeiso Griffith* (No. 2) H.C. 9/1946 (H.C.); *Matsosa* v. *Matsosa* (C.C.); *Motsiri* v. *Lintlhokoane* J.C. 79/1965 (C.C.); *Mohale* v. *Mohale* J.C. 84/1966 (J.C.); *Thokoa* v. *Seliane* (J.C.); *Molatuoa* v. *Molatuoa* J.C. 181/1967 (J.C.); *Rametsana* v. *Malelu* J.C. 27/1968 (J.C.); *Moseme* v. *Masiu* J.C. 94/1969 (J.C.); Duncan, p. 15; Ramolefe (1966), p. 19; P.D., pp. 168–9.

[2] (1969), p. 205. He proposes (at p. 207) that the law be amended to permit an estate to be declared insolvent if the liabilities exceed the assets.

[3] H.C. 9/1946.

[4] *Molatuoa* v. *Molatuoa* (J.C.).

[5] See e.g. *Tsoele* v. *Nqhae* J.C. 73/1964 (J.C., seduction); *Moshoeshoe* v. *Masilo* J.C. 239/1964 (all courts); *Thokoa* v. *Seliane* (all courts; abduction); *Moseme* v. *Masiu* (all courts; abduction); p. 136 above.

[6] *Machela* v. *Lethunya* J.C. 98/1968 (J.C.).

[7] See e.g. *Neheng* v. *Neheng* J.C. 57/1967 (J.C.) discussed at pp. 278–9 below.

family and he must administer it with the family's best interests in mind. The relationship between the heir and the deceased's widow in this respect, including his obligation to support and maintain her, is fully explored in Chapter 18 and here attention will be concentrated solely on the heir's obligations towards his brothers and sisters.

Since 1903 the Laws of Lerotholi have always contained a provision imposing on the heir a duty to share the estate with his junior brothers according to their rank, based upon the order in which their mothers were married.[1] This means, in general terms, that larger shares should go to the more senior brothers and smaller portions to the more junior. The provision is couched in extremely vague language and its specific content requires further investigation.

As we have already seen, the chief method by which the head of a polygamous household ensures that all the members of his family will be adequately cared for after his death is through the process of allocation to his different houses. Property once allocated to a house remains with that house and cannot be transferred to another house without consent, nor can it be seized by the principal heir for his own house. However, the obligation to share placed upon the principal heir now extends beyond allocated property (which does not pass to him anyway) and relates specifically to unallocated property. In terms of section 13(1) of Part I of the Laws this must be shared with his junior brothers as well as used with the deceased's widow or widows for their support.

The expression 'junior brothers' refers only to those who have attained their majority, since minors will be maintained by the heirs in their own houses or by their widowed mothers.[2] But apart from this there appear to be two practical limitations upon the application of the sharing principle. First, it seems comparatively rare today for a polygamist to leave any large amount of unallocated property on his death.[3] Usually he will have allocated virtually all he possesses to his various houses. Secondly, he will commonly have allocated more to the junior houses (where the younger wives are) and thus these will probably be better endowed than the senior house.[4] For this reason it would often be unjust to make the

---

[1] (1903), s. 14; (1922), s. 14; (1946), s. 13 of Part I; (1959), s. 13 (1) of Part I.
[2] See P.D., pp. 193–4.   [3] See P.D., p. 163.
[4] See Hamnett (1975), p. 57; P.D., p. 163.

heir share out the small amount of unallocated property with his junior brothers.

As Hamnett has explained,

Normally, where a reasonable part of the estate has been allocated to junior houses by the deceased, the principal heir is not obliged to support these houses (e.g. by providing [*bohali*] for sons being married) out of the unallocated estate. If the heir himself discharges the duty of allocating a (wholly or largely) unallocated estate, he will take such debts into account in deciding how much support he can afford to let the junior houses have, as well as other factors such as the number of dependants to be supported in each house.[1]

In a particular case it may be that the heir will have discharged his duty by paying *bohali* for a younger brother's marriage and is not liable to allocate further property.[2]

In monogamous marriages the family head may sometimes allocate property during his lifetime to his younger sons to ensure they are properly provided for after his death.[3] However, the heir's obligation to share the estate with them will still be applicable in appropriate circumstances where the allocation was comparatively small or, as is common, none was made at all.

Where a younger brother considers he is entitled to a share he should naturally bring his claim in the first instance before the family in terms of section 14(4) of Part I of the Laws of Lerotholi.[4] If he gets no satisfaction there he can proceed to the courts, but there has been a tendency on the part of the judiciary to leave the heir with complete discretion as to the amount.[5] As a result he is liable to hand over a mere pittance.

In view of this the question may be raised whether the junior brothers of the heir are adequately provided for where the deceased has made only small allocations to them or none at all.

---

[1] (1975), p. 58.

[2] See *Tseole* v. *Tseole* J.C. 39/1962 (L.C.).

[3] See *Malefane* v. *Malefane* J.C. 13/1957 (all courts); *Mohafa* v. *Mohafa* J.C. 218/1964 (J.C.); *Motleleng* v. *Motleleng* J.C. 78/1967 (J.C.); P.D., p. 188. Cf. Duncan, p. 18, *dubitante*.

[4] *Tseole* v. *Tseole* (J.C.).

[5] See e.g. *Nthathakane* v. *Nthathakane* J.C. 78/1944 (J.C., *contra* L.C. which divided the estate up); *Mokorosi* v. *Mokorosi* (1954) H.C.T.L.R. 24 (C.C.); *Tseole* v. *Tseole* (C.C. and P.C.'s Ct.); see also P.D., pp. 162–3. Casalis (at p. 179) had remarked in 1861—'. . . the younger members have nothing but what [the heir] chooses to leave for them'.

Certainly Ramolefe's statement that 'brothers and sisters of the full- or half-blood take equally'[1] is pure wishful thinking. The heir's obligation does indeed extend to supporting and maintaining his sisters, both those who are unmarried and those who have *ngala*-ed home or been divorced.[2] But it goes no further than that and, as will be seen in the following chapter, the limited nature of the support duty *vis-à-vis* the deceased's widow has given rise to a good deal of concern.

A very moderate proposal that a junior son who had worked hard on the family lands after his father's death should be entitled to retain the fruits of his labours directly rather than through a share granted by the heir at his discretion was rejected by a large majority in the National Council in 1948.[3] A provident family head is thus well advised to make full use of his power to allocate property and make testamentary dispositions.[4]

---

[1] (1969), p. 206.
[2] *Machela* v. *Lethunya* J.C. 98/1968 (J.C.).
[3] *1948 National Council Proceedings*, pp. 438–44.
[4] See Ch. 19 below.

THE STATUS OF WIDOWS

THE status of widows in Sesotho law is a matter of particular interest. As early as 1820 Chieftainess 'Mantatisi was ruling a large Batlokoa tribe as Regent for her son during his minority and from that time onwards widows have held many positions of political power as chiefs and headmen, not only as Regents for minor sons but also in their own right in the absence of male issue.[1]

Curiously, side by side with this reflection of the strength of widows' rights in public affairs there has existed the custom of *kenelo*, a form of widow inheritance. Whether a widow permitted herself to be inherited by her late husband's younger brother under this custom or managed to assert her own independence seems to have depended mainly on her character and determination.

In 1943 in *Bereng Griffith* v. *'Mantsebo Seeiso Griffith*[2] (the *Regency case*) the High Court had to decide which of the two conflicting principles should prevail in a case of great political significance. A dispute had arisen as to who should act as Regent during the minority of the present King of Lesotho, Moshoeshoe II, following the death of his father, Paramount Chief Seeiso.

The defendant was Seeiso's widow. Her right to be recognized as Regent and acting Paramount Chieftainess and to administer her late husband's estate and be the guardian of his children was challenged by the plaintiff, Seeiso's junior brother. The plaintiff contended that a widow could hold neither administrative office

---

[1] Ellenberger and Macgregor, pp. 44–51 (concerning 'Mantatisi); Ashton, pp. 197–9; Sheddick (1953), p. 40. Over fifty examples were quoted in evidence in the *Regency case*. The right of a widow without male issue to succeed to the chieftainship in her own right was enforced in *Setlokoane* v. *Setlokoane* J.C. 228/1967 (C.C. and J.C.), despite the wording of s. 2 of Part I of the Laws of Lerotholi (for which see p. 264. below). The National Council had decided in 1950 (see *Proceedings*, pp. 80–94) to amend the section to permit widows to succeed in such circumstances, but the amendment was never incorporated in the Laws and it was not until the enactment of the Chieftainship Act, No. 22 of 1968, that the change was finally introduced formally—see s. 10(4).

[2] (1926–53) H.C.T.L.R. 50.

nor property since she was not *sui juris*. On the contrary, he asserted, she fell under his guardianship because he was her late husband's junior brother and therefore he had the right to *kenela* her. Each of these claims is examined in the present chapter which explores the various aspects of the status of widows as follows:

  1. *Kenelo.*
  2. Guardianship.
  3. Rights in estate property other than land and buildings.
  4. Rights over land and buildings.
  5. Loss of rights.
  6. Remarriage.

1. 'KENELO'

The practice of *kenelo*, the Sesotho version of the levirate, was widespread during the early history of the Basotho[1] and was thought to possess the following advantages.

First, it provided the widow with care and protection and a male guardian for her children, including those whom she would bear in the future.[2]

Secondly, it was seen as a satisfactory method of increasing the husband's lineage by the addition of further children who would be fathered by a member of that lineage (known as a *mokeneli*), rather than by a complete stranger. In this way the *bohali* paid for the wife would be fully productive[3] and her future children would definitely be regarded as legitimate.[4]

Both these justifications reflect the extent to which the Basotho regarded a wife as married into her husband's family rather than exclusively to the man himself.[5] The traditional custom is presently in a state of decay, but before examining the extent of its survival, its most important features will be described.

Kenelo normally arose on the death of the husband, but it has

---

[1] *1873 Report and Evidence*, pp. 41, 44 (George and Sofonia Moshoeshoe); *1903–05 South African Native Affairs Commission*, vol. iv, p. 392 (Chief Jonathan); Ellenberger and Macgregor, p. 274; Sekese (1953), p. 18; Laydevant, p. 254; *Bereng Griffith* v. '*Mantsebo Seeiso Griffith* (the *Regency case*) (1962–53) H.C.T.L.R. 50 at 63–4.

[2] Ellenberger and Macgregor, p. 274; P.D., pp. 83–6.

[3] *Regency case* at 63–4.

[4] Laydevant, p. 254; Ramolefe (1966), p. 19; 'Restatement', pp. 2, 11.

[5] Ellenberger and Macgregor, p. 274; *Regency case* at 63–4; *Mojapela* v. *Nkibane* J.C. 305/1966 (J.C.).

been suggested by one writer that it could also occur where the husband became mad or otherwise incapable of performing his normal political and social roles.[1] Although it is often stressed that *kenelo* could only take place, at any rate so far as cohabitation was concerned, with the widow's consent,[2] it seems probable that in earliest times widows, like other women, did what they were told.[3] Today, the widow's consent is naturally required.[4]

Only one of a specified group of the deceased husband's relatives was permitted to *kenela* his widow. This group consisted of his younger brothers or other younger blood relations one of whom would be appointed by the head of the family as the *mokeneli*.[5] Elder brothers were barred on the basis that they were the widow's 'fathers',[6] and so were the deceased's sons,[7] but though it was regarded as incestuous to do so, men in both categories seem at times to have violated this rule.[8]

Kenelo had a number of deficiencies. In the first place it was in many cases oppressive to widows who were undoubtedly imposed upon. Even if they rejected cohabitation they still had to suffer one of their late husband's relatives administering the household property and they commonly alleged that he squandered the estate and used it for his own purposes.[9] The practice also led to further dissension within the family because of the possibility of jealousy between the wife of the *mokeneli* and the widow.[10]

Its decline was precipitated by two particular circumstances. First, it was strongly condemned by the Paris Evangelical Missionary Society as an immoral and heathen custom so that those who practised it were not permitted to become church members.[11]

Secondly, Paramount Chief Griffith declined to practise it himself. On the death of Paramount Chief Letsie II without male issue he was succeeded in 1913 by his brother Griffith. The question arose as to whether Griffith would *kenela* Letsie's widow

---

[1] Jones, p. 70. [2] Sekese (1953), p. 18; Laydevant, p. 254.
[3] P.D., p. 84. [4] 'Restatement', p. 4.
[5] Ellenberger and Macgregor, p. 274; *Regency case* at 63–4; 'Restatement', pp. 2, 10.
[6] 'Restatement', pp. 10–11; P.D., p. 85.
[7] Ramolefe (1969), p. 199.
[8] *1873 Report and Evidence*, p. 44 (Sofonia Moshoeshoe); Ashton, p. 84; P.D., p. 84.
[9] Laydevant, p. 253. [10] Sekese (1953), p. 18.
[11] See *The Church of Basutoland: Its Constitution, Rules and Regulations* (Morija, 1927), pp. 29, 38.

and father children for Letsie. If he had, these children would then have succeeded to the Paramountcy on his death in preference to his own issue. Griffith publicly announced that he would not *kenela* Letsie's widow and he only accepted the Paramountcy on this basis. His own son Seeiso therefore succeeded him on his death.

Kenelo gradually fell into decay in face of these pressures and this was the position in 1943 when the *Regency case* came before the High Court. A great deal of expert evidence was given and ultimately Lansdown J. dismissed the first part of the plaintiff's claim as follows:

Much evidence has been adduced to the question whether this system of *kenela* [sic][1] still exists in the social life of the Basuto people. . . . Witnesses called on behalf of the plaintiff have affirmed this to be the case. Those called on behalf of the defendant have as confidently asserted that *kenela* has either already disappeared or is fast disappearing and is no longer practised generally amongst the Basuto nation. In support of their respective contentions, the merits of the system have been dwelt upon, on the one side it being asserted that *kenela* in a polygamous society is the lifeblood of the nation, the guarantee against widows and fatherless children sinking into poverty and depravity; while on the other hand, it is contended that the system would perpetuate a degree of servitude entirely inconsistent with that stage of civilisation to which the Basuto nation has advanced. . . .[2]

He went on:

While I am not prepared to concede that *kenela* has disappeared from the memory of the present generation, and while I am of the belief that instances of the practice will still be found in some of the kraals of the country, I definitely reject the evidence of those witnesses of the plaintiff who assert that it is in present day existence amongst the nation as a universally practised custom. . . . It is established that *kenela* in the sense of a sharing of her bed could be rejected by any woman to whom it was proposed. The main purpose of the practice, namely the raising of the seed to the House of the deceased man, has thus been vitally attacked at its root; and the remaining part of the practice, namely the control of the widow with her children and the administration of the property of the deceased, has not, in my judgment, survived

---

[1] Throughout this passage the word should be *kenelo* (the noun) rather than *kenela* (the verb).

[2] At 63–4.

in such a way as to enable the Court to say that it is a long-established and reasonable custom which must be enforced as law in the Basuto family life. That there are many instances in which the wife of a deceased man receives assistance and counsel from her husband's family, including his surviving brother or brothers, does not alter this position. Nor is the situation affected by the fact that the widow of a man is, in theory, after her husband's death, still a member of her deceased husband's family.[1]

The *Regency case* received considerable publicity in the country at large and no doubt its outcome gave widows even greater steadfastness in resisting *kenelo* than they had possessed before. Of the thirty-six widows interviewed during my social survey not a single one had been *kenela*-ed, although fourteen were still living with their deceased husbands' families. The other twenty-two had either lived their married lives with their husbands away from their in-laws or else had left after their husbands' deaths.

While the *Regency case* lays down that *kenelo* cannot be enforced, it does not go so far as to declare that rights flowing from existing *kenelo* relationships should not be upheld. In *Sekake v. Tautona*,[2] decided in 1959, both the Paramount Chief's Court and the Judicial Commissioner held the offspring of a *kenelo* relationship to be the legitimate son and heir of his genitor's elder brother and thus entitled to succeed to the Chieftainship of Patlong. While the *ratio decidendi* was that all posthumous children are regarded as legitimate provided *bohali* has been paid for their mother, the following remarks of Driver J.C. are of interest:

From my own experience after fifteen years as Judicial Commissioner... I have come across several cases in which the *kenela* custom is still being practised with the consent of the widow or widows of the deceased husband. . . . Even though the *kenela* custom may be a decadent custom it is still practised occasionally . . . and in this point my assessor is in entire agreement with me.

The court then proceeded to explain that the wording of section 2 of Part I of the Laws of Lerotholi was incomplete as an expression of the Sesotho law on succession to the chieftainship when it provided

---

[1] At 67.
[2] J.C. 15/1959.

... if a Chief dies leaving no male issue the Chieftainship shall devolve upon the male issue following according to the succession of Houses.

On the face of it, this would mean that the late chief's brother's senior son would inherit if he himself had no male issue on his death. However, the court construed the words 'dies leaving no male issue' to mean 'dies leaving no male issue and his wives have not borne any male children under *kenelo* after his death and they are now past the childbearing age'.

In certain circumstances such an interpretation of the law must have given rise to uncertainty, since a long period of time could elapse while the family waited to see if the widow would bear a son. On the other hand, if the deceased's brother refused to *kenelo* his widow, as Griffith did, the matter would be resolved immediately.

Ultimately in 1968 the legal position was altered by the enactment of the Chieftainship Act which now provides that only a 'legitimate' son may succeed to the office of chief.[1] Although, as already explained, children born of *kenelo* unions are indeed regarded as legitimate it seems probable that the intention of the legislature was to outlaw them for this purpose as well as other children fathered by anyone other than the chief himself.[2] In any event it should not be forgotten that the Act is only concerned with succession to the chieftainship and it expressly leaves unaffected the rules as to the inheritance of property[3] where rights flowing from *kenelo* may still be operative.

Where a *kenelo* relationship has been entered into, the *mokeneli* is the administrator of the estate and so has an obligation to support and maintain the widow[4] and is presumably entitled, on the same basis as her deceased husband was, to claim compensation for wrongs committed against her to counterbalance his liability for her wrongs. Thus where she is seduced the *mokeneli* may claim damages and these can be utilized to support her and her children.[5] In this respect *kenelo* still serves a useful purpose in maintaining the family as a viable unit.

---

[1] Act 22 of 1968, s. 10(1).
[2] See *Molapo* v. *Molapo* H.C. Civ./A/8/1973 (H.C.); P.D., pp. 23–4.
[3] See s. 39.
[4] Ramolefe (1966), p. 19; 'Restatement', p. 11.
[5] P.D., p. 85.

2. GUARDIANSHIP

Aside from the question of *kenelo* and apart from a few remarkable chieftainesses, a widow in former times was always regarded as a minor and fell under the guardianship of a male member of her late husband's family. If her eldest son was married he would be her guardian; if he was not, or if she had no male issue, one of her late husband's brothers or the principal heir from another house would hold that position.

Today the situation has changed. It is best understood by examining three sets of circumstances—first where there is a major (i.e. married) heir, secondly where the heir is a minor, and thirdly where there is no male issue at all. The general rule is that the choice of a guardian is a matter for the deceased's family to decide[1] as it always has been, although today a widow does have a measure of choice.[2] In practical terms the position seems to be as follows.

In the first situation the widow will almost invariably fall under the guardianship of her own eldest son if he is married;[3] if he is not, but the principal heir (i.e. the heir in the senior house) is, then the latter will be her guardian.[4] However, Ashton reports that among the 'Sons of Moshoeshoe' the principal heir is expected to be the guardian of all the junior widows even if there are married heirs in their own houses.[5]

In the second situation—where her son is the principal heir and he is a minor (or she is a junior wife and the principal heir is a minor)—the widow is often herself appointed as the guardian of the heir in her own house and thus rather than being under guardianship she actually exercises it.

In the third type of case where there is no male issue at all the widow would also not appear to be under anyone's guardianship. However, in both these last two situations she will nevertheless be restricted in her rights.

The working out of these principles in terms of rights and duties is most conveniently discussed in the context of the following examination of rights in respect of estate property other

[1] *Phamotse* v. *Phamotse* H.C. 22/1952 (P.C.'s Ct., H.C.); *Leluma* v. *Leluma*, Matsieng C.C. 70/1956 (P.C.'s Ct.); *Tjotsi* v. *Tjotsi* J.C. 4/1965 (L.C. and J.C.); *Chalete* v. *Mbohla* J.C. 76/1967 (J.C.).

[2] *Tjotsi* v. *Tjotsi* (J.C.).

[3] See *Mohale* v. *Mohale* J.C. 84/1966 (C.C. and J.C.); *Moeletsi* v. *Moeletsi* J.C. 75/1965 (C.C. and J.C.).

[4] P.D., p. 194.   [5] At p. 184.

than land. The threefold classification is thought to be not only conducive to clarity of expression but also of legal significance and it serves to explain the particular wording of some of the provisions of the Laws of Lerotholi. However, hitherto it has gone virtually unnoticed by commentators.[1]

3. RIGHTS IN ESTATE PROPERTY OTHER THAN LAND AND BUILDINGS

Part I of the Laws of Lerotholi contains no less than eleven subsections dealing with the rights of widows and heirs in relation to the inheritance of property other than land. Some of the subsections are of long standing, but the vast majority were drafted by the Standing Committee of the National Council around the years 1946–8 with the assistance of the Judicial Commissioner of the day, Mr. Driver.

No one who has read them through carefully can have felt anything other than utter dismay and frustration at their complexity. In the first place they are drafted mainly with polygamous marriages in mind and their application to a monogamous marriage is often a matter of inference. While this is unrealistic in modern times it reflects the wealthy and mainly chiefly composition of the National Council at that period.

Secondly, the headings of the sections are misleading. Thus, to take but two examples, the heading of section 12 is 'minor heir' and yet section 12(4) in no way bears upon the position of a minor heir; on the other hand, section 14(3) does deal with the position of a minor heir but it is placed under the heading 'allocation of property during lifetime'.

Thirdly, there are apparent inconsistencies. Thus whereas section 12(2) prohibits a widow with a minor heir from disposing of any part of the estate without the *prior consent* of the child's paternal uncles, section 14(3) in dealing with virtually identical circumstances declares that a widow may not dispose of property without first *consulting* the child's guardian.

Fourthly, it is extremely difficult to be sure in what circumstances one provision rather than another is applicable.

Quite apart fom these deficiencies, Hamnett has rightly pointed out that 'it is precisely at the points of greatest difficulty that

---

[3] But see P.D., p. 233 where Bereng seems to be making this point.

sections 11–14 are either silent or ambiguous'.[1] However, his statement in the same breath that they 'represent a brave attempt by contemporary Basotho (and others) to "codify" and "specify" the rules' would seem to give far greater credit than is due.[2] Certainly Hamnett himself does not embark upon a systematic analysis of the operation of the various provisions, nor has this been attempted by anyone else.[3]

The threefold division referred to above will now be explored.

(a) *Where the Heir is a Major*

Of all the evidence given to the 1872 Commission, one statement made by George Moshoeshoe has assumed particular significance during the ensuing hundred years. It has not only been cited repeatedly by the courts and by commentators; it also gives rise to difficulties of interpretation since it appears to contain an ambiguity. He began by saying:

Each wife has a separate establishment. The husband apportions cattle to each house; the eldest son in each house inherits all the property which has been allotted by the father to that house . . .[4]

A little later in his evidence, however, he appeared to modify this unequivocal assertion of the heir's rights and, after explaining that the eldest son claimed the *bohali* in respect of the marriages of sisters in his house, he proceeded:

Although I have said the eldest son of the house claims the cattle, I must explain that he is only acting for his mother, who has charge of all her deceased husband's property during her lifetime belonging to her house, but at her death, then it devolves upon the eldest son of the house.

This either amounts to a contradiction in terms or it must mean that the earlier reference to the eldest son inheriting was intended to apply only after the widow's death and that during her lifetime she had control over the part of the estate that had been allotted

---

[1] (1970), p. 255.
[2] Ibid. It is only right to add that one of Hamnett's central arguments was that Sesotho law did not contain specific rules and thus he regarded it as both 'fortunate' and 'significant' that sections 11–14 were as uncertain as they are.
[3] Duncan's treatment (at pp. 11–15) is very sketchy and Ramolefe's (1969) is both confusing and, in places, erroneous (see below).
[4] *1873 Report and Evidence*, p. 41.

to her house.[1] It is far from clear exactly what George Moshoeshoe did mean and modern interpretations differ. Those who wish to emphasize the strength of a widow's rights point to the latter part of his statement while those who uphold the heir's pre-eminence rely on the former part.

Attention must next be turned to an early statement to be found in the Laws of Lerotholi. The original version in 1903 contained the following provision as section 14.

The heir . . . shall be the eldest male child of the first wife, but the heir must use the estate with his father's widow or widows and must share with his juniors[2] according to rank of birth.

The modern version of this statement is slightly different and is contained in section 13(1) which runs as follows:

. . . the heir . . . shall inherit all the unallocated property of the estate and he is obliged by custom to use the estate with his father's widow or widows and to share with his junior brothers according to their rank, which shall be according to the order in which their mothers were married.

This clearly emphasizes that the heir does inherit the estate on his father's death even if the widow survives; however, he naturally has an obligation to look after her and use the property in consultation with her.[3] It is true that section 13(1)—in a departure from the original section 14—is dealing with unallocated property whereas George Moshoeshoe was referring to property allocated to the separate houses, but for present purposes it is not thought that this distinction is of any significance. In the case of allocated property it is the heir in the particular house who must use his own house's property with his own mother; in the case of unallocated property it is the general heir who must use the property with all the houses and all the widows. Moreover, in a single monogamous marriage this will amount to the same thing and there is no necessity

---

[1] The passage is misquoted in Duncan (at p. 11), the word 'who' being replaced by 'and'. This completely alters the sense of the second part of the statement and makes it more consistent with the first part, further emphasizing the heir's rights.

[2] i.e., junior brothers (see rephrasing used in s. 14 of the 1922 edition of the Laws).

[3] See *Sekoumane* v. *Sekoumane* J.C. 295/1947 (P.C.'s Ct. and J.C.) cited in Duncan, pp. 13–14; *Ntoula* v. *Morake* J.C. 227/1960 (J.C.).

at all to create a distinction between allocated and unallocated property.

This line of argument gains some support from a new subsection drafted around 1947.[1] While no new *general* provision was drawn up to deal specifically with the relationship between the heir and the widow *vis-à-vis* allocated property, section 14(3) did purport to regulate this situation so far as *junior* houses were concerned and there seems no logical reason to confine its application so as to exclude the senior house.[2] It runs as follows:

If there is male issue in any house other than the house from which the principal heir comes, the widow shall have the use of all the property allocated to her house and at her death any property remaining shall devolve upon the eldest son of her house who must share such property with his junior brothers in his house; provided that no widow may dispose of any property without consultation with the guardian while that son is a minor, and provided further that on the eldest son reaching his majority he will assume control of the property in his house.

This subsection clearly differentiates between the heir's *control* (after attaining his majority) and the widow's *use* of the property,[3] whereas George Moshoeshoe had spoken of the widow having *charge* of the property, a concept more akin to control than use.

However, the extraordinary background to the framing of this provision must be explained. During the 1947 session of the National Council the Regent and acting Paramount Chief 'Mantsebo was endeavouring to strengthen the position of widows like herself who had no male issue and whose late husband's heir came from a junior house.[4] She pointed out that in the *Regency case* from which she had emerged victorious, Lansdown J. had referred to the second part of George Moshoeshoe's evidence with apparent approval and she sought to have this part of his statement incorporated in the Laws of Lerotholi. After considerable discussion the Council agreed to her proposal by fifty-four votes to none. Since there is no record of the attendance at that session there is no

---

[1] The Standing Committee of the National Council was assisted in the drafting by Driver J.C.—see *1947 National Council Proceedings*, p. 192.

[2] See Hamnett (1970), pp. 381–2.

[3] See *Chalete* v. *Mbohla* J.C. 76/1967 (L.C.). Ramolefe (1969), p. 202 is in error in stating that section 14(3) gives the widow *control and use*.

[4] See *1947 National Council Proceedings*, pp. 157–76.

way of knowing how many abstentions there were but some speakers certainly did oppose her. However, when the Standing Committee came to draft the new law, instead of implementing the decision of the Council they produced a section which adopted the part of George Moshoeshoe's statement which emphasized the heir's pre-eminence. Moreover, the clause was confined to the position in junior houses simply because the Council debate began with these particularly in mind.

Furthermore a new section 14(2) was introduced to deal with the position with regard to allocated property in junior houses which have no male issue in circumstances where there is an heir in the senior house. It provides that the widow shall have the use of all the property allocated to her house, but that she cannot dispose of any of this property without the prior consent of her guardian. On her death the property is inherited by the principal heir (in the absence of an heir in her own house—a situation covered by section 14(3)), who must use it for the maintenance of dependants in that house, in terms of the axiom '*malapa ha a jane*' ('houses do not "eat" one another').

Here again, then, emphasis is placed upon the widow's right to use the property subject to the control of a member of her late husband's family. The principal heir himself cannot inherit immediately, however, for the obvious reason that this would violate the above axiom.

Another new provision, section 13(2), dealt with the division of unallocated property as follows:

The question of what portion of the unallocated estate shall be set aside for the support of the deceased's widow or widows during her life shall be decided by the paternal uncles of the principal heir and other persons whose right it is under Basuto Law and Custom to be consulted.

Although the section is expressed to deal only with unallocated property, it is submitted that the rule is the same in respect of allocated property within a house. The logic of this becomes apparent when a monogamous marriage is considered. In such a marriage all the property is treated as unallocated[1] and therefore section 13(2) must govern the relationship between the widow and the heir. There seems no reason, if this is accepted, why the same

---

[1] *Lekaota* v. *Lekaota* (1963–6) H.C.T.L.R. 38 at 42 (H.C.).

should not apply with respect to property allocated to a particular house where there is a polygamous marriage.

If this contention is correct and the dichotomy between allocated and unallocated property is merely a descriptive one defining the range of persons who may have interests in it and is not one affecting the nature of these interests as between widow and heir, then the essence of the relevant sections of the Laws of Lerotholi becomes clear. The heir, if he is a major, inherits upon his father's death; if he is a minor he inherits when he attains his majority by marrying.[1] He thereupon immediately assumes control over all the unallocated property and the property allocated to his own house. Unallocated property he is bound to use with all widows and dependants; property allocated to his own house he must use with the widow and dependants in that house. Property allocated to other houses which lack male issue is not inherited by the principal heir until the deaths of the widows in those houses, although they are not free to dispose of such property without the consents of their guardians.

Aside perhaps from the last of these three situations the dominant partner in the relationship is undoubtedly the heir in the sense that he has control, though his freedom is limited by the checks which can be placed upon him by his paternal uncles and other relatives who exercise an over-all supervisory authority in case of disagreement.[2] A widow, however, is in legal theory definitely in a subordinate position, as she was in the relationship with her husband during his lifetime *vis-à-vis* property matters. While this corresponds with the first part of George Moshoeshoe's statement, if taken on its own, it is in sharp opposition to the second part and seemingly therefore to the tenor of the whole.[3]

---

[1] *Mokorosi* v. *Mokorosi* (1954) H.C.T.L.R. 24 (J.C.). It is his in the sense that it can be executed on by the court in pursuance of a judgment against him even if the property is actually situate at the widow's home—see *Lisene* v. *Ramohanoe* J.C. 166/1967 (L.C. and C.C., appeal to J.C. not proceeded with). See also P.D., pp. 188–9.

[2] Ramolefe (1969), p. 206; P.D., p. 160.

[3] Possibly George Moshoeshoe exaggerated the rights of women in order to impress the members of the Cape Commission who probably suspected that women were not afforded much protection under Sesotho law. But cf. the views of some members of the Panel Discussion who thought that traditionally widows did have control over the estate—see P.D., pp. 164–6. Moreover Sheddick (1953), p. 63, states that in modern times the widow enjoys a life interest in family property and Ramolefe (1969), p. 202, also takes the view that widows have extensive rights along the lines of George Moshoeshoe's full statement.

The analogy with a wife's status while her husband was alive is carried further when questions of *locus standi* and the execution of judgments arise. The heir is made liable for the widow's delicts just as her husband was and estate property may naturally be used to pay the necessary compensation.[1] Since the estate belongs to the heir no execution can be made upon it unless he has been made a party to the case;[2] as a result the Judicial Commissioner has held on many occasions that only the heir can sue and be sued on his own and that the widow does not possess the requisite *locus standi* to appear in court unassisted,[3] save in exceptional circumstances such as in land disputes (where widows are fully in control)[4] and where immediate action is called for and the heir is not available.[5] The parallel with the position of a wife is very close.

It must be admitted that the Basotho Courts do not generally concern themselves with a widow's *locus standi* and commonly allow her to appear unassisted.[6] Even where the point is raised by the other party the court may expressly permit the widow to continue with the proceedings.[7] However, Thompson J.C. nearly always raises the question *meru motu* on appeal, often justifying this on the basis of the difficulty of executing a judgment, though in one case he has held that a party who did not raise the matter in the court of first instance was estopped from raising it on appeal.[8]

On the broader issue of who has the right of control there have been two important decisions in the High Court and Court of Appeal during the past decade and a discussion of these will lead us into a deeper analysis of the practical solutions available to settle disputes of this nature.

[1] *Kente* v. *Foloko* J.C. 212/1963 (J.C.); *Mohale* v. *Mohale* J.C. 84/1966 (C.C. and J.C.).
[2] *Malakane* v. *Jonathan* J.C. 161/1966 (J.C.); *Motsoene* v. *Peko* J.C. 184/1968 (L.C.).
[3] *Tsiloane* v. *Tsiloane* J.C. 6/1962 (J.C.); *Kente* v. *Foloko* (J.C.); *Kapa* v. *Orpen* J.C. 120/1964 (J.C.); *Ramokone* v. *Kapoko* J.C. 136/1966 (J.C.); *Polo* v. *Polo* J.C. 137/1966 (J.C.); *Malakane* v. *Jonathan* (J.C.).
[4] *Rantja* v. *Rantja* J.C. 140/1951 (J.C.); *Motsoene* v. *Peko* (C.C. and J.C.; *contra* L.C.). See also P.D., pp. 191, 230, 233.
[5] *Ramokone* v. *Kapoko* (J.C.); *Molefe* v. *Lebopo* J.C. 337/1966 (J.C.).
[6] See the Basotho Court judgments in all the cases mentioned above in footnote 3, except *Kente* v. *Foloko*; see also P.D., pp. 231, 233.
[7] See the Local and Central Court judgments in *Kente* v. *Foloko*.
[8] *Molefe* v. *Lebopo* J.C. 337/1966 (J.C.; *contra* C.C.).

In *Lekaota* v. *Lekaota*[1] the marriage was a monogamous one. The widow claimed the return of estate property consisting of two head of cattle, two horses and the proceeds of sale of some mohair. She alleged that the heir had removed these assets from her control without her consent. Her claim was dismissed by the Local Court on the ground that she had not first brought the matter before a family meeting. Her appeal to the Central Court was dismissed as frivolous; the Court pointed out that in terms of section 13 of the Laws of Lerotholi the son was the heir, not the widow. However, the Court went on to explain to her that though she could not assert that the estate actually belonged to her, nevertheless if a son failed to provide his mother with proper support then she could lodge a complaint against him.

On appeal to the Judicial Commissioner's Court, Thompson J.C. reversed this decision. He relied upon the latter part of George Moshoeshoe's statement and purported to follow two earlier decisions of Driver J.C. in *Makupu* v. *Makupu*[2] and *Mpetsana* v. *Mpetsana*.[3] He held that the widow was entitled to the use of the estate until her death, but that she had to consult her son who was her *molisa* or guardian. However, the son could neither dispose of household assets nor even remove them from her possession without her prior consent.[4] Here although she might have been consulted, she had certainly not given her consent.

The Judicial Commissioner's decision was overruled by the High Court. Elyan J. began by quite rightly explaining that the decisions in *Makupu's case* and *Mpetsana's case* were not in point. Secondly, Thompson J.C. had considered that George Moshoeshoe's statement did not conflict with section 13, whereas such a conflict was patently obvious.[5] If the widow had charge of all the assets of the estate, how could the heir comply with section 13 and not only use the estate with the widow but also share it with his junior brothers? Thirdly, the Judicial Commissioner had described a widow's entitlement as one of usufruct,[6] which it most definitely was not.

---

[1] (1963–6) H.C.T.L.R. 38.
[2] J.C. 89/1955 (J.C.).
[3] J.C. 206/1957 (J.C.).
[4] He had reached the same decision in the earlier case of *Maleke* v. *Maleke* J.C. 22/1961 (J.C.).
[5] The point is completely missed by Duncan, p. 11.
[6] It was also so described by Driver J.C. in *Lephole* v. *Lephole* J.C. 15/1958.

Elyan J. summarized his conclusion:

> . . . I am advised by both my Assessors that where there is male issue such interest as a widow has . . . in unallocated movables including cattle remains unaffected by the death *per se* of her husband, so that save that the heir takes the place of the deceased husband in regard to the control of such property, no such widow is by reason of the husband's death beneficiary for life or otherwise of such property except as provided by the said Law 13. I might perhaps mention that my Assessors . . . add to this by way of example that in consequence of the death not affecting . . . such interest of such a widow in such property, ordinary household effects and suchlike should not be removed by the heir from the family home during the lifetime of the widow.[1]

In the particular circumstances of the case the heir had acted quite properly in his dealings with the assets of the estate.

The thrust of the judgment seems to be that a widow is to be placed in the same position as she was during her husband's lifetime.[2] As we have seen earlier,[3] as a wife she was entitled to be maintained by her husband and had a customary but legally unenforceable right to be consulted before property transactions with people outside the family took place;[4] further she could only dispose of property herself without her husband's consent in an emergency.[5] This approach is consistent with section 13(1).

In the leading case of *Khatala* v. *Khatala*[6] which was decided only a few months after *Lekaota's case* the situation was more complex. The deceased had been a monogamist, but had married a second time after the death of his first wife. The disputing parties were his first wife's son and heir and his second wife, now widowed. Each of the marriages had been contracted both customarily and by civil rites, but Sesotho law was applied by all the courts as the proper law. The case went through six courts, three of which held in favour of the son, the plaintiff, and three in favour of the widow, the defendant. The plaintiff had obtained possession of the livestock belonging to the estate, but the defendant had managed to

---

[1] (1963–6) H.C.T.L.R. at 42–3. [2] See P.D., pp. 161–2, 166.
[3] See pp. 171–2, 176–7 above. [4] See P.D., p. 162.
[5] See, in the case of a widow, *Moonyane* v. *Moonyane* J.C. 138/1955 (J.C.) (disposal not permitted); *Ntona* v. *Mothobi* J.C. 205/1968 (C.C. and J.C., *contra* L.C.) (disposal permitted in emergency).
[6] (1963–6) H.C.T.L.R. 97.

have the deceased's Post Office Savings Book altered into her own name and it was this asset that was the source of the litigation.

After the three lower courts had reached differing conclusions Thompson J.C. gave judgment in favour of the widow. He relied again on the latter part of George Moshoeshoe's statement and held that the widow was entitled to retain the book, although if she wished to make use of it she had to consult the heir who was her *molisa* or guardian. His judgment was not entirely clear as to whether the property was to be regarded as allocated or unallocated, and presumably he did not consider that this was material to the decision.

On appeal to the High Court his finding in favour of the widow was upheld. Roper J. also placed reliance on George Moshoeshoe's statement, but the vital part of his *ratio decidendi* was that the savings-bank book fell within the category of allocated property despite the scanty evidence justifying such a finding of fact. If the property had been unallocated then the heir would have been entitled to immediate enjoyment of it under section 13(1).

While it is contended, with respect, that the decisions of the Judicial Commissioner and the High Court were erroneous in law in preferring George Moshoeshoe's views to the rule in section 13(1) and further that the High Court made a false and confusing distinction between allocated and unallocated property, it must be confessed that the existing confusion has merely been further confounded by the decision of the Court of Appeal which overruled it.

Their Lordships held that in a monogamous marriage the concept of allocation was inappropriate and therefore George Moshoeshoe's statement was inapplicable because it only concerned allocated property. Since the plaintiff as the heir inherited the whole estate he was entitled to have the bank book. While the widow had the right to be maintained by the heir, she did not have the right to retain the book.

The Court's evasion of the substance of George Moshoeshoe's statement on the basis of a distinction between allocated and unallocated property is both regrettable and also surprising in view of the Court's seeming indifference to the classification, as reflected in the following remarks:

It seems to be unhelpful to seek for unallocated property when fixing the respective rights of the appellant and the respondent. Along that line one can at least as well say that all the deceased's property was unallocated as that there was one house to which it was all allocated. But preferably one should hold that allocation has no bearing on the present case.[1]

Once this stage in the reasoning is reached, George Moshoeshoe's statement has to be confined, as the Court held, to polygamous households. However, there can be no logical justification for drawing this distinction. It seems clear that in most cases, particularly among the commoners, there will be practically no unallocated property in a polygamous household.[2] Why therefore should the heir's position *vis-à-vis* property allocated to his mother's house be different in a polygamous household from his position *vis-à-vis* the whole estate (however it is classified) in a monogamous marriage?

Two writers have voiced strong criticisms of the superior courts' decisions in both of these cases. Ramolefe states that in *Lekaota's case* Elyan C.J. undervalued a widow's rights; these do not simply relate to crockery and bedding and the heir cannot remove *any* property from the widow's sight since this may interfere with her rights of use and consultation.[3] He goes on:

An even greater objection is that heirs could, with impunity, swoop down hawk-like after their father's death and drive all before them leaving the widow and other dependants only with such china as may still be serviceable at their father's death. Surely, if her interest in unallocated property remains unaffected by her husband's death, a proposition I endorse, then there can be no question of removal of anything, especially if we accept the statement that the only change is that of control passing from her husband to her son or the heir.[4]

The crux of the matter is therefore to define the heir's right of control which is derived from the same right formerly possessed by the late husband as the administrator of the household. Is it so limited that in no circumstances can the widow ever be deprived of possession of such household assets as money and livestock? We have already seen that a wife's rights were certainly not so strong as this and it can surely be argued forcefully that the rights

[1] (1963–6) H.C.T.L.R. 100.   [2] P.D., pp. 163, 166.
[3] (1969), pp. 203–4.   [4] Ibid., p. 204.

actually exercised by the heirs in the two cases corresponded closely with the control vested in a husband.[1]

Hamnett's criticism is more thoroughgoing. His view is that the approach of the courts in the two cases was directed to the fruitless task of trying to identify rights *in rem*. Instead, he argues, the courts should have concentrated their efforts on the protection of the rights of widows and heirs *inter se*.[2]

It is submitted that he is quite correct here. The vital interests in need of preservation are that the widow should be properly maintained and that the estate should not be dissipated to such an extent that nothing remains after her death.[3] It is also true that it is insufficient for the courts to be satisfied with the mere identification of the heir and the simple assertion of the heir's right of control. The further problem remains of defining what power resides within this right and how far it is restricted by the interests of the widow. In attempting to do this, it is important to place the two cases examined so far in the wider context of actual disputes which arise and the possible solutions which are available.

In the same way that the law provides safeguards for a wife during her husband's lifetime, similar processes exist to protect her after her husband's death. In fact she may well need greater protection at this time for a number of reasons. First, the heir may be distracted from the needs of the widow by the requirements of his own wife and children. Secondly, he may not be living in the same vicinity as the widow. Thirdly, the widow may not be his own mother, and therefore he may have less regard for her welfare.

A widow's right to be maintained by the heir is clear not only from sections 13(1) and 14(3) of the Laws of Lerotholi, but also from a number of cases[4] apart from *Khatala* v. *Khatala*. How is

---

[1] The Panel members agreed with both the decisions—see P.D., p. 164.

[2] (1975), p. 56.

[3] Ibid., p. 55. He also suggests (at p. 55) that certain apparent terminological contradictions in some Basotho Court judgments do not in fact indicate any substantive disagreement. 'Whether the widow or the son is said to "inherit" depends on whose rights appear to be under invasion.' However, while this may be correct, his examples are not considered sufficient to establish the point and may be explained on other grounds, including the division of the subject adopted here.

[4] See below, pp. 278–80. The extent of the maintenance required for a royal widow in terms of livestock, food, clothing, and medical attention was one of the issues decided in *'Mantsebo Seeiso* v. *'Mabereng Seeiso* (1926–53) H.C.T.L.R. 212 (H.C.).

this right enforceable and what is its relationship with the heir's right of control?

Where the widow and the heir cannot solve their differences satisfactorily among themselves the law provides for the dispute to come in the first instance before a family council in terms of that important provision, section 14(4) of Part I of the Laws of Lerotholi. This section dovetails in with section 13(2) which, it will be recalled, makes the deceased's brothers, i.e. the paternal uncles of the heir, responsible for determining the appropriate portion of the unallocated estate to be set aside for the use of the widow. Both Ashton and the members of the Panel Discussion took the view that the role of the uncles was only an advisory one and that the heir was entitled to overrule them if he disagreed with their decision.[1] However, in view of the wording of the subsection their role would seem to be more extensive than this, giving them supervisory powers over the heir so that their decision could only be upset by a meeting of the family council or a judgment of a court of law.

Three cases shed further light on the respective roles of the uncles, the family council and the courts. *Charles* v. *Macapha*[2] concerned another dispute about a savings-bank book, but this time the deceased had been a polygamist and the book was held to form part of the unallocated property. The Local Court awarded the book to the heir, but was overruled by the Central Court which divided the money in dispute. This decision was upheld by the Judicial Commissioner on the ground that a family meeting had been held at which it had been decided that the widow should have at least part of the money in the account for her maintenance. The heir had behaved in a manner which suggested that he was not willing to support the widow and this seemed to be the only satisfactory practical solution to the problem.

More recently in *Neheng* v. *Neheng*[3] the heir was failing to support the widow and had removed some livestock from her possession without consulting her. The Local Court referred the dispute to the family council, but the heir refused to co-operate or attend any meeting of the family. The Local Court thereupon ordered the heir to restore the livestock he had removed. On appeal, the Central Court ordered the entire estate to be divided

---

[1] Ashton, pp. 181–2; P.D., p. 160.
[2] J.C. 238/1963.   [3] J.C. 57/1967.

into two halves under the supervision of the paternal uncles because it had become abundantly clear that the heir was not prepared to co-operate with the widow.

In upholding the Central Court decision, Thompson J.C. summarized the over-all position in the following terms:

It is of course important to bear in mind that the heir in custom does not ever have absolute and entire rights of disposal of his father's estate. Further than that it is important to bear in mind the difference between the European law on this matter which is in very considerable contrast to customary law, and I think the main contrast there is that the head of the family is himself bound by certain coventions and customs in his handling of his family property as is his heir. He is the head of the family and as such administers the family property for that family's benefit. He cannot squander such property. Meanwhile he is not bound to adopt advice given him by his wife or wives or mother or uncles, but he is not supposed to dispose of family assets, or to liquidate them, without consulting them, without consulting the other members of the family concerned. He can be prevented from wasting family assets unnecessarily. It is often said that a widow's position in relation to her late husband's heir is very little different from her relation to her late husband during her husband's lifetime, which would mean to say that the heir could not normally deprive the widowed mother of the means of sustenance and maintenance, which she had during the late husband's lifetime.

Neheng's case was followed in *Mochele* v. *Motanyane*,[1] another case in which the heir had removed stock from the widow to his own home ninety miles away without consulting her. The widow alleged that she was not being properly maintained and claimed the return of the stock. Since the family had failed to resolve the dispute the Local Court ordered the heir to restore what he had taken away. This decision was upheld by President Noosi in the Likueneng Central Court who explained:

If the widow can show that she is not properly treated or supported and show that this is caused by [the heir's] misdeeds or wrongs the court can order that the property or stock should be taken from the control of the heir, or a portion thereof, and be given to the widow who will work with a person to be nominated by the family who will be called the guardian.

[1] J.C. 294/1969.

He went on:

Even if those things can be so placed in the hands of the widow that
does not mean that they are hers, they still belong to the heir . . . [I]t
is unfitting and a disgrace . . . that the benefits derived from the stock
or animals left by the deceased should be used or eaten by the daughter-
in-law of the deceased at her husband's home and the widow . . .
should derive no benefit . . . the mode of living which the widow is
expected to lead . . . should not differ very much from that which she
led during the lifetime of her late husband.

The Judicial Commissioner agreed and confirmed the decision
that the stock should be returned.

In both *Neheng's case* and *Mochele* v. *Motanyane* mention was
made of the fact that the widow would have to use the property
in consultation with an uncle of the heir or other relative chosen
by the family. The supervisory role of the uncle thus extends
beyond the mere decision as to the amount which should be set
aside for the widow's use.

It would be convenient if it were possible to distinguish these
last three cases from the final judgments in *Lekaota's case* and
Khatala's case on the basis of different factual situations, namely
that in the former cases the widow needed the property in dispute
if she was to be adequately maintained, whereas in the latter she
had no such pressing needs and was amply provided for otherwise.[1] However, it is clear, at all events from the facts of *Khatala's
case*, that the widow was in very straitened circumstances. The
decisions of the higher courts are therefore inadequate in their
pursuit of the limited goal of defining who has control of the
property. Greater emphasis must be placed on the maintenance of
the widow rather than the property rights of the heir whenever
circumstances justify this, as they normally do. Where the heir
has clearly manifested his unwillingness to support the widow or
to co-operate with his family over this matter there is every
justification for the court to order the handing over or restoration
of property to the widow, rather than waiting for a subsequent
claim for maintenance to arise.[2]

[1] Cf. P.D., p. 167.

[2] For similar decisions see *Mefane* v. *Mefane* H.C. 6/1942 (P.C.'s Ct.,
contra S.C.); *Malikhetla* v. *Malikhetla* J.C. 20/1958 (C.C. and J.C.). The Panel
members seemed to think that *Neheng's case* was wrongly decided and that a
separate suit for maintenance should have been brought—see P.D., p. 164.

A widow is entitled to be maintained as far as possible at the same standard of living as when her husband was alive and she must therefore have the wherewithal to run her household as she did as a wife. This will usually entail the possession of money, livestock, and farm equipment in addition to household effects and cooking utensils. It is submitted that no distinction should be made between money and livestock. Money has long been a familiar form of maintenance and wealth in all parts of the country.

However, against the requirements of the widow must be balanced the general interests of the heir, both in terms of his right to make over-all decisions about the administration and preservation of the estate property and in respect of his own beneficial use. It is to be hoped that the higher courts will adopt a flexible approach to the whole question in the future and not confine themselves within too narrow a framework of inquiry.

(b) *Where the Heir is a Minor*

The guardian of minor children is appointed by the family after the father's death. Traditionally one of the father's brothers would have been chosen[1] but the law has seen a marked shift in modern times in favour of the extension of the rights of women in this area and it is quite common for a widow to be appointed today, as will be shown. However, where the principal heir is married and thus a major he is the guardian of minor heirs in other houses as well as of minor children in his own house.[2]

Whoever is appointed as guardian of the principal heir, where he is a minor, is automatically the guardian of minors in other houses in a polygamous household. Under the maxim '*malapa ha a jane*' property allocated to one house can, of course, only be used by the guardian for the maintenance of minors in that house.[3]

The status of a widow where at the time of her husband's death his heir is a minor was one of the questions for decision in the *Regency case*.[4] No provision of the Laws of Lerotholi expressly covered the point at that time, but after hearing expert witnesses Lansdown J. concluded:

---

[1] *Kente* v. *Foloko* J.C. 212/1963 (J.C.); *Qele* v. *Ndabeni* J.C. 68/1966 (J.C.); P.D., pp. 175, 179–81, 189–91, 233.
[2] S. 12(3) of Part I of the Laws of Lerotholi.
[3] Ibid.
[4] (1926–53) H.C.T.L.R. 50.

A custom has . . . grown up and is now, I find, frequently, though perhaps not universally practised under which a wife, on the death of her husband leaving his eldest son a minor has become the controller and administrator of the affairs of her own House, subject, it is true, to the influence and advice of the male head of the family . . . or in some cases of the adult male members of the deceased husband's family collectively.[1]

He went on to explain that this often occurred in the case of widows of chiefs because they mistrusted their late husband's brothers and feared they might usurp the chieftainship for themselves if provided with a suitable opportunity. Such a widow therefore commonly assumed control of her chiefdom or ward as Regent.

It was contended for the plaintiff that, despite this, all widows were themselves under guardianship and it was sought to draw an analogy with the section of the Laws dealing with the situation where there was no male issue; there reference is made to the deceased husband's people being the widow's guardians (*balisa*). His Lordship held that *balisa* did not have the connotation attached to the English word 'guardians' and that this was therefore a mistranslation from the Sesotho version. A widow with a minor heir was not under guardianship, but rather exercised guardianship herself over any minor children as an automatic consequence of her position as Regent. Furthermore he found that the practice of the Regents had been followed, at least to some extent, by the general body of commoners.

The decision of the Court does not amount to a declaration that widows are always entitled to be made guardians of minor children because the appointment of a guardian is essentially a matter for the family.[2] However, it does establish that a widow can legitimately be so appointed and that if she is, her position is secure from challenge in the absence of adequate grounds for her removal. Moreover, the decision in the *Regency case* itself no doubt stimulated more widows to assert themselves when the question of guardianship came to be determined by the family.[3]

Where the widow is appointed as guardian she will be liable for wrongs committed by minor children[4] and will possess the

---

[1] At 54–5. [2] P.D., pp. 189–90. [3] See P.D., p. 180.
[4] See e.g. *Selia* v. *Monikazi* J.C. 198/1957 (J.C., abduction); *Mohale* v. *Setho* J.C. 77/1963 (J.C.); *Lebeisa* v. *Mabesa* J.C. 66/1966 (J.C.); Duncan, p. 7; Palmer, p. 72; P.D., pp. 190, 230.

necessary *locus standi* to appear in court on her own.[1] Thompson J.C. summarized the modern position in *Qele v. Ndabeni*,[2] a case in which a widow was sued for the return of some beasts which had been loaned to her late husband, as follows:

The impression this court has had from a series of cases . . . is that it is for a family to decide who is to administer the estate. . . . The courts from which appeals come . . . have decided frequently that it is competent to sue the widow, and that a large number of families leave the administration of the minor heir's estate . . . to the widow. In earlier days it might not have been accepted as correct custom in so far as it was normal for the family to appoint a male guardian. . . . In modern circumstances the impression the assessor and I get is that the courts normally accept a widow as being the proper guardian for a minor heir. . . .

Soon after the *Regency case* was decided new provisions were added to Part I of the Laws of Lerotholi to safeguard the prospective rights of a minor heir to inherit the estate.

Section 12(1) runs as follows:

When a man dies leaving an heir who is a minor, the person appointed as guardian of the heir and administrator of the estate shall keep a written record of the administration of the estate, and this record shall be open to inspection by the paternal uncles, and by other relatives of the heir as are permitted to do so by Basuto Law.

In the *Regency case* Lansdown J. had remarked that if any maladministration of the estate did occur the heir had a remedy which he could pursue when he attained his majority and that prior to that time the administrator could be sued by a person (presumably an uncle or other relative) representing the heir's interest.[3] However, it seems doubtful whether such rights were at all clearly established before the adoption of these new provisions.[4]

The proper interpretation to be placed upon the words in section 12(1) 'other relatives of the heir as are permitted to do so by Basuto Law' in relation to inspection of estate records, came up for consideration by the High Court in *'Mantsebo Seeiso v.*

---

[1] *Regency case* at 57; *Molapo v. Molapo* J.C. 77/1960 (C.C. and J.C., *contra* L.C.); *'Moleli v. Maisa* J.C. 286/1960 (J.C.); *Phasumane v. Mohapi* J.C. 205/1964 (all courts); *Chalete v. Mbohla* J.C. 76/1967 (J.C.).
[2] J.C. 68/1966 (J.C.).   [3] At 55.
[4] See the evidence of Chief Kelebone Nkuebe and Chief Matlere Lerotholi in *'Mantsebo Seeiso v. 'Mabereng Seeiso* J.C. 132/1949 (J.C.) below.

'Mabereng Seeiso[1] in 1950. It will be recalled that 'Mantsebo had been appointed Regent and acting Paramount Chief during the minority of Seeiso's heir, the present King. However Seeiso's heir was not 'Mantsebo's own child but a son of 'Mabereng, a junior wife. As we have seen 'Mantsebo's right to be the guardian of the heir had been upheld in the *Regency case*. In the instant case 'Mabereng claimed *inter alia* that she was entitled under section 12(1) to inspect the estate records in her capacity as the heir's mother.

The Paramount Chief's Court rejected her claim and held that only the uncles had a right of inspection, thus rendering the phrase 'and by other relatives to the heir' devoid of content. A considerable amount of testimony on the question was provided in the Judicial Commissioner's Court and many expert witnesses gave evidence. Chief Kelebone Nkuebe and Chief Matlere Lerotholi stated that the expression 'other relatives' referred in the circumstances of this particular case to the 'Sons of Lerotholi', i.e. Paramount Chief Lerotholi's sons, grandsons and great-grandsons, a royal family council spanning three generations of lineal descendants. 'Mabereng could not, in their view, inspect the records unless she was given permission to do so by the family. If she had a complaint she should take the matter up with the uncles and request them to make an inspection, and if they refused she could take them to court and enforce their performance of this duty.

On the other hand, Chief Bereng (with whom Chief Gabashane Masupha agreed) took the view that there had been a development in the law with regard to the status of a widow and that while in former times she would not have possessed a right of inspection, the heir's mother did now have this entitlement. There must have been a certain irony in this evidence. Chief Bereng had, of course, been the unsuccessful party in the *Regency case* in which the new status of women had received such dramatic public confirmation. Moreover, in view of his continuing vendetta with 'Mantsebo it is hardly a surprise to find him giving evidence against her interests, even if this did involve him adopting a view of modern Sesotho law exactly the opposite of that which he had put forward on his own behalf in the *Regency case*.

Be this as it may, the Judicial Commissioner preferred Chief

[1] (1926–53) H.C.T.L.R. 212.

Bereng's evidence and gave judgment in favour of 'Mabereng. In doing so he was merely following the logic of the decision in the *Regency case*. After pointing out that widows not only acted as regents but also had seats on the National Council and adjudicated in court proceedings, Driver J.C. went on:

By having this advanced status it is a natural assumption that women have also acquired a much greater authority in the family entity and in the management of . . . family affairs . . . It is essential that the existing estate should be carefully administered for the future owner. Who is the most appropriate person to see that such estate is carefully administered? In my opinion it is the mother of the owner of the estate.

He explained further that if the mother could only act through the paternal uncles an anomalous situation would arise because section 12(1) imposed no legal duty on the uncles to inspect; it merely gave them the power to do so.

On appeal to the High Court, Driver J.C. was overruled and the decision of the Paramount Chief's Court was reinstated. Harragin C.J. declared:

I have searched the evidence in vain to find any evidence to support ['Mabereng's] contention[1] and it is perfectly clear from the evidence as a whole that the only persons with a right to inspect . . . are the paternal uncles, and if they fail in their duty the right may exist in some other relative to take them to court and force them to carry out their duty, but that does not mean that every single relative of the heir has the right to inspect the record whenever he feels inclined . . . this does not mean that a mother . . . must stand by while her child's estate is maladministered. Her correct course should be to take the paternal uncles before the court and force them to do their duty by their nephew, if indeed she has evidence to show that the estate is being maladministered, or even that there are reasonable grounds for thinking that it is being maladministered.[2]

This decision has been criticized by Duncan[3] and was also

---

[1] This seems rather a sweeping dismissal of the evidence of Chiefs Bereng and Gabashane. However, both of them had been sentenced to death for ritual murder between the time when they gave their evidence before the Judicial Commissioner and the High Court hearing and perhaps this may have led Harragin C.J. to doubt their veracity.

[2] (1926–53) H.C.T.L.R. at 213–14.   [3] At pp. 12–13.

thought to be erroneous in the Panel Discussion.[1] A motion was brought before the National Council immediately after it was given to have Section 12(1) amended so as specifically to include the heir's mother among the 'other relatives'.[2] However, consideration of the matter was postponed on the ground that the debate was getting too bound up with the personalities in the case, particularly the Regent herself. Eventually the matter was shelved.[3]

The High Court decision seems to have been a retrograde one, going directly contrary to the judicial recognition of the growing rights of widows initiated by Lansdown J. in the *Regency case*. At all events it would appear that today a mother would stand a good chance of success in claiming to be entitled to inspect the estate records.

Apart from the heir's mother, the expression 'other relatives' would seem to encompass the sons of paternal uncles, but not the heir's maternal uncles.[4]

So far as the actual process of inspection is concerned, section 12(1) is curious in that it refers to an inspection of the written record of the estate, whereas in a society where much wealth is held in livestock one would need to count the animals themselves to be really sure of the true position. It would therefore seem to be implied that anyone inspecting the written record may check this against the physical existence of the stock. However, this may present difficulties since many stock are sent to graze in mountain pastures for part of the year and to bring them down often would not only be a cumbersome process but would also tire the animals out. Therefore inspections must obviously be arranged at proper intervals after consultations have taken place with those relatives who are entitled to inspect. They clearly cannot each arrange to have their own independent inspections whenever they wish.[5]

Attention should also be drawn to certain other provisions of the Laws of Lerotholi introduced around 1947 to safeguard the position of a minor heir.

Section 12(2) provides:

[1] P.D., p. 181.

[2] *1950 National Council Proceedings*, pp. 113–50.

[3] *1951 National Council Proceedings*, p. 156.

[4] P.D., pp. 179, 181.

[5] See the evidence of Chief Kelebone Nkuebe and Chief Bereng in '*Mantsebo Seeiso* v. '*Mabereng Seeiso* (J.C.) above.

No property belonging to the estate shall be sold or otherwise disposed of by the guardian, administrator or widow without the prior consent (*tumello*) of the paternal uncles and other relatives of the heir entitled by Basuto Law and Custom to be consulted.

This subsection is clear enough and is designed to prevent the dissipation of the estate during the heir's minority. A similar type of provision is found in section 14(2) to cover a case where a widow has no male issue in her house though there is male issue in another house. The widow has the use of property allocated to her house, but again she cannot dispose of any of it without the prior consent (*tumello*) of her guardian.[1]

Section 14(3) appears to cover more or less the same ground as section 12(2) but it is oddly inconsistent in providing a less stringent safeguard against dispositions of the estate during the heir's minority. It runs as follows:

If there is male issue in any house other than the house from which the principal heir comes, the widow shall have the use of all the property allocated to her house and at her death any property remaining shall devolve upon the eldest son of her house . . . *provided that no widow may dispose of any property without consultation (therisano) with the guardian while that son is a minor,* . . . (italics added).[2]

It may be argued that the range of this provision differs from that of section 12(2) in two respects. First, it is concerned with allocated property[3] and secondly with property in houses other than that of the principal heir. However, as explained earlier the distinction between allocated and unallocated property does not affect rights substantially but merely defines the persons interested. Moreover, there is no reason to suppose that section 12(2) does not cover houses other than that of the principal heir and therefore there is an apparent overlap and inconsistency to this extent. The explanation may be that despite the use of two different Sesotho words the reality of the concept in Sesotho custom and behaviour lies somewhere between them. Although the High Court has been prepared to draw distinctions between the two concepts[4] because

[1] The Sesotho version used to contain the word *therisano* (consultation) but in *Matela* v. *Mphana* J.C. 625/1952 Driver J.C. preferred the English version which had the word 'consent'; see Duncan, p. 15.
[2] Applied in *Chalete* v. *Mbohla* J.C. 76/1967 (L.C.).
[3] This distinction was drawn in *Lichaba* v. *Lichaba* H.C. 60/1949, discussed below.
[4] See *Lichaba* v. *Lichaba* H.C. 60/1949.

they are so different in their English translations, this may not necessarily be the best approach. The obligation to consult in Sesotho law may connote the acceptance of reasonable advice and thus often be virtually equivalent to requiring consent.

(c) *Where there is no Male Issue*

In the course of his evidence to the 1872 Commission George Moshoeshoe stated that a widow could inherit cattle belonging to her house if she had no male children at her husband's death.[1] Chief Jobo, a brother of Moshoeshoe I, also gave evidence of a widow's right to inherit in these circumstances, although he was careful to add that she could never have more than a life interest.[2]

The original version of the Laws of Lerotholi of 1903 further elaborated the position by providing

> If a man dies leaving only female children, the widow shall be heiress to his estate and property, but she must work in conformity with the wishes of her deceased husband's people who shall in all matters be deemed her guardians.[3]

Before investigating in greater detail the modern law two initial points should be made. First, where a widow gives birth to male issue after her husband's death her position automatically changes to that described under (b) above since her son would be regarded as legitimate and as the heir, whether fathered by her husband, or a *mokeneli*, or possibly even a stranger.[4] Secondly, whatever the extent of the widow's rights during her lifetime, the residue which is left on her death devolves within her husband's lineage group and never under any circumstances passes to her own natal family.[5]

When the rules about inheritance contained in the Laws of Lerotholi were being formulated and expanded in 1946–8 following the decision in the *Regency case* the law quoted above was rephrased as section 11(2) to read:

If there is no male issue in any house the senior widow shall be the

---

[1] *1873 Report and Evidence*, p. 41.   [2] *1873 Report and Evidence*, p. 50.
[3] 1903 version, section 15. Sheddick (1953) is in error when he states (at p. 33) that widows can never inherit property.
[4] See pp. 181–2 above.   [5] See P.D., p. 151.

heir,[1] but according to custom she is expected to consult the relatives of her deceased husband who are her proper advisers (*baeletsi*).

It will be recalled that during his judgment in the *Regency case* Lansdown J. had stated that the word 'guardians' in the earlier version of this section (see above) was a mistranslation of the Sesotho *balisa* and gave the false impression that a widow was under the strict control of her late husband's relatives. The Sesotho version now makes the matter clearer by using the word *baeletsi*.

By way of example, in *Maile* v. *Shea*[2] the Judicial Commissioner upheld as valid the allocation of a beast by a widow to her daughter in face of opposition from her late husband's elder brother, since the allocation had received general family pubicity and a younger brother-in-law had consented and the local chief had been informed.

The reference in section 11(2) to the 'senior widow' reflects the concentration of the Laws on the position in a polygamous marriage, but the rule is equally applicable *mutatis mutandis* to monogamous households.[3] Presumably junior widows in a polygamous household would be in a similar position *vis-à-vis* property allocated to their own houses.

Commenting on the section, Ramolefe states that where the senior widow inherits unallocated property she is obliged to use it with the other widows and share it with the sons of these widows and further, that the question of what portion should be set aside for the support of such widows is a matter for the deceased's brother and other relatives to decide.[4] In saying this he is in effect putting forward the view that once a widow is classified as the heir in terms of section 11(2) the provisions of section 13 apply and that the word 'heir' used therein is wide enough to include a widow in cases where there is no male issue.

This is a possible interpretation, but the actual wording of that section hardly seems to justify it. The situation envisaged there is

---

[1] Applied in *Mokorosi* v. *Mokorosi* (1954) H.C.T.L.R. 24 (all courts); *Moeketse* v. *Moeketse* J.C. 142/1955 (J.C.); and the cases referred to in footnote 3 below; see also *Ramokone* v. *Kapoko* J. C. 136/1966 (J.C.); *Polo* v. *Polo* J.C. 137/1966 (J.C.); *Setlokoane* v. *Setlokoane* J.C. 228/1967 (J.C.).

[2] J.C. 33/1965 (J.C.).

[3] *Lichaba* v. *Lichaba* H.C. 60/1949 (all courts—see below, pp. 292-3); *Phamotse* v. *Phamotse* H.C. 22/1952 (H.C.); *Maile* v. *Shea* J.C. 33/1965 (all courts); *Noko* v. *Noko* J.C. 187/1966 (L.C. and J.C.).

[4] Ramolefe (1969), p. 201.

clearly one where the heir is a married son. The relevant part of section 13(1) states:

... the heir ... shall inherit all the unallocated property of the estate and *he* is obliged by custom to use the estate with *his father's widow* or widows and to share with *his* junior brothers ... (italics added].

Moreover, section 13(2) makes reference to the 'paternal uncles of the principal heir'. By the principal heir it is clear that a son is meant for the paternal uncles of the widow would have absolutely no voice in the matter. Thus the very existence of such a son and heir is taken for granted in which case the senior widow could not inherit in the first place.

Ramolefe then turns to the widow's inheritance of allocated property and declares that in disposing of the property of her house she has first to obtain the consent of her guardian.[1] From the terms of his discussion it is apparent that he takes the view that section 14(2) is applicable in such circumstances. Again this is doubtful. Section 14(2) is based upon the presupposition that a principal heir exists somewhere although not in the house of the particular widow whose rights are being defined. It would seem not unlikely that the position here is rendered different by the existence of such a son and that the safeguards against dissipation by the widow might well be corespondingly more stringent. Assuming that there is a real difference between the two concepts, where there is male issue somewhere in the household she would need prior *consent* before disposing of property while if none exists she would only have to *consult* her late husband's relatives.[2]

These difficulties merely serve to emphasise the uncertainty that exists as to the proper interpretation and interaction of sections 11-14 of the Laws.

4. RIGHTS OVER LAND AND BUILDINGS

It will be recalled that for purposes of inheritance different rules apply to arable lands on the one hand and gardens and residential sites on the other.

---

[1] Ramolefe (1969), p. 201.
[2] *Semble contra* Hamnett (1975), pp. 148–9 who appears to take the view that a widow without male issue cannot dispose of property 'unilaterally'. *Quaere* whether this expression includes consultation.

(a) *Residential Sites, Houses, and Gardens*

(i) *Where the heir is a major*

The cases reveal the same conflicts between widows and heirs here as in relation to movable property. The leading case of *Lesitsi* v. *Mafa*[1] was concerned with the widow's right to occupy her deceased husband's houses just as much as with her right to use his fields, but the spotlight has been turned mainly on the latter question.[2] The heir had evicted the widow from the houses and the court of first instance upheld her claim to have her possession restored. However, on appeal, the Paramount Chief's Circuit Court preferred to emphasize the heir's rights and declared that the widow should live in a different house which had allegedly been allocated to her by the deceased (though she disputed this). The Court also ordered the heir to build a further house for the widow. Driver J.C. reversed this decision, holding that a widow was entitled to live in her deceased husband's houses up to her death and that no one could deprive her of this right.

In the more recent case of *Mahalefele* v. *Mahalefele*[3] both the Central Court and the Judicial Commissioner upheld the widow's action for possession against the heir who was attempting to force her to vacate her deceased husband's house and garden. The Central Court rightly relied on *Lesitsi* v. *Mafa*, but also based itself on the provisions of section 7(4) of Part I of the Laws of Lerotholi:

No widow shall be deprived of her land except under the provisions of paragraphs (2) and (3).

This section, however, purports to deal only with arable lands and would therefore not seem to have been applicable. It will be examined further below.[4]

The protection afforded to widows by the courts in such cases as these[5] has to be reconciled with the fact that section 7(7) of the Laws provides for the inheritance of residential sites and gardens by the heir, not the widow, as follows:

---

[1] J.C. 84/1953.

[2] See Poulter, 'The Place of the Laws of Lerotholi in the Legal System of Lesotho', (1972) *African Affairs* 144 at 159–60 and above, pp. 250–4.

[3] J.C. 61/1966.   [4] See p. 294 below.

[5] A similar decision was reached in *Mohami* v. *Mohami* J.C. 193/1965 (L.C. and J.C.).

On the death of a person who has been allocated the use of land for the growing of vegetables or tobacco, or for the purpose of planting fruit or other trees, or for residential purposes, the heir, or in the absence of the heir, the dependants of such deceased person shall be entitled to the use of such land so long as he or they continue to dwell thereon.

Clearly if the widow were to be regarded as a dependant of her husband she would only be entitled to remain in occupation in the absence of the heir, but this does not seem to be the way the courts approach the matter. The heir, it appears, only has a right to enjoy possession of this part of his inheritance after the widow's death.[1] The widow obviously has no right of dispostion either by allocation during her lifetime or by testamentary instrument.

(ii) *Where the heir is a minor*

If the heir is a minor child he would commonly be living with the widow as a dependant. Again his rights would be subject to those of the widow up to her death. She would, of course, be unable to dispose of the property without the prior consent of the heir's paternal uncles and other relatives in terms of section 12(2) of the Laws.

(iii) *Where there is no male issue*

As in the case of movable property the widow is designated the heir by section 11(2) of the Laws and she must consult with the relatives of her deceased husband who are her proper advisers (*baeletsi*). In *Lichaba* v. *Lichaba*[2] the deceased died without male issue and included within his estate was a house in the Mafeteng Reserve. All the courts held that his widow was entitled to inherit the house, but the main question for decision was whether she could sell the house in face of opposition from her late husband's brother. The lower courts held that she was not even bound to consult her brother-in-law, but the Judicial Commissioner and the High Court held that while consultation was required, prior consent was not. Harragin C.J. pointed out that the word 'consult' was used in section 11(2), whereas the expression 'prior consent' (*tumello*) was to be found in other sections of the Laws.[3] Since the

---

[1] *Contra* Ramolefe (1966), p. 19.
[2] H.C. 60/1949.
[3] But see above pp. 287–8 and also P.D., pp. 149–50.

Sesotho version also reflected this distinction he took the view that the point must have been appreciated by the draftsmen.

It is not entirely clear whether, assuming the necessary consultation has taken place, a widow possesses the right to determine the destination of the property on her death, either by allocation during her lifetime or by means of written instructions. In *Mothebesoane* v. *Mothebesoane*[1] Mapetla C.J. held a purported allocation by a widow in these circumstances to be a nullity. However, the authority of the decision is lessened by the fact that it stemmed from a concession by counsel which was based on cases where the deceased had actually been survived by male issue. The decision also appears to conflict to some extent with that in *Maile* v. *Shea*.[2]

(b) *Arable Lands*

It seems that widows were traditionally entitled to retain only two fields of the family's holding although widows of the royal lineage often managed to hold on to all the fields allocated to their husbands.[3] However, as the land shortage became more acute some chiefs started to restrict widows to a single field. This led Paramount Chief Griffith to issue the following ruling in 1936:[4]

I have already spoken to chiefs and told them that I do not approve of the practice of depriving widows of the lands which their husbands used to plough prior to their death. I informed the chiefs that they should know that the husbands of these widows have died in their country and in the service of Basutoland, or have died for this Territory, and that it is therefore fitting that their widows should not be deprived of the lands with which they have to support the orphans left by their husbands.

Chief, I inform you about this matter because there have recently been seven widows who have been crying that they have been deprived of their deceased husband's lands because, it was alleged, they did not pay tax as they were merely women and therefore they ought to be dispossessed of the lands. Certainly Chief, I should like to state that if anyone came to you with such a suggestion you would know that I definitely do not agree with such a matter. My wish is that these widows should be allowed to continue to use the lands which their

---

[1] H.C. Civ./T/14/1973.
[2] J.C. 33/1965 discussed above p. 289.
[3] (1954), p. 163.
[4] Quoted in Sheddick (1954), pp. 163–4.

husbands were in the habit of ploughing for the maintenance of the orphans left with them.

Soon after this pronouncement a new section 7(4) was added to Part I of the Laws of Lerotholi to protect the rights of widows still further.[1] It prohibited chiefs and headmen from depriving a widow of her lands except where, on inspection, she was found to have more than necessary for her family's subsistence or where she had failed to cultivate the lands properly over a period of two successive years. As we have seen both these grounds for deprivation are, in any case, of general application to all landholders in Lesotho.[2]

Subject to this, then, a widow possesses an automatic right to remain on the family lands after her husband's death and to continue to cultivate them; she does not need to be confirmed on the lands by the local chief or headman.[3]

However, since the size of the family has been reduced by the death of her husband, it would seem as if, under certain circumstances of a dire land shortage in her area, a widow might have to forfeit part of her holding after an inspection. Then, pursuant to section 7(2) the chief or headman could reallocate this part to someone who had no land or an insufficient holding. However, the figures in Table 11 based on the survey I conducted during 1970–1 suggest that this is not a common occurrence. Where a widow does have to surrender one or more of her lands she is permitted to select which she wishes to release.[4]

As in the case of estate property other than land there have been disputes over land rights between widows and heirs. However, the heir has no right to inherit the arable lands allocated to his father and this rule, buttressed by section 7(4), provides a legal safeguard for the widow against eviction by the heir.[5] During 1947–8 an attempt was made by the National Council to strengthen the heir's rights by permitting the inheritance of arable land and this brought his rights into direct conflict with those of the widow. The *cause célèbre* on this matter, *Lesitsi* v. *Mafa*, has already been fully discussed.[6]

---

[1] See section 7(4) of Part I (1946).   [2] pp. 30–1 above.
[3] *Molato* v. *Ketisi* J.C. 34/1966 (J.C.).   [4] Section 7(6) of Part I.
[5] *Lesitsi* v. *Mafa* J.C. 84/1953 (J.C.); *Mahalefele* v. *Mahalefele* J.C. 61/1966 (C.C.).
[6] See pp. 250–4 above.

TABLE 11

*Analysis of the landholdings of 36 widows in the
three villages of Lenono's, Manteko's, and Morija*

	Number	Percentage
Widows with more lands than at their husbands' death	3	8·3
Widows with the same number of lands as at their husbands' death	16	44·4
Widows with less lands than at their husbands' death	3	8·3
Widows who have no lands and whose husbands had none	5	13·9
Widows who have moved from one village to another	5	13·9
Widows whose husbands' heirs have taken over the lands	3	8·3
Widows who don't know how many lands their husbands had	1	2·8
	36	99·9

5. LOSS OF RIGHTS

The general principle is that a widow is only entitled to retain any rights within her late husband's family while she remains attached to it. Thus if she deserts or 'removes', and particularly if she remarries, all these rights come to an end.[1]

(a) *Remarriage*

The vexed question of a widow's remarriage by customary rites is discussed below, but whether she remarries customarily or civilly it is clear that she automatically surrenders her rights within her late husband's family.

In *Ntsoale* v. *Molungoa*[2] a widow was given presents consisting of clothes, blankets, and stock by a man whom she subsequently married. Both the Central Court and the Judicial Commissioner's Court held that, apart from clothing, whatever a woman acquires during her widowhood belongs to her late husband's family. Furthermore, it was held that since on remarriage she loses all

[1] Ramolefe (1969), p. 204.
[2] J.C. 235/1960 (C.C. and J.C.).

her rights within that family, she could not take the other presents with her to her new husband's home.

(b) *Removal or Desertion*

The principle applicable here was clearly stated by Chief Jobo in his evidence to the 1872 Commission:

A widow can also inherit the property belonging to her house as long as she remains with her husband's friends [i.e. extended family]; but if she leaves them, then she is obliged to give up the property . . .[1]

Some of the difficulties which arise in applying this principle to rights in respect of *bohali* cattle are apparent from an examination of the considerable recent litigation on the question within Chief Leluma's family. I start, for reasons of convenience, with the case of *Leluma* v. *Mojela*[2] in 1964. The plaintiff, Chief Leluma, claimed *bohali* from the defendant in respect of the latter's marriage to 'Matota. The bride's father had died without male issue and the plaintiff brought the claim as her senior paternal uncle's heir. However, he had not consulted with 'Matota's widowed mother Mpho and the question arose whether he had acted properly in so doing. Both the Local Court and the Judicial Commissioner held he was so entitled, the Local Court mainly on the basis that he had been appointed her guardian and Thompson J.C. because Mpho had been living at her parents' home for the last twenty-five years and had thus abandoned her rights in her late husband's family, including any claim to her daughter's *bohali*.

Within the Leluma family the dispute between Chief Leluma and Mpho had already been fomenting for some years and Mpho had twice previously brought actions against the Chief to try to recover *bohali* paid in respect of the marriages of her daughters. In his turn the Chief had complained that Mpho was failing to consult him in family matters as she ought to do. The question had been discussed within the family and Mpho had been told that she should consult with the Chief in all household affairs.

Still dissatisfied, she brought a further action in the Thabana Morena Local Court in 1967, but was unsuccessful in her third attempt to recover *bohali* from the Chief.[3] The Court held that

---

[1] *1873 Report and Evidence*, p. 51.
[2] J.C. 184/1964.
[3] *Leluma* v. *Leluma*, Thabana Morena Local Court C.C. 83/1967.

she was not entitled to it in view of her desertion, but gave her thirty days in which to return to her late husband's family and thus regain her rights. Unfortunately she did not receive notice of the hearing and the case proceeded in her absence and thus she did not know of the ultimatum laid down in sufficient time to do anything about it. However, when she did learn of the decision she neither appealed nor challenged the Court's procedure nor made arrangements to return home.

Soon afterwards Chief Leluma brought another action for *bohali*, this time against the husband of 'Mamopeli, another of Mpho's daughters who had recently married.[1] The lower courts dismissed his claim, holding that Mpho was the proper person to claim so long as her marriage still subsisted. They held she had not deserted of her own free will, but had probably been forced to leave through the neglect of her late husband's relatives; at all events the marriage had never been dissolved. However, their decisions were reversed by Thompson J.C. who relied on the earlier judgment in the Thabana Morena Local Court and held that Mpho's only recourse was to try to get reconciled with her late husband's family.

More or less simultaneously Mpho commenced her fourth action against Chief Leluma to recover *bohali* and was successful in the Thabaneng Local Court on the basis that she retained her rights until she was divorced and this had not yet happened.[2] The Central Court overruled this decision as inconsistent with the prior Thabana Morena Local Court judgment of 1967. In the Judicial Commissioner's Court, Matete Acting J.C. agreed that a widow's rights were only finally forfeited on divorce, but he also held that the earlier judgment of the Thabana Morena Local Court was correct in that a widow could not enjoy rights in her late husband's house while she continued to live apart. However, despite the expiry of that court's time limit of thirty days, she could still return.

He elaborated on the rights of a widow as follows:

She is entitled to maintenance . . . so long as she remains where her husband kept her at the time of his death or where the relatives of her husband allow her to live. It may be asked whether a Mosotho widow can never remove. I would say she can in consultation with the head

[1] *Leluma v. Mohale* J.C. 216/1968.
[2] *Leluma v. Leluma* J.C. 103/1968.

of her late husband's family. The next question would be what if the
relatives withhold their consent. We are of the opinion that she could
go to court as she would go before the chief in the olden days. The
court would then decide what was best in her interests and order
accordingly.

Matete and others put forward the same view at the Panel
Discussion and maintained that a widow could leave her deceased
husband's home and take property with her, provided she continued to keep in touch with her late husband's relatives. She
could even return to her own parents' home, and provided she had
no intention of divorcing herself and that she consulted her
deceased husband's people she could still be regarded as a member
of that family. However, there were other members of the Panel
who felt a widow could never remove and that if she returned to
her own parents' home this *ipso facto* meant there had been a
divorce and that the *bohali* cattle were liable to be returned.[1]
The probable answer is that a widow can validly remove and
still retain her rights, but she must not behave in such a way as to
indicate that she has broken off all contact with her deceased
husband's people and that she regards herself as a member of
another family. Obviously if she remarries she loses all her rights
and the difficult factual question for decision is whether her
conduct, though it falls short of remarriage, indicates a permanent
separation.
Similar considerations would seem to apply in the case of rights
over land. Such rights are undoubtedly forfeited if the widow
voluntarily and deliberately removes from her late husband's lands
and residence and cuts off her ties with her late husband's people,
since this amounts to divorce.[2] On the other hand, situations arise
where a wife who has been driven away by her husband and has
ngala-ed to her parents' home, wishes to return after his death.
It is thought that during her absence her rights have been in
abeyance and that if she does return as a widow she is entitled to
her normal rights in respect of her late husband's lands, gardens

---

[1] P.D., pp. 150–3.
[2] Sheddick (1954), p. 187; *Kobefo* v. *Kobefo* J.C. 259/1963 (L.C. and J.C.);
Tseole v. *Tseole* J.C. 136/1967 (J.C.); P.D., p. 174. It appears that a widow
ought to consult before removing (*Mabaleha* v. *Mofubelu* J.C. 31/1964 (J.C.)
and P.D., pp. 174–5), but there would seem to be no sanction if she fails to
do so.

and houses.[1] Two decisions of Thompson J.C. appear to take the view that such a widow can only reclaim her rights if she was living near her husband's home at the time of his death and not if she was residing farther away,[2] but there would seem to be no justification for such a distinction.

6. REMARRIAGE

This question is one of considerable complexity and uncertainty, graphically reflecting the continuing but haphazard evolution of the rights of women.

The earliest discussion of the problem is provided by Casalis who wrote that some 'generous families' did not assert the right to *kenela* a widow, but allowed her to remarry as she wished.[3] Sometimes her own parents would return all or part of the *bohali* received for her in order to accomplish this purpose. The *Livre D'Or de la Mission du Lessouto* published by the P.E.M.S. also specifically affirmed the legality of this latter practice.[4]

During the first session of the National Council in 1903 when the original version of the Laws of Lerotholi was in the process of being framed, the drafting committee proposed the inclusion of the following law:

It shall be lawful for a widow to be married a second time if she does not like to stop with her husband's parents. If she should be married having had no children at her first husband's, then she shall be married for her husband's parents. But if such a widow has children, then she shall be married for her birthparents.

In the light of subsequent developments the wording of this proposal is extremely significant. It shows that the movement of *bohali* was seen as depending upon whether the deceased husband's family had benefited from the first marriage by the birth of children. If they had, then the *bohali* had served its purpose and could not be recovered. Thus the *bohali* in respect of the second marriage was to be paid to the widow's own parents who would then possess two sets of *bohali* simultaneously. On the other hand, if no children had been added to the husband's lineage compensation was due,

[1] *Kobefo* v. *Kobefo* J.C. 259/1963 (C.C.); *Tseole* v. *Tseole* J.C. 136/1967 (all courts); P.D., p. 174.
[2] See *Kobefo* v. *Kobefo* J.C. 259/1963; *Tseole* v. *Tseole* J.C. 136/1967.
[3] At p. 190.   [4] (Paris, 1912), p. 48.

but instead of the widow's parents refunding the *bohali* and then accepting new *bohali* in respect of the second marriage, a payment from the second husband's family *direct* to that of the first husband was contemplated.

Those who supported the proposed law, led by Chief Maama, felt that some widows were being neglected by their in-laws and therefore ought to be free to marry again. However, as things turned out the proposed section of the Laws was not accepted by the National Council. Paramount Chief Lerotholi was opposed to the idea and his view prevailed. A similar proposal was also defeated in the Council in 1921.

Whether the law has now evolved to the stage where widows are free to remarry, and if so under what conditions, remains shrouded in the mists of uncertainty so far as the decisions of the courts are concerned and this ambivalence was amply reflected in the Panel Discussion. However, the 'Restatement' boldly declares that remarriage is permissible and that the new *bohali*, which is nominal, goes to the late husband's family.[1]

The relevant court decisions are presented below in their chronological sequence in order to draw attention to their general trend. After that the views expressed at the Panel Discussion will be analysed.

In *Mojela* v. *Mojela*,[2] the case concerning *mala* marriages which went to the Privy Council in 1927 and which was discussed in Chapter 12, the respondent's mother had been widowed and as a result the question arose whether she could subsequently have validly married the late Chief Mojela. Although this matter was not considered by the Judicial Committee, both the Assistant Commissioner's Court and the Resident Commissioner's Court held that a valid second marriage had been contracted and this despite the fact that no *bohali* had been returned to the widow's late first husband's family. The reason given was that her two children had been left with that family. This corresponds with the concept of alternative destinations for the children and the *bohali* on divorce and it will be seen that all the later decisions treat the whole matter as one of divorce.

However, in 1939 Paramount Chief Griffith was strongly maintaining the line earlier taken by his father in opposing the

[1] At p. 11.
[2] Privy Council Appeal No. 93 of 1927.

remarriage of widows and he told the National Council in no uncertain terms that this was not permissible under Sesotho law.[1] Ashton reported that this rather 'overstated' the position because he himself had found a few examples of widows remarrying, but he agreed that the conservative opinion of the older generation and of the courts prevented its proper recognition.[2]

In 1940 came the leading case on the subject, in which the matter was fully investigated by the High Court with the help of expert witnesses. This was *Motsoene* v. *Harding*.[3] The plaintiff, Joel, contended that he was entitled to be recognized as Chief of Leribe on the death of Chief Motsoene Molapo in place of Letsie Koabeng whose appointment had been notified by the High Commissioner in the Government Gazette pursuant to the decision of the family council consisting of the 'sons of Molapo'. Joel based his claim on the argument that his grandmother Selahlelo (alias 'Mamakakamela) had married the late Chief before the grandmother of Letsie Koabeng and that this automatically gave him priority for purposes of succession in terms of Sesotho law as reflected in the Laws of Lerotholi.

The vital issue was the validity of 'Mamakakamela's marriage, since she had previously been married to one Sekake who had died leaving her a widow. The facts surrounding her purported remarriage were as follows. She had come to live with Chief Motsoene and had stayed with him for about ten years, during which time she had given birth to Joel. She was treated by everyone as his lawful wife, but there was no evidence of any agreement on marriage between the two families. It was alleged on Joel's behalf that after his birth twenty head of cattle had been driven to the parents of 'Mamakakamela as *bohali*, but the defendant countered by saying that they were not *bohali* but merely sent to buy Joel back from Sekake's family to which he would otherwise belong.[4] Ultimately 'Mamakakamela left Chief Motsoene and returned to Sekake's family where she cultivated his lands until her death. Joel, however, remained at Chief Motsoene's and was always treated as his lawful son.

Huggard C.J. had to consider two questions. First, whether

---

[1] Ashton, p. 85.   [2] Ibid.

[3] The case was omitted in error from (1926–53) H.C.T.L.R. and eventually reported at (1954) H.C.T.L.R. 1.

[4] *Quaere* whether Chief Motsoene was trying to adopt Joel as his heir—see Jones, p. 81 (n. 7).

'Mamakakamela, having been a widow, was ever in a position to contract a valid marriage with Chief Motsoene and secondly, if she was, whether such a marriage had ever taken place. He treated the first question as one of divorce and rejected the expert testimony of those who contended that a widow was free to leave her late husband's family and that if the two sets of parents agreed, there was no necessity to go to court. His view that divorces could only be obtained in court has already been shown to be erroneous.[1] He further rejected the argument that if the children remained with the late husband's family, divorce did not necessarily involve the return of *bohali* and this too has been shown to be incorrect. Relying on the evidence of the expert witnesses for the defendant and particularly on that of Chief Molise he concluded:

When a husband dies the widow remains a member of the family of her deceased husband and cannot remarry unless she obtains a divorce. If she leaves her deceased husband's family and returns to her parents the matter can be taken before a Native Court which if satisfied as to her reasons for leaving her deceased husband's family will grant a divorce and order the return of the [*bohali*] cattle which were paid on her marriage by her deceased husband's people.

Chief Molise had given additional evidence regarding the set-off of the children against the progeny of the *bohali* cattle, but Huggard C.J. stated that this did not arise on the facts of the case and therefore expressed no opinion on it. However, this did not prevent him from rejecting the argument that the reason why the *bohali* cattle for the first marriage had not been returned to Sekake's people was because that family had retained the three children of the marriage. In this respect his approach differed markedly from that adopted in *Mojela* v. *Mojela*.

Having reached this conclusion on the first question, the learned Chief Justice did not need to come to a decision on the second one. He held that the presumption of marriage from the length of cohabitation (which he regarded as more easily rebuttable under a polygamous system) was here rebutted by the absence of evidence establishing a prior divorce. If there had in fact been a divorce then 'Mamakakamela's ultimate return to Sekake's family and lands would be quite inexplicable.

In two cases soon after *Motsoene* v. *Harding* the Paramount

---

[1] See p. 205 above.

Chief and his Court took the view that if the *bohali* had not been returned, a widow could not validly remarry and that she remained attached to her late husband's family.[1]

Then in 1943 Lansdown J. commented on the position in the course of his judgment in the *Regency case*. He described perpetual widowhood as 'an unfortunate position' but seemed to doubt whether remarriage was possible at all.

There is some evidence *albeit slight*, that in such a position a woman might emerge from her husband's family by an arranged divorce, leaving behind her her children and her husband's estate, with the possibility of the children being regarded as adequate compensation for the *bohali*, or of her own family being required to refund the *bohali*[2] [italics added].

Thus by this stage the courts had shown a total lack of consistency on the question ranging from total rejection to recognition of remarriage without even the necessity of returning *bohali*.

In 1952 the case of *Molapo* v. *Mahooana*[3] reached the High Court after a passage through five lower courts involving two rehearings. The plaintiff sued for a declaration that he was the legitimate son of the late Mahooana Molapo and thus entitled to succeed him. The case turned on the validity of his mother's remarriage after she had been widowed. Four lower courts found against the plaintiff on the following basis. *Bohali* of twelve head of cattle had been paid for his mother by her second husband's family. These had been delivered to her own family who had then passed them on to her first husband's family. However, during the interim period before this latter transfer her own family was in possession of two sets of *bohali*. This was held to be contrary to Sesotho law since it gave the appearance that she was simultaneously married into two different families. Her parents should have refunded the *bohali* in respect of her first marriage and only accepted *bohali* in respect of her second marriage *after* this had been done.

On appeal to the Judicial Commissioner's Court, Duncan J.C. took a different view. He posed the question in the following way.

---

[1] *Khakhau* v. *Letsina*, Quthing D.C. 12/1941 (P.C.'s Ct.); '*Mamosala* v. *Mosala*, Mafeteng D.C. 27/1941 (P.C.'s Ct.).

[2] (1926–53) H.C.T.L.R. at 67.

[3] (1926–53) H.C.T.L.R. 309.

He took it for granted that it was necessary for a widow to be divorced from her deceased husband's family and asked whether it was possible for a divorce to take place without the restoration of *bohali*. He considered that the statements to this effect were all concerned with divorces arranged between the respective families and did not cover judicial decrees of divorce. In the circumstances of the present case he held that Chief Jonathan Molapo had pronounced a decree of divorce.

From the moment that sentence was pronounced the marriage ended and a divorce was decreed. The physical possession of the cattle ceased to be of importance—they were a debt or a credit that could be settled at any time voluntarily or through the process of the court. The divorce was decreed before the cattle were sent by Mahooana to his new wife's family, and there could be nothing wrong in this.

Duncan J.C. went on to apply the presumption of marriage from the long period of cohabitation which had elapsed and the fact that they had acquired the reputation of being man and wife. Moreover, the plaintiff had been treated as their legitimate son for about forty-five years without anyone in the family raising any doubts.

The Judicial Commissioner was overruled in the High Court where Willan C.J. and his two assessors held that a widow could in no circumstances validly remarry without the prior return of the *bohali* paid in respect of the first marriage. They relied particularly on two interlocking passages from Whitfield's book, *South African Native Law*:

No other man can contract a valid union with her (i.e. a wife) by payment of *lobolo* while the first *lobolo* remains with her father or heir . . .

. . . a marriage is dissolved only by restoration of the cattle. . . . Death of the husband does not dissolve the marriage in Bantu law.[2]

In the subsequent cases of *Tlhakanelo* v. *Tlhakanelo*[3] and *Noosi* v. *Mohapi*[4] Driver J.C. followed the decision of the High Court in *Motsoene* v. *Harding*, and in *Noosi* v. *Mohapi* he found it necessary to overrule the Paramount Chief's Court which had recognized a

---

[1] At p. 64.   [2] At p. 85.
[3] J.C. 204/1954.   [4] J.C. 70/1957.

widow's divorce where the *bohali* cattle had been paid for the second marriage prior to being passed on to the first husband's family as restoration.

In the light of this diversity of judicial opinion what conclusions can be drawn?

The argument that the law absolutely forbids the remarriage of widows is only supported by the fact that a provision expressly permitting it has never been incorporated in the Laws of Lerotholi and by the tentative *obiter dictum* of Lansdown J. in the *Regency case*. Neither of these considerations can be regarded as conclusive especially in view of all the other decisions to the contrary.

The weight of judicial authority undoubtedly supports the proposition that a widow can only remarry after obtaining a divorce from her deceased husband's family and that this necessarily involves a restoration of the *bohali* and that this restoration must occur before the receipt of the *bohali* in respect of the second marriage.

However, this view is open to the following objections. Since an ordinary divorce during the husband's lifetime does not invariably require the restoration of *bohali*, is there any reason why the position should be different in the divorce of a widow? There is indeed the distinction that one of the circumstances where *bohali* is not reclaimable in ordinary divorces is when the husband has been at fault for the breakdown of the marriage. The analogy after his death would be where his family are responsible for the rift, e.g. where they have unjustifiably driven the widow away. In these circumstances and also where the late husband's family elect to keep the children of the marriage there seems no justification for insisting on the return of *bohali* as a *sine qua non*. It is not a prerequisite during the husband's lifetime[1] and the fallacy of equating Sesotho law on this matter with the position in South Africa is plain.

If the suggested approach is the correct one two possibilities arise. Either the divorce is achieved by inter-family agreement in which case such an agreement will have to be proved and this will naturally be more difficult in the absence of a physical return of the *bohali*. Alternatively, and presumably much more unlikely, a judicial decree will have been granted in which case it would seem in view of section 34(5) of Part II of the Laws of Lerotholi that

[1] Pp. 202–4 above.

no argument about the necessity for a return of *bohali* could possibly arise. The section, as already noted, now confers a discretion on the court to decide this question as seems just.

The second problem relates to a situation where the *bohali* is to be returned either because the widow has been responsible for the break with her in-laws[1] or because she has borne no children or because she is taking her children away with her. Here two further questions arise. First, must the *bohali* for the first marriage be restored before the *bohali* for the second marriage is received? Secondly, can the two transfers be reduced to one by the simple expedient of the second husband's family paying *bohali direct* to the first husband's family, as was originally proposed in 1903 by the committee drafting the Laws of Lerotholi? My own impression, based partly on further examples supplied to me of the second possibility occurring in practice and partly on the views expressed to me privately by the members of the Judicial Commissioner's Court, is that the law is in the process of moving slowly towards recognition of a widow's remarriage with the payment of *bohali* going direct to her late husband's family. However, I would admit that this is probably not yet the state of the existing law.

The lengthy debate on this question at the Panel Discussion admirably reflected the bewildering variety of opinion on the issue.[2] As the discussion proceeded some of the participants changed their minds after hearing others express different views and as the problem and its possible solutions were rephrased.

The different standpoints may be summarized as follows.

The most uncompromising attitude, which was held by more members at the beginning than at the end (and perhaps only ultimately retained by the most conservative member, Motlamelle) was that no widow could ever validly remarry under Sesotho law. When she first married her husband, she was not merely marrying him but also his family and the marriage could therefore only come to an end on her death. Whereas during her husband's lifetime she might have been able to obtain a divorce by family consent, this became impossible after his death because he was not there to agree to it. A man wishing to marry such a widow

---

[1] The 'Restatement' (at p. 21) says that a widow who becomes wayward or of loose morals or whose disrespect of her in-laws is intolerable may be divorced and the *bohali* reclaimed. However cf. P.D., p. 197 where this was denied.

[2] P.D., pp. 19–25, 240–4.

could neither make arrangements with her deceased husband's family, nor with her own parents. She was therefore only in a position to have lovers, not another husband.

The disadvantages of this situation were then pointed out by other members. These lovers begot children whom they often failed to maintain. They could not be sued for compensation for adultery or seduction and they might easily squander the assets of the widow's house. Furthermore, there was likely to be trouble over the recognition of the offspring of such unions, especially within the chieftainship. The example of Chief Mathealira, the younger brother of the present King was cited. His mother, the wife of Paramount Chief Seeiso was still a young woman when she was widowed and she conceived Mathealira after Seeiso's death.

Two alternative solutions to the problem were examined. First, was it possible for the widow's parents to return the *bohali* and thus free her from her deceased husband's family? Initially this procedure was rejected by nearly all the panel members, but when the matter was re-examined at the end of the conference Matete (who had not been present during the earlier discussion) and Molapo seemed to gain some acceptance for the idea.[1] The widow could return home to her parents and explain to them that she wished to remarry. If they agreed to this they could return the *bohali* paid for her and receive new *bohali* from her second husband's family.

Molapo stated that if a widow was in love with a man whom she wished to marry and all efforts to restrain her had proved futile he could bring *bohali* cattle to her parents' home and her parents would pass these on to the deceased husband's family. Such widows (or even wives whose husbands were alive) were known as deserters or absconders (*maphuma nkho*). However one feature of this scheme was unacceptable to Matete who maintained that part at least of the original *bohali* had to be refunded *before* the new *bohali* was received, otherwise the second marriage would be invalid. Even if the widow's parents were poor and needed to utilize the second *bohali* cattle in order to refund the original *bohali* this transaction should somehow be camouflaged to give the

---

[1] This procedure was followed in *Phoofolo* v. *Pongo* J.C. 89/1951 and none of the three courts which heard the case cast any doubts on its validity. The matter for decision here was not a remarriage but the amount of *bohali* to be returned on the divorce.

impression that the refund of part at least had occurred before the acceptance of new *bohali*.

The second possibility was for a marriage to be arranged directly between the deceased first husband's family and the family of the prospective second husband. This was supported by the example of the procedures of Chief Lipubuoa's marriage to a widow, but the validity of such a marriage was regarded as more dubious than the first possibility by most of the panel members.

Widows themselves generally believe that they are entitled to remarry under Sesotho law though they are not inclined to favour this course of action because they fear that they will have to surrender their rights over their children. Of thirty-six widows interviewed during my social survey in 1970–1 twenty-six regarded remarriage as permissible and only seven thought the law prohibited it. However, not a single one had actually remarried though some had taken lovers and as many as half of those who were under the age of thirty-nine at the time of their husbands' deaths had subsequently borne a child, and often more than one.

Perhaps it is fitting to end this chapter with a twist of colonial history. One of the first legislative acts of the Cape administration after the annexation of Lesotho in 1868 was to frame a regulation expressly permitting the remarriage of widows.[1] They clearly took the line that any custom to the contrary was offensive and had to be overridden. The British were more tolerant and subsequently repealed it. Today, if a Basotho Court were to hold that Sesotho law did prohibit remarriage it might well be successfully argued on appeal that any such rule was repugnant to justice and morality and thus unenforceable. The law may thus have come full circle.

---

[1] See section 8 of the marriage regulations promulgated under G.N. of 13 May 1870.

19

ALLOCATIONS OF PROPERTY AND WRITTEN INSTRUCTIONS

1. ALLOCATIONS

(a) *Introduction*

THE concept of allocation in Sesotho law is a complex one since it encompasses a number of different acts. In its most usual sense it refers to the allocations of property which a polygamist makes to his various houses during his lifetime for their support.[1] Land, huts, livestock, and household effects would commonly be distributed to individual wives for the maintenance of the members of their houses and the maxim '*malapa ha a jane*' operates to prevent one house taking property from another without the latter's consent. However, provided such consent is present it seems that it may even be possible for a daughter in one house to be allocated to another house.[2] This can be regarded as a form of adoption and on her marriage a part of her *bohali* would be received by the house to which she had been trasnferred.[3]

Secondly, allocations of property can be made by the family head not to a particular house but to individual members of his household, such as his wives, his children and his grandchildren.[4] Often this will be done by giving the stock of each donee a particular earmark though this is by no means a prerequisite.

---

[1] See p. 173 above.

[2] See *Mohale* v. *Mohale* J.C. 76/1963 (all courts).

[3] See P.D., pp. 185–7.

[4] See *Malefane* v. *Malefane* J.C. 13/1957 (youngest son); *Mohafa* v. *Mohafa* J.C. 218/1964 (younger son); *Motleleng* v. *Motleleng* J.C. 78/1967 (younger son); *Semoli* v. *Semoli* J.C. 159/1967 (eldest son); *Malatela* v. *Sefale* J.C. 42/1961 (daughter); *Maile* v. *Shea* J.C. 33/1965 (daughter); *Mohale* v. *Mohale* J.C. 76/1963 (granddaughter); *Bereng Griffith* v. *'Mantsebo Seeiso Griffith* (No. 2) H.C. 9/1946 (grandson). Duncan (at p. 18) doubts whether allocations within a single house are permitted, but cites no authority in support of this proposition. The cases show that valid allocations can be made by both monogamists and polygamists.

Under modern conditions the allocations could equally take the form of money deposited in an account in the name of the donee or an insurance policy with the donee as the named beneficiary. A man's purpose here is to make suitable provision for his widows and to give his children or remoter issue a start in life.

It is sometimes suggested that allocations cannot be made to daughters,[1] but this contention would appear to be untenable, particularly in the light of the unanimous recognition of the validity of such an act by all the Basotho Courts in *Malatela* v. *Sefale*.[2] The statement of the Judicial Commissioner to the contrary in that case must be taken to be erroneous and should not be followed; it is, in any event, inconsistent with a later decision of the same Court in *Maile* v. *Shea*.[3]

A variation of the second form of allocation occurs where the family head decides to make an allocation of property which is only to take effect after his death. In such cases the property remains with the family head and is not distributed to the named donee until he dies. This concept is close to that of a testamentary disposition and it was as a result of this similarity that testamentary instruments in the form of 'written instructions' came to be recognized by Sesotho law.[4]

It will be appreciated that the function served by the allocation of property in each of these ways is to provide for the various dependent members of the family. In the process tension may be created between the prospective heir and the other members of the family because the heir will naturally be concerned to ensure that the estate which passes to him will be large enough to cover the deceased's debts. Otherwise, under the principle of onerous succession, he will need to have resort to his own assets.[5] On the other hand, since the heir inherits all the deceased's unallocated property and may not satisfactorily fulfil his responsibility to support other members of the family, it is most desirable from their point of view that sufficient property is allocated to them by the family head during his own lifetime. The rules that govern the validity of allocations reflect the attempt to achieve a harmonious balance between these two opposing interests.

---

[1] See e.g. the doubts expressed in P.D., p. 148.

[2] J.C. 42/1961.

[3] J.C. 33/1965 (J.C.).

[4] See section 14(1) of Part I of the Laws of Lerotholi discussed below, pp. 315–18.

[5] See pp. 254–5 above.

In the ensuing discussion it is important not to lose sight of the practical realities of the situation. In only a small proportion of cases do families have a large amount of wealth available for allocation whether in cash or in livestock. We have already seen that the wages that most people earn are hardly adequate for their subsistence and as many as a third of all households possess no stock whatever.[1] Most of the remainder will only have a few cattle, sheep or goats. The most valuable assets will usually be the physical structures comprising the matrimonial home together with its garden, and on death these will only rarely pass by allocation to someone other than the heir, for reasons which will soon become apparent. Arable lands, on the other hand, are virtually excluded from the picture altogether. Their allocation, it will be recalled, is the domain of the chieftainship and the only allocation within the family (if it can be called such) is the informal one whereby a man allots each of his wives a part of his lands.

(b) *Conditions of Validity*

(i) *Publicity*

Despite two High Court decisions to the contrary, there is an overwhelming mass of authority, both judicial and in the works of commentators, to the effect that an allocation must take place with full family publicity and that the prospective heir must be present himself at the time or be notified afterwards.[2] This probably does not mean that he can prevent his father from making an allocation, but merely that he should be kept in the picture through the normal processes of information and consultation.[3] Publication of the allocation to members of the family

---

[1] See Morojele, *1960 Agricultural Census, Part 2*, pp. 29–30, 38.

[2] *Sekhonyana* v. *Bereng* H.C. 30/1943 (P.C.'s Ct., S.C., and H.C.); *Bereng Griffith* v. *'Mantsebo Seeiso Griffith* (No. 2) H.C. 9/1946 (J.C.; *contra* H.C.); *Tefo* v. *Tefo* H.C. A/1/1953 (L.C., J.C., *contra* C.C., H.C.); *Malefane* v. *Malefane* J.C. 13/1957 (J.C.); *Taole* v. *Taole* J.C. 265/1963 (J.C.); *Mohafa* v. *Mohafa* J.C. 218/1964 (J.C.); *Chokobane* v. *Chokobane* J.C. 69/1966 (J.C.); *Bolepo* v. *Bolepo* J.C. 296/1966 (J.C.); *Motleleng* v. *Motleleng* J.C. 78/1967 (all courts); Duncan pp. 16–17 (relying on three decisions of the P.C.'s Ct.— *Qhamaku* v. *Qhamaku* J.C. 169/1947, *Molapo* v. *Peete* J.C. 196/1947 and *Borotho* v. *Borotho* J.C. 360/1948); Hamnett (1975), p. 59; P.D., pp. 182–5.

[3] Statement of the Paramount Chief's representative, *1957 National Council Proceedings*, pp. 112–13; Duncan, p. 17; P.D., pp. 226–7. However, in *Peleha* v. *Peleha* J.C. 251/1947 the Paramount Chief's Court upheld the heir's claim that his father was not entitled to allocate livestock to the sons of a junior wife before he had made an allocation to those in the senior house. The decision

is designed to provide the necessary evidence in the event of a dispute at a later date. For this purpose it is also desirable that the local chief be notified though this is not essential.[1]

The leading case on the subject, *Bereng Griffith v. 'Mantsebo Seeiso Griffith* (No. 2),[2] concerned an allocation made within the royal household. Paramount Chief Griffith had made an *inter vivos* allocation of 100 cattle and 200 sheep to his grandson Julius Bereng, but the livestock had not been handed over to the child by the time Griffith died. Subsequently the Regent 'Mantsebo refused to deliver the stock to Julius, who was still a minor, and as a result they were claimed by his father on his behalf. The Paramount Chief's Court upheld the claim but was reversed on appeal by the Judicial Commissioner. Driver J.C. heard a mass of conflicting evidence about what constituted a valid allocation and ultimately formulated the following five conditions which were based largely on the advice of his assessor Thabo Lechesa:

(1) The intention of the donor to make the gift must be firm.

(2) The property comprised in the gift must belong to the donor and be certain.

(3) There must be publicity particularly within the donor's family.

(4) The heir of the donor should be present in person, if possible; if he cannot be present or if he is a minor then one or more of the responsible members of his house or his paternal uncles must be present so that they can raise an objection if the gift is unreasonable and to the prejudice of the heir.[3] The heir must, in any event, be notified of the gift.

(5) The donee should be present in person if possible; if he is absent or if he is a minor a responsible member of his family must be present to accept the gift and thus be in a position to identify it.

The Judicial Commissioner further decided that there was no

---

was confirmed on appeal by Driver J.C. but on other grounds—see below. See also *Borotho* v. *Borotho* J.C. 360/1948 where Driver J.C. decided that the heir's consent had not been vitiated by duress, thus giving the impression that consent was indeed necessary.

[1] *Bolepo* v. *Bolepo* J.C. 296/1966 (J.C.); *contra* Hamnett (1975), p. 59.

[2] H.C. 9/1946.

[3] See also P.D., pp. 182–5.

necessity for stock which was being allocated to be specially branded or earmarked[1] nor did it have to be pointed out to the herdboy. He found that on the facts of the case the donor's heir, Chief Seeiso, had neither been present at the making of the allocation nor been represented there, nor was he later notified of it. Moreover, the requirement of general family publicity had not been satisfied. In the upshot he held the allocation was invalid.

This finding was overruled in the High Court by de Beer J. who held that on the evidence the third and fourth requirements specified by Driver J.C. had not been established to form part of the law.[2] Regrettably he adopted the common law test for the proof of a valid custom and struck down the rules enumerated by Driver J.C. for lack of certainty. This error in his approach clearly deprives his judgment of some of its authority, more particularly since he recognized that it was consonant with Sesotho legal principle for the ultimate heir to have a voice in the disposal of the family assets during the lifetime of his father.

However, he was also influenced by a far more significant factor, namely the omission from the relevant section of the Laws of Lerotholi of any reference to the third and fourth requirements specified by Driver J.C. On the other hand, the section does safeguard the heir's position in a different way by limiting the extent of allocations made to persons other than the heir to one half of the estate. This provision which had only just been introduced into the Laws, earlier in 1946, will be examined in greater detail below and the question will be raised as to whether it ought not to be regarded as having superseded the other requirements, despite the continuing spate of pronouncements that these are still necessary. However, it should be clearly recognized that if there is a requirement that the heir must be notified of any allocation for it to be valid and if the courts continue to accept his evidence that he was not so informed as readily as they have done hitherto, this will have a tendency to reduce the rights of other donees virtually to vanishing point.

(ii) *Positive act or intention*

In *Masobeng* v. *Masobeng*,[3] which was a dispute between two houses of a polygamist, the Judicial Commissioner declared that

---

[1] See also Ramolefe (1966), p. 20.
[2] This decision was followed by Willan C.J. in *Tefo* v. *Tefo* H.C. A/1/53.
[3] J.C. 36/1965.

the fact that the livestock in question had been acquired by the deceased while he was living with his second wife (following the desertion of his first wife) did not by itself prove that they had been allocated to the second house. From this it would seem that there must be some positive act or intention to constitute a valid allocation.

By contrast, in the similar case of *Tsosane* v. *Tsosane*[1] there was strong circumstantial evidence of allocation. The deceased had been a polygamist with two houses. The disputed property consisted of a mill, bought jointly by the deceased and his second wife under a hire-purchase agreement, and a post-office savings-bank balance representing the profits of the milling business which they had run together. These facts, coupled with the expressed intention of the deceased and his second wife to marry in community of property (although this turned out to be impossible),[2] were sufficient to satisfy both Thompson J.C. and the High Court that the overwhelming probability was that these assets had been allocated to the second house. Curiously, the validity of the allocation was not challenged on the ground of lack of publicity, although the argument was made that it was void for being in excess of half the estate. This latter contention could not, however, be substantiated on the facts.

A further situation in which the courts might sometimes be willing to draw the conclusion that an allocation has been made is where the family head purchases livestock out of the earnings of one of his younger sons.[3] Here again, however, there would have to be evidence indicating that such stock were to belong to the son in question rather than forming part of the general household property.

(c) *Revocation*

The leading case on the revocation of an allocation is *Semoli* v. *Semoli*.[4] The plaintiff, who was a bedridden cripple, sued the

---

[1] H.C. Civ./A/6/1968. The first marriage was by Sesotho custom and the second by civil rites in South Africa. All the courts dealt with the case on the footing that Sesotho law was the applicable law and that both marriages could be recognized as valid side by side. This would not have been possible if South African law had been applicable.

[2] South African law would not permit this since the husband's first wife was still alive.

[3] See *Malefane* v. *Malefane* J.C. 13/1957 (J.C.).

[4] J.C. 159/1967.

defendant, his eldest son, for the return of 130 head of cattle which he had allocated him some years previously. His ground for taking this step was that the defendant had neglected him in his illness and old age. A family council had already agreed that the defendant should be compelled to return the stock. Even during the family meeting the defendant was unrepentant over his behaviour and stated that someone else should look after the plaintiff because he himself was too busy herding his stock. The family had decided to appoint the plaintiff's third son as the guardian of the house in question and as the prospective heir in place of the defendant.

When the defendant failed to carry out the order of the family council the claim was brought to court and the defendant contended that the cattle could not be recovered from him because the allocation amounted to an outright and irrevocable gift. The Local Court accepted this argument but its decision was reversed by the Maja Central Court where President T. J. Molapo applied, by analogy, the principles governing disinheritance. Provided there was a just cause for the action taken and that the matter was given full family publicity (including notification to the heir himself), a family head could disinherit his prospective heir and revoke any allocation already made. This was endorsed by the Judicial Commissioner's Court on appeal.

It is also clear that a prospective heir cannot compel his father to make an *inter vivos* allocation in his favour.[1]

2. WRITTEN INSTRUCTIONS

Testamentary dispositions in the form of written instructions have been recognized by Sesotho law since 1903, but the superimposition of this novel concept on top of the process of allocation has not proved a smooth and easy task. The matter is best approached in historical perspective so that the development of the law towards its present stance can be fully appreciated.

(a) *Historical Development*

It is beyond doubt that the traditional law did not recognize anything remotely similar to the written will of Roman–Dutch or English common law. Such testamentary instruments differ in at least three fundamental respects from the allocations which were commonplace. First, a will is almost always made in writing.

[1] See *Khomoaleburu* v. *Matala* J.C. 214/1949 (J.C.) cited in Duncan, p. 14.

Secondly, its contents are often kept secret, whereas the essence of allocations was that they were made publicly. Thirdly, bequests in a will may be made to non-relatives. Moreover, before the time of Moshoeshoe I the usual practice was for a man to make the allocations he desired during his lifetime rather than to attempt to control his property from the grave. Moshoeshoe I himself, however, seems to have allocated property both by way of *inter vivos* gifts and by leaving oral instructions as to the disposition of his estate after his death. This emerges from the following passage taken from the evidence given by his successor, Letsie I, to the 1872 Commission. Major Bell asked him: 'According to Basuto law and custom, can a man dispose of his property before his death, by making a verbal will?' He replied:

'Such a practice is very rare. I have only heard of one instance in which it has been done, and that was in the case of the Chief Moshesh, shortly before his death.'

The Chairman then took up the questioning:

'Since Moshesh has established a precedent, will the laws and customs of the Basutos recognize a will, by which a man disposes of his property?'
'Yes, if he disposes of his property justly, but not if he disinherits his legal heirs.'
'Don't you think it would be a good thing if there was a regulation providing that persons may make a written will disposing of their property and providing for the guardianship of their children as they may think fit?'
'Yes, I think it will be a good thing, as no one will be compelled to make a will; those that like can do so, but those that don't like can leave it alone.'[1]

It is clear that Moshoeshoe I did not set a precedent for the making of wills as that word is generally understood in terms of the common law; he gave oral and public instructions as to what allocations to his relatives he wished to be made after his death.[2] However, when the original version of the Laws of Lerotholi was

---

[1] *1873 Report and Evidence*, p. 48.
[2] See the statements of Counsellor Goliath Malebanye in *1950 National Council Proceedings*, p. 107 and *1957 National Council Proceedings*, pp. 111–12; *1931 National Council Proceedings*, pp. 55–63; P.D., pp. 222–3. Duncan's statement at p. 18 is rather misleading.

formulated in 1903 it contained in section 15 a provision dealing with both oral and written dispositions as follows:

. . . if a man during his lifetime has disposed of his property by will or gift, his intentions must be carried out.

This declaration took the curious form of a proviso tacked on at the end of a section which otherwise dealt with the position of a man dying without male issue and leaving only a widow and daughters. Whether it was the intention of the drafters that the proviso was only to apply if there was no male heir can only be guessed at, but the debates at the National Council in 1917–19 show that some members certainly took the view that it did only have this very narrow scope.[1]

Since the exact connotation of the word 'will' was unclear to many Basotho the new edition of the Laws in 1922 added an explanatory sentence at the end of section 15 as follows:

Will or gift[2] is a document made by a person during his lifetime stating what he desires done with his property after his death, if the estate thus willed be his *bona fide* property, and if that is in accordance with the laws and customs of the Basuto.

It thus emerged that what the Laws really had in mind was not a will in common law terms but a written document complying with Sesotho law. The difficulty here, however, was to know exactly what was meant by the need to act 'in accordance with the laws and customs of the Basotho'. On the one hand, it might mean that no disposition could be made at all if there was a male heir since he was basically entitled to the whole inheritable estate; this would clearly be the case if the section was in any event restricted to those situations where there were only female children, as some members of the National Council believed. A second possibility was that no disposition could be made which ran counter to the general rules of Sesotho intestate inheritance; thus if the deceased died without male issue but leaving brothers and daughters the former would inherit despite the deceased's desire to bequeath the estate to the latter. Thirdly, the Law could

[1] See *1917–18 National Council Proceedings* (document 16); *1919 National Council Proceedings* (document 23).
[2] In *Bereng Griffith* v. *'Mantsebo Seeiso Griffith* (No. 2) H.C. 9/1946 de Beer J. considered that the word 'gift' was meant to cover only *donationes mortis causa*. This is clearly erroneous.

perhaps be stretched to mean that the heir would have to give his consent before any disposition could be made and thus he would be entitled to exercise a power of veto over his father's wishes; however, as we have already seen, the real obligation is probably that the heir must merely be consulted or notified and this was indeed the finding of the courts in the case of *Sekhonyana* v. *Bereng*.[1]

In the result there were those in the National Council who proposed in 1943 the deletion of the words '. . . and if that is in accordance with the laws and customs of the Basuto' on the ground that this phrase was diametrically opposed to any degree of freedom of testation which they regarded as inherent in the idea of a will and which they eagerly sought for themselves so as to provide for their widows, their junior sons, and their daughters. Despite strong opposition from those who argued that if the senior house of a polygamist was not given special legal protection husbands would give all their property to junior wives or concubines, the motion to delete the offending words was carried.[2]

However, for some reason this proposal was never implemented. When the new version of the Laws appeared three years later in 1946 it contained instead an interesting compromise. The new section (renumbered section 14) ran as follows:[3]

If a man during his lifetime allots his property amongst his various houses but does not distribute such property, or if he dies leaving written instructions regarding the allotment on his death, his wishes must be carried out provided the heir according to Basuto custom has not been deprived of the greater part (*karolo e kholo*) of his father's estate.

(b) *Present Restrictions or Conditions of Substantive Validity*

This section has remained in force unamended up to the present time and it possesses three striking features. First, it only refers to allocations between various houses though this surely cannot operate to take away the general right to make allocations to individuals or to deprive a monogamist of such a right altogether. Secondly, oral dispositions intended to take effect after death are made subject to the same conditions as those made in writing.

---

[1] H.C. 30/1943 (all courts).
[2] See *1943 National Council Proceedings*, pp. 89–92.
[3] Section 14 of Part I (1946); currently section 14(1).

However, *inter vivos* allocations where the distribution of the property occurs before death are not expressly covered though the section has been held by the courts to apply to them.[1] The word 'will' with its alien connotations is belatedly replaced by the more appropriate expression 'written instructions'.[2] Thirdly, freedom of allocation is restricted to one half of the estate. The operation of this limitation must now be examined in greater detail.

Some indication of the novelty of the idea is apparent from the attitudes of the Basotho Courts in the leading case on written instructions, *Mokorosi* v. *Mokorosi*.[3] The deceased's estate was a comparatively large one comprising *inter alia* a butcher's business, various houses, a motor truck and some livestock. He had executed a will in common law form in which he had bequeathed the bulk of his property to his second and third sons. His first son had predeceased him leaving a widow, the plaintiff, and the deceased had only left her a legacy of £100.

The plaintiff initiated proceedings in the Basotho Courts[4] in which she claimed to inherit the entire estate on the basis that her late husband was the heir and therefore his vested right passed to her from the time of his death. Her claim was perfectly correct in terms of an intestacy[5] and was upheld by all three of the lower courts. None of them was prepared to recognize the will as valid since it purported to raise the younger brothers above the eldest, which was contrary to Sesotho custom. However, when the case

[1] See e.g. *Peleha* v. *Peleha* J.C. 251/1947 (J.C.) discussed below, pp. 320–1.

[2] The distinction between the two concepts is important in interpreting the Cape Law of Inheritance Act (No. 26 of 1873) which was introduced into Basutoland in 1884 and is still in force. It grants to those competent to make a will complete freedom of testation, including the power to disinherit any relative. If the Sesotho concept of written instructions were to be treated as a will then the proviso to section 14(1) of the Laws of Lerotholi would be inconsistent with the provisions of a statute and could not be applied in the Basotho Courts in terms of section 9 of the Central and Local Courts Proclamation (see Ch. 3 above). The Cape Act was obviously not designed with this objective in view, but rather to abolish the legitimate portion recognized by the Roman–Dutch common law, and therefore section 14(1) is unaffected by it—see *Hoohlo* v. *Hoohlo* Civ./A/4/1969 (C.A.) per Roper P. and Maisels J.A.

[3] (1954) H.C.T.L.R. 24.

[4] Since these courts only have jurisdiction to apply Sesotho law they did not consider whether the proper law might have been the common law. When subsequently an action was commenced in the High Court between different parties to determine which law was applicable it was held that this was the Administration of Estates Proclamation (discussed below, pp. 323–4) and *not* the customary law after all—see *Mokorosi* v. *Mokorosi* H.C. Civ./T/4/1955.

[5] See p. 231 above.

came before the Judicial Commissioner's Court both parties accepted that the will must be recognized as a legal document, but Driver J.C. held that in terms of section 14 it could only be effective up to half the value of the estate. Thus the plaintiff was entitled to receive one half and the other beneficiaries under the will the other half. This decision was upheld on appeal to the High Court.

One of the interesting points about the case is that the validity of the will was accepted in terms of Sesotho law despite the fact that the heir had neither been present at its execution nor subsequently notified of it. It may therefore be that the intention in the reformulation of the present section 14 was to replace the requirements of general publicity and informing the heir by the new one that the heir must not be deprived of the greater part of the estate. Since they both serve the same general purpose of protecting the heir's interest one can see that to have both safeguards might be regarded as superfluous. As already mentioned this was the view taken earlier by de Beer J. in *Bereng Griffith* v. *'Mantsebo Seeiso Griffith* (No. 2).[1]

A problem in relation to section 14(1) which has already been referred to in passing is that it does not expressly cover one common type of allocation, namely the situation where property is both allocated and distributed during the donor's lifetime. Instead the wording of the subsection is clearly directed at the devolution of the property comprised in the estate on the donor's death. In any event it would obviously be impossible to assess in advance of the donor's death the value of the estate he will leave in order to decide whether any particular allocation would deprive the heir of more than half of it.

Despite these formidable obstacles, immediately after the new subsection was introduced Driver J.C. held that in such cases an assessment could be made at the time of the allocation.[2] In *Peleha* v. *Peleha*[3] he granted the prospective heir an interdict to prevent his father disposing of more than half his current assets by means of an *inter vivos* gift in favour of a junior son. This approach would seem to place undue fetters on a father's freedom to

---

[1] H.C. 9/1946. See also P.D., p. 229.
[2] *Peleha* v. *Peleha* J.C. 251/1947. There is also an *obiter dictum* to the same effect by Driver J.C. in *Borotho* v. *Borotho* J.C. 360/1948.
[3] J.C. 251/1947.

administer household property for the benefit of the family as a whole (not to mention his personal property) and since it is not authorized by the subsection it is submitted that the decision should not be followed. Instead, the general rule would seem to be applicable that the allocation must take place with full family publicity and that the heir must be present himself or be notified afterwards. On this basis the heir would seem only to have the right to be kept in the picture through a process of consultation and information and not possess a power of veto over his father's actions.

In *Hoohlo* v. *Hoohlo*[1] the question was raised in the High Court whether, in calculating if the heir had been deprived of the greater part, the estate should be deemed to encompass not only the assets left by the deceased on his death but also property he had allocated during his lifetime. If this were so, the heir would have to account for what he had already received and all other allocations would have to be brought into the over-all assessment. The difficulties inherent in such a process coupled with the undesirability of allowing completed transactions to be upset, militate strongly against such a method of calculation and it is thought that Evans J. was right to reject it. The proviso in favour of the heir is clearly designed to operate on the assets existing at the date of his father's death and, as explained earlier, different rules regulate the making of *inter vivos* allocations. For the purposes of the subsection the estate consists of all the deceased's personal property together with any household property not already allocated and distributed to individuals and houses.[2] This latter property is protected by the '*malapa ha a jane*' principle.

(c) *Conditions of Formal Validity*

Since the whole concept of 'written instructions' falls somewhere between the traditional Sesotho process of allocations and the common law will, the problem arises as to whether the law should require formalities appropriate to the former or to the latter or some mixture of the two.

We have already seen that allocations are still generally thought to require family publicity and the notification of the heir, although these essential safeguards for the heir may now have been replaced,

---

[1] H.C. Civ. App'n/38/1968 (H.C.).
[2] *Bolepo* v. *Bolepo* J.C. 296/1966 (J.C.).

at any rate in relation to dispositions taking effect on death, by the restriction preventing any disposal of more than half the estate. *Mokorosi's case*,[1] for instance, recognized the latter requirement, not the former.

Wills, on the other hand, must be signed at the end by the testator (or on his behalf and in his presence by someone authorized to do so) in the presence of two or more competent witnesses present at the same time, and these witnesses must have attested and subscribed the will in the presence of the testator.[2] There would hardly seem to be much justification in demanding compliance with these stringent formalities, but the authenticity of a document purporting to be 'written instructions' would surely need to be established by suitable evidence. This could presumably be shown not only by the signatures of witnesses attesting the instructions themselves but also by persons who saw the deceased write the instructions or sign them, whether they were family members, strangers, or the local chief or headman.[3] However, it is clear that there is no requirement that the chief should countersign the written instructions themselves.[4]

(d) *Proposals for Reform*

Since 1946 a number of proposals for reforming this branch of the law have been put forward.

In 1950 the Progressive Association introduced a motion into the National Council designed to give all Basotho complete freedom of testation under customary law.[5] The Association argued that the existing law prevented people from making proper provision for their widows and married daughters and also denied them the right to make bequests to hospitals, schools, and churches which would benefit the community at large. It was further contended that if such a reform was accepted the heir's position could be safeguarded by ensuring that the bequests only took effect after the debts left by the deceased had been extinguished.[6] The motion was heavily defeated.

---

[1] (1954) H.C.T.L.R. 24 (J.C. and H.C.).

[2] Wills (Execution) Ordinance, 1845, s. 3.

[3] See P.D., pp. 225–8.

[4] *Mokorosi* v. *Mokorosi* (1954) H.C.T.L.R. 24 (J.C. and H.C.).

[5] See *1950 National Council Proceedings*, pp. 95–109.

[6] However, this failed to take account of future debts such as *bohali*, which would also need to be dealt with in any reform.

The next approach to the National Council came in 1953 but along different lines.[1] Recognizing that there was little chance of altering section 14 of the Laws of Lerotholi, the protagonists turned their attention to wills under the common law. The idea was that wealthy people and traders should be free to make wills as they pleased and that if they failed to do so their intestate estates should be administered in the same way as those of the white population. The Legal Secretary, Mr. O'Leary, explained to the Council that only a very limited class of Basotho were permitted to bequeath property by will, namely those persons whom the Master of the High Court was satisfied had 'abandoned tribal custom and adopted a European mode of life', and who if married had married by civil rites.[2] In making this assertion the Legal Secretary was relying on the wording of the proviso in section 3(b) of the Administration of Estates Proclamation, but his interpretation was probably incorrect since this enactment only deals with the machinery for winding up estates and does not regulate the capacity of persons to make wills nor the actual devolution of estate property.[3] At common law any person of sufficient age and understanding may make a will and the Law of Inheritance Act[4] grants total freedom of testation to all those competent to make a will. Thus it would *seem* that there was no need for any change in the law of testate succession since Basotho already possessed all the powers they sought.[5] Oblivious of this the President of the Council instructed the Legal Secretary to prepare a draft amendment to the law. It subsequently emerged along the following lines. Where a man entered into a civil marriage at a time when he was not a party to an existing customary marriage with another woman he would be entitled to make a will in respect of all his property and would possess complete freedom of testation. However, if he failed to make a will his intestate estate would be

[1] See *1953 National Council Proceedings*, pp. 352–68; *1957 National Council Proceedings*, pp. 101–17.
[2] Administration of Estates Proclamation, No. 19 of 1935, s. 3(b).
[3] See *Fraenkel* v. *Sechele* (1963–6) H.C.T.L.R. 70. This was an appeal in 1964 from the Bechuanaland Protectorate (as it then was) to the joint Court of Appeal which was shared, prior to independence, by the three High Commission Territories. The statutory wording which the Court had to construe was very similar to the Lesotho provision.
[4] Act No. 26 of 1873, Part II, s. 5.
[5] The position certainly cannot be regarded as crystal clear. The Legal Secretary may have been closer to the mark so far as intestacy was concerned.

governed by the rules of customary law.[1] If the husband was already married under Sesotho law to a woman other than the woman he proposed to marry by civil rites, protection would be given to the first wife and her children by placing property allocated to her house beyond the provisions of any subsequent will.

This draft amendment was debated in the Council in 1957 after being referred to the districts for their comments and a Select Committee was appointed to look into the question. When the Committee reported in 1962 they recommended the repeal of section 3(b) of the Administration of Estates Proclamation on the ground that it discriminated against the Basotho. However, they also recommended that a person should only be allowed to make a will in respect of half his estate. The other half should remain for the benefit of his household.[2] No specific steps were taken to implement these proposals and the matter was eventually dropped.

Apart from the fact that the whole inquiry seems in retrospect to have been misguided in view of the widespread misapprehension as to the state of the existing law, it can surely be argued that to seek to encourage increased use of the common law will on the ground of defects in the customary law was a far less satisfactory solution than remedying those defects themselves. Thus if greater freedom of testation was required in order to prevent the heir from being given the character of 'an all-devouring monster'[3] and to improve the position of the widow and other relatives as well as allowing bequests to charitable institutions, this should properly have been done by changing the customary law itself. In this way, everyone would have had the advantage of the reform, whereas the Legal Secretary's proposals would have restricted the benefits to Basotho who married by civil rites and who could afford the expense and trouble of going to consult an attorney with a view to making a formal will. However, it is at least clear that the time has come to dispense with section 3(b) of the Administration of Estates Proclamation with its vague and paternalistic phrasing.[4]

---

[1] Ironically, this had been the position in terms of ss. 11 and 12 of the marriage regulations promulgated under Proc. 41 of 1877 during part of the period during which Basutoland was annexed to the Cape Colony.

[2] *Report of Select Committee on Wills, Estates and Marriages* (Maseru, 1962), pp. ii, iii.

[3] This expression is used by Ramolefe (1969), p. 207.

[4] See Ramolefe, ibid.

PART III
CONCLUSION

20

SOME THOUGHTS ON THE FUTURE

IN the early nineteenth century, when Moshoeshoe I was in the process of knitting together the various groups who were to be the fathers of the present Basotho Nation, great importance was attached to the unity and integrity of the extended family. Life was generally hard with constant battles against a variety of enemies, both African and European, as well as the need to contend with drought and starvation. It was imperative in such times that the head of the family should be given unswerving loyalty and obedience by all its other members, and individual wishes inevitably had to be sacrificed to the welfare of the extended family as a whole. This fundamental principle of patriarchal authority was mirrored in a wider social context by the authority of the various echelons of the chieftainship and ultimately in the status of the Paramount Chief himself.

The legal framework of this period can be likened to a spider's web. Regular and beautifully simple in design it provided a means of spreading power and authority over groups of people in a series of ever-widening circles. A father had rights over his nuclear family, the head of the lineage over the extended family, headmen and chiefs over their respective populations, and the Paramount Chief over all. At the same time the system was sophisticated in that all members of society were tied together through an intricate mesh of relationships involving mutual rights and responsibilities. These covered such matters as allegiance, rights to land, the right of chiefs to place their sons, the right of commoners to speak at *pitsos*, the right of a father to all property acquired by members of his family and a corresponding liability to compensate for all their wrongs, the payment and receipt of *bohali*, the supervisory role of uncles and so on. In this manner a delicate mechanism of checks and balances was created to contain what would otherwise have been conflicting interests, and a very considerable degree of harmony was achieved.

This carefully constructed web soon found itself in the path of a wind of change so strong that parts of the network were bound to give way in the storm. These pressures came from the alien culture of the Europeans whose pervasive influences on many levels of Basotho life arrived virtually simultaneously. No better description survives of the impact which this advent so quickly wrought upon the Basotho people than that of a man whose cause was in the vanguard of external influence. He was the Revd. L. Duvoisin of the Paris Evangelical Missionary Society, who wrote in 1885:

Whatever reproach one may level against the ancient social system of the [Basotho] it was nevertheless an order of real value. It was the product of that instinct of preservation which is found among nations and individuals alike and which prompts them to adopt, quite naturally, the customs, the laws, the institutions most conformable with their genius, and therefore best calculated to perpetuate the national life, and to shelter it against the injurious influences to which it may be exposed. By the importance which it gave to all the family kin, by the meticulous care with which it regulated the mutual relationship, as well as the rights and duties of every member of the community, this patriarchal organisation was a mighty rampart against every kind of irruption. . . .

Under the dissolving influence of civilization and Christianity—for the latter has also had its share in this process of demolition—these ancient barriers of the patriarchal institutions were shaken; the antique severity of the customs has softened; the bonds of discipline have slackened; youth in particular has emancipated itself; it has become more or less frivolous, immoral, and whereas formerly, for example, it would have been an unheard-of thing to have it said of a young woman that she had become pregnant before marriage, the event is so common today that it is scarcely noticed.[1]

Duvoisin then proceeded to catalogue the vices and diseases which many Basotho had picked up while working in the diamond mines in South Africa. Contact with European ways had so far produced little of benefit.

Preceding chapters of this work have sought to monitor in detail the changes brought about in Sesotho family law during more than a century and a quarter of contact with extraneous forces

[1] Quoted in Germond, p. 540.

whether they have been economic, religious, educational, social, political, administrative, or judicial. But if any one general trend can be said to predominate among these changes it is surely the waning of the rights of the extended family over its individual members and more particularly the decline in the authority of the family head.[1]

Half a dozen illustrations will suffice to confirm the point. Polygyny has declined considerably so that now it is extremely rare to find a man with more than one wife, whether he be a chief or a commoner. In the past a man was positively encouraged to have many wives if he could afford them and it was an indication of his wealth and prestige that he was able to do so.

The role played by the families of the bride and bridegroom respectively in arranging, negotiating, and consenting to a marriage is much more limited today than it used to be. People now choose their own spouses and some men marry without the consent or even knowledge of their parents. Moreover, in certain instances a court can actually override the views of parents who refuse to give their consent to a marriage. The *seantlo* custom under which on a wife's death her father was obliged to provide another daughter as a substitute has almost completely died out.

The influence of the *lekhotla la lelapa* (informal family court) seems to have decreased partly through the ease of access to the official courts and partly through the weakening of kinship bonds brought about by the pattern of migrant labour. Divorce, for instance, is no longer a matter primarily for the parents of the spouses to arrange and seems to be becoming rather more frequent than before. This suggests a decline in the efficacy of traditional processes of encouraging a reconciliation.

Wives have carved out for themselves a greater freedom of action. They can bring proceedings in the courts against their husbands for maintenance and appear to have an equal right to the custody of their children during marriage. They can request dissolutions of their marriages without parental consent. They are entitled to enter into contracts of employment without their husbands' authority so as to benefit the family as a whole and can pledge their husbands' credit at local shops for necessaries without first obtaining permission to do so.

[1] In the political sphere there has been a similar development with the power and status of the chieftainship being gradually eroded.

Widows, too, have asserted themselves and gained considerable independence from the families of their deceased husbands. This is reflected in their right to reject a *kenelo* union, their capacity to be the guardians of their minor children, their power to administer (and in some circumstances actually inherit) estate property, their increased *locus standi* in the courts and above all in their right to remarry.

Nor have unmarried sons and daughters been prepared to remain under the total domination of their fathers. Apart from acquiring the freedom to choose their spouses, they have taken jobs and generally managed to control the use of their earnings and have, on occasion, even been granted rights to land.

On the other hand, despite these very considerable breaches made in the complex web of traditional family relationships the movement from a patriarchal extended family to a more individualistic nuclear family has by no means been fully accomplished. Indeed the changes in family law produced by contact with outside influences have probably been smaller than in any other branch of customary law. The question necessarily arises whether the legal position can satisfactorily be allowed to rest at what might be regarded as merely an intermediary stage or whether immediate reforms are called for.

In the remainder of this chapter I propose to consider some of the possible changes which might be introduced. There is no shortage of comparative African material on reforming customary family law,[1] but one is left with the impression that while many attempts have been made during the course of more than a century to remodel African law (usually on European lines), success in implementing them has understandably proved rather elusive. Thus the willingness of the majority of the Basotho of today to welcome such changes—or at any rate to comply with them at the behest of their political leaders—is obviously a vital factor in framing any new proposals for the future.

[1] See e.g. Anderson (Ed.), *Family Law in Asia and Africa* (London, 1968), Chs. 1 (Cotran), 2 (Morris), and 13 (Rubin); Salacuse, *An Introduction to Law in French Speaking Africa*, Vol. 1 (Michie, 1969); Schapera, *Tribal Innovators: Tswana Chiefs and Social Change* (London, 1970); Phillips and Morris, *Marriage Laws in Africa*; Roberts, 'The Settlement of Family Disputes in the Kgatla Customary Courts—Some New Approaches', [1971] *J.A.L.* 60; Read, 'A Milestone in the Integration of Personal Laws: The New Law of Marriage and Divorce in Tanzania', [1972] *J.A.L.* 19.

The first question is whether polygyny should be abolished on the ground that in modern conditions it possesses no economic or social benefits for the community at large and that it involves undesirable inequality between the sexes. The majority of Basotho would probably be prepared to accept an outright prohibition, but if this was thought to be too sweeping a reform because of the deep rooted tradition of polygyny in Basotho culture an attempt should surely be made to safeguard the usual victims of the practice, the senior wives. One method of achieving this would be to frame a new rule which made it necessary for a husband to obtain his first wife's full and free consent before taking subsequent wives.[1]

Secondly, should it still be an essential requirement for the validity of a marriage that the bride's parents have given their consent to the wedding, even where their daughter is over twenty-one? Already the corresponding requirement can be disregarded with impunity on the bridegroom's side of the family and the need for any parental consent at all can easily be evaded entirely by means of a civil marriage if both parties are over twenty-one. The present rule seeks to impose parental will upon individual choice in what must surely be seen as an increasingly personal matter and it merely serves to encourage elopement. On the other hand, it might well be desirable to fix a minimum age for customary marriages in the same way as this is done in civil marriages and make, for instance, the marriages of persons between sixteen and twenty-one subject to parental consent on both sides.

Thirdly, should the payment of *bohali* be forbidden on the ground that it is a relic of the inferior status of women and serves to strengthen the hold of a girl's father over both her and her prospective husband? Further criticisms might be levelled against the practice along the following lines:

(i) It tends to delay marriages unduly while either the prospective bridegroom or his father saves enough to make a sufficient payment. The normal age for a man to marry is presently between thirty and thirty-four and this probably means that numerous informal unions are established while the men are in their twenties.

---

[1] If, as is fairly common, the first marriage is a civil one then any subsequent 'marriage' by the husband would entitle the first wife to obtain a divorce at common law on grounds of adultery—see *Rakhoabe* v. *Rakhoabe* H.C. Civ./T/11/1968 (H.C.); *Nthunya* v. *Nthunya* H.C. Civ./T/34/1968 (H.C.).

Apart from this a couple bent on marriage will usually decide to elope. Elopement commonly leads to litigation in respect of the payment of compensation for abduction and often the legal status of the relationship between the elopers gives rise to uncertainty and difficulty.

(ii) The *bohali* custom may be exploited today by some fathers who take a purely commercial attitude towards the transaction and put a high 'price' round their daughters' necks. Partly this is a consequence of the payment frequently being made in cash and a father may be tempted to see his daughter's school fees as a profitable investment which he is entitled to exploit to the full at her wedding.

(iii) The conventional scale of *bohali* is twenty-three head of cattle which at the cash equivalent currently employed by the courts is R460 (roughly £260). In terms of market value the cost of actually purchasing twenty-three cows today would be nearer twice that figure. That such sums of money should be changing hands on marriage in a country of such dire poverty seems incredible and the fact that the majority of the male population have to put up with the appalling conditions and wages in South Africa to earn any money at all appears to make the whole process outrageous.

However, in practice the situation is far from being so shocking. The *bohali* is usually paid over a long period of time (and the debt is not always totally extinguished at that) and cattle received in respect of a daughter's marriage are used to pay for a son's marriage so that the circulation of cattle (and indeed money) is a constant process by no means exclusively dependent upon earning and saving. Moreover, this preservation of contact between the two families and their members may be seen as positively beneficial. Only a small payment is usual to start the marriage off and for the legal validity of a marriage with *bohali* only a few animals need actually be transferred at the time of the wedding. On the other hand, it does remain true to say that *one* of the economic pressures which induce people to leave Lesotho for spells of work in South Africa is the need to pay *bohali* and savings from wages earned there clearly *are* utilized for this purpose, when arguably they could be put to better use, for instance in purchasing necessary household articles and furniture for a new home.

(iv) *Bohali* is an endless source of dispute and litigation. The courts have to handle numerous cases every year involving a determination as to who is entitled to receive *bohali*, who is liable to pay it and how much is outstanding. The difficulties are generally made worse by the lack of any written evidence either as to the amount originally agreed upon or as to the amount already paid.

(v) The fact that *bohali* is prima facie payable in cattle and that for this purpose a scrawny beast is as good as a fat and healthy one means that the country is gravely overstocked and the quality of cattle depressingly low. *Bohali* is thus one of the factors militating against agricultural progress and improvement and it does constitute a hindrance to greater economic development and prosperity.

Against all these criticisms must be set the fact that *bohali* is a very central feature of Basotho culture which it would be very hard to dispense with abruptly, more particularly since it seems to be generally favoured by women who say they feel 'more married' if *bohali* has been paid for them. It might therefore be more appropriate to suggest measures of reform which, while attempting to do away with some of the harmful consequences of *bohali*, yet retained the essence of the transaction intact. One method would be to impose a limit on the amount of *bohali* which could be agreed upon and paid, somewhere well below the existing conventional scale (perhaps at ten head of cattle)[1] and to bar claims to recover *bohali* through the medium of the courts after a specified period had elasped since the marriage (perhaps five or ten years). Such reforms might successfully reduce elopement, combat commercialism, free family assets for more useful purposes, reduce the amount of litigation,[1] and help to improve the quality of livestock.

---

[1] This would link the amount of *bohali* to the *tlhabiso* ceremony referred to above, pp. 118–22.

[2] Litigation might also be reduced—or at any rate simplified—if it were made obligatory to register all marriages and at the same time specify the amount of *bohali* paid at the wedding and the amount outstanding. A marriage certificate would certainly be useful for establishing a man's status in South Africa and would clearly distinguish wives from concubines in elopement situations. The task of the courts might also be made easier if it were made compulsory to register extra-judicial divorces. The difficulty lies, however, in enforcing compliance with such rules. The sanction of nullity (or criminal prosecution) would seem disproportionate. The Cape Government's attempt to make the registration of marriages compulsory in Basutoland was unsuccessful and at the present time registration of the first customary marriage is merely optional—see Marriage Act 1974, s. 4.

Of course, they might equally turn out to have little impact on these problems and there would be the added difficulty of enforcing the rule providing for a maximum figure. A penal sanction might well be regarded as too drastic and the best approach would probably be to make any agreement for a larger amount unenforceable in respect of the excess and permit any excess already paid to be recoverable by court action.

Fourthly, should the rights of a married woman be further strengthened so that she is given greater equality with her husband? Her consent, for instance, could be made a legal prerequisite before any household property was disposed of by her husband. This might prove to be unacceptable in the present climate of opinion, but she might be allowed to administer her own separate property such as purchases made with her earnings and she could be granted full *locus standi* to sue and be sued in respect of her acts and omissions in her own name. Her right to maintenance ought, if possible, to be more efficiently enforced through arrangements whereby her husband's earnings could be attached by his employer, even if he was working in South Africa. Then there is the further question of her rights on divorce. At present her personal position is that she falls back under the guardianship of the head of her own family and her rights to any property acquired during the marriage are far from clear. It would probably be more consonant with modern conditions for her to be given full independence and an entitlement to a clearly defined share in those matrimonial assets which she has helped to acquire. Similarly, a widow's rights are in considerable need of improvement. She certainly ought to be granted a fixed share in any livestock and money left by her husband. Her rights to his lands and the matrimonial home are adequately safeguarded at present, but her difficulty in obtaining proper maintenance from the heir could be offset to a large extent if she participated more fully in capital assets. The circumstances in which she can remarry should obviously be clarified and any undue restrictions removed.

Fifthly, if kinship ties are becoming much less important and the interest of the lineage is giving way to that of the individual there would seem to be strong justification for amending some of the rules of inheritance. Why should the deceased's brothers have a claim on intestacy which is superior to that of his own daughters? Should the heir continue to have a fixed right to such a large proportion of the estate, thus restricting considerably the testator's freedom to make proper provision for the other members of his family, particularly his widow? Clearly if the heir's rights were to be cut down his liabilities would have to be correspondingly reduced and his responsibility for his father's debts would have to be limited to the extent of the assets in the estate. But assuming this could be satisfactorily achieved, is there any reason why after proper provision for the widow by means of a fixed proportion, the deceased's estate should not, on intestacy, be shared among *all* his children either in equal shares or in other fixed proportions? It is hardly likely that illegitimate children could yet be placed on an equal footing with legitimate children but should they not at any rate have stronger rights to inherit within their mothers' families than at present is the case? Furthermore, if freedom of testation were permitted a procedure could be introduced whereby a dependant might in certain circumstances obtain reasonable provision out of the estate if he had been left unprovided for without just cause.

Sixthly, despite the many inroads that have been made into the patriarchal authority of a family head over his children, there are still a number of areas where the interests of a child are subjugated to the wishes of a father. Should this position now be reversed? For instance, in determining custody questions following a divorce, the courts are required to make such orders as seem to be just in all the circumstances, but the future welfare of the child is not necessarily the main factor taken into consideration. The retention or return of the *bohali* cattle and the desires of the father are regarded as at least equally important. Moreover, if the *bohali* is returned and the children go with their mother (which is quite common) not only is the father absolved from any liability to maintain them in the future, but the wife's family are in a worse economic position than before in terms of ability to provide such maintenance themselves. Another point is that whereas the law has developed to permit some unmarried women to emancipate themselves to a considerable degree, bachelors who are over twenty-one still find that, in legal theory at any rate, they are minors and are obliged to hand over their wages to their fathers. In return for this dependent status they are entitled to look to their fathers to pay compensation for their wrongs and to make a contribution towards their *bohali*. If this were felt to be inappropriate in modern circumstances the law could be altered and made to provide that majority is automatically attained at twenty-one or earlier on marriage by both men and women. A more acceptable proposal, in my view, would be for majority at twenty-one to turn on the extent to which a person was leading his life independently of his father. A related question is whether an unmarried girl who becomes pregnant should have the right to sue her seducer for hospital expenses and maintenance for the child, instead of the right of action being vested in her father as at present. The best solution might again be for the matter to depend upon her degree of independence from her father.

The question whether or not to introduce any of these changes into Sesotho family law is happily now largely a matter for the Basotho people themselves, relatively free from the fetters of external control. However, while some of the possible reforms referred to may come about gradually through shifts in the patterns of people's behaviour and policy decisions made by the customary courts, more immediate action would need to take the form of legislative enactment. The guiding precepts for any legislative body should surely be to attempt to fulfil the natural aspirations of all members of the community to regulate their lives in accordance with their own wishes, sentiments and beliefs, while at the same time encouraging the nation as a whole to move in the direction generally thought to be the most desirable. Experience shows that legislatures which go against public opinion and try to abolish deep rooted customs and traditions do so at their peril. Reforms are far more likely to be implemented by the community at large if they do not involve abrupt reversals of current practice but rather build upon and develop further principles that have already been established. Thus the movement towards increased rights for women and unmarried persons over the age of twenty-one began long ago and has now gained considerable momentum. Polygyny has long been on the decline. On the other hand, the payment of *bohali* has remained unaffected by more than a century of missionary endeavour and is as strong a custom today as at any time in the past.

The virtues and deficiencies of both the traditional extended family and the more individualistic nuclear family must be clearly recognized and evaluated. While the dictates of personal justice and fulfilment must be given due weight, the traditional process of co-operation between a large number of people is an asset not lightly to be discarded.

Mention of legislation raises the related question of a statutory codification of the whole of Sesotho family law. The rules which are presently written down are embodied in separate parts of the Laws of Lerotholi, each possessing a different status. Those in Parts II and III are delegated legislation, whereas many of the most significant ones are in Part I which is only partially recognized as law in the higher courts. One possible reform would be to put Part I on an equal footing with the other parts by enacting it as law and thus bring a uniformity of approach to all three parts by both the superior and the customary courts. It should, however, be borne in mind that Part I consists of rules on a variety of subjects jumbled together piecemeal and amended rather haphazardly over a period of seventy years and therefore its statutory enactment would bear little resemblance to a systematic and comprehensive code covering the whole field of family law.

There is a widely held belief, fostered particularly in Southern Africa by the notorious example of the Natal Code,[1] that codification may easily lead to the petrification of rules which have long since ceased to serve any useful purpose and may thus deprive customary law of its natural flexibility and adaptability. This is not necessarily so. These deficiencies are not the *inevitable* consequence of enacting a code. The fault lies rather with an apathetic legislature or with courts which are unduly conservative and unresponsive to the changing needs of society or which, for cultural reasons or through the training of their judges, view their role as the mere application of the literal words of the code instead of in more dynamic terms. Similar reasoning would apply to the question of giving statutory form to Part I of the Laws of Lerotholi or to any officially approved restatement which was declared to be prima facie evidence of the law.[2]

More important, it seems, than the particular way in which customary law is reduced to writing are the attitudes of legislators and judges (at all levels) towards the ideal of keeping the law in tune with the values and needs of the people it exists to serve. The crucial factor is thus the commitment of those entrusted with

[1] There have been three codes, those of 1878, 1891, and 1932.
[2] The existing 'Restatement of the Sesotho Law of Marriage' has received no such official recognition to date.

the authority to change and constructively interpret the law rather than the exact legal standing of the written rules themselves.[1]

This prompts a final question—how well have the courts been acquitting themselves during recent years in handling a largely unwritten body of family law? Broadly speaking, the judges of the superior courts have had no particular interest in Sesotho law and consequently have often tended to approach it in the wrong spirit. In the upshot their decisions have on a number of occasions been erroneous. Their defence, almost certainly, would be that they had no ready means of acquiring a detailed knowledge and understanding of the law.

However, although the impact made by certain decisions of the superior courts has been considerable, the actual volume of disputes which have come before them has been minute. It is therefore the functioning of the Judicial Commissioner's Court and the Basotho Courts which deserves most attention. Three Judicial Commissioners, Driver, Duncan and Thompson have given sterling service and in the main their decisions have reflected a sound appreciation and proper respect for Sesotho law. They have administered it without paying undue heed to technicalities imported into their procedure by statute and have usually managed to achieve substantial justice. This is no mean achievement when both their immense workload and the spartan conditions in which they sometimes had to operate while on circuit are taken into account.

An over-all assessment of the performance of the Basotho Courts is a far more difficult task. The court presidents are clearly not all of even quality, their education and training needs to be improved and they are hampered by knowing so little of what is being decided in courts other than their own. Furthermore, it should not be forgotten that they are civil servants who move around from one court to another and that in each district they will find the traditional unofficial 'courts' of chiefs and headmen operating side by side with their own. We have seen that the parallel existence of these two institutions can provide a useful means of sharing the burden of dispute settlement, but the relationship between the two can equally be one fraught with conflict. This is not a very satisfactory state of affairs and the fact

---

[1] A permanent law-revision committee would be useful for keeping a constant check on developments.

that the court presidents took over the judicial powers formerly held by the chiefs during colonial rule must make the position of the former somewhat uneasy and perhaps helps to explain why they have not had enough self-confidence to embark on a course of progressive interpretation and innovation.

In the future, then, the administration of justice will best be served when there is a unified court structure, when the superior courts have access to sufficient information for them to take judicial notice of Sesotho law, when decisions are much more widely reported than they are at present, when the judges in the lower courts are better trained and when qualified lawyers are entitled to appear before them. It surely cannot be long now before all this will come to pass.

APPENDIX

Excerpts from
The Laws of Lerotholi (1959 edition)

PART I

DECLARATION OF BASUTO LAW AND CUSTOM

Succession to Chieftainship

2. The succession to Chieftainship shall be by right of birth: that is the first born male child of the first wife married; if the first wife has no male issue then the first born male child of the next wife married in succession shall be the Chief.

Provided that if a Chief dies leaving no male issue the Chieftainship shall devolve upon the male following according to the succession of houses.

Contribution to [bohali] by maternal uncles

5. A maternal uncle shall be given a portion of the [bohali] paid for the marriage of his nieces if such nieces be married by African custom and if the maternal uncle contributed towards the maintenance of his nieces. If such uncle fails to contribute towards the maintenance of his nieces he shall have no claim to a portion of the [bohali].

The portion of [bohali] to be paid to the maternal uncle shall be based upon the amount of the [bohali] received.

NOTE—'Contributing towards the maintenance' means contributing towards the clothing, initiation and entertainment, etc., of the nieces or contributing towards the [bohali] for the marriage of the brothers of such nieces.

Liability for act or debt of another

6. No African shall be liable for a wrongful act or debt of his adult relative or friend, but the head of a family may be held liable for a wrongful act or debt of his minor children (i.e. unmarried children living in his house and under his control).

Allocation of land

7. (1) *Allocation of land generally:* Every Chief and every Headman . . . is responsible, within his area of jurisdiction, for the allocation of land to his subjects. It shall be the duty of the Chief and Headman to see that land is allocated fairly and impartially.

NOTE—Land may be allocated for several purposes, e.g. residential, business, planting of trees, growing of vegetables or tobacco, cultivation of crops, burial of the dead, erection of churches for purposes of worship, building of stables and kraals, etc.

(2) *Inspection of land allocated for the growing of crops:* Every Chief and every Headman . . . shall frequently inspect all lands allocated by him in his area for the cultivation of crops and is empowered to take away land from people who in his opinion have more lands than are necessary for their and their families' subsistence and grant such land so taken away to his subjects who have no land or insufficient lands.

(3) *Deprivation of land not used or ill used:* It will be at the discretion of such Chief or Headman to take away a land or lands which he has allocated to any of his subjects who, through continued absence or insufficient reason, fails for two successive years properly to cultivate or cause to be cultivated.

(4) *Retention of lands by widows:* No widow shall be deprived of her land except under the provisions of paragraphs (2) and (3).

(5) *Provision of lands for minors and other sons on the death of their parents:*

(a) On the death of the father or mother, who ever dies last, all arable land allocated to them shall be regarded as land that has become vacant and shall revert to the Chief or Headman for re-allocation. Should however there be minor dependants left in such household, it shall be the duty of the guardian of such minor dependants, or in his absence the person who has the custody of the minors, to report the presence of such minors to the Chief or Headman, and it shall be the duty of the Chief or Headman to make provision for such minor dependants, during the period of their minority, from the land or lands of their deceased parents. If the minor dependants are sons, the Chief or Headman shall, on such sons attaining majority, confirm them on the land or lands used for their benefit during the period of their minority.

(b) In the re-allocation of lands which have reverted to the Chief or Headman on the death of the previous occupier and after the needs of any minor dependants have been satisfied as in the previous sub-paragraph (a) prescribed, the Chief or Headman shall give priority, as regards the allocation of the remaining lands should there be any, to the requirements of any adult son or sons of the deceased provided such son or sons reside in the village of the deceased.

(c) Any person aggrieved by the action of the Chief or Headman in failing to observe the provisions laid down in this paragraph (5) may complain to the Principal or Ward Chief as the case may be, and if dissatisfied with the decision of the Principal or Ward Chief he may appeal to the Paramount Chief.

(6) *Right to select which land to surrender:* When under paragraph (2) or (4) above a Chief or Headman orders that a land or lands be surrendered, the person so ordered to surrender a land or lands shall have the right to choose which land or lands shall be surrendered.

(7) *Land allocation for gardens and tree plantations, etc.:* On the death of a person who has been allocated the use of land for the growing of vegetables or tobacco, or for the purpose of planting fruit or other trees, or for residential purposes, the heir, or in the absence of the heir, the dependants of such deceased person shall be entitled to the use of such land so long as he or they continue to dwell thereon.

(8) *Land required in the public interest:* Except in the public interest it shall not be lawful for any person to be deprived of his lands, gardens or tree plantations except in accordance with the provisions of this law.

Heir

11. (1) The heir . . . shall be the first male child of the first married wife, and if there is no male in the first house then the first born male child of the next wife married in succession shall be the heir.

(2) If there is no male issue in any house the senior widow shall be the heir, but according to the custom she is expected to consult the relatives of her deceased husband who are her proper advisers.

Minor heir

12. (1) When a man dies leaving an heir who is a minor, the person appointed as guardian of the heir and administrator of the estate shall keep a written record of the administration of the estate, and this record shall be open to inspection by the paternal uncles, and by other relatives of the heir as are permitted to do so by Basuto Law.

(2) No property belonging to the estate shall be sold or otherwise disposed of by the guardian, administrator or widow without the prior consent of the paternal uncles and other relatives of the heir entitled by Basuto Law and Custom to be consulted.

(3) If the heir in any house is a minor, the principal heir, if he is of age, is regarded as his guardian. If the principal heir is himself a minor, the guardian appointed by the relatives for the principal heir shall also be the guardian of the minors in any other house. Such guardian must use the property allocated to any particular house for the maintenance of the heir, his brothers and minor sisters in such house only.

(4) Where property has been allocated to any particular house and the wife in that house predeceases her husband, the property allocated shall remain with that particular house to be inherited upon the death

of the father by the eldest son of that house and to be shared by him in accordance with Basuto Law and Custom with his junior brothers in his own house.

Inheritance

13. (1) Subject to the provisions of paragraph 14 the heir . . . shall inherit all the unallocated property of the estate and he is obliged by custom to use the estate with his father's widow or widows and to share with his junior brothers according to their rank, which shall be according to the order in which their mothers were married.

(2) The question of what portion of the unallocated estate shall be set aside for the support of the deceased's widow or widows during her life or their lives, shall be decided by the paternal uncles of the principal heir and other persons whose right it is under Basuto Law and Custom to be consulted.

Allocation of property during lifetime

14. (1) If a man during his lifetime allots his property amongst his various houses but does not distribute such property, or if he dies leaving written instructions regarding the allotment on his death, his wishes must be carried out, provided the heir according to Basuto custom has not been deprived of the greater part of his father's estate.

(2) A widow who has no male issue in her house shall have the use of all the property allocated to her house. On her death the principal heir shall inherit the remaining property but he must use the property for the maintenance of any dependants in such house; provided that no widow may dispose of any of the property without the prior consent of her guardian.

(3) If there is male issue in any house other than the house from which the principal heir comes, the widow shall have the use of all the property allocated to her house and at her death any property remaining shall devolve upon the eldest son of her house who must share such property with his junior brothers in his house; provided that no widow may dispose of any property without consultation with the guardian while that son is a minor, and provided further that on the eldest son reaching his majority he will assume control of the property in his house.

(4) Any dispute amongst the deceased's family over property or property rights shall be referred (for arbitration) to the brothers of the deceased and other persons whose right it is under Basuto Law and Custom to be consulted. If no agreement is arrived at by such persons, or if either party wishes to contest their decision, the dispute shall be taken to the appropriate Court by the dissatisfied party.

Abduction of unmarried girl

3. (1) No person shall abduct or cause to be abducted an unmarried girl over the apparent age of 16 years against her wish, whether with the concurrence of her parents or otherwise. Any person contravening this rule shall be liable on conviction to a fine not exceeding [R100] or to imprisonment for a period not exceeding twelve months or to both such fine and imprisonment.

(2) Any such girl so abducted should complain without delay to the Court.

(3) In cases where the abduction takes place at the instance of the parents the Court should not grant any compensation to such parents.

Abduction of unmarried girl against wishes of her parents

4. (1) If any unmarried girl over the apparent age of 16 years is abducted by a man with her consent but against the wishes of her parents, the parents of such girl may being an action for compensation not exceeding six head of cattle against the man or his parents.

Second abduction

(2) If the man abducts the same unmarried girl a second time against the wishes of either his or her parents, the amount of compensation to be awarded to the parents of such girl shall be at the discretion of the Court, and the Court may order the dissenting parents to arrange the marriage.

Abduction of married woman

7. Any person who abducts a married woman or causes any such woman to be abducted shall be liable on conviction to a fine not exceeding [R100] or to imprisonment for a period not exceeding twelve months or to both such fine and imprisonment; and in addition the Court hearing the case may award to the husband compensation not exceeding ten head of cattle.

Seduction of married woman

8. (1) The compensation awarded . . . for seduction of a married woman shall not exceed three head of cattle.

Second seduction of married woman

(2) If the same man again seduces the same woman, the compensation awarded shall not exceed five head of cattle.

Death resulting from seduction of married woman

(3) If the woman seduced becomes pregnant and dies in labour, the compensation awarded shall not exceed ten head of cattle.

Removal of children from care of parents, etc.

10. No person shall take away or cause to be taken away any child from the parent, guardian or person having the lawful custody of such child. Any person contravening this rule shall be liable on conviction to a fine not exceeding [R20] or to imprisonment for a period not exceeding two months.

NOTE—'Child' means any child under the apparent age of 16 years.

Marriage

34. (1) A marriage by Basuto custom . . . shall be deemed to be completed when:

(a) there is agreement between the parties to the marriage;
(b) there is agreement between the parents of the parties or between those who stand *in loco parentis* to the parties as to the marriage and as to the amount of the *bohali*;
(c) there is payment of part or all of the *bohali*: Provided that if the man dies before the woman goes to his parents' house the *bohali* shall be returned and the marriage shall be null and void.

(2) If the woman dies before all the *bohali* is paid any balance of the *bohali* which remains unpaid shall none the less be payable.

(3) A form of marriage purporting to be entered into whereby a woman is married to a fictitious person (*lebota*) or to a person already deceased (*lebitla*) is expressly forbidden.

(4) Dissolution of marriage contracted in accordance with the provisions of sub-rule (1) of this rule may be granted by Basuto Courts on the application of either party on the grounds of the wilful desertion of the other party, or to the wife for the persistent cruelty or neglect of her husband or other cause recognized under Basuto Law and Custom.

(5) A Court granting dissolution of such a marriage shall make an order regarding the retention or return of *bohali* cattle, and to whom the children, if any, shall belong, as may seem just in accordance with the circumstances in which the dissolution is granted.

GLOSSARY OF
SESOTHO WORDS

Baeletsi	Advisers.
Bathethesi	Witnesses; negotiators of a marriage agreement.
Bohali	Payment of livestock or money upon marriage, 'bridewealth', 'brideprice', 'childprice'; marriage. (Zulu equivalent—*lobolo*.)
Fomo	A sheep slaughtered for a feast by the bride's father denoting satisfaction at the payment of *bohali*.
Hlonepha	To respect, honour, be polite, avoid certain words.
Karolo	Part, portion.
Kenelo (verb, *kenela*)	A type of widow inheritance, levirate.
Koae	A sheep or goat slaughtered to celebrate the first formal visits of the bride and groom to their respective in-laws.
Lebitla	A grave, tomb, dead man.
Lebota	A wall; fictitious person.
Lefa	Inheritance.
Lefielo	A servant wife (lit. broom).
Lekhotla la lelapa	Family council.
Lekhotla la tlopho	Unofficial court of chief or headman.
Litsoa	Portion of *bohali* due to senior maternal uncle on the marriage of his niece.
Mabatho mofumahali	Principal or great wife.
Mafisa	A contract for the loan of livestock.
Mafura	Fat, oil; head of cattle slaughtered after the conclusion of a marriage.
Mala	A wife married as a seed raiser (lit. bowels).
Malome	Senior maternal uncle.
Matalenyane	Little green one (referring to the 1922 version of the Laws of Lerotholi which was printed in a green paper cover).
Maumo	The intestines of a *tlhabiso* ox.
Mojalefa	The heir.
Mokeneli	Man who inherits his brother's widow.

Mokhoa	Manner, way, habit, fashion, routine, custom.
Molao	Law, order, commandment, bond.
Molisa (pl. *balisa*)	Shepherd, 'guardian'.
Molisana	A horse forming part of *bohali* (lit. herdboy).
Moqhoba	An ox forming part of *bohali* (lit. driver).
Morero	A plan, decision, purpose.
Mpho	A gift.
Ngala	To sulk, to leave one's husband and go to one's parents' home.
Ngoetsi	Junior wives of large-scale polygamists (lit. daughter-in-law).
Nyala	To marry.
Nyatsi (pl. *linyatsi*)	Concubine.
Phahlelo	Trousseau.
Pitso	Assembly, gathering, public meeting.
Ramotsana	Village head.
Seantlo	Special form of marriage to a deceased wife's sister.
Seholoholo	One of the *bohali* cattle specifically due to the bride's mother.
Selelekela	Two of the *bohali* cattle sent first and specifically due to the bride's parents.
Seotla	An ox given to indemnify people who have brought up a child for others.
Serapa	A small field.
Serethe	Junior wife of a polygamist.
Seriti	Shadow.
Sesila	A single beast payable by way of compensation for a wrongful termination of an engagement to marry (lit. dirty, stained).
Sethepu	A junior wife, polygamy.
Setsiba	Ten sheep or goats forming part of *bohali* (lit. loin-cloth, trousers).
Tebeletso	Cattle paid by way of a deposit of *bohali* on engagement, advance, pledge, token.
Therisano	Consultation, advice.
Tja-bohobe	A sheep or goat slaughtered as part of a feast of welcome for the bride on arrival at her husband's home (lit. something to go with bread i.e. meat). Same as *koae*.
Tlhabiso	Ox slaughtered as part of the wedding festivities.
Tumello	Consent, permission.

BIBLIOGRAPHY

I. WORKS ON LESOTHO

(a) *Books*

ARBOUSSET, T., *Narrative of an Exploratory Tour to the North-east of the Colony of the Cape of Good Hope* (Bishop, London, 1852).

ASHTON, H., *The Basuto* (O.U.P., London, 1952; 2nd ed. 1967).

CASALIS, E., *The Basutos* (James Nisbet, London, 1861; repr. C. Struik, Cape Town, 1971).

DUNCAN, P., *Sotho Laws and Customs* (O.U.P., Cape Town, 1960).

ELLENBERGER, D. F., and MACGREGOR, J. C., *History of the Basuto, Ancient and Modern* (Caxton, London, 1912; repr. Negro Universities Press, New York, 1969).

ELLENBERGER, V., *A Century of Mission Work in Basutoland* (Sesuto Book Depot, Morija, 1938).

GERMOND, R. C., *Chronicles of Basutoland* (Sesuto Book Depot, Morija, 1967).

HAILEY, LORD W., *Native Administration in the British African Territories, Part V, The High Commission Territories* (H.M.S.O., London, 1953).

HAMNETT, I., *Chieftainship and Legitimacy: An Anthropological Study of Executive Law in Lesotho* (Routledge & Kegan Paul, London, 1975).

LEISTNER, G., *Lesotho: Economic Structure and Growth* (Africa Institute, Pretoria, 1966).

ORPEN, J. M., *History of the Basutus of South Africa* (Cape Town, 1857).

PALMER, V. V., *The Roman–Dutch and Sesotho Law of Delict* (Sijthoff, Leiden, 1970).

—— and POULTER, S. M., *The Legal System of Lesotho* (Michie, Charlottesville, 1972).

P.E.M.S., *The Church of Basutoland: Its Constitution, Rules and Regulations* (Sesuto Book Depot, Morija, 1927).

SEKESE, A., *Mekhoa le Maele a Basotho* (Sesuto Book Depot, Morija, 1907; repr. 1968; first part as *Mekhoa ea Basotho*, 1893; repr. 1953).

SHEDDICK, V., *The Southern Sotho* (I.A.I., London, 1953).

——, *Land Tenure in Basutoland* (H.M.S.O., London, 1954).

SMIT, P., *Lesotho: A Geographical Study* (Africa Institute, Pretoria, 1967).

SMITH, E. W., *The Mabilles of Basutoland* (Hodder & Stoughton, London, 1939).

THEAL, G. M. (Ed.), *Basutoland Records* (3 vols., W. A. Richards, 1883, and C. Struik, 1964, Cape Town).

WALLMAN, S., *Take Out Hunger* (Athlone Press, London, 1969).

WILLIAMS, J. C., *Lesotho: Land Tenure and Economic Development* (Africa Institute, Pretoria, 1972).

(b) *Articles, etc.*

ATMORE, A., 'The Passing of Sotho Independence 1865–70' in Thompson, L. (Ed.), *African Societies in Southern Africa* (Heinemann, London, 1969) 282.

COWEN, D. V., 'Land Tenure and Economic Development in Lesotho', (1967) *S.A.J.E.* 58.

CRAWFORD, J., 'Land Shortage and Land Plenty', (1967) *S.A.L.J.* 437.

HAMNETT, I., 'Some Notes on the Concept of Custom in Lesotho, [1971] *J.A.L.* 266.

JONES, G. I., 'Chiefly Succession in Basutoland', in Goody, J. (Ed.), *Succession to High Office* (C.U.P., Cambridge, 1966) 57.

KUNENE, D., 'Notes on *Hlonepha* among the Southern Sotho', (1958) *African Studies* 159.

LAYDEVANT, P. J., 'Étude sur la famille en Basutoland', Tome 1, Fascicule 11, (1931) *Journal de la Société des Africanistes* 207.

PAROZ, R., 'Le Mariage au Lessouto', (1946) *Journal des Missions Évangéliques* 17.

POULTER, S. M., 'The Place of the Laws of Lerotholi in the Legal System of Lesotho', (1972) *African Affairs* 144.

POULTER, S. M., 'An Essay on African Customary Law Research Techniques: Some Experiences from Lesotho', (1975) *Journal of Southern African Studies* 181.

RAMOLEFE, A., 'Customary Law Inheritance and Succession', (1965–6) *Basutoland Notes and Records* 18.

RAMOLEFE, A., 'Sesotho Marriage, Guardianship and the Customary Law Heir', in Gluckman, M. (Ed.), *Ideas and Procedures in African Customary Law* (O.U.P., London, 1969) 196.

SMITS, L., 'The Distribution of the Population in Lesotho and some Implications for Economic Development', (1968) *Lesotho Notes and Records* 19.

(c) *Official Reports, etc.*

Annual Reports of the Department of Agriculture.

Annual Statistical Bulletins.

Basutoland Village Population Lists (Maseru, 1960).

Cape Government Census of Basutoland (Cape Town, 1875).

DOUGLAS, A., and TENNANT, R., *Basutoland Agricultural Survey 1949–50* (Maseru, 1952).

Laws of Lerotholi (Morija, 1922; revd. 1946, 1955, 1959).

Lesotho First Five Year Development Plan 1970/71–1974/75 (Maseru, 1970).

MOROJELE, C., *1960 Agricultural Census*, Parts 2 and 3 (Maseru, 1962–3).

National Council, *Reports of Proceedings* (Maseru, 1903–58).

National Council, *Report of the Committee on Basuto Court Reforms* (Maseru, 1950).

National Council, *Report of Select Committee on Wills, Estates and Marriages* (Maseru, 1962).

PIM, SIR A., *Financial and Economic Position of Basutoland* (H.M.S.O., London, 1935).

Population Census Reports, 1911, 1921, 1936, 1946, 1956, 1966.

Report and Evidence of Commission on Native Laws and Customs of the Basutos (Saul Solomon & Co., Cape Town, 1873; repr. Sesuto Book Depot, Morija, 1966).

(d) *Unpublished works*

DEVITT, P., 'The Politics of Headmanship in the Mokhokhong Valley (M.A. thesis, University of the Witwatersrand, 1969).

HAMNETT, I., 'Sotho Customary Law' (Ph.D. thesis, University of Edinburgh, 1970).

POULTER, S. M. (Ed.), 'Sesotho Family Law Conference Transcript' (1970).

'Restatement of the Sesotho Law of Marriage' (cyclostyled, n.d., but *circa* 1968).

2. GENERAL WORKS

ALLEN, C. K., *Law in the Making* (Clarendon Press, Oxford, 7th ed., 1964).

ALLOTT, A. N., *Law and Language* (S.O.A.S., London, 1965).

——, *New Essays in African Law* (Butterworths, London, 1970).

ANDERSON, J. N. D., *Family Law in Asia and Africa* (George Allen & Unwin, London, 1968).

DANIELS, W. C. E., *The Common Law in West Africa* (Butterworths, London, 1964).

FALLERS, L., *Law without Precedent* (University of Chicago Press, Chicago, 1969).

HAILEY, LORD W., *An African Survey* (O.U.P., London, Revised 1956).

JUNOD, H. A., *The Life of a South African Tribe* (Macmillan, London, 2nd ed., 1927).

PHILLIPS, A., and MORRIS, H. F., *Marriage Laws in Africa* (O.U.P., London, 1971).

RADCLIFFE-BROWN, A. R., and FORDE, D. (Eds.), *African Systems of Kinship and Marriage* (O.U.P., London, 1950).

REUTER, A., *Native Marriages in South Africa* (Aschendorffsche Verlagsbuchhandlung, Munster Westfalen, 1963).

SALACUSE, J., *An Introduction to Law in French Speaking Africa*, Vol. 1 (Michie, Charlottesville, 1969).

Salmond on Jurisprudence (Sweet & Maxwell, London, 11th ed., 1957).

SCHAPERA, I., *Migrant Labour and Tribal Life* (O.U.P., London, 1947).

——, *Tribal Innovators: Tswana Chiefs and Social Change* (Athlone Press, London, 1970).

SEYMOUR, S. M., *Native Law in South Africa* (Juta, Cape Town, 2nd ed., 1960).

——, *Bantu Law in South Africa* (Juta, Cape Town, 1970).

WHITFIELD, G., *South African Native Law* (Juta, Cape Town, 2nd ed., 1948).

INDEX

Abduction,
  compensation, amount of, 109
  compensation, borrowed for *bohali*,
    109–10, 115–17
  compensation, recoverable on
    divorce, 110–11, 218–19
  defined, 109
  leading to forced marriage, 82
  leading to reduced *bohali*, 96–7
  liability to pay compensation, 109,
    183
  of a married woman, 169–71, 179
  repeated, 84, 91
  vicarious responsibility for, 190
  See also, delicts; elopement
Administration of estates,
  inspection of written records of,
    283–6
  statutory 'mode of life' test, 53,
    323–4
  See also, heir; inheritance; widows
Adoption,
  allocation of daughter, 309
  as heir, 233, 237–9
  definition, 237
  statutory recognition, 53
  validity, 237–9
Adultery,
  bohali debts unaffected by, 129
  children conceived in, 27, 216–18,
    230–1, 235, 239
  compensation, amount of, 168–9
  defined, 168
  justification for divorce, 208,
    210–12, 331
  of widow, 307
Age,
  minimum for marriage, 73, 331
Age of majority, 187–9, 336
  See also, majority
Agriculture, 28–32
  crop production, 28–31
  level of productivity, 24–7
  livestock production, 31–2
  See also, land

Allocations of property, 309–24
  by monogamist on remarriage, 175,
    243–5, 247, 275
  by polygamist to 'houses', 173,
    226, 243, 256, 267, 289, 309
  conditions of validity, 186, 311–14
  family knowledge of, 224
  inter vivos, 319–21
  notification to heir, 186, 311–13,
    320–1
  positive act or intention, 313–14
  publicity, 311–13
  restriction to half of the estate, 313,
    319–22
  revocation, 240, 314–15
  to daughters, 195, 233–4, 289,
    309–10
  to individuals, 309–10
  to junior 'houses', 256–7
  to junior sons, 186, 257–8
  widow's capacity to make, 289,
    292–3
  See also, 'houses'; land; property;
    testamentary dispositions; written
    instructions
Ancestors,
  belief in, 32, 41
Annulment of marriage, 212, 219–20
Arable land,
  See land
Ashton, H., 13–14

Bachelors,
  allocations of land, 186–7, 330
  contracts of employment, 186
  denied *locus standi*, 186
  earnings belong to fathers, 135,
    185–6, 190, 192, 327, 335
  inheritance of their personal
    effects, 228
  liability under contracts, 193–4
  ownership of property, 185
  possession of the vote, 186
  succession to chieftainship, 186
  vicarious responsibility for delicts
    of, 189–93, 327, 335